Those Who Can, Teach

Those Who Can, Teach

FOURTH EDITION

Kevin Ryan
BOSTON UNIVERSITY

James M. Cooper
UNIVERSITY OF VIRGINIA

HOUGHTON MIFFLIN COMPANY   BOSTON

Dallas   Geneva, Illinois   Hopewell, New Jersey   Palo Alto

*This edition is dedicated to
those who will teach*

EFGHIJ—M—89876

Printed in the U.S.A.
Library of Congress Catalog Card
   Number: 83-082566
ISBN: 0–395–34257–0

*Cover photograph by James Scherer.
Special thanks to the Angier School,
   Newton.*

Preface

Those Who Can, Teach is a book of questions. In fact, it was written in the first place to answer the question, "What are the things people beginning their formal study of education should know?" We have organized the chapters of our book around a series of questions that are likely to be of special concern to prospective teachers—and which we believe are keys to the central issues and concerns of education. We must warn you, though: the questions look deceptively simple, like an innocent packet of fishhooks. We have embellished these question-hooks with lures and baited them with dainty morsels. And, like good fishermen, all we want you to do is swallow them. We believe that, once that happens, the hooks will stick in your vitals and our work will be done. Putting aside this somewhat discomfiting metaphor, we hope that these questions provide direction and focus to your study well beyond the time you spend with this book. For those of you who are contemplating careers in teaching, we believe that pursuing answers to these questions will help you clarify your career goals.

This is the fourth edition of Those Who Can, Teach. It is intended as a basic text for courses variously titled "Introduction to Education" or "Foundations of Education." We originally wrote this book because we couldn't find the kind of textbook our students and the students of many of our colleagues needed and wanted—a book that involves prospective teachers in the real issues of schooling and education and gives them a clear view of the skills and knowledge they will need to be successful professionals.

Coverage	*Those Who Can, Teach* presents a frank and up-to-date examination of the field and foundations of education and, especially, the teaching profession. Although the text is firmly based in educational research and scholarship, it seeks to convey the important knowledge and issues in the field of education in a way that effectively bridges educational research and classroom practice. Part I ("Self and Career") examines various motivations for teaching and provides timely information on salaries and employment opportunities. Part II ("Foundations") contains totally new chapters on two core foundational subjects, the first on the philosophy of education and the second on the history of American education. In Part III ("Schools: The Present") the dynamics of school life are examined from many angles to give the prospective teacher a multilayered view of schools, from governance and financing to classroom interactions to what is taught. Part IV ("Teachers") gives readers a behind-the-scenes look at some of the common experiences of beginning teachers; describes the attitudes, skills, and knowledge essential to effective teaching; and evaluates the current status of teaching as a profession. Finally, in Part V ("Social Issues and the Current Scene") recent innovations in the field of education are discussed along with some of the more critical issues in education today, such as sex-role stereotyping, moral education, declining student performance, the back-to-basics movement, and the search for excellence in education.

Features of the Revision

New in this fourth edition is an increased emphasis on the foundations. In addition to the two new chapters on the philosophical and historical foundations of education, we have integrated throughout the text more coverage of social, economic, legal, and psychological foundations. We added this material in response to the many instructors who told us that the foundations of education were important aspects of the courses they taught and that, from their perspective, our book would be even more useful to them if we included these topics. For many students, studying the foundations may seem remote from their immediate concerns about teaching. In our coverage of foundational topics, we have tried to demonstrate their importance to prospective teachers and to present them in a lively and interesting way.

Because education by its very nature is a dynamic field with new research findings becoming available and new public priorities emerging, each chapter of the previous edition has been revised, some in a very major way. Wherever applicable we have incorporated the most recent statistics, data, research findings, and reports—including, for example, new sections on microcomputer use in classrooms, alternative schools, private education, social problems affecting the young, John Goodlad's "A Study of Schooling," and the report of the National Commission on Excellence in Education. In addition, chapter order has been changed to make the book better suited to current course structures and the concerns of the 1980s. For example, "Is There a Job for You in Education?" is now the second chapter in the book because employment outlook is a critical issue for today's education students, and the chapter on the first year of teaching has been totally recast to give much more attention to the positive aspects of teaching.

Pedagogical and Stylistic Features

Although there is much that is new in the fourth edition, there are also many features that have been retained. Chief among them is the book's lively and refreshing writing style. We have tried to communicate the seriousness surrounding professional topics and at the same time weave in humor and create a sense of conversing directly with the reader. The text describes extensively the experiences of classroom teachers, often in their own words; this gives the text a greater sense of reality.

Many pedagogical features have been included to enhance the student's learning and the text's usefulness. Dialogues appear periodically to highlight controversial points and topics of particular interest. Biographies of distinguished educators and teachers, such as Maria Montessori and John Dewey, have been placed throughout the text. Further, the book is sprinkled heavily with cartoons, photographs, newspaper items, and thought-provoking quotations. In addition, each chapter begins with a capsule overview and a list of key points and concludes with a series of discussion questions and an annotated list of suggested readings.

Ancillary

Those Who Can, Teach has a companion book of readings, *Kaleidoscope: Readings in Education,* Fourth Edition, that can be used either in conjunction with the text or as a separate volume. This collection of over sixty selections contains works by some of the most distinguished scholars in education along with the writings of practicing teachers and administrators. A mixture of topical and classical studies, the readings include diary entries, poems, letters, teacher accounts, journal articles, news stories, and government reports. There is also an easy-to-use chart that crossreferences topics discussed in *Those Who Can, Teach* with the readings in *Kaleidoscope.*

A final word about the title of the textbook. George Bernard Shaw, the great Irish playwright with the razor tongue, had many unpleasant things to say about schools and education, but one of his cruelest remarks was reserved for teachers: "He who can, does. He who cannot, teaches." The world has taken a lot of turns since Shaw wrote that line. Education is no longer a luxury of the leisure class. Teaching is a much more demanding and crucial occupation than it ever was before. Developing a person's human potential is serious work. Now those who can, teach.

Acknowledgments

Whenever any of us put pen to paper, we are indebted to many people. However, in the writing of this book, we are especially appreciative of the help given by the following individuals: Larry Laufman for his invaluable contribution to the research and writing of Chapter 4; William Geulcher for his aid in developing the case materials in Chapter 1; Ernie Lundquist for sharing with us the secrets of the Cosmic Apple and for running out for coffee and sandwiches; and our colleagues and students for their many good ideas and continuing support. We owe a special debt to Charles H. Clark, Harrisburg Area Community College, Sean Healy, Kean College of New Jersey, Jerald Hunt, Milliken University, Sylvester Kohut, Tennessee Technological University, and Jack C. Stewart, Columbus College, for their comprehensive and constructive analyses of the developing manuscript. A number of other reviewers also made key contributions to the organization and content of this edition, most notably:

Morris Anderson, Wayne State College

Peter Baldino, Youngstown State University

David S. Basler, Central Washington University

Catherine Becker, Montclair State College

Hilary Bender, Boston University

John Brothers, Central State University

Jerald M. Bullock, Brenau College

Joseph Davis, Lander College

Richard O. Davis, Edinboro State College

Ralph Dessenberger, Lock Haven State University

Dee Ann Foresman-Fine, South Dakota State University

Phil Fitch, Point Loma College

James Fouche, Northern Kentucky University

Katherine Fuller, Gainesville Junior College

George D. Gates, Idaho State University

Paulette Harris, Augusta College

Evelyn Hatfield, Mankato State University

Glenn E. Hinkle, St. Edward's University

Emily Hoover, Kent State University

Elizabeth Ihle, James Madison University

Jerry Dale Jones, Rio Grande College

George Joyce, James Madison University

Joseph Kirshner, Youngstown State University

Matthew J. Ludes, State University College

Nancy McKinley, Adult Learning Center, Laramie, Wyoming

Milton Messinger, California State College

Pam Rhodes, Oklahoma Christian College

Ivan Sanders, NW Missouri State University

Charlene Smith, California State University

Jamie C. Smith, Appalachian State University

James R. Stephan, Loma Linda University

John A. Stirton, San Joaquin Delta Community College

Patricia Ann Williams, Sam Houston State University

Lonnie H. Wood, Colorado State University

A very special acknowledgment is due to Marilyn Ryan for the substantial intellectual and psychological contributions she made to this book. Finally, we wish to express our special appreciation to our editors at Houghton Mifflin, who functioned throughout the many months of the revision process as supportive colleagues and intellectual partners.

KEVIN RYAN

JAMES M. COOPER

Contents

————————

III

SCHOOLS: THE PRESENT

135

Those Who Can, Teach

SELF
AND CAREER

I

Why Teach?

1

The purpose of this chapter is to help you answer a fundamental question: why become a teacher? This chapter is first because of the underlying importance of the question. Because we believe it is important for you to discover your own motivation for choosing a career in education, we have designed this chapter to help you in the process of answering the question.

This chapter emphasizes that:

▪ To help you decide whether to become a teacher, you can draw on a number of sources of useful experiences, including actual encounters with teachers and children, vicarious classroom experiences, guidance from friends and acquaintances in the profession, and your own personal reflections.

▪ Different teachers have different motives for teaching. By presenting three cases of representative teachers, we hope you come to understand more fully your own motivations for teaching.

*I*F YOU TEACH, it is likely that by the end of your second year of teaching you will have had both of the following experiences:

1. Someone at a party or some other social gathering will ask you what you do and how you like teaching. Shortly, the person will tell you that he or she has always wanted to be a teacher and regrets having become a stockbroker/homemaker/bookkeeper/sales rep/flight attendant/disc jockey. He or she may still give it all up and become a teacher.

2. You will get to know an experienced teacher who confides in you that he or she deeply regrets having become a teacher. In college the person felt sure that he or she was cut out for teaching, and actually enjoyed it in the beginning. But gradually he or she became bored with the whole thing— bratty kids, pushy administrators, the same old faces in the teachers' lounge, the instant-expert parents, the boring curriculum. Now the person feels trapped in teaching and can't see any way to get out.

The purpose of this chapter, then, is to keep you from becoming "the other person" in either of these two scenes. It is to help you make a good decision about what to do with your life, particularly if you are undecided about becoming a teacher.

Centuries ago, Francis Bacon told us that "knowledge is power." Much earlier still, Socrates recognized the special power of self-knowledge when he urged, "Know thyself." An understanding of one's motives in something as important as a career choice can help prevent faulty decision making.[1] A superficial motivation to teach can, and frequently does, lead to failure and disappointment. For instance, you may admire and want to emulate a former teacher. And you may, out of respect for this person, decide to teach without ever analyzing whether or not you have the capacity or drive. Or you may think it is admirable to like and help children. But in the process of actually working with, say, sixth-graders, you may discover that you can't stand sixth-graders, or that you're not even particularly interested in children.

Clarifying your motives helps you to identify your strengths as a person and a prospective teacher as well as to cope with your shortcomings.

---

[1] We are violating a time-honored textbook convention by switching voices. We find that in writing this book we sometimes speak to the reader in the third person, such as in "the reader will note" or "one might argue." At other times we use the more intimate second person, as in "you may not agree" or "we would like you to. . . ." We are inconsistent in this matter because our intention is inconsistent. We wish to speak more directly to the reader at some times than at others. We also find that we address "you" when we feel more urgency about an issue.

It has been conventional for textbooks to refer to the teacher as "he." Because teaching is an occupation chosen by large numbers of women as well as men, we have used terms that include both sexes.

Someone whose desire to teach grows out of a passion for art history has to know how to guard against hostility toward students who don't share that love of art. More than a few frustrated teachers have been heard to mutter, "Those ungrateful little wimps aren't worthy of Shakespeare" (or French infinitives, or Victorian poetry, or the niceties of quadratic equations). In any event, we have written this chapter—and, indeed, the entire book—in the hope that you will use it to gain a greater understanding of how you and a career in education might fit together.

SOURCES OF USEFUL EXPERIENCE

The major educational insight to be applied to education in recent years concerns individual differences. There is a new appreciation for the unique learning styles and, often, the unique learning problems people have. As a result, the "one-true-way" approach to education is gradually slipping by the boards.

The same insight about individual differences applies to making an intelligent career choice. Because people learn in such diverse ways and differ so much in what they already know and need to learn, we can give only sketchy guidelines here. We recognize four categories of experience that are potentially fruitful in the quest for an answer to "Should I teach?"

Real Encounters

People who plan to be teachers should test their commitment to teaching by putting themselves in actual school situations. As much as possible, students of teaching should observe in schools and participate in various activities that put them in contact with children and adolescents. Many teaching candidates avoid real contact with the young until they begin student teaching, only to find that young people are considerably different from the romantic images they had been manufacturing. "Those nasty little fifth-graders are so disgustingly . . . human!" one shocked student teacher said. Frequently, too, teaching candidates limit their encounters to normal elementary and secondary school students. They do not consider teaching mentally retarded or physically handicapped children, or even becoming a specialist such as a reading teacher. They have exposed themselves to only one segment of the opportunities and challenges of teaching.

Increasingly, school districts are employing students as teacher aides and assistant teachers, both during the regular school year and in summer school. And a large number of teacher education programs have cooperative arrangements with schools whereby college students are given opportunities to play a variety of roles within the school, often as part of their coursework in education. Schools, however, do not exhaust the opportunities. There is much to be said for nonschool contact with children, such as camp counseling, playground work, after-school recreation projects, work in orphanages and settlement houses, and youth-related church work. Other possibilities are coaching a team or sponsoring a club. The opportunities are many. The important thing, however, is to get your feet wet—to get the feel of working with children in a helping relationship.

Vicarious Experiences

Not all learning has to take place in the school of hard knocks. In fact, civilization itself requires that we be able to capitalize on the experience of others. Artists and other talented people can make the experience of others accessible to us for enjoyment, edification, or both. There are great fictional classics about teachers and schools such as *Goodbye, Mr. Chips* by James Hilton and *The Corn Is Green* by Emlyn Williams. And there are more recent novels such as Bel Kaufman's *Up the Down Staircase* and Evan Hunter's *Blackboard Jungle.* (All four of these books have been made into films.)

Films and television are another source of vicarious experience. Two relatively recent examples are the television serials "Fame" and "Square Pegs." In general, films and television experiences help us relive our own experiences in school and also help us see school in a different light. These vicarious experiences can be a valuable source of learning and testing for prospective teachers, particularly if they approach the experience somewhat more critically than does the ordinary television or movie viewer. We need to remember that books, films, and television portray school life as a much more intense and heightened set of human encounters than the normal teacher faces. Then, too, the flux and flow of life in a real school is simply not visible. The drama of teaching is quiet, long-term, and terribly real.

LAST DAY

The last bell rang.
The building filled with shouts and cheers
And emptied soon. Yet one still sat.
He looked at me, and I could see in that thin face
An awful realization no other child had known:
The year was gone.

I knew, but I was older. I could bear
The lost and sickish feeling of farewell

From simple familiarity with it.
I went back to where he sat;
I said there would be other years.
I said that I would write him letters in the summer.
Somehow he knew, this child who had never had a letter in his life,
That warm words are always somehow cold on paper,
And never take the place of being close.

Slowly he gathered up his books.
Walking toward the door, he looked around the room.
What did he see? What had this been to him?
I knew, and yet I could not know.
It was the end
Of a year.

Reese Danley Kilgo, *Phi Delta Kappan* 51, no. 475 (May 1970). Reprinted by permission of the author and publisher.

Guidance

Another aid is the advice and counsel of those who know you. Besides parents and friends (who often may be too close to you to be objective), you can consult former teachers, career placement counselors, and your college professors. The professors of education you are and will be working with can be particularly helpful, because they normally have a great deal of familiarity with the realities of teaching. You should exercise some caution here, however. First of all, choose people who know you well rather than those who have just seen you at your better moments. Second, do not expect an IBM printout of hard data with a firm decision at the end. If you get a few glimpses of insight from the person whose advice you are seeking, be satisfied. Third, be cautious, since many people are compulsive advice givers. Frequently people generalize on the basis of too little knowledge, and they are often just plain wrong. Receive advice openly, but follow it cautiously.[2]

Reflection

The most important aspect of the real school encounters, guidance, and vicarious experiences you collect is that they provide you with data for reflection. By *reflection* we simply mean the process of trying to understand fully your experiences and their implications for you. People are often so busy experiencing things, or getting ready to experience them, that they fail to reflect on what they have done in a manner that would assure their getting the most from the experience.

We cannot stress enough this point about reflection. It goes to the very heart of why we have written this book. Both of us are convinced that many people make very sloppy decisions about becoming teachers. They have not asked fundamental questions about themselves and about schools. This is precisely why we have organized this book around a series of questions such as "Why teach?" and "What is a school?" It is also why we periodically ask you to stop and reflect on a particular question. Occasionally, we ask you to commit yourself in writing, since doing so can help you clarify exactly what you mean. We have also included case studies, anecdotal material, and actual accounts by teachers. We hope that you will regard this material as vicarious experience that will stimulate your own reflection. In effect, we are much less interested in telling you something than in presenting you with some tough questions. Although questions such as "What makes a teacher effective?" may sound simple, their answers—if there are any answers—are frequently quite complex. We hope that you will use these questions not only to guide your career choice, but to help you reflect on the whole phenomenon of teaching and learning.

---

[2]Although our good friend Ernie Lundquist has tried to claim credit for this thought, we believe that Shakespeare's Polonius beat him to it.

For many people, the choice of teaching as a life's work is clear and simple. For others, the path is hidden and their journey unclear. The famed Swiss educator Johann Pestalozzi was one of those who took a less direct route. Well into middle age, Pestalozzi gave every sign of being a bungling failure. As a youth in Zurich he hated school, and afterward he pursued a long series of abortive occupational ventures. Nor was he a success as a personality. Raised by his widowed mother and a maid, he developed great sensitivity but remained overly dependent on women. In later life, the fame he achieved reportedly went to his head. But despite all his personal failings, Pestalozzi is both a hero and a model for educators.

After attending the University of Switzerland, where he finally learned to enjoy

JOHANN PESTALOZZI
(1746–1827)

studying and became active in social and political reform, Pestalozzi established an orphanage in his own home, where he taught neglected children the rudiments of agriculture and simple trades. But the orphanage failed in 1780, and Pestalozzi, in despair, went into seclusion to write *The Evening Hour of a Hermit,* a moving compendium of aphorisms and reflections.

Much later, at the age of fifty-two, he began a new career. When Napoleon's armies massacred the citizens of the town of Stans, he collected several dozen destitute children and cared for them under extremely difficult conditions. Pestalozzi made the Institute for the Poor an educational experiment, teaching the children to spin, weave, and do

farm work, as well as to study. But because he had accepted more students, including retarded children, than he could accommodate, he was forced to close the school for lack of funds. This was one more failure in an uninterrupted series, but Pestalozzi was undaunted. He had found his vocation in teaching and his happiness among children.

In 1805 Pestalozzi founded a boarding school in an abandoned castle at Yverdon, which flourished for twenty years. It quickly became famous and attracted students from all over Europe. Its curriculum, which emphasized drawing, writing, singing, physical exercise, group recitations, map making, and field trips, was based on the principle of "sense impression"—the idea that we understand only what we observe clearly, and that words and

MOTIVES FOR TEACHING

We would like you to take a moment to write down what you feel are your motives for wanting to be a teacher. If you are unsure whether you want to be a teacher (this probably applies to the majority of readers), list your motives both for and against becoming a teacher. If you do not wish to use the space provided here, we suggest that you do write down your list in some permanent place. Although the purpose of this list is to help you think about yourself and analyze your career choice, you may wish to save it for future reference.

There is a reason why we use the plural, *motives.* Most of us have mixed motives, some altruistic and some selfish, about most of the things that are important to us. Our motives often conflict, and occasionally they

ideas have meaning only when they are related to concrete objects. Pestalozzi thus put considerable stress on the importance of concrete situations in the child's learning. The study of geography involved field trips and the construction of elaborate models of whole territories. Pestalozzi anticipated modern methods of math instruction by using concrete objects to develop number competence. Four students or four chairs, for instance, illustrated the concept *four*. Students learned to read and write with slates, pencils, and alphabet cards. Pestalozzi also emphasized the importance of art in the curriculum, not only to provide an emotional outlet for the children but also to encourage creativity and develop intellectual discipline.

Pestalozzi's educational theory was built on the as-sumption that human beings are motivated by three drives: primitive impulses, social needs, and ethical yearnings. He conceived of education as the process by which ethics triumph over animal impulses. His model of learning was the family, with the teacher acting like a parent and serving as a model to be imitated. The ideal of love governed Pestalozzi's philosophy of education—love that should not be modified or withdrawn even if the student misbehaves. The teacher, he was convinced, should never punish or show disapproval, a very novel attitude in the early nineteenth century. The Yverdon curriculum offered carefully graded instruction, allowance for individual differences, and ability grouping; in general, Pestalozzi was less concerned with "meeting standards" than with the in-tegrity of the students and their work.

Misunderstood by his contemporaries, who considered him too radical and emotional and accused him of taking children too seriously, Pestalozzi nevertheless achieved fame and international influence within his lifetime. He came to be called the Christopher Columbus of elementary education because he opened up so much new territory in that field. Several foreign governments sent teachers to Yverdon for instruction—Pestalozzi's teacher-training department was unique at the time—and he was made an honorary citizen of the French Republic and knighted by the czar.

Advocates of love and acceptance in the educational process owe and acknowledge a heavy debt to Johann Pestalozzi.

are incompatible. In any event, one motive is rarely sufficient to explain a choice as complex as the career in which we plan to spend a large part of our lives.

_____

_____

_____

_____

_____

_____

_____

_____

_____

If you did not stop reading to think about your motives for wanting to be a teacher or to commit yourself in writing, you're probably like many other readers. What kept you from seriously engaging the question? Your answer to this question may tell you a good deal about yourself as a learner and, incidentally, about the educational system of which you are a product. Have you been trained to devour pages without really confronting the issues conveyed by the words? Have you learned to disregard your own views, even about issues quite central to you? Does it make you uneasy to probe your own motivation seriously? If your answers to these questions are yes, you are like many other students. However, we hope that this will be a different kind of book and a different kind of reading-questioning-thinking experience for you. We want it to be unlike so much else you read: things you pick up, spend time with, and put down again without having been moved or changed in any way. Because we are teachers, we want this book to have a very special impact on you and to help you make good decisions

© 1981 United Feature Syndicate Inc.

about whether you want to be a teacher and about what kind of teacher you want to become. For these reasons, you need to read this book in a different way. Take the book on fully. Encounter it. Participate in it. Fight with it. Laugh with it. Laugh at it. Improve it by adding yourself to it. You will be asked or nudged to do things that are not in keeping with your natural style of learning. Doing these things, however, may help you to identify more clearly how you learn best and give you a sense of the various ways you can learn and can know something.

We're asking you to invest something of yourself in this book. That old tired cliché "you get out of it what you put into it" applies here. So, again, if you didn't think about and write down your motives, go back and have a try at it.

There must be a nearly infinite number of answers to the question "What are my motives for wanting to become a teacher?" Here are a few examples you might check against your own list:

- I really like the idea of having influence on 30 (or 150) kids every day.

- I would rather be a big fish in a little pond than a little fish in some big corporation out there.

- Teachers are my favorite people, and I want to stay among them.

- I can't think of anything else to do with my major.

- Teaching seems to be a fairly secure, low-risk occupation with a lot of attractive benefits.

- The instruction I had in school was incredibly bad, and I want to correct that situation.

- I don't know what I want to do. So I'll teach for a while until I make up my mind.

- My parents would really be pleased if I were a teacher.

- I, quite simply, love children—especially the scruffy, unattractive ones everyone else ignores.

- One of my students might become a famous painter, or the president of a major corporation, or who knows what. It would be nice to have a strong influence on just one significant life.

- I've never wanted to do anything else. As far back as I can remember, I've always wanted to teach.

- I really want to become a principal (or a coach, or a guidance counselor, or a college professor, or an educational researcher), and this seems to be the way one has to start.

- Education seems as if it's going to be the action field of the future, and I want to be part of it.

- I am happiest when I'm explaining something and helping people grow.

- I don't like business and its grubby dog-eat-dog world, and teaching seems like a more humanistic option.

- I don't like what is happening to our society, and teaching seems to be a way to improve things.

DIALOGUE[3]

JIM: I'm having a little trouble with this list.

KEVIN: What's the matter? Can't you find your motive on it?

JIM: Seriously, it could be confusing to the reader. For instance, "the desire to work out one's own problems." This seems much more likely to be an unconscious motive than the others do.

KEVIN: I agree, but some of the other motives can be hidden, too, like the desire for respect and prestige. On the other hand, some people go into teaching to relieve the anxiety and discomfort they feel about particular social wrongs. They are consciously seeking to work out something that is a problem to them.

JIM: All right, but I'm troubled about another thing. The way we've separated out these motives and the way we've written the cases make it appear that individuals are driven by a single, clearly visible motive. Life just isn't that way. We are driven by many motives, some of which may contradict each other.

KEVIN: You're right. The way we've done it makes a very complex phenomenon seem too simple. But if we tried to portray the full range of human motivations in each case, we'd have three novels instead of three brief case studies. But you bring up a good point, and I hope the reader is forewarned.

JIM: One final point. This reads like THE list. We don't mean to give this impression.

KEVIN: Right, we've left out all sorts of motives. For instance, some people go into teaching because they want to coach a state championship athletic team; some women become teachers because they want an occupational "insurance policy" in case something happens to their husbands or their marriages; some people use teaching as a second job so they can support themselves in what they really want to do, such as write; and some people espouse a particular religious doctrine or economic system and are seeking converts. No, this list merely scratches the surface. We're just trying to get students to begin thinking about why they want to teach.

[3]Several times during the writing of this book, the authors had disagreements or misunderstandings or minor conflicts in points of view. We had to talk these differences through and ended by illuminating each other and coming to some agreement. We want to share these discussions or dialogues with you not only to provide extra information on the topics in question but, more importantly, to show you that the questions that are at the center of our book cannot always be answered in black-and-white terms.

The rest of this chapter is composed of three case studies that illustrate some common motives for going into teaching. Each case study is followed by a set of questions and a comment. The cases are intended as examples of how particular abstract motives take shape in teachers' lives. We offer these case studies to you as vicarious experiences to use in examining your own motivations. You may also want to discuss the cases and the accompanying questions with other people. The shared experience of reading the cases and responding to the questions should help you probe and understand your own motivations. And, finally, the cases and accompanying comments raise important issues about the nature of teaching.

The three motives we have chosen are:

1. the desire to teach a particular subject
2. the desire to work out one's own problems
3. the desire to aid in the renewal of society

*Case Number 1
The Desire to Teach a
Particular Subject*

Shari decided to be a second-grade teacher when she herself was in the second grade. So, when she graduated from college and was offered a position teaching second grade in a well-run elementary school, she felt her dreams had come true. After the first few months, Shari thought things were going very well. There was a good deal of activity in her class. The parents that she had met seemed pleased with their children's progress. The principal had visited twice and was extremely encouraging. Shari thought her second-graders were wonderful, and she was generally pleased with their behavior. Her only nagging concern was that the students often seemed sluggish or uninterested or, perhaps, simply bored.

Shari could not understand why her students might be bored, particularly when they were showing such good progress in reading. When she went home for Thanksgiving vacation, she shared her worries with her mother, who was an elementary school teacher with sixteen years of experience. Her mother offered to take a day of professional leave and observe Shari in action in the classroom. When, two weeks later, the observation day was over, the women went back to Shari's apartment for coffee and debriefing.

"Well, what did you think?" asked Shari.

"Before I answer that, let me ask you a few questions," responded her mother. "Shari, would you say that today was a typical day?"

Shari paused and reflected. "Y-e-s-s-s, I think so. If anything, it was a little too typical."

"What do you mean by that?"

"Well, nothing very special happened. One day last week, a huge dog wandered into the classroom, and I lost the class for the afternoon. Today nobody got a laughing fit or a bloody nose, and we didn't do anything really out of the ordinary, like put on a play, or have a visit from the school nurse."

"Okay. I see. But what I'm really getting at is, was the day typical in terms of what you taught?"

"I don't know what you mean by 'typical,' Mom."

"Okay, then, let me tell you what's on my mind. There is some good news and some bad news. Which do you want first?"

"Oh, the good news, of course!"

"Well, dear, there's a lot of good in what I observed today. Your class is well organized. The material is fresh and engaging. You obviously have been trained well, you're warm and creative, and you bring a good deal of yourself to what you are doing. Quite honestly, Shari, I had tears in my eyes much of the day because I was so proud of you. You're going to be an excellent teacher, Shari. Believe me, I don't think that after five years of teaching I could have done many of the things you are doing now. You look like you're having fun, and you communicate that enjoyment to the children."

"Oh, Mom, what great compliments! After that I think I'm ready for the bad news."

"My criticism, Shari, is based on today's being a typical day. And if it was, I think that your class is way out of balance."

"Out of balance?"

"Shari, all the time you were in teacher training you talked about reading, how important it is, the old and new methods that you were learning, the books on reading theory that you were reading, and your own teaching plans. In fact, you've been talking about reading for eight or nine years now. You love reading, and that's what has created a lack of balance in your teaching."

"Mom, I don't get the point. How can someone love reading *too* much?"

"It's not that you love reading too much, Shari, but that you seem to love the other subjects so little. You were with those children for four and one-half hours today, and my notes tell me that more than three and one-half of those hours were devoted to reading. What about writing and penmanship? What about arithmetic? Do you realize that you devoted only twenty-one minutes to arithmetic? And that was straight out of the workbook! During the lunch break I looked at the curricular guide for the second grade. If today was typical, you are way out of line with what the school district expects you to accomplish during the year."

"I guess I have been stressing reading pretty heavily. But it's *so* important."

"But so is learning to write, and so is getting a firm foundation in math. So is learning to work in groups, and the rest of the second-grade

curriculum. You told me, Shari, that you're worried because the children seem bored, and quite frankly, dear, I think you are stifling them with too much reading. Even the segments of instruction within reading and the free reading time are too long. The children's attention span isn't very long, and they need changes in their activities. Besides, the fact is that you are seriously impairing their academic progress by not attending to the rest of the curriculum. Shari, you are going to have to get things in balance. You are going to have to give much more time to other subjects and, most importantly, you are going to have to give *yourself* to those other subject matters. Shari, you need to show the same enthusiasm and creativity for them that you show for reading."

"Mom, it hurts to hear this, but I think you're right. In a funny way I knew that I was overdoing it, but I just couldn't bring myself to face it."

"Well, dear, what are mothers for?"

Questions

1. From the information available, how would you characterize Shari's motivation to teach?

2. What might be some other interpretations of Shari's situation that are different from her mother's assessment?

3. Shari obviously has carried into her teaching a zeal for one important aspect of the curriculum. What are some of the advantages and disadvantages associated with this situation?

4. Shari needed another pair of eyes to help her see her problem. What other sources might she have called on for feedback on her performance?

Comment

Love of subject matter or content is an important and commendable motive for teaching. A major purpose of school is to pass on to the young the best of society's knowledge. Another important purpose is to develop in young people basic skills and, especially, a love for learning. A teacher who has a passion to convey subject matter is often quite effective at both of these goals. We probably all have had certain teachers who seemed genuinely excited about their particular subject or discipline. Although such teachers often drive students very hard, they are the ones who usually make the greatest impact.

But carrying love for subject matter or content to an extreme can cause trouble. Shari's motive is not uncommon. Nor is the problem she worked herself into. Students have many needs. Second-grade students need not only a foundation in several different content areas but also diversity during the day. Staying with one subject area for most of every day is bound to take its toll. For the children, having a teacher as energetic and creative as Shari didn't compensate for getting too much of a good thing.

The other side of a strong desire to teach a certain content or subject matter often is the motive of avoidance. Many of us feel uncomfortable with elements or aspects of the curriculum that we are required to teach. For instance, it is not uncommon for elementary school teachers to have a limited background in mathematics and, consequently, to be uncomfortable with the subject. The result is that when time and energy are assigned to the various subjects, mathematics ends up being shortchanged. And the children are actually the ones who are most shortchanged. The same avoidance can be seen in many subject areas. The physical education teacher who loves basketball finds it easy to extend the program for that sport at the expense of, say, gymnastics. The English teacher who loves interpreting literature finds it easy to avoid slugging it out with grammar, punctuation, and other essential writing skills. While our tendency to avoid what we do not know or like is understandable, it is also irresponsible. Further, it is

also unfair both to the students and to subsequent teachers, who will expect students to have a command over the avoided or neglected content.

Teachers who are strongly motivated by the desire to teach particular content need to be somewhat cross-eyed. Keeping one eye on what they want to teach, they need to keep the other eye on the students, on their day-to-day progress and needs. No one ever said that it is easy to be a good teacher.

Case Number Two
The Desire to Work Out
One's Own Problems

Jean was a first-year teacher in a high school in Austin, Texas. As a result of desegregation efforts, her school was evenly balanced between Anglos and Hispanics. Jean was very pleased to be assigned to a school with such a heavy concentration of Mexican-American students, because she was interested in social justice and in using the political process to obtain one's rights. Jean had been raised in a comfortable suburb adjacent to another city in the Southwest, so she thought she had some grasp of the issues faced by Mexican-American students. Also, her parents, both of whom worked, were political activists who were usually on the side of the underdog.

Jean, like many new teachers, believed she had adequate mastery of the subject matter, but she worried about whether she would get along with the students. She was particularly concerned about her ability to relate to Hispanic students. Consequently, in the early weeks of school, she worked very hard to establish a rapport with the Mexican-American students in her classes. Some of them took Jean into their confidence, and they had long talks in her classroom after school. During one of these sessions, Miguel complained that the school by and large ignored the Hispanic students and that the Hispanic students were politically naive and unorganized. Jean suggested that they establish a student branch of La Raza, a political action group advancing the cause of Mexican-Americans.

The students became quite interested in this organization, and it began to take hold in the school. Although Jean received a good deal of satisfaction from this, she had a sense that all was not well. She had a regular monthly conference scheduled with the head of the English department, whom she both trusted and admired. At the beginning of the conference, the supervisor asked Jean what particular aspects of her teaching pleased her. Jean replied that she had good relationships with her Hispanic students. The supervisor asked how she had accomplished this, and Jean answered that she had spent a great deal of time talking with them as a group and that, under her sponsorship, the students had formed a group, Estudianta por La Raza. The supervisor, a youngish woman with a great deal of experience in urban schools serving poor children, was not so pleased with Jean's apparent success as Jean was.

"Jean," she said, facing her, "What do you really want to do here? Is it your goal to organize the Hispanic students into a power coalition? Is that what you feel you're getting paid to do?"

"Well," Jean replied, "these kids just have to get organized. The only answer to the social oppression they've been living under is to organize and begin making their weight felt as a group."

"That may or may not be true," said the supervisor, "but that's not the point at issue. You have a mixed class of children, and you're here to help them acquire some understanding of each other along with skills, knowledge, and outlooks that will help them survive and excel in society. But you wanted the Hispanic students to like you, so you identified with their feelings of separateness and their prejudices about Anglos. And, if you will, you have created two factions in your class and you treat each differently."

"*I* didn't do that!" Jean contested hotly. "Society did."

"No, Jean, you did," said the supervisor. "Instead of encouraging your students to confront and understand their prejudices, and creating an atmosphere that would allow them to emerge as individuals capable of solving their own human problems, you encouraged them to value their prejudices and to think that they were right to maintain those prejudices. As an Anglo teacher teaching Hispanics and Anglos, you have a tremendous opportunity to help Hispanics understand the Anglo. You say you understand these kids, and that's important; but it's equally important that they understand you and other people like you. Is it your goal for Hispanic students to come to you whenever they have a problem with the Anglos and have you solve it for them? What happens when you are no longer around and those kids run into that problem? Do you think they're going to love and respect you for not teaching them how to work with Anglos? Not on your life. They're going to hate you for using them and failing to teach them what they need to know to get along."

"I honestly feel that I owe them something," Jean said. "And I just can't work it out that easily. What are you telling me to do? To ignore their problems and go back to 'business as usual' with the workbooks and all that?"

"You do owe them something, but 'them' means all those kids. You've got a rare opportunity here to help both the Hispanic kids and the Anglo kids learn how to master themselves and how to handle their prejudices so that they can settle the problems of living together without depending on you and the other Anglo liberals for help. You can get these kids to confront their fears, bring them out in the open, and deal honestly and rationally with them in class. You can deal with the issue through the subject matter, through composition, through general class discussion. These kids may discover that they are much more alike than different, regardless of their cultural background."

"I really don't think it will work," said Jean. "The Hispanic kids are angry and they've heard too much discussion and too much bull to take more of it from an Anglo teacher."

"Look," the supervisor replied, "I taught psychology in a junior college twenty years ago while I was getting my master's degree. I had white kids from the ethnic neighborhoods of Chicago who weren't exactly thrilled at having a black teacher. But I knew that this class was okay when, in the middle of the unit on perception and prejudice, one of those white students said that he had thrown a stone at Martin Luther King on his march into Cicero, and that he was amazed at his own ignorance in doing such a thing. Then a black got up and said that he had actually attacked white people on the street for no good reason, and he, too, was amazed at his own prejudice. Here were some kids who were learning to see people as people. It can be done if the teacher has a clear sense of how the subject matter can help people understand themselves.

"When a student in the class began talking about 'whitey' or 'niggers,' as they did in the early meetings, we'd ask the class to stop and consider their feelings in view of the reading we'd done on fears and aggression. In that way each member of the class was forced to come face to face with his or her own doubts and fears. I'm a teacher, Jean, and I tried to use my subject matter and my objectivity to help students see themselves as the people they are. The more they understood themselves, the more they understood others in the class as people. That's why they could admit their failings in front of a whole class of people like themselves. I really feel, Jean, that teaching English gives you a good opportunity to do some of the same things. There seems to be one lesson that you have yet to learn about teaching, and that is . . ."

"Yes?"

"That teaching is a relationship to be ended, not to be continued."

"Would you explain what you mean by that?" Jean asked.

"Sure," said the supervisor. "Mature teachers prepare students for independence, not dependence. They try to get them to the point where they are able to fend for themselves. And I guess that's what I'm questioning about your relationship with your students. Are you really doing that for them?"

"I don't know," said Jean, softly. "I honestly don't know. I need to think about all this."

Questions

1. How would you characterize the personal problems Jean seems to be working out in her teaching?

2. Have you had experience with teachers who seemed to be working out personal problems in their classes? What kinds of problems? What was the effect on the class?

3. Have you ever known personal problems to be used effectively in a classroom? If not, can you imagine circumstances in which they might be used effectively?

4. How do you evaluate the advice Jean received from her supervisor?

5. If you had been Jean's supervisor, what would you have advised her?

6. What are some of the implications of the supervisor's statement that "mature teachers prepare students for independence, not dependence"? What are some ways that elementary and secondary school teachers can stimulate independence?

7. Did the supervisor think that organizing a student group of Hispanic students would have a bad effect on the school?

8. Was the supervisor simply telling Jean to teach the subject matter in which she had been trained? What instructional technique did Jean's supervisor use in dealing with the problems of her students?

Comment Insecurity is endemic in beginning teachers. They want assurance. As a result, some teachers seek to be popular with their students. There is a difference, however, between popularity and a genuine helping relationship. Popularity may make a real helping relationship impossible. In a sense, this is what Jean did with her Hispanic students. She achieved quick popularity by organizing their political aspirations, and that was why, as her supervisor pointed out, she thought she understood their needs. But she had not really given the students what they needed; she had given them only what she thought they needed. Had Jean understood better what she herself needed, as well as what she wanted, then her relationship with the students would have been more mature. Jean's experience illustrates the importance of examining one's own motives before attempting to motivate others. Perhaps if Jean had examined her own motives a bit more deeply, she would have realized that she had to overcome fear of rejection by her Hispanic students before she could teach effectively. The very fact that Jean spent much of her time worrying about relating to Hispanic students, rather than relating to Carlos, Juanita, Miguel, and Lucita as individuals, tells us that she had not grasped the importance of teaching at a personal level; she had, in truth, not yet acknowledged the individuality of those students.

One characteristic of maturity is the ability to work out one's own problems objectively. If Jean could have realized that her own fears of rejection and of confronting explosive feelings were detrimental to her, she would have seen that an important purpose of teaching is to help children discover that they can face and handle their own fears. Jean's supervisor tried to show her that she was forcing students to need her support rather than making them independent of her. She tried to tell Jean that her popularity may have been gained at the cost of her integrity as a teacher.

Case Number Three
The Desire to Aid in the
Renewal of Society

Fred was in his late thirties. His disposition was so pleasant, and a smile came so readily to his face, that one of his fellow teachers in the large metropolitan high school referred to him as "everybody's father." Fred had a remarkable ability to remain relaxed when everyone else was tense, and he frequently broke up emotionally charged situations with an appropriate quip or question.

Each year Fred asked to teach the slow freshman history class. Of course, his request was always granted, for the other teachers regarded the slow or "basic" classes as "punishment." Year after year, Fred worked happily with children nobody else really wanted.

Fred's freshman history class was one of the most active in the whole school. He took his students beyond the walls of the school on expeditions to day court, to the police station and jail, through industrial plants in the area—and he even sneaked in a baseball game one day. Yet his classes were not characterized by fun and games. The students worked very hard on long and involved homework assignments, intricate discussions of problems, and demanding tests.

At one point in a particular academic year, Fred invited another teacher to speak to the class on shipbuilding in the eighteenth century. The talk went well, and after the session the other teacher, Earl Dixon, commented to Fred that the temper of the discussion following his talk had been very different from what he had anticipated; the questions were thoughtful and displayed observation of detail that the guest speaker had not expected from a "bunch of basics."

Fred greeted Mr. Dixon's remarks with a chuckle. "You know, Earl," he said, "they really amaze me too sometimes. Most of these kids really have behavior problems, not intellectual ones. If you looked at their case histories, you'd find that the majority of them were 'dropped through the ranks'!"

"What do you mean?" asked Mr. Dixon.

"I mean that they were in regular classes a good bit of their scholastic lives. But when they became problems in class, their teachers decided that the cause of their poor behavior was that the work was too hard for them. So, the majority of children in this class really represent the rebels, the nonconformists, the 'antisocials'! They're the kids about whom teachers say, 'I don't care if they learn any history at all as long as they become good citizens.'"

"Yes, but you must admit that very few of them will go to college. Most basics just drop out," said Mr. Dixon.

"Maybe you're missing my point," said Fred. "I guess I'm saying that people can't be 'good citizens' unless they are contributing members of society, and that they should contribute something that they think is worth contributing. If they can't get the basic tools that make a person productive, how can they be good citizens? It's a lot more than getting jobs or making decent livings. If that were the case, we could put these kids through an industrial arts program and that would be the end of it. No, in some ways, I feel that these kids are much more capable than the kids we send to the university."

"In what sense?"

"In the sense that they are the least accepting of society as it exists now," replied Fred. "If you talked to some of them for an hour or so, you'd find that they really feel the school is hypocritical in many ways, and they aren't afraid to point out the hypocrisies. They'll tell you, for instance, that there are two sets of rules in the school, two sets of discipline procedures, two sets of privileges, and all the rest."

 "But I hear the same thing from my 'honors' classes," protested Mr. Dixon. "Those kids know about the double system too. They often tell me that an honor student here can get away with anything from cutting class to smoking in the john. The 'double system' isn't any secret in this school."

"You've got me wrong again, Earl. I know about that, but that wasn't what I was talking about. What these kids are saying is not that we expect too much of them, but too little. For instance, if a kid dropped from an A to a C in your honors history course, what would happen?"

"The kid would probably go in and see the counselor—by request."

Fred replied, "That's right. When someone does poorly, people get concerned. They try to help him or her take a look at what's wrong. If one of these students goes from a C to an F, though, everyone says, 'Well, what more do you expect? The kid's only a basic and doesn't have the ability to sustain a C.' And they get all the inexperienced teachers and martinets in the school. Oh, they know that if they become real problems, they'll get counseling and possibly even better teaching. But that isn't their complaint. They know that the system isn't out to punish them. It just doesn't care enough about them to want to punish them. They know that the system would rather they just go away and not bother anyone. That's the double standard in this school—those that are cared about and those that aren't: that's what these kids will tell you. It's not injustice, it's no justice at all."

"Is this why you request basic classes every year?" asked Mr. Dixon.

"That's part of it," said Fred. "But it's not the whole reason. I'm not quite that altruistic. No, I see in these kids something that frightens me. They have capability, but if it isn't developed it can become capability for hate, a hate based on fear. They're a mark for anyone who comes along with a good strong 'hate' message; I know it and it frightens me. They can rant and 'bitch,' but they have to be taught to analyze critically, to think through problems and to care about other people. In my mind, that is what good citizens do. They have developed capability for understanding, and that is what I am trying to do—develop that capability. I think these kids need that capability developed even more than the kids in the honors classes do, because that attention the honors children get in the course of their day here will pull them through. Plenty of people challenge them, listen to them, and chastise them when they need it. But with these kids it's a different story."

"You know," said Mr. Dixon, "you're not just talking about the basic classes. I think the same thing is generally true of average classes. It seems that a kid who's really bright gets a lot of attention, and so does the kid who is really slow, but it's that kid in the middle. . . ."

"You're right," said Fred. "The kids in this class are the bottom of that middle group in terms of the concern they arouse from the system. And they know it. Yet, as you saw today, they are capable. We owe them a decent set of expectations. I've maintained high expectations for the kids. I would prefer to slightly overmatch them intellectually than undermatch them, because no development is possible when you're being undermatched constantly."

"You know," said Mr. Dixon, "you make a pretty strong argument for your way of teaching, but someone could use the same argument to justify a very academic college-prep course, which would really be irrelevant for those kids."

"Only if the aim were to teach a very academic college-prep course. The course is a means to an end, in my mind, not an end in itself. My course is somewhat scholarly and academic, but it's not a waste of time for the kids. When we study the court system, for instance, we confront the problem of giving everyone his or her due. We talk about the difficulties of guaranteeing rights to the individual and rights to the group. I like to think, Earl, that the goal of schooling is not more schooling, but rather an ability to push back against society in a constructive way."

"Fred," Mr. Dixon said, "I'd like you to come to my class in American history and make the same points with them that you've made with me. You seem to be talking about several problems that have come up in our class. I just wonder how you'd fare with those kids. They have some very strong opinions of their own."

"I'll take my chances any time after next week, Earl. We're going down to the legislative session at the Capitol next week."

<table>
<tr><td>Questions</td><td>

1. How is Fred's commitment to social renewal specifically manifested in his classroom teaching?

2. According to Fred, what is the criterion for assignment to basic classes in his school? Was this true of your high school?

3. What is the double standard of which Earl Dixon spoke, and how do you explain it? What is the double standard of which Fred spoke, and how do you explain it? Did either of these double standards exist in your school?

4. In what sense are Fred's basic students more capable than the college-prep students? In what sense are they a more dangerous element in society? Do you agree with Fred's analysis here?

5. In what ways is Fred different from most of the teachers you have known? How are his expectations for his students different?

6. What does Fred see as the role of academic disciplines in education? If you had to, how would you argue against his position?

</td></tr>
<tr><td>Comment</td><td>

John Dewey, an American philosopher and educator, whose life and work are sketched in Chapter 3, called attention to our need to educate the young in the entire range of skills necessary for citizenship in a complex technological society. Many of Dewey's ideas were misapplied or corrupted. What Fred was reacting against is a case in point. In Fred's school as in many others, Dewey's concept of citizenship has been completely perverted.

During the thirties many schools adopted the policy of awarding a grade for citizenship. This grade originally was intended as a measure of the student's ability to use the processes of democracy in a profitable, efficient way. However, as the democratic processes Dewey had introduced to the classroom degenerated into empty forms, the citizenship grade became more and more a judgment of conduct. As long as the student "played the game" of democracy in the classroom, displaying a compliant attitude and voting for class officers who were officers in name only, he or she was given a high grade in citizenship. Citizenship became a code word among teachers. A teacher who was given a class of "low achievers" or "discipline problems" was sometimes told, "Don't worry about the academics with these children. Just make them 'good citizens.'" This meant that the teacher

</td></tr>
</table>

would not be expected to teach the students anything, for they were not capable of learning, but to keep them docile and out of everyone else's way. Parents were told that their child wasn't a very good student but "an excellent citizen." This meant that even though he or she didn't learn anything, the child did without question everything that students were supposed to do.

The use of the word *citizenship* as a synonym for *docile conduct* was a travesty of Dewey's intention. He envisioned training for citizenship as a process of working out in class actual problems that arise in a democracy. Dewey valued informed dissent, and he wanted children to develop the intellectual wherewithal to make reasonable decisions based on the disciplined study of alternatives. He would have considered the use of a citizenship grade as a conduct mark an absolute travesty of the system he had designed, for good citizens were not docile sheep who could be "conned"

REASONS FOR TEACHING

Different people have different reasons for selecting teaching as their career. Also, over the years there has been a shift in motivations. For several years the National Education Association has been probing the motivations for the selection of teaching. The table below summarizes its findings.

• What changes in the motivations of teachers does the table reveal? How do you account for those changes?

• Now that you have completed this chapter, how would you answer the question "What are your reasons for deciding to become a teacher?"

Principal Reasons Selected by All Teachers
for Originally Deciding to Become a Teacher, 1971–81 (percent)

Reason	1971	1976	1981
Desire to work with young people	71.8	71.4	69.6
Interest in subject-matter field	34.5	38.3	44.1
Value or significance of education in society	37.1	38.3	44.1
Influence of a teacher in elementary or secondary school	17.9	20.6	25.4
Long summer vacation	14.4	19.1	21.5
Influence of family	29.5	18.4	21.5
Job security	16.2	17.4	20.6
Never really considered anything else	17.4	17.4	20.3
Opportunity for a lifetime of self-growth	21.4	17.4	13.1

Source: National Education Association, "The Status of the American Public School Teacher, 1980–81" (Washington, D.C.: NEA, 1981). Reprinted by permission of the Association.

with impunity. Rather, they were men and women who could make the tough decisions that democracy needs in order to function as a system. Dewey realized that the schools were an appropriate place to teach students about the nature of such decisions and to give them low-risk but real practice in decision making in a context where mistakes were not "for keeps."

The long-term effect of the misinterpretation of Dewey's system was to discredit citizenship as an appropriate goal for schooling. Citizenship became too closely associated with conformity and following orders. Yet, in Fred's case, we see a person consciously attempting to develop educated citizens. Fred's visits to courthouses, legislative sessions, and factories, and the classroom study of major social problems, are very much in keeping with what Dewey had in mind when he spoke of "educating for freedom."

SOME CONCLUDING THOUGHTS

Selecting a career involves answering many questions, questions such as "Will I be happy?", "Will this career provide me with a satisfying lifestyle?", "Will I be up to the challenge, and will I find the work satisfying?", and "Will I grow in the experience?" People considering teaching as a life's work should grapple with these questions that surround the motives for choice. But there are other, and, if you will, deeper motives that need to be encountered.

Teaching, like nursing, the ministry, and social work, is a service occupation. Built into teaching is the idea of service to others. For many people the root of their decision to teach is deeper than a love of subject matter or an attraction to the life of a teacher. Many men and women select teaching for reasons that are, at heart, religious or humanitarian. We suspect that teachers who are truly satisfied are people whose choice has been grounded in this deeper motivation. And while such religiously based or humanistically motivated reasons for teaching are a private matter, it is a matter that each of us needs to explore very carefully. Of all the questions in this book, "Why teach?" is ultimately the most important one. How we answer determines not only whether or not we will teach, but what we will actually *accomplish* as teachers.

Discussion Questions

1. What questions about your own motivation has this chapter raised?

2. In your experience did your teachers ever speak to you directly about their reasons for teaching? Did some teachers "tell" you by their actions what their motives for teaching were?

3. What, to you, is the most compelling reason to answer the question "Why teach?"

4. If you are currently planning to teach, what events in your life have helped you discover why you want to teach?

5. Do you think of teaching as a calling? As a social service? If you do, why? If not, why not?

For Further Reading

Ashton-Warner, Sylvia. *Teacher.* New York: Simon & Schuster, 1963.
> An autobiographical account of the author's years teaching Maori children in New Zealand. The book is rich in detail and gives a clear statement of the author's approach to education.

Collins, Marva, and Civia Tamarkin. *Marva Collins' Way.* Los Angeles: J. P. Tarcher, 1982.
> This book takes the reader inside the world of one of America's most inspiring and controversial teachers. Marva Collins describes her method of educating the children others forgot.

Fuchs, Estelle. *Teachers Talk: Views from Inside City Schools.* Garden City, N.Y.: Doubleday, 1969.
> A collection of teachers' statements about themselves, schools, and learning during their initial four months of teaching in an urban setting. The author analyzes these statements, explicating the underlying assumptions of the teachers and suggesting alternative actions.

Good, Thomas L.; Bruce J. Biddle; and Jere E. Brophy. *Teachers Make a Difference.* New York: Holt, Rinehart, and Winston, 1975.
> A summary by three researchers of their own work and that of others. The authors offer insights into teaching and practical suggestions for the classroom.

Kaufman, Bel. *Up the Down Staircase.* Englewood Cliffs, N.J.: Prentice-Hall, 1964.
> An easy-to-read, humorous, and poignant semifictionalized account of a beginning teacher's experience in a New York City high school. A thoroughly enjoyable book.

Ryan, Kevin, et al. *Biting the Apple: Accounts of First Year Teachers.* New York: Longman, 1980.
> This book tells the stories of ten beginning teachers struggling to master their new profession.

Stuart, Jesse. *The Thread That Runs So True.* New York: Charles Scribner's Sons, 1949.
> An autobiographical account of the famous writer's experience as a teacher in a one-room school. It includes an interesting description of the problems and successes of a beginning teacher, and of life in rural America.

Stuart, Jesse. *To Teach, To Love.* New York: Penguin Books, 1973.
> A distinguished American storyteller and former teacher summarizes his views of teaching and the many purposes of schooling.

Is There
a Job for You in
Education?

2

The purpose of this chapter is to provide you with information regarding the availability of teaching positions in the elementary and secondary schools. The chapter also explores other career opportunities both within and outside the educational field. We feel that the material contained in the chapter is vital for you to make an enlightened career decision. Study the information carefully and discuss it with your instructors and your career planning and placement office. There may be some options available to you in your program of study that would increase your chances of being hired.

This chapter emphasizes that:

▪ There are many factors that influence the availability of teaching jobs (enrollments in teacher education programs, student enrollments in schools, ratios of students to teachers, geo-

graphical location, and subject matter and grade level taught). Although there is an oversupply of teachers in some teaching fields, other fields face a severe shortage of teachers.

▪ Teacher salaries remain relatively low, with the average salary of classroom teachers in 1981–82 being just under $19,000. However, salaries vary tremendously from school district to school district.

▪ Because the search for teaching positions may be competitive, you may have to spend considerable time and energy seeking a

job. Certain job-hunting strategies will increase your chances.

▪ Certification requirements differ from state to state for both general and specialized areas of teaching.

▪ A wide variety of careers are available to people trained as teachers.

▪ Should you be unable to secure a teaching position, or wish to change careers after you have taught, the skills you have acquired in teacher training can be transferred to related occupational areas.

▪ No matter what the job market may be at a particular moment, there has never been a surplus of good teachers. Better prepared teachers will find it easier to gain employment and will improve the teaching profession and its public image.

"Pupil Enrollment Below Estimates"

"School Board Forced to Release 150 Teachers"

"School Bond Issue Defeated by Voters"

"National Survey Indicates Surplus of Teachers"

"College Enrollments in Elementary Education Down"

"Nation Faces Shortage of Math and Science Teachers"

Y OU HAVE PROBABLY READ newspaper headlines similar to these and have wondered whether you will be able to obtain a teaching position when you graduate. Although we would like to answer this question for you personally, we obviously cannot. We can, however, provide you with information that may help you increase your chances of obtaining the kind of teaching position you are seeking. That is the purpose of this chapter.

WILL THERE BE JOB OPENINGS IN TEACHING?

In the 1960s the United States went through a rare social experience. It became inundated with adolescents and young adults. The number of young people between the ages of fourteen and twenty-four increased during the decade by a staggering 52 percent. This great population bulge put a tremendous strain on the social agencies serving this age group. Welfare and recreational agencies, police departments (fourteen to twenty-four are the high crime years), and schools were unprepared to handle this large number of young customers. In education, it meant a grave teacher shortage throughout much of the decade. People became used to the idea of a high demand for teachers. Apparently, few noticed (1) that a high percentage of the students in this sixties population bulge were graduating from college and becoming teachers, and (2) that the number of school-age children to be taught (and thus the number of career opportunities) was leveling off. As a result, in the early 1970s the teacher shortage was suddenly replaced by a teacher surplus. We went from famine to feast in the space of a few short years.

It seems, however, that the worst of the surplus is behind us. In fact, unless more college students go into teaching, the nation may be faced with a teacher shortage in the late 1980s. This situation would sharply contrast with the large general oversupply of teachers that existed during the 1970s and that is expected to continue, at a reduced level, into the mid-1980s. Several things are happening. First, the number of college students going into teacher education fell dramatically during the seventies. Probably as a direct response to the publicity about the very real job shortage in teaching and general uncertainty within the educational employment market, many young people chose other careers. In 1972 the number of graduates from teacher education programs was at an all-time high—317,000. By 1980 the number had fallen to 154,000, a decrease of 52 percent in just eight years.

Second, although the demand for additional public school teachers (including returnees to the profession) is projected to decrease during the mid-1980s, by the end of the decade the demand for additional teachers is expected to rise. From 1981 to 1985, 689,000 additional teachers are expected to be hired, but from 1986 to 1990 the demand for additional teachers is expected to increase to 983,000. This represents an increase in the average number of additional teachers hired each year from 138,000 (for the period 1981–85) to 197,000 (for the period 1986–90).[1]

Third, enrollments in public elementary schools are expected to continue to decrease until 1984, and then will begin to increase until 1990. When combined with a continuing gradual decline in pupil-teacher ratios (from 20.7 in 1980 to 18.8 in 1990), the number of elementary classroom teachers should reach 1.44 million in 1990, an increase of 265,000 teachers over the 1980 level (see Tables 2.1, 2.2, and 2.3). However, enrollments in public secondary schools are expected to decline and will be offset only slightly by decreasing pupil-teacher ratios. As a result, the number of classroom teachers in public secondary schools in 1990 is expected to be 893,000 —95,000 fewer teachers than in 1980.

The demand for additional teachers in the 1986–90 period is expected to average 197,000 per year, while the supply of new teachers is expected to average 203,000. However, if the percentage that new teacher graduates are of bachelor's degree recipients in the 1986–90 period remains at the 1980 level of 17 percent, then the supply of new teacher graduates will

[1]Martin M. Frankel and Debra E. Gerald, *Projections of Education Statistics to 1990–91*, National Center for Education Statistics (Washington, D.C.: U.S. Government Printing Office, 1982), p. 74.

Table 2.1 Enrollment in Grades K–8 and 9–12 in Public and Private Schools (in thousands)

	PUBLIC SCHOOLS			PRIVATE SCHOOLS		
	K–12	*K–8*	*9–12*	*K–12*	*K–8*	*9–12*
1970	45,909	32,577	13,332	5,363	4,052	1,311
1975	44,791	30,487	14,304	5,000 (est.)	3,700	1,300
1980	40,995	27,678	13,317	5,100 (est.)	3,700	1,400
1985 (projected)	39,166	26,951	12,215	5,000	3,600	1,400
1990 (projected)	41,267	30,244	11,023	5,400	4,000	1,400

Source: Martin M. Frankel and Debra E. Gerald, *Projections of Education Statistics to 1990–91*, National Center for Education Statistics (Washington, D.C.: U.S. Government Printing Office, 1982), p. 34.

Table 2.2 Pupil-Teacher Ratios in Public and Private Elementary and Secondary Schools (number of pupils per teacher)

	PUBLIC SCHOOLS		PRIVATE SCHOOLS	
	Elementary	*Secondary*	*Elementary*	*Secondary*
1970	24.4	19.8	26.4	16.4
1975	21.7	18.8	21.6	15.9
1980	20.7	16.9	19.7	15.3
1985 (projected)	19.8	16.6	19.3	15.0
1990 (projected)	18.8	15.9	18.7	14.7

Source: Martin M. Frankel and Debra E. Gerald, *Projections of Education Statistics to 1990–91*, National Center for Education Statistics (Washington, D.C.: U.S. Government Printing Office, 1982), p. 81. (Pupil-teacher ratios were derived from the figures presented on p. 81.)

average only about 160,000 per year.[2] At that level, teacher shortages would occur.

Another factor to consider is that teachers are not interchangeable units. Teachers are prepared for different specialties (special education, primary grades, all-level art, high school social studies), and the job market in each one of these subfields is different and may change frequently. It is unwise, therefore, to decide whether or not to become a special education teacher because you have heard that there is, in general, a surplus of teachers. Even throughout the worst of the teacher surplus there were serious shortages in some subfields.

[2]Frankel and Gerald, *Projections,* p. 76.

Table 2.3 Classroom Teachers in Public and Private Elementary and Secondary Schools (in thousands)

	PUBLIC SCHOOLS			PRIVATE SCHOOLS		
	K–12	*Elementary*	*Secondary*	*K–12*	*Elementary*	*Secondary*
1970	2,055	1,128	927	233	153	80
1975	2,196	1,180	1,016	255 (est.)	172	83
1980	2,163	1,175	988	276	187	89
1985 (projected)	2,128	1,199	929	280	186	94
1990 (projected)	2,333	1,440	893	309	214	95

Source: Martin M. Frankel and Debra E. Gerald, *Projections of Education Statistics to 1990–91*, National Center for Education Statistics (Washington, D.C.: U.S. Government Printing Office, 1982), p. 80.

Estimates of the supply and demand for beginning teachers by subject area are listed in Table 2.4. The estimated supply of prospective teachers to fill jobs open to beginning teachers in 1982 was least adequate in mathematics, physics, industrial arts, and agriculture. Other areas in which demand is relatively high are special education, bilingual education, science, and reading. Subjects or assignments in which the supply was estimated to exceed most widely the actual demand include men's and women's physical and health education, art, primary grades, and social studies. However, an oversupply does not mean there are no jobs. It means, rather, that job seeking is more competitive, and the teacher graduate may have to relocate in a different community or commute a great distance to work.

Another factor that influences the job market is location. Some communities have far more applications than they have teaching positions available. University towns, urban areas, and large cities usually have a great surplus of teachers. By contrast, rural America traditionally has had difficulty attracting and holding teachers. Generally speaking, teacher vacancies are greatest in the Plains (Iowa, Kansas, Minnesota, Missouri, Nebraska,

Table 2.4 Relative Demand by Teaching Area, 1982 Report

Teaching fields with considerable teacher shortage (5.00–4.25)

Mathematics	4.81
Science—physics	4.41
Industrial arts	4.36
Vocational agriculture	4.36

Teaching fields with slight teacher shortage (4.24–3.45)

Special education—LD	4.20
Bilingual education	4.13
Science—chemistry	4.13
Special education—PSA	3.98
Speech pathology/audiology	3.95
Special education—multi-handicapped	3.93
Science—earth	3.89
Data processing	3.86
Special education—MR	3.84
Special education—gifted	3.81
Special education—reading	3.73
Science—biology	3.66
School psychologist	3.56
Business	3.47

Teaching fields with balanced supply and demand (3.44–2.65)

Music—instrumental	3.28
English	3.21
Library science	3.12
Music—vocal	2.95
Counselor—secondary	2.79
Driver's education	2.77
Speech	2.76
Counselor—elementary	2.72
Language, modern—Spanish	2.68

Teaching fields with slight surplus of teachers (2.64–1.85)

Journalism	2.61
Language, modern—French	2.49
Language, modern—German	2.48
Home economics	2.43
Social worker (school)	2.34
Elementary—intermediate	2.26
Social science	2.11
Elementary—primary	2.02
Health education	1.90

Teaching fields with considerable surplus of teachers (1.84–1.00)

Art	1.84
Physical education	1.72

5 = Greatest demand   1 = Least demand

Source: The ASCUS Annual: A Job Search Handbook for Educators 1983 (Madison, Wisc.: Association for School, College and University Staffing, 1982), p. 6. Based upon a survey of teacher placement officers dated October, 1981, continental United States. Reprinted by permission.

North Dakota, and South Dakota) and in the South-Central states (Arkansas, Louisiana, Oklahoma, and Texas). There are fewer vacancies and/or more competition in the Northwest (Washington, Oregon, and Idaho) and in New England (Connecticut, Maine, Massachusetts, New Hampshire, Rhode Island, and Vermont).[3]

A large employer of teachers is the U.S. government. The Department of Defense operates approximately three hundred schools in twenty-seven countries around the world. These schools enroll more than 170,000 students and employ over 7,500 educational personnel. Salaries are comparable to those in the United States, but applicants must have at least one year of successful full-time employment as a professional educator.[4]

Although most of the data presented in this chapter refer to public elementary and secondary schools, private education is a highly significant part of the American educational system. In the 1980–81 school year, there were over 21,000 private schools with an enrollment of 5,029,000 and employing a staff of 281,000 teachers. One pupil out of every nine, or about 11 percent of the children attending elementary or secondary schools, attended a private school in 1980–81. Almost 13 percent of all teachers employed in elementary and secondary schools teach in private schools.[5] As Figure 2.1 indicates, most of the private schools in 1980–81 were affiliated with some religious group. Only 23 percent of the schools were not church-related, and these tended to be relatively small schools that enrolled only 16 percent of the pupils.

During the 1970s enrollment in both public and private schools declined. However, private institutions retained more of their enrollment between 1970 and 1980 than did public schools. While enrollments in public schools declined by 10.7 percent during the 1970s, private schools' enrollment declined by only 6.4 percent.

Since private schools employ 13 percent of all elementary and secondary teachers, they obviously offer an employment opportunity for new teachers. With 77 percent of the private schools being church-affiliated, many teachers who work in these schools do so because of religious motives. These teachers are often willing to work for less money than their public school counterparts and, as a result, the average teacher's salary in private schools is lower than the average in public schools. Lower salaries tend to be offset by other favorable working conditions, one study reported.

---

[3]*The ASCUS Annual: A Job Search Handbook for Educators 1983* (Madison, Wisc.: Association for School, College and University Staffing, 1982), pp. 4–6.

[4]For information on applying for a job with the Department of Defense overseas schools, write Teacher Recruitment, Department of Defense Dependents Schools, Hoffman Bldg. 1, 2461 Eisenhower Avenue, Alexandria, Virginia 22331.

[5]W. Vance Grant and Leo J. Eiden, *Digest of Education Statistics 1982* (Washington, D.C.: National Center for Education Statistics, 1982), pp. 48, 51.

Figure 2.1 Private Elementary and Secondary Schools and Their Enrollment, by Affiliation of School, U.S., 1980–81.

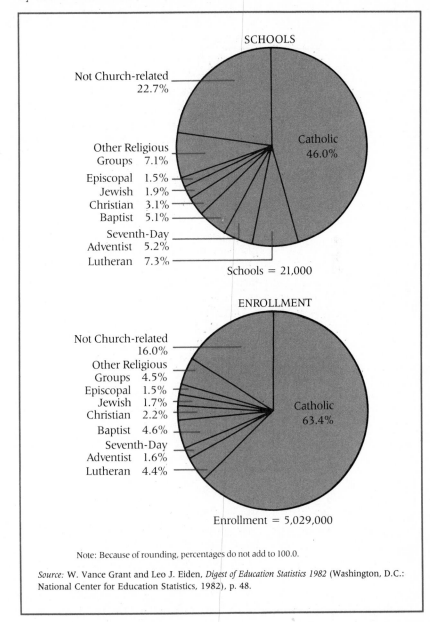

SCHOOLS

Not Church-related 22.7%

Other Religious Groups 7.1%

Episcopal 1.5%
Jewish 1.9%
Christian 3.1%
Baptist 5.1%

Seventh-Day Adventist 5.2%
Lutheran 7.3%

Catholic 46.0%

Schools = 21,000

ENROLLMENT

Not Church-related 16.0%

Other Religious Groups 4.5%
Episcopal 1.5%
Jewish 1.7%
Christian 2.2%
Baptist 4.6%
Seventh-Day Adventist 1.6%
Lutheran 4.4%

Catholic 63.4%

Enrollment = 5,029,000

Note: Because of rounding, percentages do not add to 100.0.

Source: W. Vance Grant and Leo J. Eiden, *Digest of Education Statistics 1982* (Washington, D.C.: National Center for Education Statistics, 1982), p. 48.

Compared to public schools, private schools have fewer disciplinary problems; stricter discipline, students who are less frequently absent, more supportive parents, more assigned homework, and more time spent in instruction in the central academic subjects.[6] Thus, for many individuals, teaching in a private school is an attractive alternative to teaching in the public school.

We have not had much experience in applying data on trends in population and teacher education enrollment to the educational job market. The information about employment prospects that you pick up here and elsewhere should be evaluated carefully and with some suspicion. For one thing, the educational job market may change rather rapidly. There is a great deal of movement in and out of the teaching profession, and this, of course, affects the availability of jobs. Also, these figures are affected by the economy. For instance, when economic times are favorable, more money is available for schools. The ratio of teachers to pupils goes down, creating more openings. When times are economically poor, the opposite is true. And teachers tend to hold onto their jobs more. The teachers' professional organizations have insisted for some time that what we have is an undersupply of money rather than an oversupply of teachers. They argue that there would be no surplus of teachers if we would reduce class size and get a lower pupil-teacher ratio.

As we have suggested, demographic projection and supply-and-demand forecasting are very inexact. What seems to be true as we write this may be out of date at the moment you are reading it.

Therefore, you ought to make every effort to get the most up-to-the-minute information possible about teacher supply and demand. You should consider it carefully before making a choice about a career in education and in particular about a specific subfield within education. This is especially true for people who are unable to wait for openings in their area of teaching interest. Sources of data to begin your search are your school's career counseling office, the department chairperson's or dean's office, the National Education Association, the Office of Education of the U.S. Department of Education, and the U.S. Department of Labor.

WHAT ARE
TEACHERS
PAID?

We might answer the question by saying, "Not nearly enough." No one ever went into teaching because of the lure of big money. Most of the rewards for teaching are personal rather than monetary. Most of our satisfactions come from being of service to others and helping students learn. That does not mean, however, that you have to be a pauper in order to enjoy the satisfactions that come from teaching. Salaries are a legitimate

---

[6]James Coleman, T. Hoffer, and S. Kilgore, *Public and Private Schools* (Washington, D.C.: Report to the National Center for Education Statistics, 1981).

concern for a prospective teacher; after all, everyone must have sufficient income to meet the costs of living. You will have to decide whether the salary you are likely to make as a classroom teacher will allow you to establish the type of lifestyle you want. Our purpose in this section of the chapter is to give you some objective facts with which to make your decision.

The 1981–82 average salary of classroom teachers in the fifty states and the District of Columbia stood at $18,976. Although this represented an increase of $12,355 (or 181 percent) over the 1966–67 average of $6,821, in terms of 1966–67 dollars (taking inflation into consideration), it translates to only $6,566 for 1981–82. This last figure represents a decrease of 4.3 percent in purchasing power in the fifteen years since 1966–67. Remember, also, that in periods of inflation these projected salaries will not represent dramatic increases in buying power but will probably only keep abreast of cost-of-living increases. If, however, inflation rates are brought under control, then actual gains may be realized as teachers' salaries are raised. Table 2.5 lists the average classroom teachers' salaries from 1971–72 until 1981–82. Keep in mind that these figures represent the average salary for *all* elementary and secondary school teachers, not the average for beginning teachers. The average salary for first-year teachers in 1975–76 was $8,768; for 1977–78, it was $9,739; and for 1980–81, it was $11,708.[7]

[7]National Education Association, Research Memo: "Prices, Budgets, Salaries, and Income, May 1979" (Washington, D.C.: NEA, 1979); National Education Association, Research Memo: "Teacher Supply and Demand in Public Schools, 1980–81" (Washington, D.C.: NEA, 1982), pp. 7–8.

Table 2.5 Average Classroom Teachers' Salaries, 1971–72 to 1981–82

School Year	Elementary	Secondary	Combined Average
1971–72	$ 9,424	$10,031	$ 9,705
1972–73	9,893	10,057	10,176*
1973–74	10,507	11,077	10,778
1974–75	11,334	12,000	11,690
1975–76	12,282	12,947	12,591
1976–77	12,988	13,776	13,355
1977–78	13,864	14,610	14,213
1978–79	14,692	15,455	15,043
1979–80	15,576	16,433	15,966
1980–81	17,204	18,082	17,602
1981–82	18,543	19,494	18,976

*An error exists in the original source; therefore, the combined average is not correct for the 1972–73 figures.

Source: National Education Association, Research Memo: "Estimates of School Statistics 1981–82" (Washington, D.C.: NEA, 1982), p. 17. Reprinted by permission of the Association.

Most public school salary schedules are usually determined by two factors: years of teaching experience and advanced training, usually expressed in terms of college credit-hours or advanced degrees. Thus the longer you teach and more college education you receive, the more money you will make (see Table 2.6 for an example of a school district salary schedule).

As you can see from Table 2.7, salaries vary considerably from state to state. Each school district determines what it will pay its teachers, with many states setting a minimum base salary below which the school district cannot go. Generally, the large and middle-sized school districts pay better than the small ones. Many school districts offer extra pay for special duties such as band directing or coaching athletic teams. Some also offer summer teaching or curriculum development jobs. In one survey, 10.2 percent of all teachers earned extra pay for school system employment during the summer. Another 18.8 percent earned money for outside employment during the summer. During the school year, 11.1 percent of all teachers earned money from outside employment, while 20 percent earned additional pay within the school system.[8]

Most states and school districts provide public school teachers with a number of fringe benefits, including sick leave, health and life insurance programs, and retirement benefits. When applying for a teaching position, you should be sure to ask about these benefits.

[8]National Education Association, Research Memo: "Status of the American Public School Teacher, 1980–81" (Washington, D.C.: NEA, 1982), pp. 82–83.

Table 2.6 Teachers' Annual Salary Schedule, Pasadena Independent School District, Pasadena, Texas, 1982–83

Years Experience	Step	Bachelor's Degree	Master's Degree*
0	0	$15,533	$16,552
1	1	16,018	17,054
2	2	16,435	17,650
3	3	16,982	18,390
4	4	17,592	19,131
5	5	18,214	19,887
6	6	18,953	20,653
7	7	19,711	21,530
8	8	20,478	22,421
9	9	21,354	23,309
10	10	22,255	24,196
11	10+	22,665	24,663
12	11	23,131	25,097
13–14(B.A.) 13–16(M.A.)	11+	23,580	25,571
15–16(B.A.) 17–18(M.A.)	12	24,021	25,986
17–18(B.A.) 19–20(M.A.)	12+	24,482	26,473
19–21(B.A.) 21–23(M.A.)	13	24,881	26,899
22+ (B.A.) 24–28(M.A.)	13+	25,450	27,388
29+ (M.A.)	14		27,792

*Doctorate Degree same as Master's + $500 per step.

HOW DO YOU OBTAIN A TEACHING POSITION?

It is a tight market; teaching positions are not plentiful. School district personnel are not likely to walk up to you and offer you a job, no matter how effective you may be as a teacher. You will probably have to spend considerable time and energy seeking a position. There are a number of actions you can take, however, to increase your chances substantially.

First, you must be determined to campaign for a teaching position. Make up a plan, in writing, for how you will proceed. Don't wait for happenstance. You might get lucky and land a job on your first try, but why take a passive attitude when you can do much to increase your chances of employment?

Table 2.7 Average Annual Salaries of Classroom Teachers, 1981–82

REGION AND STATE	AVERAGE SALARY OF CLASSROOM TEACHERS		
	Elementary School	Secondary School	All Teachers
50 States and D.C.	$18,543	$19,494	$18,976
New England	18,037	18,917	18,478
Connecticut	18,156	18,563	18,317
Maine	14,400	15,650	14,873
Massachusetts	19,631	20,051	19,875
New Hampshire	14,544	14,875	14,701
Rhode Island	21,559	21,428	21,494
Vermont	13,133	14,021	13,567
Mideast	20,595	21,485	21,061
Delaware	18,715	19,665	19,241
District of Columbia	24,304	24,210	24,265
Maryland	20,206	21,450	20,865
New Jersey	19,336	20,238	19,706
New York	22,600	23,000	22,826
Pennsylvania	18,820	19,720	19,307
Southeast	16,151	16,628	16,353
Alabama	15,000	16,010	15,494
Arkansas	13,591	14,361	13,984
Florida	17,157	16,613	16,907
Georgia	16,080	16,770	16,363
Kentucky	16,740	18,100	17,200
Louisiana	17,000	17,600	17,264
Mississippi	13,930	14,400	14,141
North Carolina	16,342	16,563	16,428
South Carolina	15,220	16,320	15,637
Tennessee	16,123	16,259	16,175
Virginia	16,519	17,914	17,090
West Virginia	17,023	17,450	17,209

Source: National Education Association, Research Memo: "Estimates of School Statistics 1981–82" (Washington, D.C., NEA, 1982), p. 34. Reprinted by permission of the Association.

Job seekers frequently make two common mistakes.[9] One is to try one strategy, wait for results (positive or negative), then try something else.

[9]Most of the ideas in this section are taken from John William Zehring, "How to Get Another Teaching Job and What to Do if You Can't," *Learning* 6 (February 1978): 44, 46–51.

Table 2.7 *(cont.)*

REGION AND STATE	AVERAGE SALARY OF CLASSROOM TEACHERS		
	Elementary School	*Secondary School*	*All Teachers*
Great Lakes	19,533	20,710	20,044
Illinois	20,181	22,596	21,013
Indiana	18,500	19,433	18,966
Michigan	22,113	22,609	22,351
Ohio	17,610	18,740	18,116
Wisconsin	18,900	19,870	19,346
Plains	16,763	17,934	17,340
Iowa	17,312	18,591	17,989
Kansas	16,476	16,631	16,546
Minnesota	19,152	20,596	19,903
Missouri	16,098	16,900	16,499
Nebraska	14,844	16,252	15,536
North Dakota	14,626	14,992	14,779
South Dakota	14,257	14,829	14,457
Southwest	17,110	18,065	17,526
Arizona	17,821	18,446	18,014
New Mexico	18,621	19,189	18,905
Oklahoma	16,380	17,220	16,781
Texas	17,000	18,100	17,485
Rocky Mountain	18,111	19,351	18,700
Colorado	19,142	20,102	19,628
Idaho	16,041	16,778	16,388
Montana	16,970	18,450	17,625
Utah	17,258	18,693	17,876
Wyoming	20,411	21,954	21,151
Far West	21,937	22,702	22,252
Alaska	31,810	32,060	31,924
California	22,076	22,823	22,378
Hawaii	23,767	22,537	23,261
Nevada	18,100	18,400	18,248
Oregon	19,561	20,755	20,037
Washington	21,844	22,961	22,332

What you should do is pursue many avenues or strategies simultaneously. The second common error is to block oneself out at the wrong stage in the process. Some teachers only half-heartedly write for information or never complete the application form. Others withdraw their applications prematurely. Remember: You can always say no to a job that has been offered, but you can never say yes to one that has never been offered. Keep your options open.

Next you need to get certain materials ready. These include your résumé, cover letter, credentials, transcripts, and interview skills. Your résumé allows you to present yourself the way you want to be presented to prospective employers. Its purpose is to help you get an interview with the school district officials. You should have many copies of your résumé produced. A sample résumé appears in Figure 2.2.

Your cover letters, written to prospective school districts, should be typed individually and not mass produced. The content of the letters may be the same or similar, but the recipients of the letters should not feel that they are receiving a standard letter. And, incidentally, be sure to ask for an interview. That's why you are writing the letter.

Virtually all school districts require credentials, that is, the whole package from your college recommending you for certification. Be sure to check with the career planning and placement office about how to establish your credential file and what should go into it. Do this early in your program so you will have time to accumulate the required materials. Be familiar with the Buckley Amendment, which affords you certain kinds of legal protection regarding what goes into your file. Your letters of recommendation should be recent and from people who can testify to your teaching ability.

Reproduce unofficial copies of your official transcript. Many applications require transcripts to accompany them. Since colleges charge several dollars per transcript, you can save money by reproducing the transcript yourself. Most school districts will accept unofficial transcripts (those sent from you rather than directly from the college) for the initial screening process. If you receive a job offer, you will then have to provide the school district with an official copy.

The success of your personal interview with the school district representative is one of the most important determinants of whether you get hired, so be prepared. Try to anticipate the kinds of questions that might be asked (your placement office or college library might have a pamphlet or book containing typical questions). Try role playing with a friend who plays the role of the interviewer while you play the candidate. Audiotape your "interview" so the two of you can criticize it. One survey indicated that the major factor school officials look for is whether the candidate has empathy for children. As one official stated,

> We take it for granted that a candidate who has successfully completed a teacher training program and has been recommended for certification by the dean of the college has all the technical qualifications necessary, so we don't spend a lot of time worrying over grades and the like. What we do pay a lot of attention to and look for are the personality traits that tell us a person will work well with children, that tell us a person really cares about children.

Figure 2.2 Sample Undergraduate Résumé (Candidate with Bachelor's Degree and Limited Experience)

Present Address	Permanent Address
15 Underbrook Drive	110 Main Street
Columbus, Ohio 43214	Philadelphia, PA 19127
Phone: (614) 296-3201	Phone: (315) 436-2113
Until: June 11, 1985	

EDUCATION	Present highest degree data first and work backward. Identify: major, minor, course of study, institution granting degree and date of graduation.
CERTIFICATIONS	List all subjects, grade levels, and areas able to teach.
EXPERIENCE	Include those jobs that may relate to your ability to work with people; also include all jobs of significant duration and importance. Identify employer, your title, and brief description of the duties performed, including the percentage of college expenses earned. Start with most recent employment and record data in reverse chronological order.
	Include volunteer work without pay if it pertains to a strength you see in relation to teaching.
ACTIVITIES AND INTERESTS	Include clubs, organizations, Greek affiliations, honor societies, and sports. If an officer, specify which office.
MILITARY SERVICE	If applicable, include the branch of service, dates of service, rate or rank, and experience.
SPECIAL AWARDS AND GRANTS	If applicable, note name of award, when received, and brief award description. Work in reverse chronological order.
PERSONAL	This category is optional. It can include date of birth, height, weight, marital status, health, geographical preference, date available.
REFERENCES	State that credentials and references are available upon request.

You should ask those who write letters of recommendation for you to emphasize this aspect also.

Your next major task is to find out what jobs are available and where. There are several possible strategies. Not only can your college's career planning and placement office help you set up a placement file, but it also receives hundreds of notifications of position vacancies. Contact that office frequently to see if there are any vacancies that might interest you. Another source may be the teacher employment office operated by the state department of education. About one-third of the states run such offices, and you can register with them for free or for a slight charge. These offices send registered candidates a listing of openings in their specialty area for both state and out-of-state vacancies. There are private organizations that keep current nationwide teacher vacancy lists and that will attempt to match your qualifications with those vacancies for a nominal fee. Personal contacts are often very effective in securing a position. Don't hesitate to call friends and acquaintances who might be able to help you obtain interviews. After all, they probably can't get you a job, but they may be aware of vacancies and whom you should contact. Contacting specific school districts directly is another way to determine what positions are available. Call, write, or visit the personnel office of the school districts in which you are interested. This will insure that you get current information directly from the school district.

15 RULES FOR EFFECTIVELY UPDATING YOUR RÉSUMÉ

Résumés have one purpose: to get you an interview. The interview, not the résumé, leads to the job. Jobs come through people, not through paper. If you can get an interview any other way, skip the paperwork.

There is no right or wrong way to write a résumé, although some ways are more effective and sophisticated than others. All rules are broken in this business, sometimes successfully. But each detail of the résumé-writing process should have your meticulous attention because people often are screened *out* on the basis of a poor letter and résumé. The following serve as guidelines and are based on books, arti-

cles, and the comments and preferences of hundreds of employers.

1. Résumés should be copied, preferably by offset printing. This is important because it will make your résumé stand out as professional looking. It's not expensive—about $4 for 100 copies. The *copy* of your résumé should always be accompanied by an *individually typed* cover letter.

2. Think of your résumé more as a piece of advertising than as a comprehensive data sheet. Use wide margins and plenty of spacing to make it easy to skim.

3. A listing of coursework does not belong on the résumé

because it looks amateurish. If coursework is called for, send a transcript (or send a copy of your unofficial transcript).

4. Don't use a lot of dates or numbers that make the résumé hard to skim. Eliminate dates or place them at the end of a paragraph when describing experience. Don't use them for headlines.

5. Use action verbs. Avoid using forms of "to be." Use verbs such as *initiated, created, instructed, developed, supervised, managed, counseled, negotiated, maintained.*

6. Emphasize skills, especially those that transfer from one situation to another. The fact that you *coordinated* a fifth-grade field trip to Washington

Regardless of which strategies you use, after sufficient time has elapsed remember to follow up your applications and interviews with phone calls and letters to inquire about the status of your application. The more personal the approach is, the more effective it will be. Phone calls are better than letters, and visits are more effective than phone calls. Many school districts don't know how many vacancies they will have until school opens in the fall, so don't give up too soon. This whole process sounds like hard work, and it is! Executing a campaign to find a teaching position takes effort, planning, and patience, but your chances of securing a position are dramatically increased. It's worth your while.

HOW DO YOU BECOME CERTIFIED?

All fifty states and the District of Columbia require public elementary and secondary school teachers to be certified—that is, licensed to teach—by the department of education in the state in which they work. To qualify for certification, a teacher must have completed an approved teacher education program with a bachelor's degree or higher. Besides a bachelor's degree,

leads one to believe that you could coordinate other things as well.

7. Forget your best prose. Use short, choppy phrases. Short is sweet.

8. Use positive words. Don't apologize for lack of experience or for weaknesses. This is not the place to hang out your dirty laundry. Be positive, capitalize on strengths, and leave out the negative or neutral words. If your health is "excellent," then don't say "not bad." Avoid negative prefixes or suffixes.

9. Résumés should be one or two pages. Never more. Anything longer is an autobiography, not a résumé.

10. Expound on your relevant experiences and condense descriptions of jobs or experiences that are not directly related to the work you're seeking. This means that you slant your résumé to the type of job you are seeking. Hence, you will need more than one résumé if you are applying for different types of jobs.

11. Make every word count. Use the K.I.S.S. system of writing: *Keep It Short and Simple.*

12. Omit "professional objective" or "job objective" unless you know exactly what it is and are closed to all other possibilities. Your job objective doesn't add that much to the résumé, but it can serve to screen you out. The cover letter is the best place to detail your objectives.

13. List your telephone number, including area code. Employers usually call to set up an interview.

14. At the bottom of your résumé, write: "Credentials and references available upon request." Have prospective employers request your credentials from you, not from your placement office. Don't list your references on your résumé.

15. Proofread your résumé. Then have a friend (or better, a professional proofreader) proofread your résumé. Even the pros have been known to send out résumés with humorous and embarrassing mistakes.

John William Zehring, "How to Get Another Teaching Job and What to Do if You Can't." Reprinted by special permission of *Learning,* The Magazine for Creative Teaching, February, 1978. © 1978 by Pitman Learning, Inc.

which provides the necessary liberal arts background, states require that prospective teachers have student taught and that they have taken certain other education courses. Fourteen states require teachers to have supplementary postgraduate education—usually a master's degree or a fifth year of study—after their initial certification. Some states require U.S. citizenship, some an oath of allegiance, and several a health certificate. In addition, local school districts may require teacher applicants to take written examinations or meet other requirements to be hired.

Because the requirements for certification do differ from state to state, you should become aware of the requirements for the state in which you will seek employment. Someone in your placement office or in your school of education most likely will be able to acquaint you with certification requirements. Your education library will probably contain books that list the certification requirements for all the states. Should you not be successful there, you can call or write directly to the teacher certification office in the states in which you are interested. A directory of state teacher certification offices in the United States is listed at the end of this chapter. A number of states have reciprocal agreements to accept one another's certificates as valid. If you move from one state to another, you may want to check if your teaching certificate is accepted by the state to which you are moving.

Besides the basic certificates for teaching at the elementary and secondary levels, many states require different certificates for specialization areas, such as special education, bilingual education, and kindergarten. If, as you gain experience, you want to move out of teaching into a supervi-

---

TYPICAL QUESTIONS ASKED DURING JOB INTERVIEWS

Most interviews follow a simple question-and-answer routine. Your ability to communicate effectively with a stranger in a stress situation is of critical importance. Being prepared is the best way you can avoid a disorganized answer. Questions you may be asked include:

- Why have you chosen teaching as a career?
- Why do you want to work in this school district?

- What age level children do you prefer? Why?
- What has your college preparation done to help you prepare for a teaching position?
- What are your strengths and/or weaknesses as a potential teacher?
- What are your thoughts on discipline and classroom management?

- What is your philosophy of education?
- How would you handle gifted/handicapped/disadvantaged students in your classroom?
- How do you motivate students to learn?
- Tell me about your student-teaching experience.
- What would you do for the first day of class?
- Do you have any questions for me? (*Have some!*)

sory, administrative, or counseling position, you will probably need a special certificate.

In summary, individual states use certification requirements to assure the public that the teachers teaching the youth of our society have been adequately trained. Certification requirements should present you with little difficulty, provided that the teacher education institution you attend meets the general regulations of the state department of education, and that you maintain contact with the college official responsible for coordinating the education program with the state certification requirements.

WHAT JOBS ARE AVAILABLE IN EDUCATION?

Our tendency throughout this book is to write as if education offers only a single career pattern—elementary or secondary teaching. Although it is convenient for us, it is misleading. There is great diversity within the career labeled "teaching"—you can teach anything from prekindergarten to graduate school and from remedial reading to astrophysics. Also, there are many careers in education other than teaching. Some of these occupations, such as school librarian, are closely related to schools and children, whereas others, such as project officer for the U.S. Office of Education, are physically quite remote from children.

In the same vein, we don't mean to give the impression that there is one, and only one, appropriate career in education for any given person. On the contrary, education is a field that offers many opportunities to move from one type of work to another. A common progression is from classroom teaching to a vice principalship or principalship. Besides becoming department or grade-level supervisors, many experienced teachers choose to become guidance counselors. Still others go into teacher education or a related field such as educational publishing.

On the following pages we outline the careers available in education, for three reasons. First, most people think of education as a field composed of teachers and principals, and we frankly want to expand public awareness of the wealth of careers in education. Second, we want to point out, to students who find they are not interested in teaching, the variety of non-classroom jobs available in education. Third, we want to illustrate the variety of opportunities open to people once they have embarked on a career in education.

Rapid change is characteristic of our contemporary society. More people, more problems, more technological advances, and more of everything are causing the rate of change to accelerate geometrically. The repercussions have been pronounced in almost all careers, but especially so in the professions. Until recently, though, education has been very slow to change. Many of us were taught in the same manner as were our parents, because traditional ideas and approaches seemed perfectly adequate. Those quiet days seem to be over, though; the pace of change is catching up with the schools. Social philosophers and future watchers are anticipating massive

changes in the ways children learn, teachers teach, and schools operate. The computer revolution has already arrived and is leaving its imprint on all aspects of education. (See Chapter 13 for a discussion of the impact of microcomputers, for example.) In addition, revised decisions about what should be learned in schools, instruction by new media, learning drugs, manipulation of the genetic code—all will have an explosive impact on education in the decades ahead.

Although it may be reassuring to know that there will continue to be important, attractive careers in education, right now your career choice is what matters most. Your personal happiness will depend in large measure on the decision you make. We see a direct relationship between the number of unsuited and unsatisfied people in education and the casualness that all too often characterizes career choices in education. We urge you, then, to use the resources available to you—your experience, the counsel of others, the data available from agencies, and, most important, your own thoughtful reflections—in planning your future.

Pre-elementary, Elementary, and High School Education (public and private)

Paraprofessional (assistant teacher, educational technician, teacher aide)

Teacher
  nursery school and preschool, kindergarten, elementary, junior and senior high school

Supervisor (most supervisory positions are combined with teaching responsibilities)
  grade-level supervisor, department head, critic teacher, master teacher

Consultant (for curriculum, teaching process, specialized areas, affective education)

Guidance counselor
  academic counselor, personal counselor, career guidance counselor, college placement counselor

Administration
  principal, assistant or vice principal, special project director, associate superintendent (business, maintenance, personnel, curriculum), superintendent

School specialist
  librarian, school psychologist, nurse, dietitian, coach, research director, attendance officer

Junior College, College, and University Education

Teacher
  teaching assistant, instructor, lecturer, assistant professor, associate professor, full professor

Department head

Adminstration
  dean (of the faculty, of students, of instruction, and so on), vice president, provost, president

Special services
  registrar, career guidance and placement officer, admissions officer, research director, librarian, health service personnel

Government

State department of education (curriculum, instruction, certification, research, and so on)

Federal agencies
Department of Education (Washington, D.C., and regional offices), research and development centers, regional laboratories, overseas schools sponsored by the state and defense departments for dependents, UNESCO and other international education agencies

FOUNDATIONS

Executive
program officer or staff member
researcher or writer

BUSINESS

Communications industry
television or radio reporter, newspaper educational reporter, freelance or magazine writer on education, writer for professional journals (such as *English Journal* or *Today's Schools*)

Publishing
textbook editor or writer, curriculum materials developer, sales representative for educational materials, computer educational software developer

Private consulting firms providing specialized expertise to schools, such as computers, new technology, inservice training, research services

Training and education departments in large businesses or corporations, responding to personal growth or work-related competencies of employees[10]

Private training or educational firms, providing services not available in public schools, such as advanced reading skills, more effective child-rearing techniques, and others[11]

PROFESSIONAL ORGANIZATIONS

National Education Association and American Federation of Teachers
executive, staff member, researcher or writer, field worker

Specialized education associations, such as National Association of Mathematics Teachers, National Association of Secondary School Principals

Educational fraternities, such as Phi Delta Kappa and Pi Lambda Theta

---

[10]We believe that the last quarter of the twentieth century will see a major growth in this sector of the educational community.

[11]See footnote 10.

IF YOU DON'T TEACH, WHAT THEN?

Suppose that despite all your job-seeking efforts you are unsuccessful in finding a position. Or suppose that after teaching a few years you decide that teaching is not for you. What will you be prepared to do after receiving training as a teacher? Has your training equipped you with skills that are in demand in fields outside education? For many different reasons, a substantial number of teachers each year find themselves looking for jobs outside education.

What generic or transferable skills are you likely to have developed in your preparation as a teacher that are needed in most businesses and professions? Since teachers are constantly making lesson plans based on certain objectives and activities, you have undoubtedly developed certain planning and decision-making skills, along with the ability to organize and implement these plans on a daily and long-term basis. You have learned to work under pressure and meet deadlines. You have learned to keep accurate and usable records. By keeping track of each student's work and tests in order to evaluate his or her performance, you have developed this capability of record keeping. You are familiar with libraries and audio-visual resources and have knowledge of research skills.

Teachers are also required to develop human relations skills, to relate with both children and adults. One of the major reasons why many people choose to enter teacher education programs is that they enjoy being around and working with people. In this regard you have probably developed and will continue to develop further sensitivity and empathy for other people. Communication skills are developed and refined in teacher education programs and are essential in almost any job that requires human interaction. Being able to manage groups of people in a flexible manner is a skill needed in many types of jobs. In short, many of the skills required by teachers are also required for other types of work. Naturally, additional training may be necessary, depending on the exact type of work. Now let's examine some alternative careers.

Remember the list of educational occupations that appeared on pages 51–52? A number of educational careers besides teaching—librarian, counselor, supervisor, administrator, school psychologist—were among those listed. Although these roles don't involve teaching children, they usually require a minimum of two or three years of teaching experience and additional certification. All these roles are important in the educational enterprise, should you decide that you are still interested in education but that teaching is not for you. You could also investigate employment in early childhood education and day care centers. Because early childhood education is a growing field, numerous new occupations are developing within it, such as reading specialists to help diagnose learning abilities and curriculum specialists to help plan the studies. State, local, and federal government agencies need researchers, planners, evaluators, and many others to administer the growing number of early childhood projects they fund. Government agencies, such as the U.S. Office of Education, hire many former teachers to help administer projects that are funded by federal government.

Many large businesses conduct extensive training programs for their employees and require the services of people who can design and implement training programs. Many people who have been trained as teachers find their way into such jobs.

The field of recreation and leisure activities attracts many people trained as teachers. Workers in this field plan, organize, and direct individual and group activities that help people enjoy their leisure hours. They work with people of various ages and socioeconomic groups; the sick and the well; the emotionally and physically handicapped. Employment settings range from the wilderness to rural to suburban and urban, including the inner city. Examples of recreation program jobs include playground leaders; program specialists in dance, drama, karate, tennis, the arts, and other physical activity; recreation center directors; therapeutic recreation specialists; camp counselors and wilderness leaders; senior citizen program leaders; civilian special services directors in the armed forces; and industrial recreation directors. About 135,000 people were primarily employed year round as park, recreation, and leisure service workers in 1980.[12] The majority worked in public tax-supported agencies such as municipal and county park and recreation departments.[13]

The publishing industry affords numerous job opportunities for writers, editors, and salespeople. If you are a good writer, you might be interested in helping develop or edit textbooks that can be used in elementary and secondary schools and in colleges. If you enjoy meeting people and traveling, sales work might appeal to you. Another growing area is the development of computer software related to education. Having good computer programs that students and teachers can use for instructional purposes means that jobs are available for persons with educational and computer programming backgrounds to help develop these programs.

Training as a teacher is also important for work related to professional organizations such as the National Education Association and the American Federation of Teachers, Phi Delta Kappa and Pi Lambda Theta, and the National Association of Mathematics Teachers and the National Council for the Social Studies. These organizations, and others like them, hire people for field work, writing, research, and other staff positions.

[12]"Social Service Occupations," reprinted from the *Occupational Outlook Handbook, 1982–83 Edition* (Washington, D.C.: U.S. Department of Labor, Bureau of Labor Statistics, 1982), Bulletin 2200, pp. 61–62.

[13]Information about careers in parks, recreation, and leisure services is available from National Recreation and Park Association, Division of Professional Services, 3101 Park Center Drive, Alexandria, Virginia 22302.

To discuss all occupation areas in which your training as a teacher would benefit you is not possible within the scope of this chapter. We have described only a few possibilities here. Should you decide to seek a job outside teaching, more information would be available to you from your college career counseling and placement center and from the books listed at the end of this chapter.

POSITIVE ELEMENTS OF THE TEACHER SURPLUS

One of the side benefits of the recent teacher surplus has been that schools have been able to be more selective. Instead of having to take whoever came along, schools have had the rare opportunity to choose the better-prepared teachers among those available. The fact that not just anyone (or any college graduate) can become a teacher will improve the teaching profession and its public image.

Another consideration is that there has never been a surplus of good teachers. No matter what the job market may be at a particular moment, if you and your credentials are good, there will be a place for you.

And, lastly, America has become an education-oriented society. We are realizing that the achievement of our individual and national goals depends on achieving high levels of education. This means we are committed to more and better education, to lifelong learning in and out of schools. Over fifty years ago, President Calvin Coolidge said, "The business of America is business." Today and into the future, "the business of America is education."

Teaching is where the action is and will continue to be!

Discussion Questions

1. What is the present and projected teacher supply in the field that currently interests you most? in the geographic area?

2. Are you prepared to leave your current location to find a teaching position? Are you willing to teach in an urban school? a rural school? a private school?

3. Is the average beginning teacher's salary about what you expected? Is it sufficient money for you to maintain a lifestyle that is comfortable for you?

4. What ways can you think of to increase your chances of being hired when you are ready to teach?

5. What are some effective job-hunting strategies?

6. Reflect on the list of careers in education on pages 51–52. If you were to graduate today, what position would you choose? What position might you eventually aim for? Are there any positions listed that you have never considered before but might be interested in? What effect might an over-supply of teachers have on your decision?

For Further Reading

The ASCUS Annual: A Job Search Handbook for Educators. Madison, Wisc.: Association for School, College and University Staffing.

> An annual publication designed to assist both new and experienced educators in their job search. The *Annual* is usually distributed through career planning and placement offices in colleges and universities, but it may also be obtained from the ASCUS office, Box 4411, Madison, Wisconsin 53711.

Dilts, Harold. *Teachers' Guide to Teaching Positions in Foreign Countries.* 7th ed. P.O. Box 514, Ames, Iowa 50010.

> An overview of how to obtain a teaching position overseas.

Fine, Janet. *Opportunities in Teaching Careers.* Skokie, Ill.: VGM Career Horizons, 1977.

> A paperback that explores job opportunities in education today.

Pollack, Sandy. *Alternative Careers for Teachers.* Harvard, Mass.: The Harvard Common Press, 1979.

> A very useful book for teachers considering a career switch.

Zehring, John William. "How to Get Another Teaching Job and What to Do if You Can't." *Learning* (February 1978): 44, 46–51.

> An excellent, brief article about how to find a teaching job, and if you don't, what other options are open to you.

REFERENCES FOR LOCATING SOURCES OF JOB VACANCIES

Academic Journal: The Educators' Employment Magazine. The Academic Journal, Box 392, Newtown, CT 06470. Published biweekly.

Affirmative Action Register. 8356 Olive Blvd., St. Louis, MO 63132. Published monthly.

American Education. U.S. Department of Education, 400 Maryland Ave., S.W., Washington, DC 20202. Published ten times a year.

Boarding Schools. National Association of Independent Schools and Colleges and Secondary School Admissions Test Board, 4 Liberty Square, Boston, MA 02109. Published annually.

Career Guide to Professional Associations: A Directory of Organizations by Occupational Field. Rev. 2nd ed. Cranston, R.I.: Carroll Press, 1980. A detailed alphabetical directory of more than 2,500 professional organizations, it also lists organizations by occupational field.

Changing Education. American Federation of Teachers (AFL-CIO), 11 Dupont Circle, N.W., Washington, DC 20036. Published quarterly.

Colgate, Craig, Jr., and Broida, Patricia, eds. *National Trade and Professional Associations of the United States and Canada and Labor Unions.* Washington, DC: Columbia Books, 1980. Published annually and contains descriptions of 6,300 associations, 550 of which are education-related.

Directory of Public School Systems in the U.S. Association for School, College, and University Staffing, Box 4411, Madison, WI 53711. Published annually.

Elliott, Norman F., ed. *Patterson's American Education*. Educational Directories, Inc., 716 E. Northwest Highway, Mount Prospect, IL 60056.

Encyclopedia of Associations. Detroit: Gale Research Co., 1980. Published annually and contains over 14,000 associations, 930 of which are education-related.

Handbook of Private Schools. 60th ed. Boston: Porter Sargent Publishing, Inc., 1980. Published annually.

Harris, Shirley S., ed. *Accredited Institutions of Postsecondary Education: Programs, Candidates: A Directory of Accredited Institutions, Professionally Accredited Programs, and Candidates for Accreditation*. Washington, DC:

American Council on Education, 1979. Published annually.

Today's Education. National Education Association, 1201 Sixteenth St., N.W., Washington, DC 20036. Published quarterly.

The Ascus Annual: A Job Search Handbook for Educators 1983 (Madison, Wisc.: Association for School, College and University Staffing, 1982), p. 37. Reprinted by permission.

DIRECTORY OF STATE TEACHER CERTIFICATION OFFICES IN THE U.S.

Alabama

Coordinator of Teacher Certification
State Department of Education
Montgomery 36130, 205-832-3133

Alaska

Coordinator of Teacher Education and
    Certification
State Department of Education
Pouch F. Alaska Office Building
Juneau 99811, 907-465-2857/2831

Arizona

Teacher Certification Unit
1535 West Jefferson
P.O. Box 25609
Phoenix 85007, 602-255-4367

Arkansas

Coordinator, Teacher Education and
    Certification
State Department of Education, Room
    202-A
Little Rock 72201, 501-371-1475

California

Executive Secretary
Commission for Teacher Preparation
    and Licensing
1020 "O" Street
Sacramento 95814, 916-445-0185

Colorado

Supervisor, Teacher Education and
    Certification
State Department of Education
201 E. Colfax
Denver 80203, 303-866-3075

Connecticut

Chief, Bureau of School Services
State Department of Education
P.O. Box 2219
Hartford 06115, 203-566-2670

Delaware

Supervisor of Certification and
    Personnel
Department of Public Instruction
Townsend Building
Dover 19901, 302-736-4686

District of Columbia

Chief Examiner, Board of Examiners
District of Columbia Public Schools
415 12th Street, N.W.
Washington, D.C. 20004, 202-629-4940

Florida

Administrator, Teacher Certification
Department of Education
Knott Building
Tallahassee 32301, 904-488-2317

Georgia

Director, Division of Teacher
    Education and Certification
State Department of Education
State Office Building
Atlanta 30334, 404-656-2406

Hawaii

Administrator (Certification)
Office of Personnel Services
State Department of Education
P.O. Box 2360
Honolulu 96804, 808-548-6384

Idaho

Director of Teacher Certification and
    Related Services
State Department of Education
State Office Building
Boise 83720, 208-334-3475/3476

Illinois

Manager, Teacher Certification and
    Placement
Illinois State Board of Education
100 North First Street
Springfield 62777, 217-782-2805

Indiana

Director, Division of Teacher
  Education and Certification
State Department of Public
  Instruction
Room 229, State House
Indianapolis 46204, 317-232-6636

Iowa

Director, Division of Teacher and
  Certification
State Department of Public
  Instruction
Grimes State Office Building
Des Moines 50319, 515-281-3245

Kansas

Director, Certification Section
State Department of Education
120 East 10th Street
Topeka 66612, 913-296-2288

Kentucky

Director, Division of Teacher
  Education and Certification
State Department of Education
Frankfort 40601, 502-564-4606

Louisiana

Director of Teacher Education,
  Certification and Placement
State Department of Education
Baton Rouge 70804, 504-342-3490

Maine

Certification Officer, Division of
  Professional Services
State Department of Education,
  Station 23
Augusta 04333, 207-289-2441

Maryland

Assistant Superintendent in
  Certification and Accreditation
State Department of Education
200 West Baltimore Street
Baltimore 21201, 301-659-2141

Massachusetts

Director, Bureau of Teacher
  Preparation Certification and
  Placement
Quincy Center Plaza
1385 Hancock Street
Quincy 02169, 617-770-7517

Michigan

Director, Division of Teacher
  Preparation and Certification
  Services
State Department of Education
P.O. Box 30008
Lansing 48909, 517-373-1924

Minnesota

Manager, Personnel Licensing and
  Placement
State Department of Education
Capitol Square Building
550 Cedar Street
St. Paul 55101, 612-296-2046

Mississippi

Supervisor of Teacher Education,
  Certification and Placement
State Department of Education
P.O. Box 771
Jackson 39205, 601-354-6869/6870

Missouri

Director of Teacher Education and
  Certification
State Department of Education
P.O. Box 480
Jefferson City 65101, 314-751-3486

Montana

Director of Teacher Education and
  Certification
Office of Public Instruction
Helena 59620, 406-449-3150

Nebraska

Administrator of Teacher Education
  and Certification
State Department of Education
301 Centennial Mall South
Box 94987
Lincoln 68509, 402-471-2496

Nevada

Supervisor of Teacher Certification
State Department of Education
400 W. King Street
Carson City 89701, 702-885-3116

New Hampshire

Director of Teacher Education and
  Professional Standards
State Department of Education
410 State House Annex
Concord 03301, 603-271-2407

New Jersey

Director, Bureau of Teacher Education
  and Academic Credentials
State Department of Education
3535 Quakerbridge Road
Trenton 08619, 609-292-4477

New Mexico

Certification Officer, Division of
  Teacher Education Certification and
  Placement
State Department of Education
Santa Fe 87503, 505-827-2892

New York

Division of Teacher Education and
  Certification
Cultural Education Center
Room 5A, 11 Empire State Plaza
Albany 12230, 518-474-3901

North Carolina

Director, Division of Certification
State Department of Public
  Instruction
Raleigh 27611, 919-733-4125

North Dakota

Director of Teacher Certification
State Department of Public
  Instruction
Bismarck 58505, 701-224-2264

Ohio

Director, Division of Teacher
  Education and Certification
State Department of Education
Columbus 43215, 614-469-3593

Oklahoma

Administrator, Teacher Certification
State Department of Education
2500 North Lincoln Blvd.
Oklahoma City 73105, 405-521-3337

Oregon

Superintendent of Public Instruction
Oregon Department of Education
700 Pringle Parkway
Salem 97310, 503-378-4769

Pennsylvania

Bureau of Teacher Certification
Department of Education
333 Market Street
Box 911
Harrisburg 17108, 717-787-2967

Puerto Rico

Certification Officer
Department of Education
Hato Rey 00900, 809-764-1100

Rhode Island

Coordinator for Teacher Education,
  Certification and Placement
State Department of Education
Roger Williams Building
Hayes Street
Providence 02908, 401-277-2675

South Carolina

Director of Teacher Education and
  Certification
State Department of Education
Columbia 29201, 803-758-5081

South Dakota

Director, Office of Teacher Education
  and Certification
Division of Elementary and Secondary
  Education
Kneip Office Building
Pierre 57501, 605-773-3553

Tennessee

Director, Teacher Education and
  Certification
State Department of Education
125 Cordell Hull Building
Nashville 37219, 615-741-1644

Texas

Director, Division of Teacher
  Certification
Texas Education Agency
201 East 11th Street
Austin 78701, 512-475-2721

Utah

Supervisor of Teacher Certification
Staff Development Section
Utah State Office of Education
250 E. Fifth South
Salt Lake City 84111, 801-533-5965

Vermont

Director, Adult Education Services
State Department of Education
Montpelier 05602, 802-223-2311

Virginia

Coordinator of Teacher Certification
Division of Teacher Certification
State Board of Education
Richmond 23216, 804-225-2098

Washington

Supervisor of Certification
Office of the Superintendent of Public
  Instruction
Old Capitol Building
Olympia 98504, 206-753-6773

West Virginia

Director, Office of Educational
  Personnel Development
State Department of Education
Capitol Complex, Room B-304
Charleston 25305, 304-348-2696

Wisconsin

Administrator, Teacher Certification
Bureau of Teacher Education and
  Certification
State Department of Public
  Instruction
125 E. Webster Street
Madison 53702, 608-266-1027 or 266-
  3390

Wyoming

Director, Accreditation Services Unit
State Department of Education
Hathaway Building
Cheyenne 82002, 307-777-6261

St. Thomas/St. John District

District Director
Educational Personnel Services
Department of Education
St. Thomas, Virgin Islands 00801, 809-
  774-0100

St. Croix District

District Director
Educational Personnel Services
Department of Education
P.O. Box 1
St. Croix, Virgin Islands 00820, 809-
  773-1095

The ASCUS Annual: A Job Search Handbook for Educators 1983 (Madison, Wisc.: Association for School, College and University Staffing, 1982), pp. 36–37. Reprinted by permission.

FOUNDATIONS

II

What Are the Philosophical Foundations of American Education?

3

This chapter is about the role of philosophy in the work of the teacher. Philosophy, a key foundational discipline in education, is described, five different philosophies are outlined, and their applications to the classroom are discussed.

This chapter emphasizes that:

■ Philosophical knowledge has a fundamental role in clarifying questions of education.

■ Philosophical thought has distinct characteristics. Four branches of philosophy—metaphysics, epistemology, axiology, and logic—relate rather directly to the work of the teacher.

■ Five philosophies of education (perennialism, essentialism, progressivism, existentialism, and behaviorism) not only are abstract systems of thought but also have practical implications for the classroom teacher.

■ Teachers need to have a philosophy to guide their practice.

A MEDICAL STUDENT who wants intensely to be a surgeon, has marvelous hands, and displays a high level of technical skill, but who does not know how the body functions or what constitutes health, can hardly be called a doctor.

An aspirant to the ministry who loves to work with people and possesses a marvelous gift of speaking, but who has no opinion about humanity's relationship to God or about the purpose of religion, can hardly be said to be suited for religious ministry.

And a person who has a great desire to be with young people, wants to live the life of a teacher, and possesses great technical skill, but who lacks purpose and direction, is hardly a teacher.

These three individuals are like wind-up toys, moving along blindly without a plan or an intellectual compass. And although this image may be somewhat dramatic, there *are* people who prepare for professions without getting to the core meaning of what those professions are all about. Such thoughtless and robot-like behavior can cause problems in any occupation or profession, but particularly so in teaching. What kind of a teacher can someone be who does not have a view of what people are and a vision of what they can become? Who cannot clearly define right and wrong in human behavior? Who doesn't recognize what is important and what is unimportant or can't distinguish clear thinking from sloppy thinking? The person who would take on the responsibility for educating the young without having seriously wrestled with these questions is, to say the least, dangerous, for he or she is going against the very grain of what it means to be a teacher. In fact, it is safe to say that such a person is not a teacher, but a technician.

This chapter introduces you to philosophy, one of the foundational subjects in education. It, along with history and psychology and, to some degree, sociology and anthropology, forms the intellectual foundation upon which the practice of education rests. The image of two houses, one built on sand and the other on a sturdy foundation, may help here. The teacher who grounds his or her teaching in a well-thought-out philosophy will be able to withstand shifting pressures and strong controversies. However, the teacher who has based his or her practice on intellectual sand will be buffeted about.

Many people use the word *philosophy* casually. We have all heard people talk in vague language about heady issues and then say off-handedly, "Well, I'm just philosophizing," as if that were another term for simply thinking out loud. In addition, some people debase the meaning of the term *philosophy* by speaking of their "philosophy of education" when they are merely giving their ill-considered opinions on whether children should have recess in the morning or in the afternoon. This trivialization of the concept of philosophy is unfortunate, because a philosophy of education should be very precious to the teacher. Schools attempt to do many things for children, from teaching them to get along with others to helping them develop their physical skills. But, at heart, schools are teaching the process of thinking and are attempting to put children in touch with the best ideas that humankind has produced. The study of philosophy, therefore, aids the teacher in systematic and careful reflection on issues and questions that are central to education. It also assists the teacher in considering what is known about such basic concepts as *learning, teaching, being educated, self-education,* and *the good life.*

WHAT IS PHILOSOPHY?

The word *philosophy* is made up of two root words, one being "love (*philo*)" and the other "wisdom (*sophos*)." Philosophy, then, is the *love of wisdom.* While all people do not love wisdom in the same way or to the same degree, we humans are all questioning beings—seekers of answers. As children we are preoccupied with such lofty questions as "How do I get less veggies and more dessert?" We progress to such questions as "How does the teacher always know to call on me when I don't have the answers?" and "What do I need to do to get a decent grade in geometry?" and "Which is the best college for me?" Ultimately, we may move to more advanced levels of questioning: "Who am I?" "What is the purpose of life and what am I doing here?" "What really does it mean to be a good person?"

Until relatively recently—about one hundred years ago (prior to the growth of the social sciences)—most people relied on religion and philosophy for answers to these questions. Whereas religion is said to represent the revealed word of God, philosophy represents a human attempt to sort out by reason the fundamental questions of existence. Many of the great thinkers of Western civilization—Plato, Aristotle, St. Thomas Aquinas, René Descartes, Jean-Jacques Rousseau, Immanuel Kant, John Locke, John Stuart Mill, William James, and John Dewey—have been philosophers. Because from the beginning education has always been a central human concern, philosophers have thought and written a great deal about education and the questions surrounding it.

Only a few people in our society are professional philosophers, who earn their daily bread (usually a rather meager fare) by pursuing answers to the fundamental questions of life. However, all of us who wrestle with such questions as "Who am I?" and "What am I doing with my life?" are engaged in philosophical activity. Although there is a distinction between the few professional philosophers and the great number of us who are amateurs, the questions we ask and the answers we glean are of great importance and usually have a major impact on the practical affairs of our lives and on how we choose to spend our life force. The very practical decision whether to become a teacher or a real estate broker or whatever almost always has its roots in a person's philosophy of life. In developing a philosophy, we draw on many influences: our experiences in life, our religious views, our reading of literature and history and current events. A major difference between professionals and amateurs, however, lies in the precision of their methods.

Philosophy is an extremely pure and abstract science. Philosophers do not work with test tubes or white rats. They do not use telescopes or microscopes. They do not fly off to remote societies to observe the natives. The method or process of philosophers is questioning and reasoning; their product is thought—often very wise thought. Basically, philosophers are concerned with the interpretation of meaning. They want to understand the real meaning of words. We said above that "humans are all questioning beings." A philosopher, to understand more fully the meaning of our statement and thus to be able to judge its value, would want to determine what we mean by *questioning.* Do we mean that to be a human one must put questions to others? Or that humans must question themselves? Are the questions simple questions ("Am I hungry now?") or lofty ones ("What is the most significant way I can spend my life?"). A philosopher would ask a similar set of questions about what we mean by the word *being.* The philosopher's method, then, is to ask questions to get at the real meaning of things, believing that the answer is often less important than the question, because the question often brings accepted practice under new scrutiny.

Although some philosophical discussion and writing involves technical language, it generally uses "plain language," the ordinary language of people. However, philosophers try to be extremely clear and careful about their use of terms. They do not want their ultimate prey—meaning—to be lost in the thicket of fuzzy language. Also, philosophers engage in a dialectical process: they proceed from raising questions to proposing answers to examining carefully the implications of those answers. This process usually leads to more questions, which are, in turn, probed. The philosopher Robert Zend could have been speaking for the majority of his colleagues, and at the same time kidding them, when he said, "Being a philosopher, I have a problem for every solution."

Because philosophers deal with the abstract and use pure reason as a tool, one might think that philosophy is a dull and quiet subject and that a philosopher is a peaceful scholar who sits in a field and gazes abstractedly into the distance. Perhaps it would be more accurate to envision the philosopher as sitting in a mine field or a briar patch. People occasionally turn against and challenge the philosopher. As the great ancient Greek philosopher Socrates learned, question asking is not always well received: it is seen by some people as "rocking the boat." In Socrates' case, his fellow citizens were made so uncomfortable by his questioning that they forced him either to capitulate intellectually or, as he ultimately chose, to take his own life. Although it seems that philosophy deals with simple issues in simple language, behind the philosopher's questions—for example, "What is a human?"—are raging debates about profound issues that can have far-reaching implications: for example, when can a fetus be aborted, if it should be at all? what rights do the extremely retarded have? and on and on.

In the first century A.D., the philosopher Epictetus went to the heart of the discipline when he wrote, "Here is the beginning of philosophy: a recognition of the conflicts between men, a search for their cause, a condemnation of mere opinion . . . and the discovery of a standard of judgement." The American philosopher William James said, "There is only one thing a philosopher can be relied on to do, and that is to contradict other philosophers." Nevertheless, it is from these intellectual conflicts and contradictions that much of humanity's wisdom has emerged.

THE TERRAIN OF PHILOSOPHY

Philosophy covers a large range of intellectual turf. The terrain of philosophy is divided into several areas, including four that are particularly important to the teacher: metaphysics, epistemology, axiology, and logic. These terms may be foreign to you, but we assure you that they are central to the educative process and, in fact, speak directly to the work of the teacher.

Metaphysics

Metaphysics involves the attempt to explain the nature of the real world, the nature of existence. Metaphysics tries to answer the question, "What is real?" And it tries to answer this question without appealing to the authority of religion or revelation. Further, metaphysics is more akin to a theoretical than to an empirical science. The metaphysician characteristically believes that in order to answer questions regarding such matters as the nature of humanity and the universe, simply collecting data and attempting to formulate statistically significant generalizations is not adequate. From most metaphysical perspectives, the nature of humanity cannot be captured by measuring or counting, though the metaphysical stance of some behaviorists (whom we'll discuss later) comes close to this approach.

In probing the nature of reality the metaphysician asks a whole array of questions: "Does life have meaning?" "Are human beings free or totally

determined?'' ''Is there a purpose to life?'' ''Is there a set of enduring principles that guide the operation of the universe?'' ''Can these principles be known?'' ''Is there no such thing as stability, but, rather, an ever-changing world?''

These abstract questions are ones that the educator cannot dismiss. Ultimately, the purpose of education is to explain reality to the young. The curriculum and how we teach it represents one statement of what that reality is. Other metaphysical questions are also woven into the fabric of schooling. Whether or not a particular school system emphasizes vocational education depends very much on someone's decision about the nature and purpose of humanity. Although teachers may not actually be metaphysicians, they do take a stand on metaphysical questions.

Epistemology

Epistemology deals with questions regarding knowledge and knowing. The epistemologist seeks the true nature of knowing and asks such questions as ''What is truth?'' and ''Is truth elusive, always changing and always dependent on the truth seeker's particulars of time, place, and angle of vision?" Some people, whom we call *agnostics,* are convinced that knowledge of ultimate realities is an empty hope. Some, whom we call *skeptics,* reject this position and hold instead to a questioning attitude toward our capacity to really know the truths of existence.

Epistemology deals not only with the nature of truth, but also with the way in which we know reality, and the way in which knowledge is acquired. There are a variety of ways by which we can know, and each of these ways has its advocates and detractors. Among the ways of knowing are: by divine revelation, by authority, through personal intuition, from our own senses, from our own powers of reasoning, and through experimentation.

Questions concerning knowledge and knowing are, almost by definition, of great concern to the teacher. Identifying what is true and then finding the most suitable means of transmitting this knowledge is central to the teacher's role. Even if the teacher is not particularly interested in these issues, other people are interested, and sometimes they are also interested in knowing the teacher's viewpoints. Of paramount concern to many people is the question of the true origin of humankind and how one knows it. This issue is sometimes called the *creationist controversy.* One faction insists that the public schools should present the evidence of our origin that is given in the Book of Genesis, which we know by divine revelation. Another viewpoint insists that the way to know the truth of the origin of the human race is through the scientific theory of evolution. So behind this ongoing educational and social conflict is a fundamental question of epistemology.

Because there are many different things for people to know, and because these things differ so greatly in fundamental character, it seems unlikely that there is one, and only one, method of knowing. Much of the teacher's work is helping the student find the correct way of knowing for a particular question.

Axiology

Axiology focuses on the nature of values, inquiring about the various kinds of values and which of those values are most worth pursuing. As human beings we search for the correct and most effective way to live. In doing this, we are engaging questions of values. And, of course, different people look at life and come up with very different sets of values. For instance, hedonists believe in seeking pleasure and living for the moment. On the other hand, stoics have an austere way of looking at life and seek to be unaffected by pleasure or pain. Many people answer the question, "What is a value?" from a religious perspective, asserting that God gives value to life, and thus makes existence meaningful.

Most people would agree that schools have a dual responsibility—to make people smart and to make them good. To the degree that teachers accept the second function, they are grappling with an axiological issue. In fact, teachers are intimately involved with questions of values. Young people are seeking ways to live lives that are worthwhile. Also, society expects a teacher to help children establish values that will help them both as individuals and as contributing members of society. Values, such as honesty, respect for other people, and fairness, are necessary if we are to live together in harmony. But although there are some values that a majority of people agree on, such as avoiding violence in the settling of disputes, there are other value issues that will always be controversial. Sexual behavior, capital punishment, and abortion are examples of contemporary social issues that involve a wide range of viewpoints about what is right.

Axiology has two subtopics: ethics and aesthetics. *Ethics* takes us into the realm of values that relate to "good" and "bad" behavior, examining morality and rules of conduct. As the subject of ethics speaks to a way by which we can intellectually ascertain the "right" thing to do, it often is used to represent a particular set of standards—a code of ethics. *Aesthetics* deals with questions of values regarding beauty and art. Many discussions about the value of a particular film or book or work of art are attempts to come to some aesthetic judgment on the value of the work.

Logic

Logic is the branch of philosophy that deals with the science of reasoning. One of the fundamental qualities that distinguishes human beings from brutes is that humans can *think*. The great technological progress that we have made in the last few thousand years is largely attributable to our progress in thinking. We have learned not only how to think clearly but how to communicate effectively with one another. Logic focuses on reasoning and modes of arguing that bring us to valid conclusions. The pursuit of logic is an attempt to think clearly and avoid vagueness and contradictions. Certain rules of logic have been identified, and they comprise the core of this branch of philosophy.

A primary task of the schools is to help children think clearly and communicate logically. There are two types of reasoning that are commonly used in schools: deductive and inductive logic. In the first, *deductive reasoning,* the teacher presents a general proposition and then illustrates it with a series of particulars. For instance, the teacher might assert that "people are reasoning beings" and then amplify the student's understanding of the general proposition by giving a series of examples ("humans are problem solvers"; "humans make laws"), all of which support the claim of human rationality.

Inductive reasoning works in the opposite fashion. The teacher sets forth particulars, from which a general proposition is derived or "induced." For instance, after presenting a series of specific examples of people engaging in reasoning activities, the teacher may claim that these are evidence for the general proposition that "people are reasoning beings." One of the on-going debates among educators is between advocates of deductive and inductive teaching. As is true for most controversial issues, good cases can be made for both sides of the argument.

Besides using logic in teaching, teachers also need logic for two other aspects of their work. They need logic to evaluate the reasoning of students, and they need it to evaluate the validity of new information that is presented for possible inclusion in the curriculum.

These four branches of philosophy—metaphysics, epistemology, axiology, and logic—are the major topics that concern the teacher. The answers they suggest to the teacher and the implications they have for actual classroom practice are areas to which we now turn.

SCHOOLS OF PHILOSOPHY

Answers to the philosophical questions that pepper the preceding section have almost infinite variety. Over the years, however, certain answers by certain philosophers have been given more attention and allegiance than others. These more enduring sets of answers or world views represent schools of philosophy. Some started with the early Greek philosophers and have grown and developed through the centuries. Other schools of thought are more recent and represent fresh, new formulations to ultimate questions.

We have chosen to present five philosophies of Western culture. We have selected these not because they are our pick of the "Top Five on the Philosophical Hit Parade," but because each viewpoint is currently influential in educational thought and practice. In fact, one philosophy, behaviorism, may not formally qualify as a true philosophy. Behaviorism does, however, possess many aspects of a philosophy and, as a school of thought, it clearly has an impact on schooling in this country. In the case of each of these philosophies, we present you first with a brief statement of the core ideas and then with a statement by a teacher (fictitious) who is committed to that particular philosophy. We have attempted to demonstrate that these philosophical positions are not just windy abstractions or the preoccupations of ivory-tower thinkers. Rather, these philosophical positions shape what people teach and how they teach it.

Perennialism

Perennialists view nature and, in particular, human nature as constant, as having little change. Beneath the superficial differences from one century or decade to the next, the rules that govern the world and the characteristics that make up human nature stay the same. The perennialist, too, is quite comfortable with Aristotle's definition of human beings as rational animals. Education is of crucial importance to perennialists, because it develops a person's rationality and thus saves the person from being dominated by the instinctual or animal-like side of life. It is a person's intellect, not body or emotions or instincts, that sets him or her apart from the beasts. To develop intellect means to learn how to dominate and direct instinctual and emotional energies toward higher, more rational purposes. Therefore, the nourishment of the intellect is believed to be the essential role of the school.

For the perennialist, the intellect does not develop merely by contact with that which is relevant or satisfying. The intellect is nourished only by truth. Truth, since it resides in the nature of things, is constant and changeless. And although our grasp of it is incomplete, truth is best revealed in the enduring classics of Western culture. Classical thought, then, is emphasized as a subject matter of schools. Perennialists believe that instead of focusing on current events or students' interests, the curriculum of the schools should consist of the teaching of disciplined knowledge, the traditional subjects of history, language, mathematics, science, and the arts. Perennialists place particular emphasis on literature and the humanities, because these subjects provide the greatest insight into the human condition. Although this view of the curriculum is evident in many places in education, in its most complete form it is known as the "Great Books approach," developed by Robert Maynard Hutchins and Mortimer Adler. The Great Books, which comprise a shelf of volumes stretching from Homer's *Iliad* to Albert Einstein's *On the Electrodynamics of Moving Bodies,* are the perennialist's ideal curriculum. Through immersion in these great works, students are aided in reaching the perennialists' goal, which is a state of human excellence the ancients called *paideia*. This is a state not only of enlightenment, but also of goodness. And, as such, it is a goal that perennialists believe all humans should seek. Education, then, is of great importance to the perennialists; but it is an education that is rigorous and demanding. They hold that education should not attempt to imitate life or be lifelike. Rather, education is a preparation for life. Students should submit themselves to the classical wisdom rather than try to search for what might seem to be personally meaningful.

In summary, the perennialists' view is that one learns by encountering the great works and ideas of the past. It is a view that leans heavily on the authority of the collected wisdom of the past and looks to traditional thought to guide us in the present. Further, it sees education as protecting and conserving the best thought from the past. In this sense, the perennialist favors a very traditional or conservative view of education.

THE PERENNIALIST TEACHER   I came into education twelve years ago for two reasons. First, I was appalled by the nonsense in the curriculum and by all the time I, and other students, wasted. All the time devoted to "relevant" curriculum! All those electives on trendy topics. All of those fake attitudes of teachers who told us our sharing of ignorance and those endless discussions were somehow important. My second reason for becoming a teacher is a more positive one. I am convinced that our society, our culture, has great ideas—ideas that have been behind our progress in the last 2,500 years. We need to share these ideas—no, teach these ideas to the young.

Essentially, I see my job as a teacher as passing on to the next generation, as effectively and forcefully as I can, the important truths: for instance, human dignity and the capacity of people to do evil. That has always been the teacher's role, until recent times when we have lost our way. I am convinced that a society that doesn't make the great ideas and the great thoughts the foundation of education is bound to fail. And nations and societies do falter and fall. The last fifty years has seen several formerly prominent nations slip to the wayside while other younger, more vigorous cultures have risen. I am convinced that most of those countries have failed because of the inadequate education they provided. I am dedicated to the goal of that not happening here.

I think kids are just great. In fact, I've given my life to work with them. But, believe me, I'm not about to allow them to set the rules, decide what they want to learn, or tell me how to teach it. My job is to teach; theirs is to learn. And in my classroom those functions are quite clear. Students have a lack. They don't know yet what are the really important things to learn. They don't know what they need to know. As a teacher, as a representative of society, that's my responsibility. Turning that responsibility over to students is just ridiculous. No, it's perverse! I have another currently unpopular idea: I believe that students should be pushed. School should be very demanding, because life is very demanding. All of us, when we are young, are lazy. We would much rather play than work. All of this trying to make school like play is just making it more difficult for students to really acquire the self-discipline needed to take control of their lives. What schools are turning out right now—and it pains me to say this—is a lot of self-important, self-indulgent dummies. And it's not their fault. It's our fault as teachers and parents.

And the answer is so simple! We just need to go back to the great ideas of the past and make them the focal point of education. Also, when we achieve this goal, the students don't mind working. I'm known around here as a slave driver. However, I don't pay attention to the moaning. But I do pay attention to the large number of students, both college bound and not college bound, who come back two or three years out of high school and tell me how much they value having been pushed.

Progressivism

Progressivism is a very young philosophy. It came to prominence in the 1920s through the work of John Dewey. The fact that this philosophy rather quickly had a major impact on American education almost guaranteed that it would become controversial.

Progressivism views nature as being in flux, as ever-changing. Therefore, knowledge must continually be redefined and rediscovered. Whereas other philosophies see the mind as a jug to be filled with truth, or as a muscle that needs to be exercised and conditioned, the progressive views the mind as a problem solver. People are naturally exploring, enquiring entities. When faced with an obstacle, they will try to get around it. When faced with a question, they will try to find an answer.

For the progressive, education aims at developing this problem-solving ability. The student should start with simple study projects and gradually learn more systematic ways to investigate, until he or she has finally mastered the scientific method. Method is of great importance to the progressive. On the other hand, knowledge—formal, traditional knowledge—is not given the same honored place. For the progressive, there is really no special, sacrosanct knowledge. The value of knowledge resides in its ability to solve

human problems. Regarding the school curriculum, progressives believe that a student can learn problem-solving skills from electronics just as easily as from Latin, from agronomy just as well as from geometry. Progressive teachers often use traditional subject matter, but they use it differently from the way it is used in a traditional classroom. The problems that the students are trying to solve are of paramount importance. The subjects contribute primarily through providing methodologies to help solve the problems, but they also provide information that leads to solutions. The focus is on *how* to think rather than on what to think. Progressive educators believe that the place to begin an education is with the student, rather than with the subject matter. The teacher tries to identify what the students' concerns are and tries to shape those concerns into problem statements. The student

---

John Dewey, the father of progressivism, is widely considered the single most influential figure in the history of American educational thought.

No prodigy as a child, Dewey attended public schools and the University of Vermont. As a graduate student in philosophy at Johns Hopkins University, he met and was deeply influenced by William James, the philosophical pragmatist. Dewey recognized the implications for education of James's argument that ideas are valuable only insofar as they help solve human problems. Calling his own philosophy *instrumentalism,* to emphasize the principle that ideas are instruments, Dewey argued that philosophy and education are identical, both involving the practical, experimental attempt to improve the human condition.

JOHN DEWEY
(1859–1952)

The public school curriculum in the nineteenth century was scholarly and classical, designed to improve the mind by filling it with large doses of approved culture. Dewey denounced this curriculum as the invention of a parasitical leisure class, totally unsuited to the demands of industrialized society. He claimed that the schools were divorced from life, and that they failed to teach children how to *use* knowledge. The schools, he said, should teach children not what to think but how to think through "continuous reconstruction of experience." In *Democracy and Education,* published in 1916, Dewey pointed out that Americans were being called on to make crucial political decisions unprecedented in history, and that the

schools offered no preparation for the responsibility of citizenship in a democracy. Dewey called for concentrated study of democratic processes as they are manifested in the units of political organization with which the child is familiar—the school, the local community, and the state government—in ascending order of complexity. But his most radical suggestion was that students be given the power to make decisions affecting life in the school in a democratic way. Participation in life, rather than preparation for it, he considered the watchword of an effective education.

In 1893 Dewey established an elementary school at the University of Chicago. It was experimental in two senses: in its use of experiment and inquiry as the method by which the children learned, and in its

---

motivation to solve the problem is key. The teacher helps students shape the problem, to move from hunches about the solution to a development of hypotheses, and then on to methods of testing those hypotheses. Rather than being a presenter of knowledge or a task master, the teacher is an intellectual guide, a facilitator in the problem-solving process. Students are encouraged to be imaginative and resourceful in solving problems. They are directed to a variety of sources, from reading books and studying the traditional disciplines to performing experiments and analyzing data.

The progressive school has a unique atmosphere. It is not the storehouse of wisdom or a place with clearly defined roles and authority structures. Rather, the school is a small, democratic society, a place where people are not simply preparing for life but are living it.

role as a laboratory for the transformation of the schools. The activities and occupations of adult life served as the core of the curriculum and the model teaching method. Children began by studying and imitating simple domestic and industrial tasks; in subsequent years they studied the historical development of industry, invention, group living, and nature. This curriculum was in keeping with Dewey's argument, espoused in *The School and Society,* that we must "make each one of our schools an embryonic community life, active with types of occupations that reflect the life of the larger society and permeated with the spirit of art, history, and science." Dewey also believed it to be the absence of cooperative intellectual relations among teachers that caused young children's learning to be directed by a single teacher and older children's learning to be compartmentalized.

From the late 1920s to the early 1940s—the era of progressive education—a massive attempt was made to implement Dewey's ideas, but the rigid manner in which they were interpreted led to remarkable extravagances in some progressive schools. Some considered it useless to teach geography because maps changed so rapidly. Some would encourage students who, when asked why they were not studying for an exam, replied that they wanted to come to it fresh! The role of subject matter was gradually played down in progressive schools; the method and process were regarded as more important. The rationale was that it was more important to produce a "good citizen" than a person who was "educated" in the classical sense. Dewey fought vehemently against these corruptions of his views well into his nineties.

Throughout his long life, Dewey was a social activist, marching for women's right to vote, heading a commission to investigate the assassination of Trotsky, organizing a protest against the dismissal of a colleague at the City College of New York, and the like. Though he had enormous influence on the schools and on American intellectual life, his advocacy of a socialist economy and welfare state caused him to be characterized by some as an archfoe of the American way of life. In recent years, Dewey has once again been championed by educational critics and practitioners who consider his ideas a blueprint for more relevant and humanistic schooling, even in our own times.

Progressive educators believe that the school should be democratic in structure, so that children can learn to live well in a democracy. Group activity and group problem solving are emphasized. Implicit in this approach is the belief that children not only should learn to solve their own problems, but also must develop the view that they can and should be involved in the problems of their neighbors. Often, then, the problem-solving activities of the progressive school spill out into the community, dealing with issues like ecology and poverty. In this way, students learn an important principle of progressive education: knowledge should be used to redesign the world.

Progressive education is seen by many persons as a new philosophy of education for a new people. As opposed to other philosophies, it is very American. It has no undue reverence for the past or authority; rather, it is future-oriented and practical.

THE PROGRESSIVE EDUCATOR   I'm a progressive educator and proud of it. I'm not ducking that label just because it is under attack these days. And, for the life of me, I cannot understand how a teacher can be anything *but* a progressive educator.

I'm dedicated to a few simple and, I believe, obvious principles. For one thing, children are, by their very nature, "good." And, as such, we should treat them that way rather than try to dominate them. Instead of rejecting their curiosities, I believe we should build on them. Schools should be exciting, involving places where students are caught up in interesting activities.

I really think that I'm a progressive educator because I looked at my own experiences. I know I learn best when I'm trying to solve a problem that really interests me. And somehow I've always been able to get much more interested in how we're going to solve the problems of keeping the Americans and Russians out of war than in the affairs of the Athenians and Spartans. I can get much more involved in a research problem about which stereo system gives the best value for the dollar than about some dry economic problem presented to me by a teacher. And I really don't think I'm different from the overwhelming majority of students.

I see my fellow teachers spending all their energy damming up the curious energy of students and busily imposing work on them and then wondering why they're so tired or why they're burnt out. I'm sure it's quite tiring trying to convert children into file cabinets and stuffing facts into their heads all day.

It's not that I think that ideas and content and the traditional subjects are worthless. Far from it. I teach much of the same material as the other teachers. However, I get there by a different route. I let the issues and problems emerge and then give the students a chance to get answers and to solve problems. And, as they quickly learn, they have to know a great deal to solve some of the problems. Often they get themselves involved with some very advanced material. The only difference is that now they want to. Now they have the energy. And, boy, once they get going, do they have energy! No, it doesn't always work. I have students that coast, and I've had projects that have failed. But I'd put my track record against those of my traditional colleagues any day.

One of the things that sets me apart from others is that I'm not so hung up as others are on what I call the "talky" curriculum. I am convinced that students learn most effectively by *doing,* by experiencing events and, then, reflecting on and making meaning out of what they have experienced. I think more science is learned on a nature walk than from the same time spent reading a textbook or hearing teacher explanations. I think students learn more abstract principles, such as democracy, from trying to set up and maintain a democratic society in their classroom than from a lot of learned lectures on the subject. I'm trying to get to their hearts and their heads. The traditional approach gets neither place.

To me life is a matter of solving problems. New times have new problems and demand new knowledge. I don't want my students to be ready for life in the eighteenth century, or even the twentieth century. I want them to be effective, functioning, curious citizens of the twenty-first century. They are going to need to be able to develop solutions to fit new and unique problems. While much knowledge is important, they need to realize that knowledge is only today's tentative explanation of how things work. Much of what we know now is incorrect and will have to be replaced. We should share that "truth" with students. But, more important, we must help them to be problem solvers.

Essentialism

Essentialism is another uniquely American philosophy of education, but it has had more impact and meets with more favor outside the United States than does progressive educational thought. Essentialism, in fact, began in the 1930s and 1940s as a reaction to what were seen as the excesses of progressive education.

Essentialism has its philosophical origins in two older philosophies and draws something from each. From idealism, it takes the view of the mind as the central element of reality: the mind is our tool to use to know the essential ideas and knowledge that we need to live well. From realism, it takes the tenet that the mind learns through contact with the physical world: therefore, the basic tools for observing and measuring the physical world are essential.

The essentialists believe that there exists a core of information and skill that an educated person must have. Further, essentialists are convinced that the overwhelming number of children can and should learn this core

TAKE BASIC EDUCATION: DRILL, TEST AND BORE THE CHILD.

IT WORKED FOR AWHILE, BUT IT FAILED.

TAKE PROGRESSIVE EDUCATION: MODIFY TEACHINGS TO FIT THE NEEDS OF THE CHILD.

IT WORKED FOR AWHILE, BUT IT FAILED.

TAKE OPEN CLASS ROOMS: ENCOURAGE NATURAL CURIOUSITY TO MOTIVATE THE CHILDS LEARNING SKILLS.

IT WORKED FOR AWHILE, BUT IT FAILED.

AFTER AWHILE, ALL EDUCATION FAILS.

KIDS BUILD ANTI-BODIES.

© Jules Feiffer

of essential material. The school, then, should be organized to transmit this knowledge and skill as effectively as possible.

Essentialism begins to sound a lot like perennialism. Although these two views have much in common, there are some important differences between them. For one thing, the essentialists do not focus so intently on "truths" as do the perennialists. They are not so concerned with the classics as being the repository of all worthwhile knowledge. They search for what will help a person live a productive life today, and if the current realities strongly suggest that students need to graduate from high school with computer literacy, the essentialist will find a place for this training in the curriculum. In this regard, the essentialists are very practical and pragmatic. Whereas the perennialist will hold fast to the Great Books, the essentialist will make more room for scientific, technical, and even vocational emphases in the curriculum. Essentialists see themselves as valuing the past, but not being captured by it.

For essentialists, the aim of education is to teach the young the essentials that they need in order to live well in the modern world. To realize this goal, the school should teach the child the essentials of organized knowledge. Since the established disciplines are the "containers" of organized knowledge, these disciplines are what should be taught in schools. The elementary years, however, should concentrate on the basics—the "three

R's'' and the other foundational tools needed to gain access to disciplined knowledge that one begins to come in contact with in high school.

Although there is some debate about what is "essential" in the curriculum, essentialists believe that this is not a debate to which children can contribute fruitfully. Therefore, the role of the student is simply that of learner. His or her interests and motivations or psychological states are not given much attention. Nor are the essentialists much captured by what they would call a "romantic" view of children as naturally good. They do not see the students as evil, but rather as deficient and needing discipline and pressure to keep learning. School is viewed as a place where children come to learn what they need to know. Teachers are not guides, but authorities. The student's job is to listen and learn. Given the imperfect state of the students, teachers must be ingenious in finding ways to engage the imaginations and minds of students.

Progressive and essentialist educators each claim that their particular approach is the true American philosophy of education. A case can be made that they both are, but that each reflects different aspects of the American personality. Progressivism represents the antiauthoritarian, experimental and visionary side; essentialism speaks to our more conservative, structured side. Many of the tensions in education today are between these two philosophical strains.

THE ESSENTIALIST TEACHER   In my view, the world is filled with real problems, and the young people who leave school have to be ready to take up the challenge of life and solve those problems. So for me the watchword in education is *usefulness*. I think everything that is taught has to pass the test of whether or not it is useful. My job as a teacher is to find out what is useful and then to make sure the students learn it.

I believe that school should be relevant to the young. However, my view of what is relevant is very different from the views of lots of other people. For me relevance is not what is personally "meaningful" or a "do-your-own-thing" approach. What is relevant is what helps the individual live well and what benefits humanity. For that we need to look very carefully at the past and sort out the most valuable learnings. That is what should be taught and what should be learned. I find the back-to-the-classics approach quite valuable. However, most advocates go too far. They also stress the humanities and the arts a little too much and tend to underplay science and technology. If children are going to function in today's world, and if our world is going to solve all the problems it's confronted with, we have to give more attention to these subjects than we have in the past. But, clearly, the past is the place to begin our search for the relevant curriculum.

It's not the most pleasing or satisfying image, but I think the concept of the student as an empty jug is the most accurate one. Certainly kids come to school with lots of knowledge and lots of interests. However, the job of school is to teach them what they don't know and teach them in a systematic and organized way. It's not to fill their minds with isolated fragments of information, but to fill them with systematic knowledge. They need tools to learn and, as they get older, they need human insights and skills that come from the disciplines. Given the fact that there is so much to learn, this emphasis on student interest and projects and problem solving is quite wasteful. There is plenty of time for that outside of school or when school is over. Inside the school, the teachers are the authorities, and the students are there to learn what they don't know. The environment should be task-oriented and disciplined. It doesn't have to be oppressive or unjust or any of that. I tell my students that learning is not necessarily going to be fun, but that at the end of the year they will have a great sense of accomplishment. I'd take accomplishment over fun anytime. By and large, most students do, too.

Existentialism

Although the foundation of existentialism was laid by the Danish minister-philosopher Sören Kierkegaard in the nineteenth century, modern existentialism was born amidst the pain and disillusionment of World War II. Its main proponent, Jean-Paul Sartre, broke with previous philosophers and asserted that existence comes before essence. His approach was different from most philosophers, who defined the nature of humans as rational animals or problem solvers or what-have-you, and then spoke about existence. To Sartre, existence comes first; then we define ourselves in some sort of relationship to that existence. In other words, the existentialist believes that we should not accept any predetermined creed or philosophical system and from that try to define who we are. We've got to take as our own responsibility making that decision of who we are. The process of answering the question "Who are we?" has a start but really no ending. It begins at a very crucial event in the lives of young people. Sartre calls that event the *existential moment.* The existential moment is that point somewhere towards the end of youth when we realize for the first time that we exist as an independent agent. We are suddenly struck with the fact that *I am!* With that realization come the existential questions, "Okay, I exist, but who am I and what should I do?"

The European brand of existentialism tends to be a very austere philosophy. These existentialists tend to reject all other philosophies. Although there is a vital school of existentialism, called Christian Existentialism, with roots in the work of Kierkegaard, "mainline" existentialists reject God and the concept of a benevolent universe. They believe that we live an alien, meaningless existence on a small planet in an unimportant galaxy in an indifferent universe. Whatever meaning a person can make of life has to be his or her own meaning. There is no ultimate meaning. Whereas some people might be paralyzed by this view, existentialists find the definition of their lives in the quest for meaning. The very meaninglessness of life compels them to instill life with meaning.

The one thing the existentialist is sure about is that we are free. This freedom, however, is wrapped up in a search for meaning. To the existentialist we define ourselves—that is, we make meaning in our world—by the choices we make. In effect, we are what we choose. No more. No less. No God will throw us a life preserver. No circumstance will shade our responsibility. We are responsible for what we do and what we are.

The one thing the individual can be sure of is death—the complete ending of any kind of existence. Existing in a meaningless world with no afterlife provides the ongoing tension in the existentialist's life. "Why struggle, why continue if there is no hope?" It is in accepting this question and the "death dread" buried in it, that the existentialist can gain some dignity.

Existentialism has affected American education in a somewhat softer view. The *meaningless universe* aspect is downplayed, and the *quest for personal meaning* is emphasized. Existentialism has entered American education not under the flag of existentialism, but under several different flags: "the Human Potential Movement," values clarification, and individualized instruction. Its influence in the schools has been strong but somewhat subtle. Given the fact that by law our schools must be theologically neutral (they cannot advocate any religious world view), there is, by default, an unanswered question about the meaning of existence. The existentialists' approach of finding meaning through a quest for self has filled this gap. Children are warned not to accept anyone else's answers or values, but to search for their own. They learn that they should make their own choices and their own commitments in life, rather than being told what they should choose and to what they should commit themselves.

As it exists in the classroom, existentialism is not a set of curricular materials. Rather, it is a point of view that imbues what the teacher teaches and how he or she teaches. It tries to engage the child in central questions of defining life. It tries to help the child acknowledge his or her own freedom and accept the responsibility for that freedom. It aims to help the child realize that the answers imposed from the outside may not be real answers. The only real answers are the ones that come from inside each person, that are authentically his or her own.

On the other hand, the existentialist is against not only the heavy hand of authority, but also the group emphasis in education. Homogeneous grouping and group projects and social adjustment are always keeping from the child the ultimate truths: you are alone and you must make your own meaning. The group, or social emphasis in the form and content of education, is a drug or anesthetic that prevents perception of the ultimate nature of the way things are. On the other hand, movements and activities that help the child confront his or her own freedom go to the essence of what school should be all about.

THE EXISTENTIALIST TEACHER   When I was in college the last thing I thought I'd become was a teacher. I was really turned off by education—all of that fact cramming and mind bending. I still am quite negative about most of the education that is going on around me. I get along with most of my fellow teachers and, I guess, I look like them on the surface, but I look at the world in a very different way and that makes some of them uneasy. They are busy trying to give the kids this dogma, that dogma—whether it's democracy or the scientific method. And nothing makes them quite so uptight as students seriously questioning what they have to say. Students questioning in order to see if they have it right so they can get it right on the test are fine. But, probing or challenging questions are signs that the students reject what they're getting, and that really makes teachers nervous.

What drives me is getting the kids to listen to their own rhythms. So much of their lives are programmed from home, from television, from the crazy peer-group fads and the press of group-think in the school. I'm trying to get them to break through all that. I want them to begin to find out who *they* are and what *they* feel and what *they* think. I want them to have authentic reactions to things and realize that those are the ones that are the important ones, not what the world's authorities tell them is important. It sounds quite simple, but it is very difficult. They find great security in not thinking. I guess we all do. It's so much easier to take someone else's answers and pretend that they are ours. But that is just another form of slavery. People sometimes call what I do a radical approach, and I think that's more bunkum. The aim of education has always been the examined life. Socrates said it long ago: "Know thyself." That's what I'm aiming at.

This may sound like I have them look off into space and have them ask the question, "Who am I?" Far from it. I try to get my students passionately involved in life. I try to get them to have peak experiences, whether from watching a sunrise or hearing a Mozart sonata. This often leads to their own insight. Also, they have a lot to learn about the way the world works and they have lots of skills they have to learn. And, I'm busy getting them ready to take on that task. What I don't do is spend a lot of time on all these grouping—or what I call, leveling—activities. I let them know that they are individuals, and I have a very individualized instructional approach. I spend a lot of time on individual tasks, and they always go at their own rate. If there is anything that I emphasize, it's managing their own freedom. The major message of school for me is that you've got lots of choices, but you are responsible for what you do with them. This is the reason I stress *values clarification*. This approach makes them discover their own values and take the whole issue of values quite seriously.

The other thing I stress is *freedom*. They need to know that freedom is at the core of being a human being. I'm not talking about a "do-your-own-thing," pleasure-oriented freedom. I mean a freedom that fully embraces one's responsibility. It is this kind of freedom that allows a person to become heroic. This may sound silly, but I found my educational philosophy at the back end of a car. A couple years ago I was driving home from school and at a red light I saw a New Hampshire license plate ahead of me that said, "Live free or die." That's it. That's the whole ball game.

Behaviorism

Behaviorism is an increasingly popular intellectual movement that has philosophical roots in scientific realism. Although behaviorism has philosophical origins, the real development of behaviorism has come through the discipline of psychology. For many people, however, behaviorism functions as a total system of thought, a complete world view.

In the early years of this century, an American psychologist, John B. Watson, taught and made popular the idea that *behavior* (rather than thought or intention or sentiment) is what is important. Drawing on his own work and that of the Russian psychologist Ivan Pavlov, Watson claimed that all human behavior is a result of various stimuli and the responses that follow. Whether one is talking about a child's learning to walk or the performance of a virtuoso pianist, behavior can best be understood in terms of stimulus and response. Watson was convinced that this link between stimulus and response is the key to human perfectibility. He claimed that if he were given control over the stimuli in a child's environment, he could make the child virtually anything from an architect to a beachcomber, from a surgeon to a thug.

Many of Watson's assertions were only dramatically stated speculations. However, it was not until the work of Harvard psychologist B. F. Skinner became popular in the 1950s that behaviorism had a second wind and became wildly influential. Through his utopian novel, *Walden Two*, and his psychological experiments, Skinner made a basic advance in the earlier ideas behind behaviorism. In experimental research, first with animals and then with humans, Skinner showed that the important principle of behaviorism was not stimulating to get a certain response, but providing a pleasant stimulus immediately *following* a desired response. That is, instead of rewarding the child in the hope of encouraging good performance, wait for the good performance and then encourage it. Or, "catch the child doing good." This frequently means waiting for small movements in a particular direction, such as for the child to stand up on two legs, and then reinforcing that behavior. Then, waiting for the next movement in a long chain of movements that will gradually lead to the child's learning how to walk. Skinner's view is that behavior that is reinforced persists, and that which is not desists. For the behaviorist, this, in a nutshell, is the way the world works.

All of our behavior is the result of this process of behavioral response plus reward or punishment. Behavior is being shaped all the time, all around us. In order to know why robbers rob or salespeople sell or singers sing, one should not examine their statements of intention or such words as "sin" or "inspiration," but rather should examine what behavior has been

---

B. F. SKINNER
(1904–   )

B. F. Skinner is one of the United States' most famous scientists. His scholarly works have reshaped the field of psychology, his social ideas have excited the imagination of people around the world, and his educational applications have left few schools untouched. Nevertheless, he remains one of the most controversial figures in American life. One of his critics has described him as "the man you love to hate."

Skinner's notoriety and the sharp views which surround him stem from his beliefs about human behavior, which he explains in terms of physiological responses of organisms to environmental stimuli. People, he claims, are totally the products of their environment; control the environment and you control the individual. While this view sends a chill through many people and causes some to picture Skinner as a power-mad scientist endeavoring to enslave humanity, Skinner dismisses these charges. His

theory that people's behavior is shaped by their environment is not something, like the laser beam, that he "invented"; rather, Skinner asserts, it is simply a description of the way the world works. Further, he suggests that to ignore the principles of the scientific study of human behavior (usually referred to as *behaviorism*) is not only an error but a risk, for you are then vulnerable to being controlled by others. More positively, Skinner urges people to take steps to control their environment rather than merely being controlled by it.

Burrhus Frederic Skinner, called "Fred" by his friends, was born in 1904 in Susquehanna, Pennsylvania, into a middle-class family. He went through twelve years of public school and then attended Hamilton College in Clinton, New York. This future giant of psychology majored in English literature and took a classical liberal arts program. During college, Skin-

ner became very interested in writing fiction and decided to become a writer. After graduation, he moved to Greenwich Village in New York City, at that time the artistic center of the country. Reflecting on those years, Skinner, ever the realist, said, "I discovered the unhappy fact that I had nothing to say, and went on to graduate study in psychology, hoping to remedy that shortcoming." And remedy it he did. He received his doctorate from Harvard in 1931 and then began an academic journey that took him, first, to the University of Minnesota (1936–1945), second, to the University of Indiana (1945–1948), and then back to Harvard, where he still remains as an active emeritus professor.

While the bedrock of B. F. Skinner's reputation rests on his work in experimental psychology and his influential research on changes in the behavior of animals, his impact on educational thought has come as well from his roles

reinforced in their lives. On the other hand, if one wants to change the way people act, no amount of understanding or preaching will have any effect. If you want to change their behavior, you must change how they are reinforced. You must shape the desired behavior. Religions and classical philosophies are wrongheaded and wasteful speculations. And it is here that this world view becomes an educational philosophy.

For behaviorists, if you say you are an educator, you are, by definition,

as novelist, crib maker, and machinist. Although Skinner gave up his career in fiction in the 1920s, he began writing a novel some twenty years later. For many years Skinner had been interested in Utopian communities, groups of people trying to live together in ideal circumstances. Skinner began a fable about a community built on his principles of behaviorism, a community where all things are owned in common, people share both their labor and their talents, and everyone works to be happy. Skinner quickly became consumed by his writing and completed the book in twenty-eight days. Because his community is one in which everything is reduced to the Thoreauvian ideal of simplicity, Skinner named his novel *Walden Two*. Although never a best seller, the novel has been enormously influential and has become a key text on many campuses.

Skinner-the-crib-maker is more the product of distortion than fact. Skinner was well known among psychologists for his inventiveness, particularly for making equipment to advance his experiments. After observing his own daughter behind the bars of her crib, he designed what he believes was a more healthy and humane environment for an infant, his "air crib," a large, air-conditioned, soundproof, germ-free box with a sliding window of safety glass. His daughter could play and sleep in it free from the confinement of blankets or clothing. When word got out about Skinner's air crib, it was immediately confused in the minds of many with the "Skinner box," his instrument to observe and condition pigeons and animals. Visions were conjured up of the mad scientist experimenting with his own child. These stories are a source of considerable amusement to both Skinner and his daughter, now grown and an internationally respected artist.

Another of Skinner's inventions brought him more directly into education. That was the development in the 1950s and 1960s of teaching machines and programmed instruction. Using the machines, students followed a series of short steps arranged in such a way as to lead them to the acquisition of complex behavior, such as solving a mathematical problem or parsing a sentence. In effect, the machine and its program shaped the learners' behavior so that they behaved in new and better ways. These principles, or what Skinner calls the technology of teaching, have been applied widely in education and are quite evident today in computer-assisted instruction. Skinner believes we, as a species, are in a race for survival, the success of which is dependent on our developing a technology of teaching.

While others despair of human nature, Skinner remains essentially optimistic: "No one knows what the human organism is capable of because no one has yet constructed the environment that will push human achievement to its limits."

someone committed to behavior change. They would like, however, to purge from the educator's vocabulary words such as *knowledge, appreciation,* and *wisdom.* In turn, they are concerned with conduct, actions, and skills—all of which are terms that refer to observable behavior.

The role of the educator is to identify those behaviors which promote the social good, be they food making or music making, and to arrange the school environment so that those behaviors are shaped and developed. This, of course, is easier than it seems. It means knowing what reinforcements lead to what behaviors and which students are reinforced by what reward, whether it be a gold star, candy, time to run on the playground, or free time to read quietly in the corner. It requires a clarity of knowing exactly what should be the various outcomes of schooling, and this has often been lacking in education. The behaviorist, then, does not conceive of the teacher as a guide to the treasures of Western culture, but rather as an engineer of human behavior.

THE BEHAVIORIST TEACHER   It hurts me to admit it, but I taught for a long time and really didn't know what I was doing. I wanted to be a good teacher. I wanted kids to learn. I wanted to teach certain key things. And I worked hard. But it was strictly a hit-and-miss situation. For the most part, the bright kids with a history of doing well "hit," and the slower kids with a history of failure "missed." I knew something was wrong, but I just couldn't put my finger on it. I was almost getting to the point of saying, "Well, that's just the way things are," when something happened.

A book salesman convinced me to try out a short programmed text. The text broke everything down into very fine steps. There was a continuing series of short tests. When students made a mistake, they were directed to the right answer. I thought the kids would hate it. Wrong again! They loved it. They liked the self-tests. They liked the little charts they kept. They liked being able to work at their own pace. From that point I got very interested in programmed learning and the principles behind it. I had been told about behavioral objectives when I was in teacher training, but like a lot of other things, they had gone in one ear and out the other. I began structuring my teaching around behavioral objectives, and that switch subtly but strongly changed the whole direction of my teaching. It gave great clarity to what I was doing and what the students were doing. It was no longer a sort of me-against-them situation. Now we had our objectives, which we often agreed on as a group and worked on together to achieve.

What made me a convert to behaviorism, though, was reading Skinner's *Walden Two.* That book had a profound effect on me. Perhaps having seen the principle work in my own classroom made me ready to understand it more fully. But I began then, not by structuring my own classrooms along the lines of behavioral engineering and operant conditioning, but in my own life. I came to understand why I'd been doing a lot of things that I didn't really approve of, like smoking. And I learned how to quit. After a couple of disastrous experiences on a dance floor, I had defined myself as a "nondancer." Using behaviorist techniques, I've become a very good dancer in a short time. And there are dozens of other examples. What this approach has helped me do is take control of my own life. To be clear about my goals. To own my own life. To identify what reinforces me and to set up strategies to reach my goals. And I take this same approach in the classroom.

As a behaviorist teacher, I try to teach students not only skills that they need in order to function well in society, but also to be their own behavior shapers. They never hear a word about Skinner or behavior modification, but I do teach them, largely through the way we do things in the classroom, to become their own managers of learning, to be behavior modifiers. And the great majority of them really take to it. I also set up a good conduct program, where individual students in the class can earn points towards special activities like field trips. It works like a charm. I haven't had a serious discipline problem in three years.

I think behaviorism has unlocked the secret of learning. It should be a basis of all schooling. For me, it just wiped the cobwebs away and has made my teaching and my life more sensible and more enjoyable.

BEHAVIORAL OBJECTIVES

"Behavioral objectives identify goals and describe outcomes or performances learners should have as a result of participation in an activity." (H. H. McAshan, *Writing Behavioral Objectives* [New York: Harper & Row, 1970], p. 8.) The behavioral objective specifies not only the goal but also the behavior the learner will have to manifest as a means of determining success in achieving the goal.

Objectives are often stated so ambiguously that they are subject to different interpretations. Consider the following general objective: "The students should know the difference between a revenue tariff and a protective tariff." Does the teacher who chose this objective want the student to be able to write definitions of the two terms? Or to identify correctly written descriptions of the two terms? Or, given a description of a specific tariff, to identify orally what kind of tariff it is?

You can see that the objective as stated is too vague for students to determine exactly what they are supposed to know about tariffs. Here is the same objective written behaviorally: "Given written definitions of both revenue and protective tariffs, the student will be able to correctly identify orally to the instructor the name of each type of tariff on the first attempt." The clarity and specificity of this objective are the advantages of behavioral objectives. Programmed instruction, computer-assisted instruction, and systems for individualizing instruction depend on the translation of their goals into behavioral objectives.

YOUR PHILOSOPHY OF EDUCATION

At this point you may very well be confused, and possibly discouraged. To expect to be able to evaluate critically every aspect of each philosophy is to expect of yourself what few professional philosophers are able to do. What you have just finished reading is a précis of some of the major ideas of Western civilization. Some of these ideas have been around for centuries, and some are the fruits of great twentieth-century thinkers. Selecting the philosophy by which you will live and by which you will guide your professional activities takes much more investment of time and energy than reading our short chapter.

Some teachers, like the teacher-philosopher spokespersons in this chapter, settle on one philosophical view, and that view structures all of their work. Others prefer the position of philosophical eclecticism. The eclectic teacher selects what he or she believes to be the most attractive features of several philosophies. He or she might take from existentialism a search for the authentic self, and from essentialism a curricular viewpoint dominated by the usefulness criteria, and from behaviorism a certain instructional strategy.

Eclecticism is quite popular,[1] but often for the wrong reasons. It sometimes appears as the easy way out of philosophical uncertainty. Why not simply take what you please from the philosophical cafeteria of ideas? One problem is the possibility of inconsistency. To take one's view of society from the existentialist, which gives primacy to the individual, and one's teaching methodology from the progressivist, who stresses group membership and democratic process, is liable to keep everyone confused. Selecting eclecticism cannot be an excuse for lazy thinking.

A related problem has to do with the criterion for selecting eclectically from different philosophies. A difficult criterion is the individual's judgment based on "what works." For instance, you may use the classroom control techniques of the behavior modifiers because, in your judgment, they work. The problem here is that the basis for judgment or criterion of what constitutes "working" must be consistent. Having a common criterion of what constitutes "what works" becomes the real problem. If you work this out and, in effect, have a basis for judgment of "what works" in different situations, then you have gone a long way toward establishing a consistent and unified philosophy of education. Such a criterion is the basis for selecting teaching procedures. Therefore, the eclectic position is unnecessary. Nevertheless, an eclectic philosophy of education may provide a defensible way station or temporary stopping place for the individual who is working toward a unified philosophy of education.

Coming to fully understand questions about the true nature of reality or the purpose of existence is a life's work. On the other hand, the great

[1] In the process of writing this chapter, we discovered that we are really traditional, behaviorally oriented, but progressive essentialists who are searching around for a Great Books Club to join.

majority of the readers of this book are in the college years. We are not suggesting that readers sit themselves down, think through all these issues, and come up with a tight set of philosophical answers that will last a lifetime. Rather, we hope that we have focused—or refocused—your attention on some of life's essential questions and on some issues that are at the very core of teaching. In fact, the college years have always been considered a time of questioning and a time of testing the ideas which have, up to this point, been largely imposed on people by their education and cultural milieu. The undergraduate years should be a time of searching for answers to the basic questions of human identity. The uncertainty that goes along with this searching process is often an important step in self-growth. The college curriculum is designed to aid this frequently unsettling process. A major purpose of the college curriculum is to present the student with a spectrum of society's best thinkers and their attempts to understand their own existence. The reason for the general education component of teacher education programs is to provide a chance for future teachers to think through these fundamental issues of human existence. Often, however, this obvious purpose gets lost, and students go through the courses in a mechanical way, untouched by the philosophical content of the curriculum. On the other hand, the infamous college bull sessions may be where the real philosophical inquiry goes on; they are frequently thinly veiled discussions of what really counts in life and what one should try to do with his or her life. In effect, then, both the formal apparatus of college and the curriculum, and the informal opportunities to meet, talk, test your ideas with a variety of people should help you discover where you stand on some of these essential human questions.

As we said at the very beginning of this chapter, the teacher who is going to be more than a technician has a special obligation to take philosophical issues and questions seriously. Teachers owe it to themselves and to their students to know where they are going and why they are going there.

Discussion Questions

1. At the present time where are you in your own evolution or development of a philosophy of education? At the beginning of the quest? Just tying up some loose details?

2. What role, if any, does your religion play in your philosophy of education?

3. First, think back on the characteristics of your favorite teacher. Are you able to match up his or her views with any of the teacher-spokespersons or schools of philosophy mentioned in this chapter?

4. Which of the four branches of philosophy mentioned in this chapter (metaphysics, epistemology, axiology, and logic) is the one with which you feel most at home? What do you believe are the implications of this for your own teaching?

5. At this point, which of the philosophies of education (perennialism, progressivism, essentialism, existentialism, and behaviorism) appeals to you most? Why? What do you see as the most telling argument against this philosophy of education?

6. Which of these philosophies of education appeal to you least? Why? Are there any aspects of these philosophies or their application to the schools that you like and could endorse?

For Further Reading   Duck, Lloyd. *Teaching with Charisma.* Boston: Allyn and Bacon, 1981.
A new textbook which summarizes the major philosophical positions and the key questions of schooling to which each of these philosophies is addressed and does so in a readable and lively style.

Gutek, Gerald L. *Philosophical Alternatives in Education.* Columbus, Ohio: Merrill, 1974.
This textbook lays out several of the competing schools of philosophy that relate to education. It is well organized and well written.

Morris, V. C., and Y. Pai. *Philosophy and the American School.* 2nd ed. Boston: Houghton Mifflin, 1976.
An excellent textbook which summarizes the major philosophical positions and addresses how they bear on schooling in our current society.

Phenix, Phillip H. *Realms of Meaning: A Philosophy of the Curriculum for General Education.* New York: McGraw-Hill, 1964.
A superb book that describes the several ways men and women come to know the world. The author distills the essence of several disciplines and shows how they contribute to our sense of meaning. Highly recommended.

What Is the History of American Education?

4

American schooling and education did not develop overnight into our current system. Numerous social, political, economic, and religious forces have affected the development of American education. To understand our present educational system, its successes and failures, and the problems it still faces, we must look to our past. This chapter reviews the history of schooling and education in the United States, pointing out the important forces that have influenced their development and examining the contributions that significant men and women have made.

This chapter emphasizes that:

▪ Education in colonial America was originally religious in orientation but differed in form according to the geographical areas of the colonies. Schooling in colonial America was primarily for white males.

▪ During the nineteenth century, influenced by ideas of Thomas Jefferson and Benjamin Franklin and led by such reformers as Horace Mann, free public education became a reality. Common schools at the elementary level were tax supported and open to all children in an attempt to cultivate a sense of American identity and loyalty.

▪ The nineteenth century also saw the development of public high schools that were designed to prepare young people for either vocations or college within a single institution—a goal that was unique to American education.

▪ Private education has always played an important role in American history, particularly in our nation's early days. Even today, over 11 percent of the children of elementary and secondary school age attend private schools.

▪ Teacher education during the colonial period was practically nonexistent, but during the nineteenth and twentieth centuries, dramatic changes occurred to upgrade the training and status of teachers.

▪ Equal educational opportunities for minorities and women have not always existed in America. Ethnic groups such as blacks, Hispanic-Americans, and Native Americans, as well as women, have had to fight uphill battles to attain educational rights and treatment equal to those afforded white males.

*I*T IS A RARE COLLEGE STUDENT who feels a burning urgency to answer the question, "What is the history of American education?" Unless you are a history buff, you will probably ask yourself, "Why do I need to know this stuff? How will it help me do a better job in the classroom?" In truth, knowing something about the history of American education probably will not directly affect your classroom practices. So why should you study this aspect of education? There are, we think, some very good reasons.

First, understanding American educational history will give you a sense of perspective. Educators are occasionally accused of being faddist, which implies that we blindly follow each new approach or idea, thinking it is the greatest thing since sliced bread. On the other hand, we are sometimes accused of reinventing the wheel, spending a great deal of energy discovering something that has been in the educational literature for years or was a significant part of the education program of a different culture.

Second, although studying the history of American education will not give you answers to the immediate problems you are likely to face in your classes, what it will do is enable you to understand better the culture and context in which you will be working. It will help you obtain the "big picture" of why things operate as they do in today's schools.

Finally, studying the history of education will help you to appreciate better its truly noble heritage. Schools have been a progressive instrument in the lives of the majority of the people who have attended them. They have freed people from superstition and false information, and have given them new skills, positive values, and world-expanding visions of what each individual can become and what we as a people can become. Some of the greatest people who have walked the earth—Socrates, Jesus, Gandhi—saw themselves essentially as teachers. Teachers, then, are part of an old, progressive, and, indeed, inspirational human endeavor. Knowing our educational history and acquiring a historical perspective will help you live up to and extend this tradition.

THEMES IN AMERICAN EDUCATION

Reading this book, surrounded by college classmates and friends, may seem a natural step in your educational career. Kindergarten or nursery school led to elementary school; then on to junior high or middle school, which was followed by high school and now college. You may have taken this progression for granted, assuming that that's the way things have always been.

Not so. You are sitting at a level of education that was attained only by the elite of earlier generations. You are already close to the top of an educational pyramid for which the foundation was laid almost 350 years ago. The growth of the pyramid has been shaped and energized by five major forces in American educational history:

1. *Universal education*   In the colonial period, education was reserved for a small minority. Slowly, often in one-room rural schools, universal elementary education was achieved by the end of the nineteenth century; universal secondary education was attained by the early twentieth century; and, today, a college education is generally available to all who actively seek it.

2. *Public education*   In the colonial period, education was generally private and primarily for the middle and upper classes. Nationhood brought not only the spread of publicly supported education but, by the early twentieth century, compulsory education as well. Nevertheless, private education still remains as a small but important part of the whole educational system.

3. *Comprehensive education*   The basic abilities to read, write, and do arithmetic were once sufficient to prepare most children for their adult roles in society. However, the growth of urban, industrial life in America of the nineteenth and early twentieth centuries demanded also that people be educated for work. The result was the comprehensive public high school, which includes both training for trades and preparation for college.

4. *Secular education*   In earliest colonial times, the purpose of education was religious training. Beginning in the eighteenth century, and then progressing through the twentieth century, the function of American education has become increasingly secular, concerned with producing socially responsible citizens. Religious study has remained primarily in the private sector.

5. *Changing ideas of the basics*   Literacy and classical learning were the main goals of colonial education, whereas practical skills for a pragmatic, democratic society were the aims of the nineteenth-century schools. Technical and scientific literacy have become the basics in the computer- and space-aged twentieth century.

As you read the rest of this chapter, try to keep in mind these key trends. You might want to refer back to this list after you complete each of the chapter's major sections to see how many of these trends you can identify.

ELEMENTARY EDUCATION

Colonial Origins

In the 1600s, some girls received elementary instruction, but formal colonial education was primarily for boys (particularly those of the middle and upper classes). Both girls and boys might have received some preliminary training in the four Rs—reading, writing, arithmetic, and religion—at home. Occasionally, for a small fee, a housewife offered to take in children, to whom she would teach a little reading and writing, basic prayers, and religious beliefs. In these *dame schools*, girls also learned some basic household skills, such as cooking and sewing. The dame schools often provided all the formal education some children, especially girls, ever received.

Throughout the colonies, poor children were often apprenticed or indentured to local tradesmen or housewives. Apprenticeships lasted three to ten years, generally ending around age twenty-one for boys and eighteen for girls. During that time, an apprentice would learn the basic skills of a trade and might also be taught basic reading and writing, and perhaps arithmetic, as part of the contractual agreement.

Although the lines were not drawn hard and fast, the three geographic regions of the colonies developed different types of educational systems, which were shaped by each region's particular settlement patterns. New England colonists emphasized community-controlled, religiously oriented schools. Settlers in the South tended toward private education and tutors, with community schools seldom getting much support. The Middle Colonies saw the development of private venture and denominational schools.

NEW ENGLAND TOWN AND DISTRICT SCHOOLS In New England, the Puritans believed it was important that everyone be able to read the Bible and interpret its teachings. As early as 1642, Massachusetts passed a law requiring parents to educate their children. That law was strengthened in

1647 by the famous *Old Deluder Satan Act.* Because Satan assuredly would try to keep people from understanding the Scriptures properly, it was important for all children to be taught how to read. Therefore, every town of fifty or more families was obligated to pay a man to teach reading and writing. With these schools, known as *town schools,* New England set the precedent that if parents would not or could not educate their children, the government was obligated to take that responsibility.

As long as the villages remained compact and people lived close to one another, the town school system thrived. However, when settlers spread out, seeking better farmland, the town schools began to disappear. What emerged in their place was the so-called *moving school,* a schoolmaster who traveled from village to village, holding sessions in each place for several months before moving on. One can imagine how much actual learning occurred under such circumstances!

Discontent with this system of education led to the development of the *district school.* By this scheme, a township was divided into districts, each having its own school, which was taught by its own master and funded by the town treasury. The district school system soon entrenched itself in New England, as it was inexpensive to finance and afforded some measure of schooling to every child.

Some towns allowed girls to have one or two hours of instruction between 5:00 and 7:00 A.M., when boys were not using the school building. For the most part, however, girls had no access to the town elementary schools until after the Revolution.[1] Despite laws to the contrary, compulsory attendance was not very strongly enforced and, if few girls went to school in the towns, even fewer did so in the outlying districts.

SCHOOL LIFE IN COLONIAL NEW ENGLAND   The town and district schools were unlike today's schools in many respects. The schools were usually crude, one-room buildings, housing twenty or thirty students. The interiors were, typically, colorless and cold. Heating was such a prevalent problem that students generally were required to provide firewood.

Boys and girls entered school around the age of six or seven and stayed in school for only three or four years. They learned their ABCs, numerals, and the Lord's Prayer from a *hornbook,* which consisted of a page that was laminated with a transparent material made from boiled down cows' horns and then attached to a flat piece of wood. Having learned these basic elements, students graduated to the *New England Primer,* an illustrated book composed of religious texts and other readings. Although there were other primers and catechisms, the *New England Primer* was the most famous and remained the basic school text for at least one hundred years after the first edition of 1690.

[1]Willystine Goodsell, ed., *Pioneers of Women's Education in the United States* (New York: AMS Press, 1970/1931), p. 5.

In Adam's Fall
We finned all.

Thy Life to mend,
God's Book attend.

The Cat doth play,
And after flay.

A Dog will bite
A Thief at Night.

The Eagle's Flight
Is out of Sight.

The idle Fool
Is whipt at School

As runs the Glafs,
Man's life doth pafs.

My Book and Heart
Shall never part.

Job feels the Rod,
Yet bleffes God.

Proud Korah's troop
Was fwallow'd up.

The Lion bold
The Lamb doth
hold.

The Moon gives light
In Time of Night.

Foolishness is bound up on the heart of the child; but the rod of correction shall drive it from him.

— NEW ENGLAND PRIMER —

The learning atmosphere was repressive and grim. Students were under orders to keep quiet and do their work, and learning was characterized by an emphasis on memorization. Group instruction was almost unheard of; each child worked independently: one on ABCs, another on spelling, and another on the catechism. Class recitation was nonexistent. Instead, the master, sitting on a pulpit in the front of the room, called students up to recite to him one at a time.

If students did well, they were praised and given a new task. If they did poorly, they were criticized harshly and often given a rap across the knuckles or on the seat of the pants. It was believed that if children did not pay attention, that was simply a sign of how easily the devil could distract them from the path of righteousness. Such views continued to serve as a justification for severe classroom discipline throughout the first 250 years of American history.

EDUCATION IN THE SOUTH Conditions in the South were quite different from those in New England. Many upper-class Englishmen emigrated to the South, where they established large estates. As opposed to the more centralized geographic conditions in New England, the great distances between southern settlements encouraged plantation owners to educate their children with private tutors, who were often local ministers or itinerant scholars. In addition, most southern settlers were members of the Anglican Church and did not share the Puritan belief that everyone had a religious obligation to learn to read.

In the towns of the South, schools were established by governmental authority, but their administration was usually delegated to a group or corporation, which could collect tuition, own property, hire and fire teachers, and decide curriculum content. As in England, education of the poor and orphans was often undertaken by the Anglican Church or by religious groups such as the Society for the Propagation of the Gospel in Foreign Parts. Whereas the plantation owners could hire tutors or send their children to private schools, the lack of concern for general education of the entire community caused public education in the South to lag behind other sections of the country for many generations.

EDUCATION IN THE MIDDLE COLONIES Unlike Puritan New England and the Anglican Southern Colonies, the Middle Colonies were composed of a variety of religious and ethnic groups. Quakers, Catholics, Mennonites,

---

PRIVATE SCHOOLING IN THE SOUTH

In the South's few large communities, private venture schools offered secondary level studies. In these schools secular, rather than religious, studies were emphasized, and the practical courses took precedence over classical studies. Two advertisements for Charleston private schools illustrate these points.

At the house of Mrs. Delaweare on Broad Street is taught these sciences

Arithmetic	Dialling
Algebra	Navigation
Geometry	Astronomy
Trigonometry	Gauging
Surveying	Fortification

Reading Writing, Arithmetick vulgar and decimal, Geometry, Trigonometry plain and spherical, Mensuration of solid and superficial Bodies, Navigation, Surveying, Gagin, and many other useful Branches of the Mathematicks, Euclid's Elements, Italian, bookkeeping and Grammar, etc.: explain'd and taught in the clearest manner by Archidbald Hamilton, who may be heard of at Mr. Coon's Taylor in Churchstreet. N. B. He attends at any time and Place requir'd to teach, or to keep Books; and is willing upon a reasonable and speedy Encouragement to undertake a School in Town or Country for teaching all or any Part of what is above specified, otherwise to go off the country.

Sheldon S. Cohen, *A History of Colonial Education, 1607–1776* (New York: John Wiley, 1974), p. 133.

What Is the History of American Education?

In her study of classroom behavior in nineteenth-century schools, Barbara Joan Finkelstein writes that teachers were so committed to discipline that they believed that "the acquisition of knowledge represented a triumph of the will as well as the intellect. Consistently, in every kind of teaching situation, we find that teachers treated academic failure, not as a reflection of their own inabilities as instructors, but as evidence of the students' personal and moral recalcitrance; and this tendency was institutionalized on a grand scale in the village and city schools of the 1850's, 1860's, and 1870's. Indeed, the evidence suggests that teachers in every setting only rarely distinguished between the intellectual and the social aspects of student behavior as they meted out rewards and punishment." To many teachers, corporal punishment or humiliation seemed appropriate treatment for children who did not learn their lessons, for academic incompetence was considered a sign of moral laxity.

Reprinted from David B. Tyack, *The One Best System* (Cambridge, Mass.: Harvard University Press, 1974), p. 55.

Huguenots, Baptists, and others each wished to train their children in their respective faiths; Dutch, German, and Swedish settlers also wanted a separate education for their children. As a result, *private venture schools*, which were licensed by the civil government but not protected or financed by it, flourished, and the use of public funds to educate everyone's children did not become customary.

In these private schools, the teacher was paid directly by parents on a contractual basis. The instructor himself managed the school and curriculum, accepting or rejecting students as he desired. The denominational schools in the Middle Colonies shared the New Englanders' concern for proper religious training as a primary goal, but they also began early to offer, in addition to the basics, practical subjects such as bookkeeping or navigation.

The Common Schools

Prior to the Revolution, the term *common school* referred to education for the average person, but not necessarily at public expense or available to all. The American Revolution brought with it a new ideal of the common school, which, like the Revolution itself, was nevertheless rooted in the colonial period. The early New England laws had already set the precedent that all children should be taught how to read and that the civil government had authority over education. This implied a communal obligation to provide *universal education*—that is, schooling for everyone. However, even in

If a nation expects to be ignorant and free, in a state of civilization, it expects what never was and will never be.

— THOMAS JEFFERSON —

colonial New England, it was the students' parents who had to pay for the schooling.

In the first blush of the new republic, however, conditions began to favor the idea that some sort of elementary education should be provided free, at public expense and under public control, for everyone who could not afford or did not want private schooling. Even though the Constitution had relegated control of education to the states, the impetus for such public schooling came from the federal government, in particular as a result of the enactment of the Land Ordinances of 1785 and 1787. Concerning the sale of public lands in the Northwest Territory (from present-day Ohio to Minnesota), Congress passed the Land Ordinance of 1785. Every township was divided into thirty-six sections, of which one was set aside for the maintenance of public schools. Congress reaffirmed, in the Ordinance of 1787, that "Religion, morality, and knowledge, being necessary to good government and the happiness of mankind, schools and the means of education shall forever be encouraged."[2]

ARGUMENTS FOR THE COMMON SCHOOL   The common school was the ideal of educational reform in the first half of the 1800s, because liberal thinkers began to view education in a new light. They emphasized, first, the political significance of universal education. Following the American Revolution, it was recognized that a democratic government would be only as strong as the people's ability to make intelligent choices, which in turn depended on a basic education for all. It was also argued that education was a natural right, just like the very rights for which the Revolution had been fought. Benjamin Franklin and Thomas Jefferson suggested educational plans, as did other leaders of the Revolution.

The early period of independence saw an increased concern for citizenship and nationhood. The War of 1812, coming so soon after the Revolution, impressed upon Americans the idea that their separate national backgrounds had to be put aside if the new nation was to remain united and free. A system of common schooling would strengthen that, unity. Similarly, an influx of immigrants in the 1840s and 1850s, following a period of upheaval in Europe, further stimulated demand for an educational system that would serve to Americanize the waves of foreigners and keep society stable.

Many supporters of the common school also focused on its economic and social effects. Unlike the European social structure, class membership in America was rather fluid: a person's wealth and social status in this country were not dependent so much on the social class into which he or she was born. Since there was no inherited class of nobility, one's own

---

[2]R. Freeman Butts and Lawrence A. Cremin, *A History of Education in American Culture* (New York: Holt, Rinehart and Winston, 1953), p. 245.

initiative and talent became the criteria for success, and it was believed that a common education would fuel everyone's upward mobility. Universal education was thus seen by the newly evolving working class as a means of equalizing economic and social opportunities. As a result, another reason given for spreading educational opportunity was that better-educated people would increase productivity and enhance everyone's prosperity while diminishing crime and reducing poverty.

Whereas the *New England Primer* reflected the religious orientation of much colonial education, the textbooks of the nineteenth century emphasized morality and Americanism. No other book was more popular than the six-volume series of *McGuffey Readers,* which sold more than 100 million copies between 1836 and 1906. Besides training students in (American) English language and grammar, these texts introduced poetry and the writings of statesmen, politicians, moralists, and religious leaders. "They assumed the Fatherhood of God, the brotherhood of man, the wickedness of war, crime, and inhumanity, and above all, they buttressed the concept of the sacredness of property and bulwarked the position of the middle class in society."[3]

[3]Charles W. Coulter and Richard S. Rimanoczy, *A Layman's Guide to Educational Theory* (New York: Van Nostrand, 1955), p. 130.

NOAH WEBSTER
(1758–1843)

Although best remembered today for his *American Dictionary of the English Language,* which was first published in 1828, Noah Webster was best known in the nineteenth century for his *American Spelling Book* (also known as the *Blue-Backed Speller*). This small, blue-backed booklet appeared in 1783 and became the most widely used schoolbook during the early nineteenth century.

A native of Connecticut, Webster attended and graduated from Yale University.

During the course of his lifetime he was a lawyer, schoolmaster, politician, and writer. Although Thomas Jefferson, expressing his opinion of Webster in 1801, wrote, "I view Webster as a mere pedagogue, of a very limited understanding," Webster's intellectual interests were of an astounding breadth. He wrote a paper on epidemic and pestilential diseases, edited John Wingate's historical journal, wrote several scientific treatises, discoursed on banking and insurance, and along the way,

mastered twenty-six different languages, including Sanskrit!

Webster was an intensely patriotic individual who believed that America had to shed itself of its British influence and develop its own sense of American cultural identity and unity. The best way to do this, he believed, was to reshape the English language and literature so that it would reflect the unique American culture and create a national language that was free of localism. The creation of an American language

Although universal education at this time was meant only for whites, the same arguments advanced by its advocates were used later to extend universal education to include minorities. The desegregation efforts of the 1950s and 1960s were based on the idea of creating equal educational opportunities for everyone regardless of race. For further discussion of this issue, see pages 124–129 of this chapter and pages 389–399 of Chapter 12.

ARGUMENTS AGAINST THE COMMON SCHOOL   As proper as these thoughts may sound to the modern ear, they often encountered opposition. The arguments against the common school were based on economics as much as on educational or political principles. The question concerned who would have to pay for this universal education: why should one family pay for the education of another's children? The same question had been asked in the colonial period, and many people still felt that schooling, especially for the poor, should be the responsibility of religious groups. Still others felt that a free public school would gradually weaken or dilute the particular culture or religion that they had sought to establish in America. If ethnic groups commingled, what would be the fate of each one's native culture and language?

would bind the people together and help produce a strong sense of nationalism. In his dictionary there appeared for the first time ever such American words as *plantation, hickory, presidential,* and *pecan.*

Webster knew that if Americans were to develop this sense of national identity and pride, the process would best be started at an early age. Accordingly, he wrote his blue-backed speller, one of the most successful books ever written. Roughly 100 million copies were printed, and it is estimated that more than a billion readers used the book—a record surpassed only by the Bible. Oftentimes the *American Spelling Book* was the only book schoolchildren had, as it served as a combination primer, reader, and speller. The book abounded in moral stories and lessons, as well as word lists and guides to pronunciation. Webster must be credited with the fact that Americans differ from the British in writing *color* instead of *colour* and *center* instead of *centre.* Not only did he set the style for American spelling, but he made it the liveliest subject in the class-room. Spelling bees and other spelling games brightened up what otherwise was typically dull instruction.

Known as the "schoolmaster of the republic," Noah Webster campaigned for free schools for both boys and girls, where children could learn the virtues of liberty, just laws, patriotism, hard work, and morality. He was an educational statesman whose work, more than anyone else's, helped to create a sense of American language and national culture.

And what was to be done about religious study? The ability of different religious groups to exist together in one school, as in democracy itself, demanded that no one religious group be favored over another. Although there were many competing proposals, the common schools ultimately settled on the teaching of basic moral values, such as honesty and sincerity, as substitutions for direct religious instruction. However, reduction to this least common denominator did not satisfy many religious groups.

It is important to note that both the supporters and the opponents of common schools felt they were defending the ideal of freedom in American life. The issue of what role the schools should play in developing values, morals, and ethics continues today, as our discussion of moral education and religion and the schools in Chapter 12 indicates.

VICTORY OF THE COMMON SCHOOL   Many seeds of the common school movement were sown in the form of one-room schools, mandated in the early New England school laws and in the Northwest Ordinances of 1785 and 1787. Between 1820 and 1920, the establishment of common schools made steady progress around the country. By the middle of the nineteenth century and certainly by the end of the Civil War, the ideal of universal elementary education was generally acknowledged, if not universally practiced. By 1850, two states had passed compulsory attendance laws in addition to making common schools generally available. By 1900, thirty-two states had such laws, and all states did by 1930. In the North and West, states gradually passed laws for school systems to be supported by tax money and controlled by the state.

As a result, between the Civil War and World War I the number of students in schools grew enormously. In 1870, 57 percent of children between five and eighteen years old were enrolled in some form of schooling. By 1918, more than 75 percent of that age range were enrolled.[4] In 1870, average attendance was forty-five days a year; in 1918, more than ninety days. Thus, the hundred years between 1820 and 1920 witnessed extraordinary growth in the commitment to free, publicly supported, universal education.

Other Developments   **EUROPEAN INFLUENCES**   From Europe came new ideas about proper education. One of the most far-reaching experiments was the *kindergarten,* a "children's garden," where pleasant children's activities, such as songs and stories, were used to lay a foundation before formal education began. The first American experiments were actually made before the Civil War, but in 1873 a public school kindergarten was established in St. Louis, and the idea spread rapidly.

[4]Butts and Cremin, *Education in America,* p. 408.

European influence also resulted in attempts to incorporate more physical activity and manual training in the curriculum. This innovation was not designed specifically to train technical workers, but rather to complement and round out traditional intellectual instruction. In these ways, the thought of Johann Pestalozzi and other European educators entered American education. (Pestalozzi is covered in greater detail in Chapter 1.)

CURRICULUM CHANGES   During the colonial period, it was hardly necessary for a person to have knowledge beyond the three Rs unless one were wealthy and wanted to go on to college. In the early and mid-nineteenth century, the common school curriculum simply expanded on the traditional curriculum. The primary concern was less with religious training and more with obtaining functional knowledge for life after school. Subjects such as spelling, geography, history, and government were added because they were considered important for good citizenship. Natural science, physical training, and mechanical drawing were also included to provide a complete, well-rounded education.

In 1893 the Committee of Fifteen was appointed by the National Education Association to study the issue of curriculum, and the committee's report highlighted the needs and structure of a subject-centered curriculum. The eight-year elementary curriculum was to concentrate on the study of grammar, literature, arithmetic, geography, and history. Around this core, subjects such as drawing, natural science, hygiene, music, physical education, algebra, and morals would be intertwined. The eight-year sequence of the curriculum not only reflected the considerable expansion since the early days of the common school but also showed a clear commitment to a traditional, subject-centered orientation.

APPLICATION OF PSYCHOLOGY TO EDUCATION   Among various new developments in the early 1900s was the growth of psychology and its application to education in theories of learning and behavior. These theories challenged traditional educational wisdom on scientific grounds. Statistical methods and standardized testing were increasingly used to evaluate intelligence and educational achievement. Although far from perfect, these methods began to provide a basis by which educational standards and the effectiveness of different methods of instruction could be measured objectively around the nation.

CONSOLIDATION   The growth of school enrollments, especially outside the cities, would not have been possible without the consolidation of smaller school districts into larger, unified systems. Although the one-room school had served well in the days of the frontier, as areas developed it became clear that the smaller, poorer districts could not provide the educational opportunities available in larger, wealthier ones. As early as 1869, Massachusetts allowed two districts to merge. In 1910, more than half the states allowed such unification. By the 1920s, the growth of industry and the invention of the automobile (and the school bus) helped consolidate the large number of one-room schools around the country into centrally located, modern facilities that could serve larger areas better than the old district schools.

THE PROGRESSIVE EDUCATION ASSOCIATION   John Dewey (who is discussed more fully in Chapter 3) and other educators tried to create new, experimental, child-centered schools in the early 1900s. In 1919, the establishment of the Progressive Education Association was a formalized attempt to reform education according to the following principles:

1. The child should have freedom to develop naturally.
2. Natural interest is the best motive for work.
3. The teacher is a guide, not a task master.
4. A student's development must be measured scientifically, and not just by grades.
5. Students' general health and physical development require attention.
6. The school and the home must work together to meet children's needs.
7. The progressive school should be a leader in trying new educational ideas.[5]

The progressive school movement eventually went in several different directions. Some educators argued for letting children be free to do whatever they wanted; others tried to make the school into a community center for recreation, adult education, and even social reform. Critics ranged from traditionalist advocates of the subject-centered curriculum to some progressives, like Dewey himself, who argued that the ties between society and the child are broken when total freedom is granted for children to do whatever they wanted.

The 1940s brought a rather conservative reaction to the progressivism of the previous generation. However, it is good to remember that many ideas we take for granted now—such as teaching through student projects, field trips, and nonlecture methods of instruction—were hotly debated innovations that were introduced by progressive educators. Many "new" ideas that are in vogue today were in fact first tried by progressives: inquiry-based discovery learning; mastery learning, in which students move at their own pace through sequenced problem solving; performance contracting for individualized learning; differentiated staffing, in which staff are trained for different skills so as to create an educational team; flexible scheduling, in

[5]John D. Pulliam, *History of Education in America,* 3rd ed. (Columbus, Ohio: Charles E. Merrill, 1982), pp. 157–159.

Table 4.1 Types of Elementary Schooling

Type of School	Location	Time Period	Purpose
Dame schools	Most of the colonies	Seventeenth century	Private school held in housewife's home; taught basic reading, spelling, and religious doctrines
Town schools	New England	Seventeenth and part of eighteenth century	Locally controlled institution, public but not free; simple curriculum of reading, writing, catechism, and arithmetic
Moving schools	New England	Eighteenth century	Provided schooling for communities spread out over wide areas; an itinerant teacher moved from village to village
District schools	New England, primarily	Mid-eighteenth to mid-nineteenth century	Replaced town and moving schools; public but not free; each district hired its own schoolmaster, again with emphasis on basic skills
Private tutoring	The South, primarily	Seventeenth to early nineteenth century	For children of wealthy
Private venture schools	Primarily Middle Colonies, but widespread	Eighteenth–nineteenth century	Private schools, offering whatever subjects the schoolmaster chose and parents wanted for their children
Common schools	New England, Middle Colonies, and the South	1830–present	Provided free, public, locally controlled elementary schooling; curriculum emphasized basic skills, moral education, and citizenship
Kindergartens	Widespread	1855–present	Emphasized play and constructive activities as preparation for elementary schools

which school time is not necessarily bound to calendar time of specific hours; open classrooms, in which students can move about freely in a variety of activities and learning centers; team teaching; and nongraded schools, in which students can move at their own pace with variable requirements.[6]

Since the progressive education movement, elementary education has been influenced by several major forces. During the 1960s a number of national curriculum projects were developed and implemented in the elementary schools, particularly in mathematics and science. These curricula stirred up controversy, because many individuals believed that they were too theoretical and not practical enough. As achievement test scores declined during the 1970s, many parents, politicians, and educators argued that the schools had tried to accomplish too much and had lost sight of their basic purposes. A return to the basics seemed to be the cry of the late 1970s and the early 1980s. Some public schools also responded to conflicting demands of different groups by creating alternative schools within the public school system, allowing parents to choose from among different approaches how they want their children to be educated. (Chapters 6, 7, and 13 describe in more detail life in present-day schools, the current elementary school curriculum, and the innovative approaches affecting elementary schools today.)

SECONDARY EDUCATION

In the history of American secondary education, there have been four major institutions. The first type of secondary school, prevalent in the early colonial period, was the *Latin grammar school,* whose main purpose was to prepare students for college. The *English grammar school,* established in the latter half of the colonial period, was intended to provide a practical alternative education for students who were not interested in college. The third type of school, which flowered in the early national period, was the *academy.* Although its major purpose was to combine the best of both types of grammar schools, the academy gradually took on a college-oriented direction in the nineteenth century. Finally, evolving naturally from the elementary common school, the *public high school* became the predominant form of secondary education in America in the twentieth century. A uniquely American institution, the high school provides, within a single institution, both a preparation for college and a terminal vocational education.

Early Forms

LATIN GRAMMAR SCHOOLS   In the colonial period, all secondary education (that is, all education beyond the elementary level) served the sole purpose of training for entrance to college. The earliest secondary institution was the Latin grammar school, whose name gradually came to mean "col-

[6]Pulliam, *History of Education,* pp. 178–180.

lege preparatory school''; the term *prep school* still carries that classical connotation today.

A boy entered a Latin grammar school around age seven or eight and spent the next seven years learning Latin texts written either by ancient Romans or medieval scholars. Much work was memorized and, over three or four years, the student learned composition and writing of Latin verses. Following this, the student studied Greek, moving in the final year to classical Greek writers and the New Testament. He also might have given some attention to the study of the Hebrew language.

The first Latin grammar school in the colonies is generally considered to have been established in 1635 in Boston. It was public, open to boys of all social classes. The Old Deluder Satan Act of 1647, which required communities of fifty or more families to establish elementary schools, also required communities of one hundred or more families to establish Latin schools. By 1700, there were twenty-six such secondary schools throughout New England; however, enrollment was generally small and was limited primarily to the upper class. Only 202 students were enrolled in both Boston Latin schools in 1769.[7] At first, Latin grammar schools were found primarily in New England; a bit later they were instituted in the Middle Colonies. Wealthy families in the South generally either hired tutors or sent their sons back to England for college preparation.

ALTERNATIVE FORMS OF COLLEGE PREPARATION　During the colonial period, especially in the South, many students received their secondary education from tutors or at private venture schools, which were more common in the Middle Colonies. Instruction provided by a single schoolmaster obviously lacked variability and dependability. Gradually, corporate schools were developed; these institutions were governed by a board of trustees or directors and were able to continue as a corporate endeavor beyond the tenure of any particular teacher.

ENGLISH GRAMMAR SCHOOLS　The growth of middle-class businesses in the 1700s led to the demand for a secondary education that would provide practical instruction in everything from navigation and engineering to bookkeeping and foreign languages. Thus there arose private English grammar schools, which catered to the growing number of students who needed more than elementary instruction but were not interested in preparing for college. Classes were offered at various times and places, sometimes to girls as well as to boys. Commercial subjects, rather than religious ones, were taught. Some subjects, such as music, art, and dancing, were actually not practical, but were meant to be used for socializing in polite company.

---

[7]Edward A. King, *Salient Dates in American Education, 1635–1964* (New York: Harper & Row, 1966), p. 3.

SECONDARY EDUCATION OF FEMALES   In the 1700s, private venture English grammar schools were more flexible than the Latin grammar schools and, as a result, were the first secondary institutions to accept female students. Depending on the sophistication of the particular school and the preferences of its clientele, girls typically studied the three Rs, geography, and French, but they also sometimes learned English grammar, history, and Latin. Some practical vocational subjects such as bookkeeping were occasionally taught along with such traditional and socially accepted skills as art and instrumental music.

Because of the somewhat larger number of private venture schools in the Middle Colonies, girls who lived there probably had greater educational opportunity than girls who lived elsewhere. Quaker leaders, including William Penn and French-born Anthony Benezet, were concerned with and supported the education of several deprived groups, such as blacks, Native Americans—and women.

In the South, the daughters of the wealthy landowners could receive traditional instruction in the various arts and letters, such as music, dancing, and French, which would give them the social skills appropriate for the lady of a household. By the end of the colonial period, there was a double track education that was as clearly set for middle- or upper-class girls as it was for boys in the English or Latin grammar schools.

The Academy   A new type of secondary school grew up during the second half of the eighteenth century. The academy was an attempt to combine Latin and English grammar schools through separate Latin and English departments within one school. Academies were unlike the Latin grammar schools in that the primary language of the academy was English; they were unlike the English grammar schools in that classical subjects were also included in the curriculum. Gradually, the academy took the place of both other types of school.

BENJAMIN FRANKLIN'S ACADEMY   In 1751, Benjamin Franklin established an academy in Philadelphia. Its curriculum was typical of that offered at most academies. It differed from Latin grammar schools in that it focused on practical, useful studies rather than on college preparatory courses. It was an English school, emphasizing the reading and writing of English grammar, rhetoric, and literature to facilitate the communication that one would need in business and trade. Arithmetic, geometry, and astronomy were the forms of mathematics studied. History, in English translations, geography, political science, religion, and morality were also taught. Both classical and modern languages were offered, and students chose languages appropriate for the type of occupation they eventually would enter.

Although Franklin's academy offered all these courses when it was first established, over the years the emphasis shifted back to the classical languages and curriculum. This gradual change was not uncommon in academies, but the ideal of a utilitarian curriculum remained.

GROWTH OF ACADEMIES   The number of private academies grew rapidly following the American Revolution, in response to the growing need for practical business training. As many as one thousand academies existed by 1830, but the highest point was around 1850, when about six thousand academies were in operation.[8] Compared with the Latin grammar schools, the academies included instruction for a larger age range, which on the low end overlapped the curriculum of the common schools, and on the upper end sometimes provided instruction that was as extensive as that of colleges. Because they were private institutions, the academies were also at greater liberty to accept girls.

FEMALE ACADEMIES   The real surge of development in education for girls and young women came in the first half of the 1800s, with the growth of academies and seminaries that were established especially for young women. Female academies were established by Emma Willard in Troy, New York (1821); by Catherine Beecher in Hartford, Connecticut (1828); and by Mary Lyon in South Hadley, Massachusetts (1837). A secondary education acquired at one of these institutions was often the highest level of education women would ever receive. Eventually, some of these academies themselves became colleges.

The female academies had to buck the established tradition against formal education for women, who, in many quarters, were still considered intellectually inferior to men. The schools compromised somewhat by offering courses related to home economics in addition to more classical subjects.

In practical terms, the leaders of the women's education movement were committed to two goals. One was to produce women who could handle the domestic chores of wives and mothers intelligently and wisely, so as to "become companions rather than satellites of their husbands."[9] The curriculum of female academies, therefore, was designed to include subjects similar, but not identical, to those at men's institutions. Domestic skills were presented as practical applications of the more abstract traditional subjects. The other goal of women's education was to train women as teachers.

[8]Butts and Cremin, *Education in America,* p. 260.

[9]Merle Curti, *The Social Ideas of American Educators,* 2nd ed. (Totowa, N.J.: Littlefield, Adams, 1959), p. 183.

Public High Schools

Although the private academies reflected the democratic independence of the middle class, their tuition and fees effectively cut out participation by the poorer working class. In the years following the Revolution, the growing demand for free public elementary education understandably provided a basis on which to argue for free secondary education. Such schooling at public expense was the educational system most appropriate for democracy, it was argued, and the only system that could maintain democracy.

At the beginning of the 1800s, the appeal of the academies had been to provide training in studies that prepared students for practical livelihood and not necessarily for college. By the 1840s, the same goal was being demanded of public high schools. Seen in retrospect, the academies were really a link between the earlier grammar school and the later high school.

Less than ninety years after establishing its first Latin school, in 1821 Boston created the first public English high school; a second one, for girls, was established in 1826. The number of high schools throughout the states increased slowly but steadily as an extension of the common school system. Unlike the academies, high schools were governed by the public rather than by private school boards. By no means universally accepted, the argument for free public high schools was a logical one, being based simply on the inherent inequality of providing elementary schools for all and secondary schools only for those who could afford tuition.

Opponents of the idea of public high schools did not dispute the need for common elementary schools. They did argue, however, that secondary school was a luxury and was not within the domain of the taxing authorities. In 1874, however, in the famous *Kalamazoo* case, the Michigan courts ruled that the school district could tax the public to support high schools as well as elementary schools.

Debate Over the Secondary Curriculum

In the late nineteenth century, debate shifted from whether public secondary schools should be supported to what the content of the curriculum should be. Guidelines for the curriculum were derived largely from the goals that were expressed for the schools. One goal was to reduce social tensions and strengthen the democratic form of government by bringing together all social classes and ethnic groups. Another goal was to provide better preparation for Americans to participate, upon graduation, in the full range of industrial occupations. In addition, the high schools were to offer specialized vocational and technical training. Finally, the high schools were supposed to provide both a terminal educational experience for most students and also a bridge to higher education for those who were capable and chose to pursue further studies.

THE ARTICULATED CURRICULUM   The question of how to achieve these goals generated much debate between 1880 and 1920. The issue was one of *articulation*, referring to the smooth joining of different parts in the ed-

© 1962 United Feature Syndicate Inc.

ucational pyramid. In the case of public high schools, several types of articulation were debated. Outside the pyramid, the concern was to provide a curriculum that matched the objectives of different sectors of society. Inside, the concern was how to link the high school curriculum with that of the elementary school, on the bottom, and with college entrance and occupational requirements, on the top.

Industry and organized labor made it clear that they wanted high schools to give sound training in technical, commercial, and vocational fields. On the other hand, like a recurring echo, other voices made the case for the teaching of a basic set of cultural subjects, which, they argued, had practical application in that students would be trained how to think well, whatever the specific topic.

THE NEA COMMITTEES   In the 1890s, the National Educational Association commissioned several committees to investigate these matters: the Committee of Fifteen on Elementary Studies (1893), the Committee of Ten on Secondary Studies (1892), and the Committee of Thirteen on College Entrance Requirements (1895). The Committee of Ten was probably the one that had the most far-reaching impact. However, to put it mildly, one senses a bias in the composition of the committee: there were five college presidents, one professor, two headmasters, one high school administrator—and no high school teachers![10]

All three committees tended to be subject-matter oriented. They subscribed to the now discarded theory of mental discipline, which holds that a subject, in and of itself, can train the mind to reason better, in the way that exercise affects the body. Essentially, the committees sought to standardize elementary and secondary education as a pre-university experience. The Committee of Thirteen developed the idea that standardized numbers of high school course units, similar to credit hours, in foreign language,

[10]Pulliam, *History of Education,* p. 101.

mathematics, English, and so forth, should be required for college admission. So, while lip service was given to the terminal and vocational aspects of secondary education, courses for the traditional curriculum still guided educational decision making.

THE COMPREHENSIVE HIGH SCHOOL   Between the Civil War and World War I, the secondary curriculum shifted considerably. The basic mathematics courses in arithmetic, geometry, and algebra tended to be taught in a more commercial and practical context. American literature began to compete with English literature, and commercial English was added to the study of literary English. The classical languages continued to give way to the modern foreign languages. In science, to physiology, chemistry, physics, botany, and astronomy were added meteorology, zoology, forestry, agriculture, and geology. Physical education was added to the curriculum. In the social studies, the number of courses in American history grew, although European history continued to be central. To history were added civics and citizenship. Moral philosophy fell away completely and was replaced by purely commercial courses such as typing, stenography, commercial law, domestic science and home economics, industrial arts, and manual training. Of significance was the increasing number of parallel curricula, such as English, college preparatory, manual training, science, and so forth, that might be offered in a single high school.[11]

Twentieth-Century Development

GROWTH OF JUNIOR HIGH AND MIDDLE SCHOOLS   Despite the NEA Committee recommendations, how to divide grade levels for elementary and secondary training was an issue that was debated for some time. The main question was when to stop teaching basic skills and to start teaching content: should there be eight elementary grades and four of secondary school, or six elementary and six secondary? The pattern of ending elementary school after sixth grade, with six grades of secondary school, gradually gained acceptance, but this division came under fire for several reasons. Educators wanted to introduce new studies to the curriculum. They sought to give greater attention to the pupils as individuals and to gain greater understanding of adolescent development in general. There was also growing concern for keeping pupils in school past the elementary level.

In an attempt to resolve these issues, educators began to experiment with various ways to reorganize the grades. Finally, in the school year of 1909–1910, in both Columbus, Ohio, and Berkeley, California, a separate program was established for the intermediate grades 7, 8, and 9. The new grouping was called *junior high school.* By 1916, 184 urban school systems had some form of intermediate school, with grades divided in patterns of six elementary-two intermediate-four secondary, or six elementary-three

[11]Butts and Cremin, *Education in America,* p. 443.

intermediate-three secondary. By 1926, over 800 systems had a six-three-three organization, and that pattern has predominated since then.[12]

Since the 1960s, however, the system of five elementary-three intermediate-four secondary grades has become more popular, with a middle school for grades 6, 7, and 8 rather than a junior high school. In recent years, middle schools have come to focus more on the individual student, using nongraded programs with interdisciplinary team teaching, flexible scheduling, and independent study.[13]

VICTORY OF THE COMPREHENSIVE HIGH SCHOOL   In the twentieth century, public high schools continued to spread. The process of consolidating school districts, which we discussed earlier in the context of combining the one-room schools, also made the comprehensive high school available to many students who otherwise would not have had access to it. In 1890, students in public high schools were only 1.6 percent of *all* students enrolled. By 1920, they represented 10.2 percent of all students; by 1950, 22.7 percent, and by 1980, 32.9 percent of America's school enrollment was in public high schools. In actual numbers, over 2 million students attended public high schools in 1920; by 1950, 5.7 million were attending, and by 1980, the number had risen to 13.7 million.[14]

SECONDARY EDUCATION TODAY   The most remarkable observation that can be made about secondary education today is how little it has changed over the last forty years. There have been changes, of course, but they have been small relative to the changes that have occurred in American living patterns, values, technologies, and careers. The curriculum revolves around subjects that are taught by specialists and are not very different from the subjects that were offered in schools during World War I. As we will point out in Chapter 6, Larry Cuban's recent study of schooling in the secondary schools reveals that instructional practices in the secondary school have changed very little from 1900 until the present day. The reason lies in the basic structure of the high school. Its organizing framework, developed in the nineteenth century, persists today across all regions of the country. High schools are complicated organizations, requiring considerable orchestration in order to work efficiently. To change one part of the system means that other parts must also change in reaction to the first change. As a result, relatively little change occurs.

[12]William T. Gruhn and Harl R. Douglass, *The Modern Junior High School*, 3rd ed. (New York: Ronald Press Company, 1971), pp. 46–53.

[13]Joseph Bondi, *Developing Middle Schools: A Guidebook* (Wheeling, Ill.: Whitehall Company, 1978), pp. 9–12.

[14]W. Vance Grant and Leo J. Eiden, *Digest of Education Statistics 1982* (Washington, D.C.: National Center for Education Statistics, 1982), p. 35.

Table 4.2 Types of Secondary Schooling

Type of School	Location	Time Period	Purpose
Latin grammar schools	New England, Middle Colonies; a few in the South	Seventeenth and eighteenth centuries	Emphasized Latin and classical studies; designed to prepare young men for college
English grammar schools	Middle Colonies and New England; a few in the South	Eighteenth century	Private secondary schools designed to provide practical rather than college preparatory studies
Academies	Middle Colonies, New England; a few in the South	Eighteenth and nineteenth centuries	Private secondary schools designed to prepare young people for business and life; emphasized a practical curriculum, but gradually shifted back to college preparation
High schools	New England, Middle Colonies at first; now universal	1821–present	Provided public secondary schooling; combined functions of Latin grammar schools and academies (college preparation and preparation for life and business)
Junior high schools	First in California; now universal	1909–present	Designed to provide students in grades 7–9 with better preparation for high school
Middle schools	Universal	1950–present	Designed to meet the unique needs of preadolescents, usually grades 6–8; an alternative to junior high schools

If you would like a more complete picture of what life in secondary schools is like, or what is taught, see Chapters 6 and 7. Chapter 12 will give you a better idea of some of the problems facing secondary education, and Chapter 13 discusses new approaches and innovations.

PRIVATE EDUCATION

Private schools have always been part of American education. Historically, they have served three major purposes in providing (1) instruction for various religious denominations, (2) an exclusive education for the wealthy, and (3) an alternative for any group that finds the available forms of education unsatisfactory.

For more than 150 years, until the growth of the common school movement in the early 1800s, *most* education in America was private. The vast majority of elementary schools, the Latin grammar schools, the academies, and all the colleges of the colonial period were tuition-supported private schools or semiprivate institutions, controlled by independent, self-perpetuating boards of trustees. Even the "public" schools of colonial New England required the students' parents to pay tuition. As we discussed previously, the academies served as a link between the earlier Latin grammar schools and the public high schools. However, the fact that academies charged tuition limited them largely to the middle and upper classes. Although some academies were sponsored by various religious denominations, even those not specifically denominational often had a clearly religious orientation. The women's academies, for instance, often had a distinctly religious tone in their dual goals of preparing young women for family life and training teachers who would educate their students to become good, God-fearing citizens.

Since the middle of the nineteenth century, by far the largest private school enrollments have been in schools run by the Roman Catholic church. The earliest Catholic schools existed primarily in the Spanish-speaking Southwest and in French-speaking Louisiana. However, Irish and Italian immigration, after 1840, increased the support of Catholic institutions in the North and East. The total number of Catholic schools grew from about one hundred in 1840, to about three thousand in the 1880s, eight thousand in 1920, eleven thousand in 1950; it dropped to about ninety-five hundred in 1980–1981.

Despite the growth of Catholic schools, by 1890 only about 12 percent of all elementary and secondary students were enrolled in private schools. The number continued to decline to a low of 7.3 percent in 1920, but then gradually increased to a high of 13.6 percent in 1960. It is currently over 11 percent. The steady reduction in percentage of private school students was not only a sign of public school strength: it also reflected outright discrimination and pressure against those who wanted to be "different." An extreme case followed World War I, when Nebraska passed a law prohibiting the teaching of German in either public or private schools. However, in 1922, the Supreme Court ruled that a state could not interfere with the prerogative of parents to educate their children as they see fit, in this case at a private school that taught the German language, simply on the grounds of desiring to "foster a more homogeneous people with American ideals. . . ."[15] When, in 1925, an Oregon law required all children to attend

[15]Herbert M. Kliebard, ed., *Religion and Education in America: A Documentary History* (Scranton, Pa.: International Textbook Company, 1969).

public school, a Roman Catholic school and another private school successfully challenged the law on the grounds that their Fourteenth Amendment rights were being abridged.

It is significant not only that, over the past one hundred years, public schools have become clearly the principal mode of education in America but also that private education has remained an important alternative to the public schools for about 10–15 percent of the population. These figures reflect a paradox. On the one hand, from early days, private schools have represented the freedom of immigrant groups to pursue life in America and to train their children as they chose. That privilege was essential to the young democracy and still represents a basic freedom of choice in America.

On the other hand, some argue that private education supports a caste system that is, in principle, not democratic. In addition, they argue, private education inherently casts the quality of public education in a harsh light. The very existence of private forms of education can be viewed as an implied criticism either of the quality of public education or of its availability on equal terms to all comers, irrespective of class, religion, or race.

But supporters of private education respond that the public schools present an educational monopoly, and they point out that, in any case, the strained economic resources of the public schools could not handle the additional enrollment of about 5 million students who are now in nonpublic schools. Tensions between private and public education continue to exist, raising in one area, abating in the next. Sometimes the tension is creative; sometimes destructive. The issue is far from being resolved.

TEACHER EDUCATION

The education of teachers for their profession has made extraordinary strides since the colonial period, when the only real criterion was that a teacher had to know more than the students. The expansion of the common schools required larger numbers of teachers, and the development of public high schools required that the quality of elementary teaching be improved. These demands gradually have resulted in increasingly higher standards for teacher education. By the 1900s, new theories about psychology, learning, and the nature of teaching made professional training even more necessary. Normal schools, colleges, and universities began to offer sophisticated programs, which, in recent years, increasingly have become subject to public pressure for teacher accountability.

Colonial Teachers

QUALIFICATIONS Most teachers in the colonial period were not guided by any particular professional or long-term motivation. Teaching was generally viewed as a temporary position that was all right until something better came along. Teachers had to be acceptable, usually in terms of their religious orthodoxy, civil loyalty, and moral standards. For instance, in

1653, the head of Harvard College was fired because, unlike the Puritan authorities, he did not favor infant baptism. Prior to the Revolution, teachers were required to sign loyalty oaths of allegiance to the crown of England; once the Revolution started, they had to sign loyalty oaths to the various states. Even though moral behavior was variously defined, it was a criterion for teaching in virtually every community.

Although much emphasis was placed publicly on the religious, political, and moral worthiness of their teachers, the public had very low expectations concerning the professional training of teachers. There were no specialized schools to train teachers; the only educational training any teacher had was simply to have been a student. Generally, a teacher was expected to know enough about the subject matter to be able to pass along this knowledge to the pupils. Many contracts with elementary teachers required only that the teacher be able to read, write, or calculate as qualifications for teaching these subjects.

Throughout the colonial period much attention was paid to ensuring that teachers lived up to the expectations of the people who controlled education. In New England, teachers were approved by town meetings, selectmen, school committees, and ministers; in the Middle Colonies and the South, teachers were issued certificates by governors and religious groups.

STATUS   The highest salaries and status were granted to college teachers, the next best to secondary school teachers (Latin grammar schools), and the lowest to elementary school teachers. Salaries were often irregular in payment and were frequently supplemented with payment in produce or livestock. The colonial teacher received wages equivalent to those of a farmhand.

Teaching was hardly considered to be a profession in colonial America. Schools were poorly equipped, and students attended irregularly. The school term was short, in many cases making teaching a part-time occupation. Many patrons of education felt that teaching was a fairly undemanding task, and they would add to the duties of the teacher such custodial chores as cleaning out the church, ringing the assembly bell, providing a baptismal basin, running errands, serving as messenger, digging graves, assisting the pastor in reading the Scriptures, leading the singing at church services, keeping records, issuing invitations, writing letters, visiting the sick, and generally being useful. The teacher was often "boarded round," living with a different family each week in order to stretch out meager school funds.

As a result of these and other indignities, the turnover rate among teachers was high and contributed to keeping the status and quality of teachers low. In many ways, the idea of teachers being a professional group, with a "calling" to their vocation, did not develop until the 1800s.

Teachers for
the Common Schools

THE EARLY NINETEENTH CENTURY The common school movement, with its consequent demand for better-trained common school teachers, was one of the most exciting periods in the history of American education. In no other period do we find greater emotional and intellectual challenges, in speeches and pamphlets, to place education at the center of the endeavor to maintain democracy. In no other period do we find more compelling calls to raise the standards of academic training, salaries, and professional qualifications for teachers. The vocation of teaching was put forth as an intellectual, religious, and patriotic calling.

In the period between 1820 and 1865, educators began to call for special training to prepare teachers for their vocation. The academies were, by and large, the teacher training institutions during this period, but as the name implies, the academies provided training in academic subject matter only, not in the principles of teaching. Educators called for coupling academic secondary education for teachers with education in the principles of teaching. There were European models, such as those that existed in Prussia, where such methods were used to create a national school system that brought different geographic regions together with a sense of national patriotism. The implications for Americanizing European immigrants in this country seemed obvious.

WOMEN TEACHERS As in colonial times, teachers' salaries were quite low. Wages continued to reflect a general attitude that teachers were considered to be people who were unable to hold a regular job, or were a bit eccentric, or were women who had nothing much else to do anyway. Indeed, it was at this time that a shift from men to women teachers began in the elementary schools. (The result of that trend is still evident today, 150 years later. In 1980–1981, women teachers in the public schools outnumbered men by 2-to-1.) There were several reasons for this change. With the growth of popular democracy and the beginnings of the common school movement, the idea developed that practically anyone, including women, could function as public servants. Another reason, perhaps the major one, was that the increase in the number of schools also increased the number of teaching positions. Each of these positions had to be paid for, and women, quite frankly, could be paid less—in some places only about one-third the salary that men teachers received.

Other factors facilitated the greater involvement of women in education in the 1830s. Industry was gradually replacing housewives with machines in formerly hand-crafted production, such as embroidery. Seeking a higher standard of living, men began to move either westward or to the industrializing cities. As a result, when the common schools began to require better-quality teachers, the female academies, seminaries, and normal schools began to provide them.

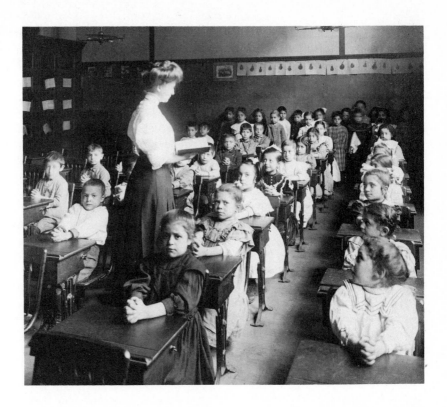

NORMAL SCHOOLS AND COLLEGES   The idea of the normal school originated in Europe. The term *normal* referred to teaching teachers the *norms,* or rules, of teaching. The first two normal schools in the country were established in 1823, in Vermont, and 1827, in Massachusetts. Here again we see New England at the forefront of educational development. The normal schools were essentially private academies that offered additional training in teaching methods and classroom discipline. A decade later, in 1837, Catherine Beecher became a full-time advocate of normal schools to train women for teaching. The first two public normal schools were established in 1839, also in Massachusetts. Around the same time, Beecher established the National Board of Popular Education, which sent over four hundred Eastern women teachers to the West. By 1860, there were twelve public normal schools in eight states. There were also informal teachers institutes offered for six-week sessions between teaching schedules, and colleges even began to offer an odd course or two on teaching methods.

AFTER THE CIVIL WAR   Following the Civil War, the greater demand for public secondary education carried with it the inherent demand for more highly trained teachers. Problems that were first acknowledged prior to the

Civil War intensified after the war and centered on "professionalism." The issue could not be avoided because the success of the common schools now demanded the training of more teachers.

In addition to the sheer increase in the number of available teaching positions, new educational theories and techniques and the development of the field of child psychology all required greater training if a teacher was to implement the new strategies in the classroom. It became less and less tolerable that so many reasons other than educational criteria were used as qualifications for teaching positions. All these concerns added fuel to the burning issues of salary and job security.

Professionalization   **BEFORE WORLD WAR I**   By the turn of the century, there had been developed balanced teacher-training programs that included instruction in the academic content the teacher was going to teach, the foundations of

---

HORACE MANN
(1796–1859)

Horace Mann was the radical educational reformer of his day. Though trained as a lawyer, he became eminently successful as an educator and politician. Asked why he had exchanged the practice of law for education, he answered that "the interests of a client are small compared with the interests of the next generation."

Born in Franklin, Massachusetts, not long after the Revolutionary War, Mann received only the most rudimentary schooling until he was fifteen. Most of his education was self-acquired, a circumstance that profoundly influenced his philosophy of education. He studied diligently in order to be admitted to Brown University, where he became a brilliant student. In 1827, Mann was elected to the Massachusetts House of Representatives, and a luminous political career lay ahead of him, but he became committed, instead, to education and to the use of political methods to bring about educational reform.

Mann made it his aim to abolish the cruel floggings that were then routine in the public schools. Schoolmasters believed it their duty to drive the devil out of their students, and many schools administered from ten to twenty floggings a day. Most schoolkeepers believed flogging to be an aid to learning. Not only were students treated cruelly; attendance at school was itself a punishment. Schools were often little better than hovels: the lighting was poor and many buildings were unsanitary and unsafe. Mann criticized corporal punishment and inadequate facilities in public

speeches, lectures, and letters, and lobbied for reform in the state legislature and in Congress.

Horace Mann strongly believed in the ideals of the common school and championed its cause throughout his career. He saw education as a tool of liberation by which the poor could raise themselves, blacks could become emancipated, and handicapped children could adjust to their disabilities. After all, Mann reasoned, education had brought him fame and position. It was over 150 years ago, then, that the idea of social mobility through education was born in America.

In order for education to be as powerful a force as he envisioned it, Mann thought it imperative to lengthen the school term and to raise teachers' salaries. To make learning

educational theory, the administrative aspects of teaching, child psychology, and pedagogical strategies. Every state had at least one public normal school. Most schools accepted students who had about two years of high school background. Most graduates became elementary school teachers after two years, although some took a four-year program to become high school teachers and administrators.

College-level teacher training grew with impetus from two directions. One was the expansion of normal school course offerings into four-year curricula; the other was the development of university courses and, eventually, departments of education. Both were stimulated by the increasing demand that high school teachers, if not elementary school teachers, should have some college training. By 1900, there were thus several ways to acquire teacher training: normal schools, teachers colleges, university departments of education, and the less formal teachers institutes.

more relevant and enjoyable, he helped introduce new textbooks designed to illustrate the relationship between knowledge and the practical problems of society. Mann organized libraries in many schools, making books readily available to students. He believed less in the formal curriculum than in individual learning—undoubtedly because of his own self-education.

Mann was responsible for the establishment of the Massachusetts Board of Education, and for the founding in 1839 of the first public normal school (a two-year school chiefly for the training of elementary teachers), in Lexington, Massachusetts. Although the normal school opened with only three students, the concept spread and was widely imitated throughout the country.

Mann was intensely interested in teacher training, and he believed that teachers should be intellectual, moral, and cultural models for their communities.

Many of Mann's ideas were controversial, but he was most violently denounced for his position on religion in the schools. Though a religious man, he believed that religious training belonged outside the schools, which should be run by the state. As a result of his views, Mann was attacked from many Boston pulpits.

Mann did not limit his reformist zeal to educational issues. When he was elected to Congress in 1849, he denounced slavery and attacked the industrial system, urging that workers be better paid, child labor be abolished, factories be made safer, and slums be eliminated. No educator, he said, could remain neutral

about social injustice. Theories and ideals must be put into practice in society; otherwise, he argued, education is mere empty words.

Mann was regarded as a dreamer and a visionary by many of his colleagues. When he took over the presidency of Antioch College in 1852, opened its doors to all races and religious sects, and admitted women on an equal basis with men, some educators predicted that these measures would promote the collapse of higher education. Mann aroused further annoyance by remarking that many Antioch students were more brilliant than their professors. Were he alive today, Mann might still be fighting for ideas he espoused more than a century ago. Many people have not accepted these ideas yet.

After World War I   Normal schools continued to become four-year colleges, which quadrupled in number between 1920 and 1940, from about forty-five to more than two hundred. The Great Depression actually helped to raise the standards for teachers, simply as a function of supply and demand. With more people than there were jobs, school districts could require additional training for qualification.

A number of major changes in teacher training can be traced over the first fifty years of the twentieth century. For one thing, we can speak of *teacher education,* not just teacher training. By 1950, most teachers had at least a four-year college degree, with a specific content area of instruction, professional courses in teaching methods and educational psychology, and some period of practice through observation, laboratory experience, and student teaching. It was also recognized that both elementary and secondary school teachers need the same amounts of educational preparation.

Today, about a dozen states require teachers to have five years of college education before they can be certified. Many teacher educators, believing that adequate teacher preparation cannot be accomplished in four years of college, are calling for extended teacher preparation programs of up to six years. With the public's concern about teacher competency, we may well see a further lengthening of the preparation time required for teachers. (For a discussion of more contemporary issues related to teacher professionalization, see Chapter 11.)

EDUCATION OF MINORITIES

The picture of American education drawn up till now has been quite rosy, because the educational achievements of this country over the past 350 years are indeed impressive. There is, however, a less pleasant side to the picture. The history of education provides insight into people's values in general, and the educational experience of minorities tends to reflect how a society relates to them. The somewhat idealized image of the melting pot begins to break down when we look at the experience of nonwhite groups.

Ethnic minorities such as blacks, Hispanic-Americans, Native Americans, Japanese-Americans, and Chinese-Americans traditionally have not been afforded equal educational opportunity in America. It was not until the late nineteenth century, for example, that the federal government made any serious effort to provide education for Native Americans. Prior to that time what formal education they received usually came from missionary groups. American society is still suffering today from the effects of educational neglect of various minority groups. For example, whereas almost 70 percent of white students complete four or more years of secondary school, only 49 percent of blacks and 42 percent of Hispanics achieve the same level of education.[16]

[16]*The Condition of Education, 1981 Edition* (Washington, D.C.: National Center for Education Statistics, 1981), p. 32.

Education
of Black Americans

BEFORE THE CIVIL WAR   As is true of colonial education generally, the earliest motivation to educate blacks was religious. In New England, as early as 1717, the Reverend Cotton Mather started an evening school for slaves. In the South, the first attempts to educate blacks were carried out by clergymen, particularly English representatives of the Society for the Propagation of the Gospel in Foreign Parts. To dubious slave owners, ministers defended the education of slaves not only as a religious duty to save their benighted souls, but also because conversion to Christianity, it was believed, would make them more docile.[17]

In the North, schools were established for free blacks. In 1731, Anthony Benezet, a French-born Quaker, started a school for slave and free black children in Philadelphia. Another school was begun by Benjamin Franklin, as president of the Abolitionist Society, in 1774. In 1787 an African Free School was established in New York City with an enrollment of forty students, which grew to over five hundred by 1820. The city provided funds in 1824 and took over the school in 1834, thus providing education for blacks before many white children were receiving it.

Yet conditions were not all bright in the North. In 1833, Prudence Crandall, a white schoolmistress in Canterbury, Connecticut, began to take in black girls. The villagers boycotted the school, threw manure into its well, and attempted to burn it down. Finally, a mob broke the windows, and the school was ultimately closed.[18]

In the South, following slave rebellions in the early 1800s, states gradually prohibited altogether the teaching of black children, whether slave or free. Some slaves were taught to read by favorably disposed masters. However, slave owners generally reasoned, probably correctly, that reading would lead to thinking, and thinking would lead to the desire for freedom. As the Civil War approached, abolitionist agitation often came from the few liberal colleges, such as Oberlin, in Ohio, and Bowdoin, in Maine, which allowed the enrollment of black students.

SINCE THE CIVIL WAR   It was in the period following the Civil War that the seeds for the education of blacks that had been sown before the war slowly began to sprout. During the period of Reconstruction, from 1865 into the 1870s, the federal government, through the Freedmen's Bureau and the occupying army, attempted to promote black voting registration and schooling. Help also came from private and religious philanthropies in the North. Because it was hoped that whites also would benefit from these endeavors, schooling was advocated for the general public as well. As we pointed out earlier, the common school movement was weakest in the

[17]Earle H. West, ed., *The Black American and Education* (Columbus, Ohio: Charles E. Merrill, 1972), pp. 7–8.

[18]C. Eric Lincoln and Milton Meltzer, *A Pictorial History of the Negro in America*, 3rd ed. (New York: Crown Publishers, 1968), pp. 108–109.

South, and at first most whites refused to participate not only in integrated schools but also in segregated schools, both of which they felt the Northern carpetbaggers were forcing on them.

By the end of Reconstruction, Southern whites began to allow the existence of separate, but unequal, schools. Black enrollment in the schools, which had been only 2 percent in 1850, was 10 percent by 1870 and 35 percent by 1890, though it dropped somewhat after that due to a period of severe repression by the new white state governments.[19] During this period "Jim Crow" laws were passed, separating blacks from whites in all areas of life. The vote was effectively taken from the newly enfranchised blacks by poll taxes and "grandfather rules," which allowed the vote only to those blacks whose families could vote before the Emancipation, thereby excluding all the freed slaves.

Into these conditions, a young black teacher named Booker T. Washington (1859?–1915) was called to start a black normal school in Alabama, at the Tuskegee Institute, in 1881. What he found there were only a few students, no physical plant, and a hostile white community. Washington, who had been born a slave, realized that the traditional curriculum of the classics would neither fit his students to help other blacks learn nor help to ameliorate the tensions with the white community. Believing strongly in the idea of learning by doing, Washington instructed his students to build the school themselves. In this process, they learned practical skills, grew produce that could be sold to the white community, and in general showed the whites that black people could be productive members of society. Booker T. Washington gradually came to be considered the outstanding black leader of the time by the white establishment.

But there were a growing number of young blacks who, unlike Washington, had not been born into slavery and who felt that Washington's policy of conciliatory training for menial positions in white society would not profit black people in the long run. They believed that practical training is necessary, but that there must also be an intellectually sound and academically rich program of study for the "talented tenth" who would form the black intellectual leadership. This was the view of W. E. B. DuBois (1868–1963), an intellectual and scholar who held a doctorate from Harvard.

In 1896, in the case of *Plessy* v. *Ferguson,* the Supreme Court upheld the constitutionality of *separate but equal* accommodations for blacks. Originally in reference to seating in a railroad car, the ruling was quickly extended to the schools. The practical significance of this ruling was to add federal sanction to the legal separation of black schoolchildren from white, most notably in the South, for the next sixty years.

[19]*Historical Statistics of the United States,* p. 370.

That the Southern schools for blacks were not equal to those for whites is woefully clear from looking at financial expenditures alone. In 1912, the Southern states as a group paid white teachers $10.32 per white child in school but paid black teachers only $2.89 per black child.[20] In the 1930s in ten Southern states, black children made up 34 percent of the school population but received only 3 percent of the funds available for school transportation. As a result, the percentage of Southern black children attending school ranged from 13–17 percent less than white children enrolled; black children also attended school an average of twenty-one fewer days a year than did white children. Consequently, it took black children from one to four and one-half additional years to complete the eight years of elementary education. During this same period, 55 percent of Southern black schools were still housed in one-room buildings, and an additional

[20]E. Franklin Frazier, *The Negro in the United States,* rev. ed. (New York: Macmillan, 1957), p. 427.

19 percent were in two-room buildings. Of the $21 million spent by the federal government for rural schools between 1933 and 1935, 80 percent was allocated to the Southern states, but only 8 percent went to black schools.

Most Northern states did not have legal segregation of schools, but the crowding of blacks into isolated neighborhoods often resulted in segregation. Furthermore, the large numbers of Southern black children who migrated with their parents to Northern cities often had to be demoted because they had not mastered the same amount of material as their Northern agemates. Generally, even in the North, black teachers taught black children.

Although these conditions continued in varying degrees through the 1940s, some gains were nevertheless achieved. The average daily attendance of black children increased and approached that of white students. The salaries of black teachers also increased, as compared with the salaries of white teachers with equal training. After having served in two world wars to "save democracy," black organizations like the National Association for the Advancement of Colored People, founded in 1909, began taking their cases to the courts. Beginning with universities rather than elementary schools, they succeeded in getting the courts to rule various law school programs to be separate yet clearly unequal. In 1950, the Supreme Court ruled that the University of Texas had to admit a black student to its old, established law school rather than force him to attend a new and separate school that had been built especially for blacks. Similarly, the University of Oklahoma was obliged to allow a black student full access to all university facilities.

The stage was finally set for the precedent-shattering case of *Brown v. Board of Education of Topeka* (1954), in which the Supreme Court ruled that separate educational facilities are inherently unequal. At the time, the case seemed a climax to one hundred years of struggle to gain educational equality together with so-called emancipation. As the events of the past thirty years have shown, the task has not yet been achieved. (Recent efforts to achieve desegregation and equal educational opportunities are discussed in Chapter 12.)

Education of Native Americans

As early as 1622, in an ominous forecast of future policies, one colonist wrote back to England that it was easier to conquer the Indians than to civilize them.[21] The education of Native Americans received less public attention than that of blacks, because Native Americans were considered

[21]R. Freeman Butts, *The Education of the West: A Formative Chapter in the History of Civilization* (New York: McGraw-Hill, 1973), p. 279.

an impediment to westward expansion, they were far from major population centers, and their dealings were largely with the federal government.

Initially, the education of Native Americans, like that of blacks, had a religious purpose. Once they had been put on reservations, the Native Americans received schooling from missionaries, who attempted to "civilize" them through the three Rs and, of course, the fourth R—religion. These missionary schools were gradually replaced in the 1890s by government schools, which tried to assimilate Native Americans by teaching them skills associated with white society.

The people who had been Native Americans for twenty thousand years finally became American citizens in 1924. By the 1960s, 55 percent of Native Americans of secondary school age finished high school, and 45 percent entered some form of postsecondary education.[22] Ironically, although the government-supplied education in English was for the purpose of assimilating Native Americans, it provided them with a common language with which to begin an alliance of tribal efforts to stop the loss of traditional ways.

Education of Hispanic Americans

As with the Native Americans, the first contact Spanish-speaking people had with the United States was often as a result of annexation and warfare. Although they had lived in the continental United States for over four hundred years, Hispanic people came into contact with Anglo-Americans only about 150 years ago, and almost from the beginning, there was a cultural clash. Hispanic children first attended religious mission schools, which were gradually replaced by secular public schools. In the process, Spanish language and Hispanic culture were subjected to a type of discrimination that was perhaps less blatant than that against blacks, but just as pervasive. The common school, although it opened educational and social opportunities in Anglo-America, often sealed off those opportunities for Hispanic-Americans. Hispanic children tended to receive lower scores than Anglo children on English-language IQ tests, which not only were written in a language that was not their own but also reflected Anglo middle-class values. Thus, an image of the Hispanic children's intellectual inferiority was reinforced.

Since the 1940s, the courts have acknowledged de facto segregation between Anglo and Hispanic schoolchildren and have required corrective integration plans. Another response has been the establishment of bilingual education programs to provide general instruction in the mother tongue at the same time that students learn English. As a result, students can enter the English-language curriculum at the appropriate age level for their grade.

[22]Butts, *Education of the West,* p. 317.

Table 4.3 Significant Dates in the History of American Education

1635	Establishment of the Boston Latin grammar school
1636	Founding of Harvard College, first English-speaking college in the Western Hemisphere
1642	Massachusetts first education law
1647	Massachusetts Old Deluder Satan Act: Towns of fifty families or more must provide instruction in reading and writing; towns of one hundred families or more must establish grammar schools
1687–1690	First edition of the *New England Primer*
1701	Episcopal Society for the Propagation of the Gospel in Foreign Parts is founded to begin educational activities in the colonies
1751	Opening of Benjamin Franklin's Philadelphia Academy
1783	Noah Webster published the *American Spelling Book*
1785, 1787	Northwest Ordinance Acts, requiring new states in that territory to set aside land for educational purposes
1821	First public high school in the United States opened in Boston; Emma Willard established first school for women's higher education
1823	First private normal school in the United States opened in Concord, Vermont
1827	Massachusetts law requiring public high schools
1837	Horace Mann made secretary of Massachusetts state board of education
1839	First public normal school in the United States established in Lexington, Massachusetts
1855	First German-language kindergarten established in the United States
1860	First English-language kindergarten established in the United States
1862	Morrill Land Grant College Act established college of agriculture, engineering, and military science in each state
1872	*Kalamazoo* case, court decision legalizing general taxes for high schools

Table 4.3 *(cont.)*

1896	*Plessy* v. *Ferguson,* Supreme Court decision used to support constitutionality of separate schools for whites and blacks
1909	First junior high school established in Berkeley, California
1910	First junior college established in Fresno, California
1919	Progressive Education Association established
1925	Oregon court decision against making private education illegal
1932	New Deal programs during the Great Depression provided federal funds for education of the poor
1944	GI Bill of Rights provided federal funding for the continued education of veterans of World War II (later extended to veterans of the Korean and Vietnam Wars)
1954	*Brown* v. *Board of Education of Topeka* decision of the Supreme Court requiring eventual racial integration of public schools
1957	Soviet Union launched Sputnik, leading to criticism and re-evaluation of American public education
1958	National Defense Education Act provided funds to improve science, math, and modern foreign language instruction, as well as guidance services
1962	Supreme Court decision against Bible reading and prayer in public schools
1964	Economic Opportunity Act provided funds for Job Corps and Head Start
1965	Elementary-Secondary Education Act provided more federal aid to public schools
1972	Title IX Education Amendment passed outlawing sex discrimination in educational institutions receiving federal financial assistance
1975	Education for All Handicapped Children (Public Law 94–142) passed
1979	Department of Education established in federal government with cabinet status

Bilingual education is just one facet of a general concern for multicultural education that removes ethnic stereotypes and tries to give a more adequate representation of the Hispanic-American experience. (See Chapter 13 for further discussion of multicultural and bilingual education.)

A FINAL WORD

There are many people who believe that the greatest contribution the United States has made to the world has been its system of free public education. It is hard for us today to appreciate what a dramatic departure from the educational systems of the rest of the world the American experiment was. It has not worked perfectly, but there is no other country in the world with a population comparable to ours that has come close to offering such extensive educational opportunities to so many people. We owe a great deal to those men and women in our history whose efforts and contributions to improve our educational system have left us a rich legacy upon which we can continue to build.

Discussion Questions

1. Why did the educational development of colonial America differ among the New England, Middle, and Southern colonies? In what ways were the educational systems different?

2. What factors contributed to the development of the common school movement? Who were some of the leading advocates of this movement toward universal, free education?

3. What made the development of the American secondary school so unique in the history of the world?

4. What has been the role of private education in our history?

5. What basic changes have taken place in teacher education in America's history?

6. In what ways were the histories of the education of minority groups and women similar?

For Further Reading

Best, John Hardin, and Robert T. Sidewell, eds. *The American Legacy of Learning: Readings in the History of Education.* Philadelphia: Lippincott, 1967.
   An excellent book of readings that pursues the major themes of public education.

Butts, R. Freeman. *Public Education in the United States: From Revolution to Reform.* New York: Holt, Rinehart and Winston, 1978.
   An interpretative history of public education viewed in the context of the social, political, economic, religious, and intellectual development of American civilization from 1776 to 1976.

Cremin, Lawrence A. *The Transformation of the School: Progressivism in American Education, 1876–1957.* New York: Knopf, 1961.

A Pulitzer Prize–winning book on progressive education.

Meyer, Adolphe E. *An Educational History of the American People.* 2nd ed. New York: McGraw-Hill, 1967.

A lively, flamboyantly written history of American education. Readers will be delighted with his "nontextbook" use of language.

Pulliam, John D. *History of Education in America,* 3rd ed. Columbus, Ohio: Charles E. Merrill, 1982.

Tyack, David B. *The One Best System: A History of American Urban Education.* Cambridge, Mass.: Harvard University Press, 1974.

A moderate, yet critical view of American urban education.

SCHOOLS:
THE PRESENT

III

What Is a School?

5

The purpose of this chapter is to help you examine the nature of schools and schooling in our society today. We mention a number of different avenues for you to take to reach an understanding of schools. In addition, you will be confronted with different views of a school and models of schooling. At the end of the chapter, your role in the reform of schooling will be touched on.

This chapter emphasizes that:

■ Education is a larger, more encompassing endeavor, whereas schooling is simply one aspect of education.

■ The purpose of school determines much of what happens in school. Among the ways to determine the aims of school are to read formal statements of purpose and to rely on one's own experiences in and observations of schools.

■ Schools can be defined by comparing them to models or abstract representations of reality.

■ Schools play a critical part in passing on a society's values to the young.

■ Schools in our culture are both similar and different in many ways. The teacher's role varies a great deal depending on the type of school.

■ Because there is much unfinished work in our schools, there is a place for committed and energetic young men and women in the teaching profession.

*W*HAT IS A SCHOOL? This may not strike you as a particularly profound question. In fact, it probably seems rather tame. School is an everyday thing. We have all spent vast stretches of our time there. Much of what we are—intellectually, socially, and emotionally—can be traced to our experiences in school. School is just . . . school. However, behind the familiar words and images lie thorny issues that have baffled theoreticians and practitioners of education for years. Quiet communities have been split into warring camps because of their inability to agree on an answer to this question. Let us see if you can answer the question "What is a school?" In the space below, jot down a definition or two of *school*.

_____

_____

_____

_____

_____

Your answer to the question reflects who you are and what your experience with school has been. Perhaps you responded in one of the following ways:

- A school is an agency that weans children from the protective warmth of the family and readies them to contribute to the world of work.

- A school is a bunch of bricks and mortar, chalkboards, and water fountains (usually with wadded gum in them) arranged in a predictable way.

- A school is a place where they fix your mind so you think like everyone else.

- A school is where children fall in love with learning.

- A school is a tax-supported babysitting agency.

- A school is a place where young savages become civilized citizens.

- A school is where we learn how good or bad we are (at many different skills and tasks), compared with bunches of people our own age.

- A school is a place where we explore who we are and how we can become full, creative human beings.

- A school is where children learn to be virtuous.

- A school is a place where the children of one generation come together to unite against the generation in power.

- A school is a fun palace.

- A school is a fact factory.

- A school is a tax-supported institution where the dead wisdom and worn-out skills of the past are force-fed to the young.
- A school is where education takes place.

Each of these descriptions says a great deal about the school experience of the person who formulated it. What does your definition say about you and your experience?

EDUCATION AND SCHOOLING

It is commonly believed that school is where people go to get an education. Nevertheless, it has been quipped that today children interrupt their educations to go to school. The distinction between *schooling* and *education* implied by this remark is important. Like *school, education* has myriad definitions. We have sprinkled a few such definitions here and there throughout the book for you to sample. For the moment, however, let us say that *education* is a process of human growth by which one gains greater understanding and control over oneself and one's world. It involves our minds, our bodies, and our relations with the people and the world around us. Whereas education takes many institutional forms, strictly speaking it is a process, an activity characterized by continuous development and change. The end product of the process of education is learning.

Education is much more open-ended and all-inclusive than schooling. Education knows few bounds. It can take place anywhere, whether in a tavern or on a tractor. It includes both the formal learning that takes place in schools and the whole universe of informal learning, from hooking a worm on a line to burping a baby. The agents of education can range from a revered grandparent to the guests on a late-night television talk show, from a retarded child to a distinguished scientist. Whereas schooling has a certain predictability, education quite often takes us by surprise. We go to the movies to relax and come home with a vivid sense of poverty's corrupting influence on the human spirit. We get into a casual conversation with a stranger and discover how little we know about other religions. People are engaged in education from the cradle to the grave. Infants learn how to satisfy themselves by sucking their thumbs. A high school-educated grandmother reads about life on an Indian reservation and goes on to become passionately involved in helping Native Americans. Education, then, is a very broad, inclusive term. It is a lifelong process, a process that starts long before we begin school and that should be an integral part of our entire lives.

Schooling, however, is a specific, formalized process, whose general pattern varies little from one setting to the next. Throughout the country, children arrive at school at approximately the same time, take assigned seats, are taught by an adult, use the same or similar textbooks, do homework, take exams, and so on. The slices of reality that are to be learned,

All of us have two educations: one which we receive from others; another, and the most valuable, which we give ourselves.
— JOHN RANDOLPH —

whether they are the alphabet or an understanding of our governmental system of checks and balances, have usually been specified in advance. What is learned as a result of schooling is also limited by the boundaries of the subject being taught: if a little boy wants to learn what a girl *really* looks like, he just knows that school is not the place to make his investigations. In the same way, high school students know they are not likely to find out in their classes how practical politics in their community really operates or what avant-garde film makers are up to. Finally, schooling tends to be limited to the young. There are, then, definite conditions surrounding the formalized process of schooling.

The Role of the School

Schools are created for the express purpose of providing a certain type of educational experience, which we call the *curriculum*. The curriculum, which will be discussed more fully in Chapter 7, "What Is Taught?," represents what a community believes young people need to know in order to develop into good and useful adults. Or, at least, the curriculum includes what the school policy makers in a particular community believe young people need to know.

 Teachers are trained and hired to fulfill the purposes of the curriculum. In simpler societies, when a boy could learn to be a man by following his father around and imitating the men of the village, schools were not necessary. Formal schooling became a social necessity when the home and the community were no longer effective or competent at training the young for adulthood through informal contacts. Societies have realized that education is too important to be left to chance. Whereas important things are sometimes learned on street corners, and grandparents often are excellent teachers, the formal educative process is simply more reliable. There is an excellent possibility that if education is acquired randomly the young will grow up with a lopsided understanding of the world and poor preparation for adult life. The chance schooling of the street has educated many in such skills as how to exploit one's fellow humans, and it has produced many a

SCHOOLS: THE PRESENT

champion penny pitcher who can't read. Occasionally we see families with the intellectual resources, skills, and time to educate their young themselves, but this is all too rare amid the complexities and demands of modern life. Also, for each individual set of parents to educate its children—even with the help of older children, grandparents, and neighbors—is wasteful and socially inefficient. So schools have been established.

The distinction between education and schooling is often blurred because the two concepts are undifferentiated in most people's minds. Keeping the differences between these two concepts clearly in mind is often particularly difficult for the people who should be most sensitive to them, that is, teachers who "do" education "in" schools. People enter teaching because they wish to educate. However, the everyday experiences of working in a school cause their allegiances to shift from abstract educational ideals to the network of personalities and ideas surrounding the particular schools where they teach. For this reason alone it is important for the teacher to keep alive the questions "What is a school for?" and "What is my contribution to this child's, or this class's, education?"

DISCOVERING THE PURPOSES OF SCHOOL

By distinguishing between education and schooling we may have clarified the question "What is a school?", but we have not yet answered it. We need to think further about the goals of a school. The following offer some means to search out a school's purposes and functions.

Formal Statements

The most direct method is to read official statements of purpose. Like most institutions, our schools have occasioned many official attempts to explain what they are all about. A few illustrations may suffice. In 1960 John Gardner, the founder of Common Cause, contributed the chapter on education to the report of the President's Commission on National Goals. Discussing the purposes behind our society's support for schools, he wrote, "Our deepest convictions impel us to foster individual fulfillment. We wish each one to achieve the promise that is in him. We wish each one to be worthy of a free society, and capable of strengthening a free society."[1]

A year later, the Educational Policies Commission of the National Education Association issued a statement entitled "The Central Purpose of American Education," in which the last paragraph reads:

> The purpose which runs through and strengthens all educational purposes—the common thread of education—is the development of the ability to think. This is the central purpose to which the school must be oriented if it is to accomplish either its traditional task or those newly accentuated by recent changes in the world. To say that it is central is not to say that it is the sole purpose or in all circumstances the most important purpose, but that it must be a pervasive concern in the work of the school. Many agencies contribute to achieving educational objectives, but this particular objective may not be generally attained unless the school focuses on it. In this context, therefore, the development of every student's rational powers must be recognized as centrally important.[2]

Both these statements by high-level groups are representative of official views of the purposes of the schools. They are eloquent, but they are also highly abstract. They may point teachers in the general direction they should be traveling, but such statements have little value in the fast-moving world of the classroom. When a teacher is struggling to come up with an approach to a map-reading lesson, statements of purpose such as "to foster individual fulfillment" and "to develop the ability to think" are rarely specific enough to be helpful.

There is, also, the question of validity. To what degree do these statements reflect the real purposes and functions of school? One harsh estimate of their accuracy is offered by Terry Borton.

[1]American Assembly, *Goals for Americans: Programs of Action in the Sixties,* ed. President's Commission on National Goals (Englewood Cliffs, N.J.: Prentice-Hall, 1960), p. 81.

[2]Educational Policies Commission, *The Central Purpose of American Education* (Washington, D.C.: National Education Association, 1961), p. 15.

There are two sections to almost every school's statement of educational objectives: one for real and one for show. The first, the real one, talks about the academic excellence, subject mastery, getting into college or a job. The other discusses the human purpose of school: values, feelings, personal growth, the full and happy life. It is included because everyone knows that is important, and that it ought to be central in the life of every school. But it is only for show. Everyone knows how little schools have done about it.[3]

Another factor limiting the value of statements of purpose is their after-the-fact quality. Purposes and goals are determined for public consumption, not as guides to moment-by-moment behavior. They are not intellectual cornerstones for real curricular decisions about what should be taught and how it should be taught. They do not affect a school's decision to teach the children to read or not to push other children or not to talk while the teacher is talking. These lessons will be taught in schools that have opposing goals, and in schools that have no written statements of purpose at all. In other words, schools do not come into existence to fulfill their stated purposes. Some years ago the noted educational psychologist J. M. Stephens speculated that "the very existence of schooling may stem not from a deliberate decision of groups or societies, but from blind, spontaneous tendencies which are developed by evolutionary demand and which are found to be prevalent in human beings, although more pronounced in some people than in others."[4]

A final point about statements of purpose is that they may mask completely contradictory practices. For instance, it is common for schools to espouse in their charters the idea, also proposed in the Educational Policies Commission's statement, that the schools should develop the child's ability to think. Although many schools do this and much more to help students develop into adulthood, some children come away from their schooling believing, in fact, that they cannot think. Many children, as a result of what they are made to learn and how they are taught, leave school believing they are "stupid" and that the life of the mind is not for them. For them, school is an intellectually discouraging place where they learn what they are not capable of rather than what they can do. But these schools, too, repeat noble phrases attesting to their dedication to teaching children to think.

Personal Experience If the formal statements by commissions and individuals can be misleading, why can't we simply rely on our own experience? We have all spent a large portion of our lives in schools, and each of us has a rich store of ideas and impressions to draw on. Personal experience is undeniably a very im-

[3]Terry Borton, "Reach, Touch, and Teach," *Saturday Review* 52 (January 18, 1969): 56.
[4]J. M. Stephens, *The Process of Schooling, A Psychological Examination* (New York: Holt, Rinehart and Winston, 1967), p. 8.

portant source of data to help us come to know what a school is. Understanding the school from personal experience has, however, two limitations. One is the angle from which we have seen our own schools; the other is the narrowness of that angle. The position from which the student observes, experiences, and comes to know the school is just one of several vantage points. Teachers have another very different point of view; administrators another; parents another; students actively involved in school affairs another; and foreign visitors to our schools another. For instance, the students in a seventh-grade American history class finish the year confused and upset because their teacher has raised serious and unanswered questions about the administration of justice in our country. But the teacher feels that unsettling the students, and goading them to asking new questions, is exactly what should be accomplished. The principal, on the other hand, is worried about all the calls from the children's parents, some challenging what the teacher is doing and threatening to withdraw their support of the school. Many of the parents think their children are too young to deal with complex social issues. One community group has condemned the

Spend a few minutes reflecting on one of the schools you attended before coming to college. Recall its physical characteristics, the dominant colors, how it smelled, the architectural imagination it reflected. Think of the moods you associate with this school. Then write down all the descriptive words and phrases that have come to your mind. Don't be concerned with order or form, but try to write at least twenty such phrases.

Now that you have recorded these bits of description, pick out the five you feel to be most important. Write them below in order of importance.

teacher as un-American, unprofessional, and a troublemaker. Another organization has come to the teacher's defense for making education socially relevant and for personifying American idealism. A foreign visitor may be confused by all the uproar, shocked by the lack of respect afforded the teacher, and disturbed that the teacher told the students so little and asked them so many questions. The angle from which we perceive, then, affects what we see of a school and the judgment we make about it. We have somehow to make up for the limitations of our angle of vision if we are really to know what a school is.

The angle of perception is not the only limitation of personal experience; the narrowness of the slice of experience we observe is also a factor. You have just composed a word picture of a school you have attended. Contrast your word picture with these two:

- strong smell of disinfectant and human sweat in the air / gritty sound of chalk scraping blackboard / fear of getting beat up on the way home / drab, greenish paint everywhere / hundreds of broken windows.

- bright colors and sunny rooms / same alphabet cards as grade school on top of board / knowing everyone—all 105—in the school / bonfire pep rally for whole community before regional football championships / two-year-old desks with carved-up tops!

Certainly, the two word pictures differ immensely. It is quite doubtful that their authors went to the same school. The first place sounds like a rather run-down school in a slum. The second could be a relatively new school in a rural area. The point is that the same word, *school,* conjures up very different images in two minds. This is because schools, and the experience of going to school, vary radically within this country. The public school in a small citrus-growing town along the Rio Grande River, serving mainly Mexican-American children, is worlds away from the private preparatory school for boys on the outskirts of New Haven, Connecticut. The newly integrated elementary school in a tense working-class neighborhood can be profoundly different from the busy, innovative elementary school in a quiet suburb just fifteen freeway minutes away. When we call on our own experience to answer the question "What is a school?", we must remember that each of us has had quite limited experience. A great variety of people, motives, activities, and outcomes are covered by the simple word *school.* Nevertheless, there *are* many points of commonality in the school experiences of people in this country, and we will explore these points later in this chapter and throughout this volume.

MODELS OF SCHOOLS

A *model* is a representation of reality. All of us create mental models to help us sort out the hundreds of thousands of sounds and sights we encounter daily and to organize them into sensible patterns. Scientists, in particular, use theoretical models in their efforts to predict events and to explain why certain things have occurred. Models can be similarly useful to us as we attempt to answer the question "What is a school?" A number of descriptive

---

WHAT THE SCHOOL IS

The school is an entry into the life of the mind. It is, to be sure, life itself and not merely a preparation for living. But it is a special form of living, one carefully devised for making the most of those plastic years that characterize the development of *homo sapiens* and distinguish our species from all others. School should provide more than a continuity with the broader community or with everyday experience. It is primarily the special community where one experiences discovery by the use of intelligence, where one leaps into new and unimagined realms of experience, experience that is discontinuous with what went before. A child recognizes this when he first understands what a poem is, or what beauty and simplicity inhere in the idea of the conversation theorems, or that measure is universally applicable. If there is one continuity to be singled out, it is the slow converting of the child's artistic sense of the omnipotence of thought into the realistic confidence in the use of thought that characterizes the effective man.

Reprinted from Jerome Bruner, *On Knowledge: Essays for the Left Hand* (Cambridge, Mass.: Belknap Press, Harvard University Press, 1964), p. 118.

models have been developed to explain the purposes and functions of a school. A few such models are briefly described in the following paragraphs.[5] As you read, think about how well each model describes the schools you know.

The School as a Factory

The school prepares children for industrial work. The modern school, which was in fact designed during the Industrial Revolution, pre-adapts children to the world of work by immersing them in a crowded, noisy environment ruled by a time clock and dominated by the production mentality. Large numbers of students (raw material) are brought together to be processed by teachers (workers), who are overseen, in turn, by administrators (supervisors). As in a factory, regimentation, lack of individualization, and systemization (seating, grouping, grading) are the major operating principles. The final product of the school is "a good worker."

The School as a Preparer for College

The school prepares the student for more schooling. The goal of the school is to ready the boy or girl for admission to college. As a result, the here and now is not nearly so important as the future is. Using this model, the curriculum of the secondary school is justified to the degree to which it

[5]Several of the models described are adapted from Bernard Spodek's "Early Learning for What?" *Phi Delta Kappan* 50 (March 1969): 394–396.

prepares students to do college-level work. Likewise, the elementary school curriculum is justified to the degree to which it prepares students for success in secondary school. In this model, the "prestige" of a school as a stepping stone to a "good college" is an important consideration.

The School as a Bureaucracy

The school is a training ground for life in a bureaucratized society. According to this model, the school is a set of experiences that wean the child from the protective and highly personalized care of the family so that he or she can deal with the governmental and economic bureaucracies to be encountered in later life. School teaches us how to cooperate and interact easily with large numbers of people we do not know well. We learn how to live by rules in whose formulation we had little or no voice. According to this model, the school helps modify individuals so that they will not oppose the bureaucracy, thus assuring the safety of the system.

The School as a Babysitter

The school relieves the parents of full-time responsibility for their children. The school is valued as a repository or "dumping ground," which enables parents, particularly mothers, to pursue new alternatives. In an industrial state such as ours, releasing women from extended childrearing frees them for other work. A variant of this is the mean babysitter model: the parents are free to be continually loving and permissive to the child, while the school dispenses discipline and sometimes punishment.

The School as a Developer of Human Potential

The school attempts to insure that each individual develops her or his capacities—intellectual, social, and physical—to the fullest possible measure. The teachers are specialists in identifying students' strengths and needs and matching the instructional program to these strengths and needs. The cor-

SCHOOLS: THE PRESENT

nerstone of the school is the uniqueness of each child, and the school is designed to be flexible and have a positive impact on the child. By aiding each child to develop human potential, the school sees itself as a major contributor to a richer, more humane society. In effect, the school provides a running start to the goal of lifelong learning.

The School as an Acculturator

The school brings together people of divergent backgrounds to accommodate themselves to and share one culture. The school's role is to teach "the American Way of Life," and to pass on the customs, values, and social patterns of the dominant group to immigrants and others who have been

---

STUDENTS TALK ABOUT SCHOOLS AND TEACHERS

All things considered, like lack of money and big classes, I think schools do a good job. I mean, you can't always do what you want to do. Somebody always has to get you to move your butt.

RURAL INDIANA SENIOR

Schools should teach us all the different alternatives that are open to society, but they should also show that there's a basic foundation to life.

NORTHEAST STATE STUDENT COUNCIL PRESIDENT

Schools usually have one thing in common—they are institutions of today run on the principles of yesterday.

15-YEAR-OLD STUDENT

In my view, the sooner we all get out of the stuffy classroom, the better it will be for every-

body. Life is much more interesting if you can go out and see something instead of just sitting in a desk and being loaded with information about it.

LYNNE, 15

The best teacher I ever had . . . she didn't give you busy-work, like read then answer questions. She let you speak and listened to your opinions. She helped us think about ourselves. In her classroom, the class was run by the class.

CHICAGO JUNIOR

A teacher can be very rude and cruel to a child, but any objection on his part is treated as impertinence. Education is a search after the truth, and to find the truth one must be

humble. This is impossible if teachers are too proud to admit when they are wrong.

JANET, 16

Schools should give us guidance to understand the nature of life and existence. I find myself in a vacuum groping for the meaning of life.

SCOTTISH SENIOR

We've got great teachers. They're like family. They respect us and joke with us and we work together.

DROP-IN STUDENT, CHICAGO INDUSTRIAL ARTS CENTER

Third, fourth, and sixth quotation from Edward Blishen, ed., *The School That I'd Like* (Harmondsworth, England: Penguin Books, 1969). Other quotations from Catherine McKenzie Shane, "Coping, Caring, Communicating: Youth Looks at the Future," *Phi Delta Kappan* (September 1976): 120. Reprinted by permission.

excluded from full participation in this society. According to this view, the school is a melting pot whose function is to minimize the influence of minority ethnic, racial, and religious influences and to teach the "American" way of life.

A cautionary note: A phenomenon as varied and widespread as a school cannot be explained by a single model. And a model is only as good as its ability to explain reality to us. Therefore, a model of a school has value to the degree that it helps us understand what we already know about schools and to make sense of the new information we receive.

THE TRANSMISSION OF CULTURE

The last model of school, the school as an acculturator, perhaps needs a bit more explanation. Possibly the point can be made best by referring to a commonly stated claim that the task of the school is to interpret the world. This assertion is faulty on two counts.

First, obviously, the world in all its variety—people, anteaters, hurricanes, eggplants, computers, ballets—is simply too much to deal with. Schools have to be selective. They must choose fragments from the universe

MOST IMPORTANT

of knowledge. The goal, of course, is to select those bits and pieces that can be used by people to discover more and more. The second error is more subtle: although educators may think they are interpreting the world to the young, what they are ordinarily doing is transmitting their own culture and its values.

By *culture* we mean the system of norms and standards that a society develops over the course of many generations and that profoundly influences the everyday behavior of people in that society. More simply, culture is as people do. The implication, clearly, is that American public schools teach the American way of looking at the world and the American way of doing things. By and large, this is not a conscious process. It was not consciously introduced into the curriculum. If we ask educators what, broadly speaking, they are trying to do, they are likely to reply that they are teaching reality and how to deal with it. But, in fact, our schools teach our version of reality and our way of handling the real world. And so, too, do the schools of other countries. Schools in northern India differ markedly from those in Ghana, and neither have much in common with American public schools. However, the schools of each country are attempting to perform a similar function: to transmit the unique culture of the country to its newest members, the young. This desire to insure that the young share the common culture may explain why in many school systems we teach American history in the third grade, the seventh grade, and again in the eleventh grade, and why, for instance, we give little attention to the history of China. China is, however, the most populous nation in the world, and it has one of the oldest and richest cultural heritages. Most scholars and foreign policy experts are sure that China will loom large in the future of this country. Nevertheless, until recently the American people had developed the habit of ignoring China, and as a result its existence is hardly acknowledged in some schools.

There is danger inherent in this tendency of schools to concentrate on transmitting the dominant culture. Just a few decades ago there was little apparent need for different cultures to understand and appreciate one another, but electronic communications, nuclear weapons, and jet travel have changed all that. If schools offer the young an understanding of only the prevailing culture, the result may be an attitude of smug cultural superiority, a phenomenon that frequently leads nations to foolish actions. In cultural terms, what we do not know we frequently do not respect. Without mutual respect people easily become enemies.

WHAT ARE SCHOOLS LIKE TODAY?

Similarities

Schools in the United States are remarkably similar to one another. Or, said another way, the culture that is transmitted by the school varies very little from one system to another. A major component of this commonality, particularly among public schools, is the curriculum of our schools, the content or subjects taught. However, another primary reason for this similarity is the general uniformity of schooling procedures. For instance, the number of hours of instruction and days in the school year is practically the same throughout the United States. (On the other hand, the Japanese school is open forty-five days more each year than our schools.) Other similarities in schooling procedures include the length of classes, the time between classes, the use of bells, the number of pupils in each class, the awarding of credits (Carnegie units) for the completion of courses, the requirement of a fixed number of Carnegie units for graduation, the types of extracurricular activities, the bureaucratic structure within the school systems, and the sources of educational funding. Also similar are the school rituals, such as book fairs, pep rallies, and graduation ceremonies.

In addition to schooling procedures, curricular offerings are similar in American schools today. Not only has the education of youth been mandated by state legislation, but also certain types of educational programs or competencies are being adopted by state legislatures across the country. For instance, as of 1983, sixteen states have passed legislation requiring students from schools throughout the state to pass a minimum competency test before they receive their high school diplomas. This, plus the fact that an additional twenty-three states have some form of minimum competency testing, is a strong pressure for curricular uniformity. Course content also is similar, because the expressed societal goals are quite uniform throughout the United States. Additionally, much of what is taught in schools is influenced by the books and materials that are used. Because the large textbook companies sell books and series of books from state to state and from coast to coast, commonalities are further emphasized. You can rest assured that ninth-grade math courses are just about the same whether you are in Portland, Poughkeepsie, or Punxsutawney.

In addition to schooling procedures and curricular offerings, actual teaching methods provide another element of uniformity in schools today. Verbal explanations, presentations and questioning, and assigning seatwork and drill on new material are among the main tools of the teaching trade.

Differences

But although there are many similarities and commonalities from school to school, at another level there are great differences. All American schools today are *not* alike, and the actual experience of teaching in one school may be profoundly different from that in another school. Some schools stress certain types of goals and focus on certain specialties. These specialties may be in the form of a vocational trade, a college preparatory program, or even in a certain type of learning style, such as informal education. Then, of course, we need to consider the intensity with which a set of procedures is being followed. Some schools have more rigid structures than others, with more rules and regulations for both teachers and students. Also, the model of the school as described earlier is determined by the community, and thus schools have different philosophical emphases.

Funding for schools is another source of difference. Whereas one district may have enough money to support numerous extracurricular activities, special workshops and enrichment programs for its teachers, and material support for its curricular offerings, another district may have to struggle simply to keep a supply of relatively up-to-date textbooks. The working conditions and morale of the faculty would certainly be affected in those two districts. Also connected with the funding issue is the socioeconomic status of the community and the attitudes of students coming to the school. A community composed of families who are struggling to put food on the table may not have a large revenue base to support its schools, and this affects the quality of the material support in the school. Furthermore, the child coming from a home with a constantly blaring television set, no books, and little money even for a daily newspaper will enter the school with a set of experiences and expectations entirely different from those of the child whose family has the means to subscribe to five magazines, allows only moderate television watching, and encourages reading. In some communities, many educated parents are ready and willing to help teachers with enrichment units and transportation and chaperoning for field trips. In such communities parents rarely fuss excessively if students bring home requests for five dollars to get a special enrichment book or ten dollars for some special program. Thus the school's socioeconomic setting will affect curricular offerings, instructional activities, schooling procedures, teacher morale, and a host of other interconnected factors.

Finally, there are the differences among the nation's public, parochial, and private schools. In 1978, more than five million students attended parochial or private schools. This figure represents 12 percent of the country's elementary and secondary school children, and the percentage is growing because many parents specifically want for their children a different type of education from that being provided by their public schools.[6]

Four Categories of Schools

So, amid the similarities are some very real differences. After studying the elementary schools in a major American city, Russell C. Doll came up with four categories into which fitted, with more or less comfort, all the schools he examined:[7] type A is highly academically oriented; type B is average academically oriented; type C is low academic–semi-problem oriented; and type D is highly problem oriented.[8] What does this mean for teachers?

---

[6]W. Vance Grant and Leo J. Eiden, *Digest of Education Statistics 1981* (Washington, D.C.: National Center for Education Statistics, 1981), pp. 47, 50.

[7]Russell C. Doll, "The Defining and Limits of Educational Innovation and Change," in *Innovative Practices in Teacher Education: Preservice through Inservice,* ed. Barry L. Klein et al. (Atlanta: Georgia State University, 1977), pp. 374–406.

[8]Because there are four categories, the reader should *not* infer, as Ernie Lundquist did, that a quarter of the American schools fit into each category.

*Children enter school as
question marks
and leave as periods.*
— THE YOUNG SAGE —

Teacher activities will be quite different in each of the four types of schools. For instance, in the highly academically oriented school, teachers generally operate in an atmosphere supportive of quality teaching, academic planning, and program review and improvement. Parents and students normally perceive little need for sweeping changes, since the schooling process is working well in these settings.

Type A schools tend to resist educational fads and stick to the fundamentals. Parents do not expect the teachers to be innovative, but they do expect teachers to insure that the children can read well, compute, and write with foundational skill to edge out close competition in the upper grades. In these schools, teachers feel the pressures from parents and students to "turn out the work." Whereas there is little need for the teachers to be disciplinarians, they frequently feel the strain of continually having to perform with excellence.

In type B schools (the average academically oriented schools), there is often a strong climate of acceptance and encouragement for educational change. The school situation for the most part is stable; the majority of students are academically talented, but some are academically slow. Teachers are comfortable and generally feel accepted. However, the school is very open to innovation, and change causes the teachers to be involved in a turmoil of shifting programs and priorities. Administrators, parent groups, or groups of teachers are continually pushing the latest educational fads. The brunt of implementing these fads and ill-conceived innovations falls on the classroom teacher. Doll compares the staffs of these schools to "well-conditioned marathon runners who, at each quarter mile, were given two ounces of lead to carry. Little by little teachers are worn down by mundane and trivial things that add up to drains in time and energy."[9]

In type C (low academic–semi-problem oriented) schools, teachers try to maintain an academic program and climate like those in the type B schools. However, they continually deal with extraneous concerns: discipline problems, truancy, student transferrals in and out, special government or district aid programs, and interminable record keeping. Most stressful for the teacher is the continual strain of trying to teach content while maintaining good classroom management, a major preoccupation in these schools. In other words, the teacher needs to be a combination of a good teacher and a good classroom manager. The amount of physical and emotional energy demanded merely to cope leaves many teachers with little left to devote to the teaching programs.

The name of the game in type D (highly problem oriented) schools is "to keep order and to survive." Multiple forces keep teachers from devoting their time and energy to the instructional program. The teachers

[9]Doll, "Defining and Limits," p. 384.

focus on ways to improve classroom management rather than on the teaching of content. Teacher absenteeism is high as a consequence of the stress inherent in this type of school. Indeed, these schools can sometimes be physically dangerous to both the students and the teachers.

The reader should keep in mind that Doll's description is based on one study of one city's elementary schools at one rather turbulent moment in history. Although the picture that emerges strikes us as being overly harsh, we believe the study points out the falsity of the view that a school is a school is a school. The physical, emotional, and learning climates can be distinctly different in each type of school and thus can affect each teacher's performance. But it must be kept in mind that teachers are different, too. Many teachers find deeply satisfying human and professional rewards from teaching in a trouble-ridden, type D school, and they would be unhappy in a type A school. So, too, for each of the types. The point is that teachers should consider the circumstances and qualities of the school district and the school when selecting a teaching position. They should assess their own abilities and preferences before deciding to teach in a particular type or category of school.

With an understanding of the differences in schools and an understanding of their own abilities, teachers should be able to move into teaching positions that are best for them and, at the same time, best suited for the school and students.

THE UNFINISHED WORK OF THE SCHOOLS

It is probably clear by now that there is no single satisfactory answer to our question "What is a school?" This and many other questions that we ask in this book are too large and complex to be adequately answered here. We pose them and talk about them anyway to aid you in your investigations into the issues behind the questions. People contemplating careers in education must commit themselves to working out answers to these questions. It seems unlikely that you can make a good career choice if you lack an understanding of the institution you are considering entering. And if you hope to survive and be happy within an institution, you will need to know how it works. You need to know what the institution says it is doing ("we are training future workers," or "we are educating well-rounded citizens prepared to excel in college") and what it actually does. You need to know what a particular school's expectations of you, as teacher, will be, so you can decide how to respond or if you wish to respond at all. Finally, if you hope to improve the schools, that is, make them better because of your involvement with them, you need a realistic view of what is now going on in the schools and a vision of what the schools can become.

Schools are a human invention. As we established earlier, people bring schools into being for particular social purposes. The overall purposes of school are to advance the common good and to help people live happy and successful lives. However, if schools are to serve society, they must at least keep pace with the society. Many people who are concerned about our schools feel that they are moving very slowly while the rest of society experiences dynamic change. In effect, the schools are out of phase with and lagging behind the society they are supposed to be serving. There are, also, situations where the schools get ahead of the rest of society. For instance, in the 1970s American universities produced many more Ph.D.s in the hope that there would be a continuing expansion of higher education. They tried to lead society in a direction in which it did not want to go. The result is tension. As happens frequently in times of tension, views polarize in the manner suggested by John Gardner's statement on this page. Nevertheless, the purposes for which schools are brought into being are still vital. People still desire good schools for their children. And, as you will see later in this book, many excellent ideas are being generated and movements are underway for the renewal of our schools.

Some readers may be uncomfortable with the idea that it is their job to renew the schools. Many may feel that becoming a good classroom teacher is enough. The teachers, however, are more than technicians in charge of their classrooms. As professional people, they and their colleagues *must* have a voice in deciding how their services are rendered. It follows that the teacher is not responsible simply for his or her own performance, but bears responsibility for the total educational enterprise. To live up to this responsibility requires a deep understanding of the schools and much hard work, but it is the very critical nature of the problems confronting the schools that makes teaching such an exciting occupation today. Schools are becoming increasingly important in the life of each individual and to the well-being of the society. Strong pressures exist for reforms and for changes in public education. In the immediate future, education is where the action will be. We have a chance to complete the unfinished work of the schools.

Discussion Questions

1. Can you think of some pieces of information you picked up on the street that you later "unlearned" in school? Can you think of some things you learned in school that your experience later taught you were untrue? Which has happened more often? How do you react to this?

2. To what extent did the schools you attended serve the purposes suggested by the various models we described? Can you suggest any models we have overlooked?

3. Which of the models of schools we have discussed is illustrated by the cartoon on page 148? Is it inappropriate to any of the models we have discussed? Does it seem to you an apt comment on your own education?

4. How do you feel about the school as transmitting the culture rather than "the truth" or "just the facts"? What are some of the problems with the school being a transmitter of cultures? What happens if the state takes a very strong hand in this? Are there any examples in history in which the state used schools to promote a particularly dangerous culture?

5. What are some commonalities of schools that have not been mentioned in the text? What are some of the dissimilarities or unique features from one school to the other that you have observed?

6. Did your elementary school fit into one of Russell C. Doll's categories? Where did it fit and why? If not, how was your school unique? And, perhaps more importantly, why do you think it was unique?

For Further Reading

Cusick, Philip. *Inside High School: The Student's World.* New York: Holt, Rinehart and Winston, 1973.
> Based on his experience as a participant-observer, the author gives us a "student's eye-view" of schools, a vision many have forgotten. An interesting and insightful book.

Dreeben, Robert. *On What Is Learned in School.* Reading, Mass.: Addison-Wesley, 1968.
> A sociologist's perspective on the nature of schooling and its link to the surrounding institutions of family, occupations, and politics. It focuses on the relationships between the school structure and the learning outcomes and the relevance of those outcomes to the surrounding institutions.

Goodlad, John. *A Place Called School: Prospects for the Future.* New York: McGraw-Hill, 1983.
> The author reports on a major study of American schools. Although what Goodlad finds going on in schools will disturb many people, he offers many stimulating suggestions for change.

Joyce, Bruce, et al. *The Structure of School Improvement.* New York: Longman, 1983.
> The author examines why change in schools is difficult but, more important, lays out a plan for school improvement.

Rutter, Michael, et al. *Fifteen Thousand Hours.* Cambridge, Mass.: Harvard University Press, 1979.
> Based on an extensive study of British schools, this book details the effects of fifteen thousand hours of classroom time. It proves that schools do make a difference.

Sarason, Seymour B. *The Culture of the School and the Problem of Change.* Boston: Allyn and Bacon, 1971.
> An examination of school cultures and the problems inherent in attempting to bring about change. The author particularly highlights the important role of the principal in any change process.

Tyack, David. *The One Best System: A History of American Urban Education.* Cambridge, Mass.: Harvard University Press, 1974.

> This book not only describes the growth and development of our urban school system, but reveals the drive toward bureaucratic standardization in schools.

Wise, Arthur. *Legislated Learning: The Bureaucratization of the American Class-room.* Berkeley: University of California Press, 1979.

> The author identifies a new and powerful element in American education, the courts. Until recently, legislators, lawyers, and judges had little to do with schooling; the author describes this radical change.

What Is Life in Schools Like?

6

This chapter attempts to describe school environment and classroom life as reported by a number of social and behavioral scientists. It examines some of the characteristics of student life, the language of the classroom, relationships among students, and the school as a social system. In addition, descriptions of three innovative schools are presented to illustrate environments that differ considerably from more traditional schools and classrooms.

This chapter emphasizes that:

▪ The relationship between environment and conditions for learning is important. For learning to occur, learners must interact with their environment.

▪ Studies of life in elementary classrooms reveal that students spend time waiting, experience frequent interruptions, are continually distracted, and frequently experience delayed gratification and denied desire.

▪ A review of instructional practices in high school classrooms from 1900–1980 reveals that life in high school classrooms hasn't changed much since the beginning of the twentieth century.

▪ Classrooms are places where verbal exchanges occur. Research studies describe the nature of the language of the classroom.

▪ The school is a social system, and the role of peer groups in that social system is extremely influential.

▪ Effective schools are characterized by a "coherence" of positive elements, including agreement on the goals of the school, effective communication, consistent enforcement of rules, and regular monitoring of pupils' academic progress.

▪ Although life in some schools is not the exciting experience it should be for students, many schools are innovative and stimulating and encourage creativity and independence.

*E*ACH OF US perceives reality differently. As you read this chapter you will undoubtedly react to particular passages by thinking, "That's just what life in my school was like!" or "It wasn't like that at all." Someone who attended the same school as you did, but whose background and experiences were different from yours, may remember the school in an entirely different light from the way you remember it. There is no standard version of reality. Moreover, different socioeconomic groups, different communities, and different sections of the country may produce schools that are dissimilar in certain respects. Even two schools in contiguous neighborhoods may be markedly different, and a single school can change radically in a few years' time. But, despite these important qualifications, the authors—and other observers—believe that certain conditions are more typical of schools than they are idiosyncratic and that some observations are authentically generalizable. Let's look at life in the schools and see what we can find out about the school as an environment.

THE SCHOOL AS AN ENVIRONMENT

The relative importance of heredity and environment is an old issue among philosophers and educators, and one that seems unlikely to be resolved in the near future. Perhaps it's insoluble. But one thing seems clear—both heredity and environment deeply influence an individual's capacity to learn. We all feel intuitively, though we'd probably have trouble proving it, the crucial importance of environment in shaping who we are. John Dewey, the American philosopher and educator (see pages 76–77 for his biographical sketch), contended that environment

> leads [an individual] to see and feel one thing rather than another; . . . it strengthens some beliefs and weakens others . . . it gradually produces in him a certain system of behavior. . . . In brief, the environment consists of those conditions that promote or hinder, stimulate or inhibit, the characteristic activities of a living being.[1]

Environment and Learning

If school represents a major aspect of the environment of every child, how important is the school environment in facilitating or impeding learning? For the environment to affect learning, interaction must occur; mere physical proximity to a stimulating environment does not guarantee stimulation. This is why taking a group of children from an inner-city ghetto to an art museum to expose them to cultural riches usually has little or no impact on their lives. As George Leonard, an educational innovator, states:

> No environment can strongly affect a person unless it is strongly interactive. To be interactive, the environment must be responsive, that is, must provide relevant feedback to the learner. For the feed-

[1] John Dewey, *Democracy and Education* (New York: Macmillan, 1916), p. 13.

back to be relevant, it must meet the learner *where he is*, then program (that is, change in appropriate steps at appropriate times) as he changes. The learner changes (that is, is educated) through his responses to the environment.

Within these constraints, the human organism is incredibly flexible. If there are limits on the human ability to respond to learning environments, we are so far away from the limits as to make them inconsequential. Throughout human history to date, it has been the environments, not the human beings, that have run up against limitations.[2]

An environment must, then, be interactive in order to exert a strong influence.

The school environment also tends to suffer in comparison with other learning environments that are a part of children's lives. At one time in history school was the child's major source of learning about the world. Just the fact that schools possessed books about the world made schools a rich source of information. But today the schools are competing with other learning environments, such as those provided by television, records, transistor radios, videogames, video and audio cassettes, and improved recreational and social facilities. As a result of interacting with these other environments, children are far more sophisticated and knowledgeable. Schools that ignore this fact and do not provide a stimulating, interactive environment for children will continue to produce discontented students.

Conflicting Environments It is often argued, in defense of the schools, that they are not the children's sole environment. In fact, the home and the street are ordinarily more influential in a child's life. This is of particular concern when the school environment is in direct conflict with the rest of the child's experience. The value system of the school is likely to honor work for its own sake and to stress obeying rules and preparing for the future by delaying gratification. The culture of the neighborhood, on the other hand, may regard work as exploitation or as a necessary evil, hold the law in low regard, and value action and excitement above order. The child's parents may have adopted a philosophy of "eat, drink, and be merry" as a defense against despair. How fully are neighborhood values assimilated before the child even begins school? How are children affected by inconsistency in their environments?

 Nevertheless, psychiatrist William Glasser argues that when children do not learn it is the school, not the parents or the neighborhood, that has failed; the students have not been taught in school to gain and to maintain a sense of identity and self-worth through social responsibility. Students, Glasser maintains, have learned a lot about the world by the time they

[2]Excerpted from the book *Education and Ecstasy* by George B. Leonard, pp. 39–40. Copyright © 1968 by George B. Leonard. Reprinted by permission of Delacorte Press. Reprinted by permission of The Sterling Lord Agency, Inc. Copyright © 1968 by George B. Leonard.

enter school and have, within the limits of their age, learned to cope with it; whatever their environment, they are optimistic about the future.

> Very few children come to school failures, none come labeled failures; *it is school and school alone which pins the label of failure on children*. . . . Whatever their background, children come to school highly receptive to learning. If they then fail to continue to learn at their rapid preschool rate, we may if we wish blame it on their families, their environment, or their poverty, but we would be much wiser to blame it on their experience in school.[3]

STUDIES OF LIFE IN CLASSROOMS

Whereas the total environment of a school is highly significant, some educators are more concerned with specific dimensions of life there. Before reading about their findings, try this brief exercise: Listed here is a series of words representing the opposite extremes of a continuum, each pair connected by a row of boxes. Place a check along any point in the continuum in the box that you think best represents a child's experience of life in an elementary classroom. Do this quickly, giving your immediate responses rather than thoughtful consideration.

distraction	□	□	□	□	□	□	□	□	□	□	concentration
delay	□	□	□	□	□	□	□	□	□	□	promptness
boredom	□	□	□	□	□	□	□	□	□	□	excitement
postponing	□	□	□	□	□	□	□	□	□	□	doing
unexpressive	□	□	□	□	□	□	□	□	□	□	talkative
confusion	□	□	□	□	□	□	□	□	□	□	order
restriction	□	□	□	□	□	□	□	□	□	□	freedom
interruption	□	□	□	□	□	□	□	□	□	□	continuity
denial	□	□	□	□	□	□	□	□	□	□	satisfaction
repetition	□	□	□	□	□	□	□	□	□	□	freshness

Check back later to see how your responses compare with the findings discussed in the following pages. Do your perceptions of life in an elementary classroom agree with these findings?

The Significance of Routine

An excellent perspective on how time is typically spent in the elementary classroom is provided by Philip W. Jackson's *Life in Classrooms*.[4] Anthropologists have taught us that the humdrum aspects of human existence

---

[3]William Glasser, *Schools Without Failure* (New York: Harper & Row, 1969), p. 26.
[4]Philip W. Jackson, *Life in Classrooms* (New York: Holt, Rinehart and Winston, 1968).

have cultural significance, and Jackson asserts that we must look at the most routine events in an elementary classroom if we are to understand what happens there. Are certain trivial acts repeated innumerable times? How frequently do they occur? What is their cumulative effect on the child? What do they teach the child? Jackson's observations of elementary school classrooms demonstrate how revealing the answers to these questions can be.

Have you ever figured out how many hours a child spends in school? In most states the school year is 180 days. The day typically begins at nine and ends at three, a total of six hours. Thus, if a child doesn't miss a day of school, he or she spends over a thousand hours in school each year. Including kindergarten, the average child will spend over seven thousand hours in elementary school. How are those hours typically spent?

You may think first of the curriculum—so many hours of reading and language arts, so many hours of mathematics, science, play, social studies, music, art, and so on. But what do students really *do* when they are studying these subjects? They talk individually, to the teacher and to one another. They read silently and aloud. They yawn. They look out the window. They raise their hands. They line up. They stand up. They sit down. In short, they do a number of different things, many of them commonplace and trivial.

And what about the teacher? Jackson has observed that the elementary teacher engages in as many as a thousand interpersonal interchanges each day. What is the nature of these interchanges? The teaching-learning process consists, for the most part, of talking, and the teacher controls and directs discussion. The teacher acts as a gatekeeper, deciding who shall and who shall not speak. (One may debate whether or not this *should* be the teacher's role, but clearly most teachers function this way.)

The teacher also acts as a dispenser of supplies. Since both space and resources are limited, and the number of students wishing to use them at any one time is likely to be greater than the supply, the teacher must dole them out. A related function is the granting of special privileges to deserving students—passing out the milk, sharpening the pencils, taking the roll, or operating the movie projector. Although little teacher time is involved in the awarding of these special jobs, they are important because they help structure the classroom socially as a system of rewards and punishments.

REWARDS

Timekeeping is another teacher responsibility. It is the teacher who decides when a certain activity ends and another begins, when it is time to stop science and begin spelling, and when to go outside for recess. In some schools the teacher is assisted in timekeeping by bells and buzzers that signal when a "period" is over. As Jackson observes, things happen because it is time for them to occur and not because students want them to.

These teacher functions can all be seen as responses to the crowded conditions in the classroom. If the teacher were dealing with one student

at a time in a tutorial situation, gatekeeping, granting special privileges, dispensing supplies, and timekeeping would become superfluous. But since this is not feasible, much time and energy are spent keeping order. The resulting atmosphere has unavoidable effects on the students. What are some of the consequences for students in crowded classroom conditions?

WHAT STUDENTS EXPERIENCE   One of the inevitable outcomes for the students as a result of what Jackson calls the teacher's "traffic-management" functions is delay. Since students' actions are limited by space, material resources, and the amount of teacher attention they can command, there are definite limits on their freedom in the class. In addition, since the class ordinarily moves toward a goal as a group rather than as individuals, the pace of progress is often determined by its slowest members. Waiting is a familiar activity for elementary school children—waiting in line to get a drink of water; waiting with arm propped at the elbow to be called on to answer a question; waiting to use the paper cutter; waiting until others have finished their work to go on to the next activity; waiting until four other students have finished reading aloud for a chance to do so.

Denial of desire is another common experience for the elementary student. A question goes unanswered, a raised hand is ignored, talking out of turn is not permitted, relief of bodily functions is allowed only at specified times. Some denial is necessary, and some is probably beneficial, but one thing is certain—delayed gratification and denied desire are learned in school. Though you as a teacher will invariably be kept busy, this is not the case for your students, and a certain amount of student frustration is bound to develop as a result of delay and denial.

Students also experience frequent interruptions and social distraction. Interruptions are of many sorts—interruptions of seatwork by the teacher to give additional instructions or to clarify one student's question, mechanical interruptions when the motion picture film starts to flicker, interruptions when messages from the principal's office are read aloud to the class, interruptions for fire drills, interruptions when the teacher is working with one student and another student misbehaves, and so on. Students are expected either to ignore these intrusions or quickly to resume their activities. The emphasis on an inflexible schedule contributes to the sense of interruption by making students frequently begin activities before their interest has been aroused and stop at the height of their interest when the schedule dictates that they must begin another task.

A related phenomenon is social distraction. Students are often asked to behave as if they were in solitude, when in fact they are surrounded by thirty or so other people. At certain times during the day students are assigned seatwork and required to work on their own. At such times communication among students is often discouraged, if not forbidden. To be

surrounded by friends, sometimes seated across from each other at a table, and not be allowed to talk is a difficult and tempting situation. As Jackson remarks, "These young people, if they are to become successful students, must learn how to be alone in a crowd."[5]

Delay, denial, interruption, and *social distraction,* then, are characteristic of life in elementary classrooms. How are children affected by these class-

[5]Jackson, *Life in Classrooms,* p. 18.

BEGINNING TEACHER EVALUATION STUDY

A study sponsored by the National Institute of Education, the Beginning Teacher Evaluation Study (BTES) was developed to identify teaching activities and classroom conditions that foster student learning in elementary schools. The study focused on instruction in reading and mathematics at grades two and five. From this study we have obtained additional quantitative data on how elementary school children spend their time.

1. *Time allocations.* About 58 percent of the school day is allocated to academic activities, about 23 percent to nonacademic activities (e.g., music, art, physical education), and about 19 percent to noninstructional activities such as transitions between activities and class business.

2. *Engaged time.* On the average, students spent one hour and thirty minutes (second grade) and one hour and fifty-five minutes (fifth grade) actively engaged in reading and math activities. In the highest classrooms the engaged time was about thirty minutes longer, and in the lowest classrooms it was about thirty minutes less than the average.

3. On the average, students were engaged about 73 percent of the allocated time in reading and math.

4. During allocated time for academics, students were not engaged about sixteen minutes an hour, on the average. Half of this nonengaged time was taken up with interim activities (e.g., passing out and collecting papers) or waiting for help, and the other eight minutes were when students were clearly off task.

5. *Seatwork.* Overall, students spent about two-thirds of the allocated academic time in seatwork (or self-paced activities) and about one-third of

their time working with an adult. Engagement was higher in teacher-led settings (about 84 percent) than in seatwork settings (about 70 percent). An inevitable fact of classroom life is that if a teacher working alone divides a class into three groups, students will be working alone two-thirds of the time.

6. Student engagement during seatwork increased when there was substantive interaction between teacher and student during seatwork. Such substantive interaction consisted of a teacher (or aide) monitoring seatwork and holding students accountable by asking questions. Such substantive interaction was most effective when it occurred 11 percent or more of the seatwork time.

Barak V. Rosenshine, "How Time Is Spent in Elementary Classrooms," *The Journal of Classroom Interaction* 17 (Winter 1981): 23–24.

SCHOOLS: THE PRESENT

room facts of life? It is difficult to measure their effect, because they are present to a greater or lesser degree in every classroom. Also, different students have different levels of tolerance for these phenomena. It would seem, however, that the student who either possesses or quickly develops patience will find school more tolerable than the student who lacks it. The ability to control desires, delay rewards, and stifle impulses seems to be necessary to the "mature" student. Jackson explains:

> Thus, the personal quality commonly described as patience—an essential quality when responding to the demands of the classroom—represents a balance, and sometimes a precarious one, between two opposed tendencies. On the one hand is the impulse to act on desire, to blurt out the answer, to push to the front of the line, or to express anger when interrupted. On the other hand is the impulse to give up the desire itself, to stop participating in the discussion, to go without a drink when the line is long, or to abandon an interrupted activity.[6]

The necessary balance is achieved by the majority of students. Others may respond in either of the two ways just described, or in still another manner. If you as a teacher are to understand why children act as they do, an understanding of the dynamics of the classroom is a necessity. Jackson's book offers considerable insight into life in elementary classrooms.

Instruction in the High School Classroom

In a review of instructional practices in high school classrooms from 1900–1980, Larry Cuban concludes that the high school of today is remarkably similar to high schools at the beginning of the twentieth century.[7] Concentrating on classrooms in the academic subjects (English, history and social studies, science, foreign language, and mathematics), Cuban examined how classroom space and furniture were arranged; what manner of grouping the teacher used for instruction (whole class, small group, and so forth); what amount and type of classroom talk were used by teacher and students; what instructional activities were used in the classroom (recitation, discussion, tests, lecture, film, student reports, and so forth); and how much physical movement students were allowed within the classroom. The overall picture showed that there is a striking uniformity between today's high schools and those of the early twentieth century. Certain elements were similar in both classrooms regardless of size, region in which the schools were located, and whether the schools were rural or urban: persistence of whole-group instruction, domination of teacher talk over student talk, question/answer format drawn largely from textbooks, and little student movement in academic classes.

[6]Jackson, *Life in Classrooms*, p. 18.

[7]Larry Cuban, "Persistent Instruction: The High School Classroom, 1900–1980," *Phi Delta Kappan* 64 (October 1982): 113–118.

A National Science Foundation (NSF) study conducted in 1977 and reviewed by Cuban randomly sampled more than five thousand U.S. high school teachers on their teaching methods. All math, science, and social studies teachers said that they used lecture and discussion more than any other technique. Next in frequency to lecture and discussion were tests and quizzes (for math and social studies teachers) and student use of lab materials (for science classes). Roughly one-half to two-thirds of the teachers said that they taught their classes as an entire group.

Another study reviewed by Cuban was John Goodlad's "A Study of Schooling," which placed observers in 525 high school classrooms. As part

An eight-year study in which over one thousand classrooms were observed has yielded interesting data on how teachers teach and how time in classrooms is used. The amount of classroom time actually spent on instruction was about 70 percent at the elementary school level and 75 percent at the senior high level. At the typical high school, about 70 percent of the time spent on instruction involved verbal interaction or "talk," with the typical teacher "out-talking" his or her class of students by a ratio of three to one. Of the approximately 150 minutes of talk each day, only 7 minutes involved teachers' responses to individual students.

The way in which students spent most of their classroom hours varied from level to level. At the elementary school level,

---

HOW STUDENTS SPEND CLASSROOM TIME

---

about 60 percent of students' time during a day was spent preparing for and cleaning up after assignments. At the junior high school level, approximately 59 percent of the students' time was spent listening to teachers explain or lecture. Students at the senior high school level spent 54 percent of their time fulfilling written assignments.

The study found that there was very little instructional variability. The major activities of the classroom were lecturing, written assignments, and quizzes, particularly in the academic subject areas. In the arts, physical education, and vocational education, there were more demonstrations, discussions, various types of physical performing, and production of products other than written ones, although the differences between these sub-

jects and the academic ones was less than the researchers expected.

Teachers were very much in control. Students were rarely involved in planning or evaluating activities. Instruction usually involved the total class; small-group activity was rare. Overall, there was minimal student movement in the classroom, minimal student-to-student or student-to-teacher interaction, and low, nonintimate affect (either positive or negative).

The researchers conclude that the formal and informal experiences of teachers and the messages they receive from the internal and external context of schooling all reinforce the status quo.

John I. Goodlad, *A Place Called School* (New York: McGraw-Hill, 1983).

of that study, it was observed that in the typical class the teacher explained and lectured to the whole class, asked factual questions, or watched students work. Generally, students listened or answered teachers' questions. Five activities consumed, on the average, two-thirds of each high school period: (1) preparing for assignments, (2) explaining/lecturing/reading aloud by the teacher, (3) discussing, (4) working on assignments, and (5) taking tests.

The apparent invulnerability of high school classrooms to substantial instructional change leads Cuban to conclude that such change is not likely to occur. There are many structural givens: the school day is sliced into periods of less than an hour; teachers face between 125 and 170 students a day in groups of 25 to 35; a teaching load consists of five classes and two or more different lesson preparations; and there are a dozen other external requirements of grading, credits, and exams. Coupling these factors with the facts that teachers are isolated from peers and are infrequently supervised, teachers often complete a school day without once reflecting with colleagues on what pedagogy was practiced or what successes and mistakes occurred. Cuban concludes that rectifying this situation would mean modifying teachers' class loads, altering their amount of contact time with students, and controlling any of a vast number of identifiable variables.

The Language of the Classroom

In any elementary, junior, or senior high school classroom, at any given moment, the chances are very good that someone will be talking. Who will it be? Will he or she be talking about something related to instruction, or to management of the classroom, or about something extraneous to the lesson? These kinds of questions have been asked by researchers for years, but only in the past twenty-five years have effective techniques and instruments for analyzing the language of the classroom been developed.

INTERACTION ANALYSIS   One of these instruments, developed by Ned Flanders and called Flanders's Interaction Analysis, enables the observer to categorize both teacher and student verbal behavior. See Table 6.1 for a description of Flanders's ten categories. Developed to facilitate extensive research into teacher influence on student attitudes and achievement, Flanders's system measures a primary component of teacher influence: verbal directness or indirectness. The amount of intellectual freedom the teacher grants to students can be estimated by determining the proportion of directness and indirectness in the teaching. Direct verbal behavior on the part of the teacher—lecturing, giving directions, reciting facts, criticizing—tends to minimize the variety of possible student responses. Indirect behavior—eliciting student statements, accepting and making use of student ideas, praising, encouraging, varying strategies in response to the situation—increases the freedom of the student.

Table 6.1 Flanders's Interaction Analysis: Summary of Categories for Interaction Analysis

TEACHER TALK		STUDENT TALK	OTHER
Indirect Influence	Direct Influence		
1. *Accepts feeling:* accepts and clarifies the feeling tone of the students in a nonthreatening manner. Feelings may be positive or negative. Predicting and recalling feelings are included. 2. *Praises or encourages:* praises or encourages student action or behavior. Jokes that release tension, not at the expense of another individual, nodding head or saying "uh huh?" or "go on" are included. 3. *Accepts or uses ideas of student:* clarifying, building, or developing ideas or suggestions by a student. As teacher brings more of his own ideas into play, shift to category five. 4. *Asks questions:* asking a question about content or procedure with the intent that a student answer.	5. *Lectures:* giving facts or opinions about content or procedure; expressing his own idea; asking rhetorical questions. 6. *Gives directions:* directions, commands, or orders with which a student is expected to comply. 7. *Criticizes or justifies authority:* statements intended to change student behavior from nonacceptable to acceptable pattern; bawling someone out; stating why the teacher is doing what he is doing, extreme self-reference.	8. *Student talk-response:* talk by students in response to teacher. Teacher initiates the contact or solicits student statement. 9. *Student talk-initiation:* talk by students, which they initiate. If "calling on" student is only to indicate who may talk next, observer must decide whether student wanted to talk. If he did, use this category.	10. *Silence or confusion:* pauses, short periods of silence, and periods of confusion in which communication cannot be understood by the observer.

*There is no scale implied by these numbers. Each number is classificatory; it designates a particular kind of communication event. To write these numbers down during observation is to enumerate, not to judge, a position on a scale.

Source: Edmund Amidon and Ned Flanders, "Interaction Analysis As a Feedback System," in *Interaction Analysis: Theory, Research, and Application,* ed. E. Amidon and J. Hough (Reading, Mass.: Addison-Wesley Publishing Co., 1967), p. 125. Used by permission.

Flanders's initial research project involved 147 teachers, representing all grade levels, six different school districts, and two counties.[8] In summarizing his findings, Flanders discovered the "rule of two-thirds": during about two-thirds of classroom time, someone is talking. About two-thirds of that time, the person talking is the teacher. Two-thirds of the teacher's talk is spent giving directions, expressing opinions and facts, and occasionally criticizing students. Flanders also discovered that superior classes—those that scored above average on constructive attitudes toward the teacher and the classwork—also scored higher on content achievement tests, after test results were adjusted for initial ability.

In studies of seventh-grade social studies and eighth-grade mathematics classes, Flanders found that the teachers in superior classes talked only slightly less than the teachers in the other classes, 50 to 60 percent of the time, but that only 40 to 50 percent of their teaching was directive. In other words, the teachers whose classes had constructive attitudes and scored higher on content achievement were more flexible than others in the quality of their verbal influence.

By contrast, the analysis of classes below average in constructive student attitudes and in content achievement showed that their teachers spoke over 75 percent of the time, and that over 75 percent of their talk was devoted to giving directions, expressing opinions and facts, and, occasionally, criticizing students. For these teachers, the rule of two-thirds becomes the rule of three-fourths plus.

LANGUAGE MOVES   In another study Arno Bellack used a totally different conceptual framework to study classroom language patterns. Utilizing 15 teachers and 345 pupils in "Problems of Democracy" classes in high school, Bellack viewed classroom discourse as a game played with language.[9] His analysis of classroom language yielded several valuable insights:

1. Teachers dominate verbal activities. The teacher-pupil ratio in terms of lines spoken is 3:1; in terms of moves, the ratio is about 3:2.

2. Appropriate teacher and pupil moves are implicitly but clearly defined—the teacher is responsible for structuring, soliciting, and reacting, whereas the student is ordinarily limited to responding. (This evidence corroborates Flanders's finding that teachers dominate classrooms in such a way as to make the students dependent.)

3. Teachers initiate about 85 percent of the cycles. The basic unit of verbal interchange is the *soliciting-responding* pattern. Verbal interchanges take place at a rate of slightly less than two cycles per minute.

[8]Ned A. Flanders, "Intent, Action and Feedback: A Preparation for Teaching," *The Journal of Teacher Education* 14 (September 1963): 251–260.

[9]Arno Bellack et al., *The Language of the Classroom* (New York: Teachers College Press, 1965).

4. In approximately two-thirds of the moves and three-fourths of the lines, talk is content oriented.

5. Fact stating and explaining account for between 50 and 60 percent of the total discourse in most classrooms.

Bellack's empirical evidence suggests that the classroom is teacher dominated, centered around subject matter, and fact oriented. The student's primary responsibility seems to be to respond to the teacher's soliciting moves. Thus student initiative does not seem to be characteristic of the high school social studies classes sampled. It is, once again, dangerous to generalize from a limited sample. Yet evidence from studies such as Bellack's indicates that, for a large number of classes if not the majority, this is the case.

QUESTIONING   In a third study of classroom language, James Gallagher investigated the kinds of questions that teachers ask. His study involved 235 boys and girls in ten different classes for gifted children at the junior and senior high school level.[10] Gallagher differentiated between four categories of questions:

1. *Cognitive-Memory* questions require the student to reproduce facts or other remembered content through the use of such processes as recognition, rote memory, and selective recall. An example of a cognitive-memory question would be: "Can you tell me where Christopher Columbus first landed in the Americas?"

2. *Convergent* questions require the student to generate new information that leads to the correct or conventionally accepted answer. Given or known information usually determines the correct response. An example of a convergent question might be: "Could you summarize for us the author's major point?"

3. *Divergent* questions require the student to generate his or her own data independently in a data-poor situation, or to take a new perspective on a given topic. Divergent questions have no "right" answer. An example of a divergent question is, "How might the history of the United States have been different if the Pilgrims had landed on the west coast instead of the east coast?"

4. *Evaluative* questions require the student to make value judgments and decisions regarding the goodness, correctness, or adequacy of information, based on a criterion usually set by the student. For example, the evaluative question "Which president did more to enhance the office of the presidency—Jefferson or Jackson?" requires the student to decide on criteria to judge what enhancing the office of the presidency means, and then to compare Jefferson and Jackson with respect to those criteria.

The results of Gallagher's study show that in practically all class sessions, cognitive-memory questions constitute 50 percent or more of the total questions asked. The more the class tended toward a lecture mode rather than a discussion mode, the more often teacher questions and student responses fell into the cognitive-memory category. Convergent questions were the second most frequent category, with very few divergent or evaluative questions and responses. In fact, Gallagher surmises that class discussion could operate normally if only the first two categories of question were available.

Gallagher also found an extremely close relationship between the type of teacher questions and the pattern of thought expression observed in the students' responses. To a large extent, he observed, the teacher controls the expressive thought patterns of the class.

[10]James J. Gallagher, "Expressive Thought by Gifted Children in the Classroom," *Language and the Higher Thought Processes* (Champaign, Ill.: National Council of Teachers of English, 1965), pp. 56–65.

"I was trying so hard to look as if I were paying attention that I didn't hear what you said."

© Joe Buresch. First published in *Today's Education*.

NONVERBAL COMMUNICATION   When we think of language we ordinarily think of words. A number of researchers have recently become interested in another kind of language—the silent language of gestures, facial expressions, bodily movements, and other means of nonverbal communication. In his book *The Silent Language*,[11] anthropologist Edward Hall maintains that much of the content of a culture is communicated nonverbally. Hall has helped train American diplomats to understand how gestures and expressions that communicate one thing in our culture may be interpreted quite differently in another culture. He uses as an example the differences between American and Arab culture regarding the appropriate distance between two conversing people. If two Americans are carrying on a conversation at a distance of twenty feet, they will consider the distance unacceptable and will move closer together until both are more comfortable.

[11]Edward T. Hall, *The Silent Language* (Garden City, N.Y.: Doubleday, 1959).

The exact distance they choose will vary, depending on how well they know each other, but about three feet is the norm. However, in Arab cultures the appropriate distance is less than three feet. Therefore, when an American and an Arab are conversing, the Arab is trying to get closer while the American is trying to move backward in order to establish the "appropriate" distance. Hall reports that he has seen this situation occur with the result that the Arab wonders what is wrong since the American seems repelled, while the American *is* repelled by what seems to be pushy behavior.

An interesting story, but what does it have to do with teaching? The answer: a great deal. Most teachers are totally unaware of their nonverbal communication patterns. That they may be saying one thing verbally and communicating the opposite nonverbally does not even occur to most teachers. For instance, the third-grade teacher who puts her arm around the white students in her class, or pats their heads fondly, yet maintains a certain distance with the black students, is definitely communicating a message. Yet, if asked if she discriminates between her students, she would be likely to reply indignantly in the negative. In fact, research indicates that lower-class youngsters rely heavily on nonverbal communication to understand meanings in the classroom.[12] We maintain that if there is a discrepancy, the message a teacher communicates nonverbally is probably more valid and truthful than the verbal message, because it is much easier to conceal real feelings in words than in actions.

Since nonverbal communication is more difficult to conceptualize, define, interpret, and measure than verbal communication, relatively little work has been done to date in this area. Charles Galloway has, however, developed guidelines for observing a teacher's use of *space, time,* and the *body.*[13]

SPACE   A teacher's use of space can convey meaning to the students. For example, when and where a teacher chooses to travel in a classroom has significance. A teacher who never ventures far from the desk at the front of the room may convey insecurity to the students—a reluctance to leave "home base." Some teachers rarely venture into the students' territory except to monitor their seatwork. A teacher's unwillingness to mingle with students will certainly be detected by them.

TIME   How teachers use classroom time is often an indication of the value they place on certain activities. The elementary school teacher who

[12]Basil Bernstein, "Social Structure, Language and Learning," *Educational Research 3* (1961): 163–176.

[13]Charles Galloway, "Nonverbal Communication," *Theory Into Practice* 7 (December 1968): 172–175.

spends a great deal of class time on social studies but very little on math is conveying a message to the students that they will almost surely detect.

BODY MANEUVERS   Teachers frequently use nonverbal tactics to control students' behavior. The raised eyebrow, the finger to the lips indicating silence, the hands on hips, and the silent stare all communicate unmistakable meanings. Galloway notes that when the teacher's verbal and nonverbal communications are in contradiction, the students read the nonverbal cues as a truer reflection of the teacher's real feelings and act accordingly. You can see this happening when a teacher verbally reprimands a student for talking but acts in such a way that the student knows the teacher doesn't really feel strongly about it. Shortly thereafter, the student begins talking again.

How can you analyze or become more aware of your nonverbal communication? Perhaps the best and most accessible cue the teacher receives is feedback from students, though teachers vary considerably in their ability to recognize student responses and to utilize this information to analyze their own behavior. You can also make a videotape of yourself teaching and analyze the tape to identify inconsistencies between your verbal and nonverbal behavior. The videotape recorder is a tremendous boon to teachers in that it allows them or others to evaluate their performances relatively objectively.

We have seen in our brief survey that decoding language of the classroom can shed considerable light on what happens there. The techniques and systems that Flanders, Bellack, Gallagher, and Galloway have developed to look at the language of the classroom can also be used by teachers to analyze their own communication processes and messages. How much do you want to dominate discussion when you become a teacher? Do you want to have a direct or indirect influence on students? Do you want the students to become dependent on you, or do you want to foster independence? Do you know when you are communicating one message verbally and another nonverbally? What kinds of thinking do you want your students to practice—recall and recognition, or analysis and evaluation? The kind of thinking they do is in part a product of the kinds of questions that you ask them. If you feel it is important to understand your experience, it would make sense for you to develop competence in one or more of these language evaluation systems during your teacher-education program.

THE SCHOOL AS A SOCIAL SYSTEM

Socialization can be defined as the general process of social learning whereby the child learns the many things he or she must know to become an acceptable member of society. The major socializing agencies in the life of a child are the family, the peer group, the school, the church, the youth-serving organizations, political and economic institutions, and the mass media. Some of these agencies, such as the school, are formal, and some, such as the peer group, are informally organized.

The school has its own subculture—a set of beliefs, values, traditions, ways of thinking and behaving—that distinguish it from other social institutions. The school attempts to socialize children by getting them to value those things the school teaches. The more successful students tend to accept these values, whereas many of the less successful students reject the ways of thinking and behaving that the school values.

Most schools differentiate students according to achievement. In the elementary school, achievement is defined along two lines: cognitive, or the learning of information and skills, and social, which includes such aspects of learning as respect for the teacher, consideration of other students, good work habits, initiative, and responsibility. With its variety of personnel, activities, and subject matter, the high school offers the student a wide variety of choices in both the cognitive and social areas of achievement.

As a subculture, schools have not only their own rules for behavior, but also their own rituals and ceremonies. School assemblies, athletic events, graduation ceremonies, honor society inductions, and school songs and cheers, are among the ceremonies and rituals commonly found in schools.

Schools differ from one another in many ways. In some schools the relationship between teachers and students is warm and cordial; in other schools it it cool and formal. Competition among students is encouraged in some schools, yet in others it is de-emphasized. Some schools engender among the students a sense of pride in the school and its accomplishments, whereas in other schools the students are apathetic or even hostile. Student achievement levels in some schools are consistently higher than those in schools that are comparable in terms of material resources and student characteristics. Why these differences occur has been the object of many recent studies on characteristics of effective schools, a topic to which we now turn.

CHARACTERISTICS OF EFFECTIVE SCHOOLS

Some researchers regard effective schools as those that enable disadvantaged children to attain a basic skills mastery comparable to the minimally successful level of middle-class children. Ron Edmonds, drawing on his own work and on that of other researchers, argues that schools that accomplish this feat share six common characteristics:

1. They have strong administrative leadership.
2. They have a "climate of expectation" stressing acquisition of basic skills for all students.
3. They have an orderly rule-bound atmosphere that emphasizes instruction.
4. They emphasize learning over nonlearning activities.

5. They divert, when needed, resources from noninstructional to instructional areas.

6. They use some method to monitor pupil academic progress systematically.[14]

In a ten-year study of 140 schools, Edward Wynne identified a number of characteristics that distinguish successful from unsuccessful schools.[15] "Coherence" was the characteristic most commonly associated with the successful schools in Wynne's study. By *coherence* he means that the positive elements in a school were pervasive. In contrast, schools lacking in coherence were never all bad, but negative elements seemed mixed with displays of efficiency or caring. Coherence came from an appropriate meshing of many elements.

Staff conduct is one such element. In the effective schools, each staff member worked hard at his or her job, simultaneously striving to relate that work to the aims of the whole school. *Staff* includes not only teachers and administrators, but also counselors, lunchroom attendants, security guards, custodians, and other school employees. In effective schools the staff, and even the students and parents, knew what constituted good performance. For example, they all knew that a good teacher "cares" and that caring is displayed in overt conduct, such as regular and timely attendance, well-organized lesson plans, reasonably orderly classes, routinely assigned and appropriately graded homework, friendly but authoritative relations with students, purposeful use of class time, and supportive relations with colleagues. Teachers also set performance goals for students and translated these goals into precise objectives.

Coherence was not maintained successfully unless most members of the school community were kept well-informed. In a typical school there are many barriers to adequate information flow, but in the better schools a variety of strategies were used to overcome the problems. For example, numerous methods or techniques were used for communicating between the school and home: handbooks for students and parents, report cards, periodic newsletters to parents, notes from teachers, regular parent-teacher meetings, and diverse activities to encourage parents to visit the school often.

Good schools tended to create vital subgroups of teachers. These subgroups were assigned relatively clear, plausible tasks: to plan and evaluate curricula, shape homework policies, redesign report cards, and the

---

[14]Ron Edmonds, "Effective Schools for the Urban Poor," *Educational Leadership* 37 (October 1979): 15–27.

[15]Edward A. Wynne, "Looking at Good Schools," *Phi Delta Kappan* 62 (January 1981): 377–381.

like. These tasks gave subgroup members the reward of their own sense of accomplishment in working collectively toward important and valuable ends. Members of the subgroups who failed to perform their tasks received strong group disapproval. Erring staff members tended to change or to seek work somewhere else.

Effective schools were very good in creating a wide variety of school-wide incentives, such as honor societies and public recognition of achievement, to foster and encourage learning. The weaker schools used some of the same tactics, but with fewer resources and less energy.

Rules for student discipline were precisely and clearly stated and consistently enforced. Punishment for rule infractions was incremental; that is, repeat offenders received harsher punishments. All staff members enforced the rules equally, considering such enforcement as a professional responsibility. Rules were reviewed periodically, and obsolete or unenforceable provisions were removed.

Extracurricular and student service activities were important in good schools. Most of these activities were socially constructive in nature, in that

---

CLASS SIZE AND STUDENT LEARNING

For many years teachers and their professional organizations have argued strongly for the need to reduce class sizes if education for children is to improve. There was little evidence in the research literature, however, to support their arguments that the reduction of class sizes would lead to an increase in student learning. Using new statistical techniques, a team of educational researchers headed by Dr. Gene V. Glass has concluded that there is a relationship between class size and pupil learning. Reviewing nearly eighty studies of the relationship between class size and pupil achievement (some dating back as far as 1900!), these researchers found that average pupil achievement increases as class size decreases. They discovered that the typical achievement of pupils in instructional groups of fifteen and fewer is several percentile ranks above that of pupils in classes of twenty-five and thirty. Additionally, they discovered that for every pupil by which class size is reduced below twenty, the class's average achievement improves substantially more than for each pupil by which class size is reduced between thirty and twenty. The real benefit to learning, then, seems to occur when classes are reduced below twenty students, as opposed to the benefits accruing from reductions between thirty and twenty pupils.

Allotting all teachers fifteen pupils per class would, of course, be an expensive proposition. The authors suggest that small classes may be more justifiable for remedial instruction and in the primary grades to allow students the opportunity for a good start.

Gene V. Glass, Leonard S. Cahen, Mary Lee Smith, and Nikola N. Filby, "Class Size and Learning—New Interpretation of the Research Literature," *Today's Education* (April–May 1979): 42–44.

they promoted conduct that was helpful to others. Effective schools conceptualized, articulated, and publicized some criteria of good pro-social performance. Pro-social behavior was recognized and rewarded in numerous ways, such as by the issuance of certificates. In addition, school spirit in good schools was believed by teachers, supervisors, and students to be important.

It would appear, then, that the schools that are most successful in socializing students to behave in ways that schools value are ones in which the principal and staff agree on what they are doing, communicate their expectations to students, consistently enforce rules, provide an environment conducive to accomplishing the task, and monitor pupil academic progress regularly.

Peer Groups

Operating both within and outside of the school is another influential socializing agency—the peer group. Children are members of two social worlds: the world of adults and the world of their peers. As members of the adult world, children are always in a position of subordinate status; adults have privileges and rights that children don't. In the peer world, children have equal status and learn from one another. As members of the adult world, children are expected to show deference and respect for authority. As members of the peer world, they can express their own attitudes, explore personal relationships, and test themselves out against others.

POPULARITY TOP GOAL OF STUDENTS POLLED

Denver (UPI)—A survey of Colorado high school students shows being popular is more important to them than getting good grades or "being in the newspaper or on TV."

In fact, school officials said, getting good grades ranked only ninth—slightly ahead of "being smiled at"—on a list of 15 types of recognition the high school youngsters would like to get.

Being publicized in the newspaper or on television ranked last.

The State Board for Community Colleges and Occupational Education said it surveyed students at four high schools and asked each of them to choose the types of recognition they would most like to receive.

"Being popular" was first among the 15 choices offered

and was followed with "being loved or appreciated" and "helping people."

The survey was part of an eight-state research project initiated by the national headquarters of Future Homemakers of America and Home Economics Related Occupations.

Houston Chronicle, October 5, 1978. Reprinted by permission.

SCHOOLS: THE PRESENT

Sociologist James Coleman's studies of peer relationships among adolescents have resulted in some very interesting observations.[16] Coleman believes that industrial society, by shifting much of the responsibility for the training of a child from parents to the school and by extending the necessary period of training, has made the high school into a social system of adolescents. The values and activities of this adolescent subculture are quite different from those of adult society, and its members' most important associations are with one another rather than with adults. Society has created for adolescents a separate institution of their own; home is merely a dormitory, whereas "real" living consists of activities unique to the peer group.

Sociologist Jere Cohen has identified three types of students, or teen subcultures: academic, delinquent, and social.[17] The *academic* students are the ones who identify most completely with the values of the school. They have intellectual interests and want to achieve high grades so they can go to the more selective colleges. They tend to participate in activities such as debate, theater, the literary magazine, intellectually oriented clubs, and student government. The *delinquents* reject the school's values. In the last fifteen years or so, this subculture has split into two branches—the "greasers" and the "freaks."

The greasers have been around since the 1950s. Their typical dress consists of a black leather jacket, boots, and tight pants. In many respects, the greasers have the most highly refined code of behavior of all the high school subcultures. The gangs in which they gather operate according to sophisticated conventions and codes. Greasers tend to get C's and D's in their classes. Although they are not particularly interested in studies, they don't cause any trouble in school. They tend to study the trades, and their techniques for customizing and modifying cars have given rise to a popular art form. Generally, school is an irrelevancy for the greasers, rather than a target for adolescent rebellion.

Freaks, on the other hand, are those shaggy-haired, drug-ingesting, rock-music fans who have been giving high school educators problems since the late 1960s. One student summarizes the freaks' behavior:

> Freaks in our high school—20 percent of the kids—have been getting high since grade school. When they get to high school, they party every day before school starts. They're into chemicals—Quaa-

[16]James S. Coleman, "The Adolescent Subculture and Academic Achievement," in *Society and Education*, ed. R. Havighurst, B. Neugarten, and J. Falk (Boston: Allyn and Bacon, 1967), pp. 109–115. Coleman's findings were reported in 1960. Do you think his observations are still valid today?

[17]Christopher Johnson, "From Freaks to Rah Rahs: Subcultures in the High Schools," *Today's Education* (April–May 1981): 30GS–32GS.

ludes, PCP, angel dust, LSD—while other students use marijuana or cocaine. They get their money for drugs either by working or by dealing.

According to Stephen Buff, another describer of teen subcultures, music, drugs, and nonconformist dress and behavior are all ways of upsetting "a square adult world which has nothing to offer them except condemnation, discrimination by storekeepers and neighbors, police repression, deadly boring jobs . . . , (and) rules of dress and conduct in schools which teach them nothing."[18]

The teen subculture that enjoys the greatest degree of status among other students is the *social* type, consisting of the jocks and the "rah-rahs"—athletes and their admirers. The social types are also active in other conspicuous activities, such as student council. This group tends to emulate college fraternity lifestyles, often throwing big weekend parties. As one student states, "In our school, the cheerleaders and girls who date jocks are the most sexually active, but they still have good reputations because they're popular." The social types demonstrate the continuing importance of athletics, moderate academic success, and involvement in student government as the key elements for status among teenagers.

Membership in these teenage subcultures begins to form in the junior high schools as cliques develop around particular interests such as athletics, academics, student government, cars, or drugs. These groups strengthen as the teenagers begin to move away from their families, and peer membership becomes a type of new family where comfort and support are found.

[18]Christopher Johnson, "From Freaks to Rah Rahs: Subcultures in the High Schools," p. 31GS.

DIALOGUE

KEVIN: Freak is a rather cruel term, isn't it?

JIM: I think so. I believe Johnson was trying to capture the "planned outrageousness" of some of these students.

KEVIN: And what do you mean by "planned outrageousness?"

JIM: Well, in the last several decades we have seen those students who really have a tough time fitting into school and who feel alienated from the academic students, the athletes, and the vocational students forming groups who symbolize their alienation by their dress and appearance. They assume the appearance of "freaks."

KEVIN: That's right, in the sixties before long hair became "in" and stylish, it was a symbol of alienation. Right now in the mid-eighties, student "freakism" has taken a different form.

JIM: What's that?

KEVIN: Punk, friend. Punk.

By the sophomore year of high school, the subcultures have stabilized so much that it is difficult for individuals to move from one group to another. By senior year, however, the hold of the subcultures on students begins to weaken. At this age the students are developing more self-confidence, and they start seeking greater freedom. At this point the friendship group becomes a drag on their autonomy.

Until that happens, however, the teen subcultures exert strong influence on the values of their members, and this can cause problems for the high school educator. Conflict between the subcultures often occurs, especially between the jocks and freaks. Each group views with contempt the values dominant in the other group. Jocks reject the use of drugs (other than marijuana) and hold in contempt the freaks' resistance to authority and achievement. Freaks are equally contemptuous of the jocks' interest in student government and athletics.

Most high schools have done a reasonably good job in making the academic and social types an integral part of school life. The schools have not been very successful in doing so with subcultures like the freaks and the greasers. In fact, the schools may be reinforcing the alienation felt by the freaks and greasers, because these groups reject the school's values.

Trying to find ways to bring members of alienated subcultures into participation in their schools is a major challenge for high school and junior high school educators.

THE SCHOOL AS POTENTIALITY

It appears that life in schools is not the exciting experience it should be for many students. The difference between eager first-graders and blasé teenagers, or even between first-graders and fifth-graders, is an object lesson on the effects of schooling. As students spend time in school they are inevitably shaped by it. Many become docile, they question authority less, they learn to think of themselves as successes or failures, they perform rituals without knowing why, they are asked to memorize things they do not care about—and this is called learning.

All schools are not this way, however. There are many innovative and stimulating schools that encourage creativity and independence in a truly interactive environment. Let's look at three of those schools.

High School for the Engineering Professions

The Houston Independent School District (HISD), Houston, Texas, is the sixth-largest school district in the United States, and operates one of the most varied and successful magnet school programs in the country (see Chapter 12 for a discussion of magnet schools). One of the most successful

---

TEENAGERS' ATTITUDES TOWARD HIGH SCHOOL

"A majority of secondary school students are proud of their schools, have a sense of belonging, and believe that teachers really care whether they learn. They feel less positive about school administration, however."

These conclusions stem from a survey of over ten thousand students from twenty-two states, representing twenty-five school systems, most of which are located in cities of moderate size. Students perceived their teachers as explaining clearly what assignments to do and how to go about them. Regardless of grades, students believed they were "learning a lot," and generally agreed that schools were teaching those things they needed to know "right now." They were also satisfied with their treatment by counselors, and they perceived school spirit as high at their schools. However, a significant minority responded negatively even to those items that the majority rated quite positively. About one student in six was not proud of his or her school; more than one in five did not feel that teachers care whether students learn. Two out of five students expressed negative feelings about school administrators. One out of three was unhappy with school counseling services.

These data tend to support Jere Cohen's conclusions that for certain subcultures in today's high schools, school does not meet their needs.

Clinton I. Chase, "Teenagers Are Mostly Positive About High School," *Phi Delta Kappan* 62 (March 1981): 526.

---

of these magnet schools is the High School for the Engineering Professions (HSEP). Designed to promote desegregation by offering an academic program that will attract diverse types of students, HSEP emphasizes applied mathematics and science. It attempts to provide a superior academic program for highly talented college-bound youth who may wish to major in engineering. One hundred percent of its graduates through its first three years of existence have gone on to college, including many prestigious colleges and universities.

HSEP has seven periods per day instead of the usual six. Most students earn seven credits per year, so a student who starts in ninth grade will complete all of the regular high school requirements by the end of the eleventh grade. In addition to the usual history, English, and physical education courses, HSEP offers algebra, geometry, trigonometry, calculus, biology, chemistry, physics, logic, and economics. Students also take four courses in computer sciences, courses in engineering drawing, creative design, engineering lab, engineering analysis, and a course in electronics. Whereas the engineering courses emphasize theory, math, and analytical thinking, the lab provides ample equipment to encourage "tinkering" by students who may not have had much opportunity to take motors apart or fix lawnmowers. The curriculum was planned with the help of an advisory group of deans of colleges of engineering.

HSEP is successful in attracting students from both within and outside the HISD, with many of the students having to rise between 5:00–5:45 A.M. in order to catch buses to this unimpressive building, located in a dingy industrial-residential neighborhood. Students often endure bus rides in rush-hour traffic of up to two hours each way because they believe they are getting the best education to be had in the Houston area. As one senior states, "You learn earlier than most teenagers that you are working for your future." A ninth-grader says she loves "the freedom to work at your own pace." A tenth-grader who transferred from a nearby affluent suburban school district says, "In most other high schools, serious people are in the minority. Here I can pursue the fields that interest me the most and feel challenged."

The school has been successful in two other areas as well: recruiting minority and female students into a professional field where they are embarrassingly underrepresented (only 1 percent of engineers in this country are black), and involving local businesses and industry in the school. Twenty-six major companies have provided $300,000 in funds and equipment to HSEP. Experts from Houston's engineering industries have also volunteered time to assist students on projects and to help educators in planning curriculum changes and purchasing equipment. A technologist from a major oil company who has become closely involved with HSEP comments, "At HSEP, there are college recruiters standing in line in one of the most ghettoized areas of Houston to offer kids a four-year scholarship. It's proven that you can get quality kids if you don't lower your standards.''[19]

Amherst Middle School The Amherst Middle School, located in Amherst, New Hampshire, is a handsome modern structure set in the middle of seventy-six acres of land. The school was designed and operates on the premise that students between the ages of ten and fourteen go through rapid physical and psychological changes, and the school building and curriculum must reflect and accommodate these changes.[20] Because students in this age group attain almost 90 percent of their adult size during these years, the school and its program was designed to be flexible enough to accommodate the children's need for physical activity.

Parental involvement is a hallmark of the school's program. Teachers keep parents informed of problems by communicating directly with parents. The school offers parent information nights where as many as four hundred parents attend sessions on topics such as age and learning characteristics, and how to watch TV with their children with the idea of exchanging viewpoints and values. Coffees are held during the day to get parents into the building to see what is actually occurring within the school. Parents are also involved in the building advisory committee, where they meet with teachers and administrators to talk about the program and to voice any concerns they might have.

The curriculum of the school is highly interdisciplinary. For example, the students and teachers actually operate a farm on the acreage surrounding the school. The basic philosophy is that, given the limited supply of food in the world and the possibility that sometime there could be famine in this country, students should learn how they can supplement their own food supply. The students built their own greenhouses in shop. In science classes seeds are planted, and the seedlings are transferred to the greenhouses until time for planting. When the food is harvested it is sent to the home economics class, where students learn how to preserve the food by canning. Finally, the math class figures the cost-effectiveness—whether it is cheaper to grow your own food or simply buy it at the supermarket. Once the original costs of clearing the land and purchasing equipment were discounted, the students discovered that it was cheaper to grow their own food. Students are now branching out into making decorative gourds from Indian corn, building a sugar shack to make maple syrup, and planting fir seedlings so that in eight years they will be able to harvest and sell Christmas trees.

[19]Nancy Stancill, "A High School for Engineers," *American Education* 17 (June 1981): 18–22.

[20]Paul L. Houts and Sally Banks Zakariya, "The Very Model of a Model Middle School: A Conversation with Paul D. Collins," *The National Elementary Principal* 59 (June 1980): 28–33.

The building is organized in teams of four—with one teacher from each of the four major disciplines (social studies, science, math, and language arts). Each team is assigned approximately one hundred students, and each team has the responsibility for the academic program for those students. Teams develop their own themes for study. One recent project was advertising. Students studied advertising as it appears in newspapers and on television, even computing per-page costs for advertising and texts. Another theme is consumer education. Students learned how to analyze the meat content in certain soups to determine what percentage of the soup is meat and what portion consists of other ingredients. There is a structured curriculum, but within broad limits teachers have the freedom to develop their units according to their own teaching styles.

Paul Collins, the school's principal, stresses that the key to a model middle school is a real understanding of the preadolescent student. Because of the many changes the students are experiencing in themselves, the first prerequisite in any middle school, he believes, has to be the development of positive self-concepts. "They have to feel good about themselves; they have to feel that they can be successful; they have to be happy," he states. His philosophy seems to be summed up in his words," . . . where there is caring, schools can be successful."

The Zoo School

Life in the last half of the twentieth century has been characterized by the constancy of change. New knowledge has been created or discovered at a rate unprecedented in human history, making much of what we have already learned obsolete. If this change is to continue, how can the schools best prepare students to cope and survive? One approach to this problem of preparing youth for an unknown and changing future is that employed by the John Ball Zoo School in Grand Rapids, Michigan, a one-year alternative program for highly motivated sixth-graders.[21] This school's philosophy is that the best way to prepare youngsters for an uncertain future is to teach them the skills that will help them learn whatever is necessary to cope with new problems, find jobs, survive, and prosper. In other words, the school tries to teach students *how* to learn rather than focusing on any specific body of knowledge.

The school consists of two classrooms serving fifty-two students. It is not an elitist school in terms of academic qualifications, but has only one criterion for admission: a willingness to work hard at learning. Located adjacent to the city zoo, the school has a program that focuses on environmental education and global education, the latter stressed through daily study of current events. The students make extensive use of the zoo, but the model is adaptable to any site. For example, a similar program with a

[21]Phil Schlemmer, "The Zoo School: Evolution of an Alternative," *Phi Delta Kappan* 62 (April 1981): 558–560.

focus on history might be located in a museum; or one concentrating on research might be housed in a library. No specific site is essential to carrying out the task of teaching children to learn independently.

Eight specific independent learning skills are taught at the Zoo School: reading, writing, research, planning, problem solving, self-discipline, self-evaluation, and presentation. These skills are emphasized in every course, and students are graded on how well they learn to use them. The first third of the school year is spent introducing each skill and presenting a rationale for learning it. This part of the year is highly structured, with students working in unison on tasks. The second phase of the program centers on individualized learning, with students following outlines that describe the steps of specific projects. The steps within these projects leave the student with individual decisions that make each project unique. A typical project in zoology, for example, might have each student studying a mammal and designing a presentation to teach classmates about that animal's characteristics, including habitat, food, reproduction, and methods of rearing its young. Students are evaluated on their ability to use the eight independent learning skills. In the final phase of the year, the students work on individual, independent projects. They choose from several projects that have already been planned and outlined and proceed without constant direction from the teacher. Students who have not mastered the eight skills by this time are assigned projects with more structure to insure that they do not suffer academically. There is considerable freedom for students to make major decisions about the final forms their projects will take.

A survey taken of students who attended the school during its first six years of operation and of their parents indicated high marks for the school. One hundred percent of both students and parents said they would advise a highly motivated student to attend the Zoo School. Over 80 percent of the students and parents described the Zoo School experience as "very enjoyable." As one student said, "What I like most about this school is the freedom that we have to work on our projects, and the closeness between the teachers and students here at the zoo." The school was given similar high ratings for teaching the students independent study skills, research skills, written and oral presentation skills, study skills, self-discipline, self-confidence, personal responsibility, how to accept challenges, and how to work with others. For students willing and able to work hard and assume responsibility, this type of program should help them to become productive, thinking adults.

A FINAL WORD

Having read about many educational researchers' observations in schools and classrooms, you may want to compare what they have observed with your own observations. The appendix that begins on page 190 describes several different techniques that will enable you to learn something about life in schools by direct, first-hand observation. The appendix includes guidelines about how to get the most out of your school and classroom observations, as well as specific details on how to gather information by note taking, observation systems, analysis of classroom materials, and interviews. If you are planning on observing in schools and finding out what life there is like, this appendix should be most useful to you.

Discussion Questions

1. How would you describe the importance of the environment in contributing to a child's learning?

2. Did any of Jackson's or Cuban's findings surprise you? If so, which ones and why?

3. Which research findings from the studies on the language of the classroom have the most meaning and importance for you and your approach to teaching?

4. Which characteristics of effective schools, as identified by Edmonds and Wynne, seemed to fit the high school you attended? Which characteristics were definitely absent?

5. Did your high school contain the three student subcultures that Cohen identified? To which group did you belong? Were you aware of the effects of peer pressure on your behavior?

6. What reactions did you have as you read the descriptions of the High School for the Engineering Professions, the Amherst Middle School, and the Zoo School?

For Further Reading

Goodlad, John I. *A Place Called School: Prospects for the Future.* New York: McGraw-Hill, 1983.

> The result of an eight-year study on schooling, this book gives new and fresh insights into how teachers teach and how classroom time is used.

Jackson, Philip W. *Life in Classrooms.* New York: Holt, Rinehart and Winston, 1968.

> An anthropological analysis and categorization of everyday occurrences in classrooms. To understand life in elementary school classrooms, Jackson believes we have to appreciate the cultural significance of its humdrum elements, such as repetition, waiting, interruptions, frustration, and constant rapid-fire interchanges between teacher and students.

Kaufman, Bel. *Up the Down Staircase.* Englewood Cliffs, N.J.: Prentice-Hall, 1964.

> An easy-to-read, humorous, and poignant semifictionalized account of a beginning teacher's experience in a New York City high school. A thoroughly enjoyable book.

Kohl, Herbert. *36 Children.* New York: New American Library, 1968.
    A popular account of a Harvard graduate teacher's first year in a ghetto school in Harlem. Kohl describes the students' initial hostility and the ways he overcame it. The book also describes vividly the difficult conditions under which teaching is practiced in some sections of New York City.

Mehan, Hugh. *Learning Lessons: Social Organization in the Classroom.* Cambridge, Mass.: Harvard University Press, 1979.
    A detailed analysis of the tacit rules that organize the social interactions of the classroom. Based upon a year of videotaped observations of an inner-city elementary school class.

Metz, Mary Haywood. *Classrooms and Corridors: The Crisis of Authority in Desegregated Secondary Schools.* Berkeley, Calif.: University of California Press, 1978.
    A detailed study of two desegregated secondary schools in an urban setting that examines the relationship among education, orderly conduct, and authority.

Sarason, Seymour B. *The Culture of the School and the Problem of Change.* 2nd ed. Boston: Allyn and Bacon, 1982.
    An examination of school cultures and the problems inherent in attempting to bring about change. The author highlights the importance of the role of the principal in any change process.

Smith, Louis M., and William Geoffrey. *The Complexities of an Urban Classroom.* New York: Holt, Rinehart and Winston, 1968.
    An intensive analysis of a single seventh-grade classroom with a middle-class teacher in a slum school. Beginning with a description of the behavior of the teacher and pupils as the school term starts, the authors use these data to develop a framework of initial social structure and process in the classroom.

APPENDIX: CLASSROOM OBSERVATION

This appendix is designed to help you develop skills in observing classrooms and schools. You will probably benefit most by reading the rest of this section rather quickly now and rereading it carefully before you observe schools and classrooms. The material on the following pages is somewhat technical in nature, and it is probably best assimilated when you know that you will be making use of it soon.

Virtually all teacher education programs provide opportunities for the prospective teacher to observe experienced teachers. Observation may take place "live," or it may involve viewing videotape recordings of classroom sessions. Either alternative can be extremely valuable if it offers an opportunity for insight into how a classroom is organized, how the teacher relates to different students, or how different forms of instruction can be used. On the other hand, observation of a classroom can be boring, tedious, and educationally irrelevant. What is it that makes observation valuable or worthless? The difference is a matter of knowing specifically what you are attempting to observe and why, being able to gather information accurately, and interpreting your data in order to learn from it. Thus, to really benefit from observing an actual classroom you must have some training in observational techniques.

It is physically and mechanically impossible to record *everything* that occurs in a classroom, let alone in an entire school. Thus any technique used to gather data about the classroom environment must of necessity be selective. This is a built-in and unavoidable limitation of all recording instruments and techniques of observation.

Furthermore, the background and training of the observer influence the classroom phenomena he or she chooses to focus on and the ways in which he or she interprets them. If the variable in question is aggressive behavior among students, for example, an educational psychologist may interpret a classroom outbreak as a result of the teacher's inconsistent reward pattern. An anthropologist might view it as a normal event within the youth subculture. A student teacher, because of personal needs and anxieties, might assume that the students are misbehaving because they don't really like him or her. For this reason, objective interpretation is as much of an impossibility as is comprehensive observation. But knowing the limitations of observational techniques will help the observers to interpret the data better, and being aware of their own particular perceptual habits will help them to exert caution in interpretation.

Data-Gathering Techniques

The observational methods used in education were developed by the behavioral and social sciences to gather data about and interpret complex environments; they were later found to be appropriate for use in schools as well. This section will introduce you to some of these tools and approaches, and to the kinds of preliminary decisions and subsequent interpretation which give meaning to observation. The scrupulous observer must ask certain questions: What specifically will be observed? Which method of gathering data will be most effective? What do these data mean? To learn from observation, then, the observer needs (1) objectives, (2) a way to record observations, and (3) a way to interpret observations with respect to objectives.

Observation should not be aimless. If you are to find out what life in the classroom is like, you must decide which aspects you wish to focus on. Your objective may be very broad, such as, "What does the teacher do and say during a class period?" Or it may be as narrow as "How many times does a particular student speak to another student?"

From the data that you collect you can form a hypothesis about why certain things occur, and you can test this hypothesis by making predictions about what should happen if it is correct. If your prediction is not validated, you can re-examine your data and try to develop another explanation. If your prediction is validated repeatedly, you will know that you are moving in the direction of understanding what is happening in the classroom and, possibly, why. For example, suppose your objective is to examine the teacher's verbal interaction with each individual student. After performing frequency counts—recording how many times the teacher calls on each student, or how many times each student volunteers information or asks the teacher a question—over a period of a week, you might hypothesize about the frequency distribution for the following week. If your predictions are validated you should then try to interpret your findings. Was the teacher displaying a bias against certain students? Did the teacher systematically ignore the students seated in a particular part of the room? Were certain groups of students treated in particular ways, e.g., girls, or certain socio-economic groups? Caution must be exercised in drawing conclusions, however, because rival hypotheses may explain the same phenomena.

The point to be emphasized is that in order to understand the happenings in a classroom, you must select objectives which provide you with a focus. Since you can't see, hear, and interpret everything, you must be selective. To be selective, you must establish the purpose of your observation.

You may find one of the following techniques of data gathering particularly appropriate, given your objectives, the equipment available, and the degree of access you have to a school. All have been used profitably by classroom observers.

NOTE TAKING   Probably the most common means of gathering data in the school is note taking. The method is borrowed from cultural anthropologists, who take copious notes of their observations while living with the natives of an unfamiliar culture. You can use the same approach to accumulate information about the interpersonal relationships, values, or social status of individuals in a class.

If you choose the note-taking approach, certain preliminary decisions will have to be made. First, how comprehensive should your notes be? You will be attempting to record everything you see that relates to your objective. Thus the broader your objective, the more you will have to record. In many instances it will be difficult for you to decide quickly on the relevance of a specific event. A handy rule of thumb: when in doubt, write it down. Too much information is better than not enough, for insufficient data can lead to frustration and to erroneous conclusions.

Second, should you write a description of what you see and hear, or should you simply record what is said verbatim? Should you write down your impressions of incidents, or should you be as objective as possible? We recommend that, whenever possible, data be recorded verbatim. In trying to summarize or describe what takes place you are likely to substitute your own perceptions of what took place for what was actually happening. If you wish also to record your impressions, insights, inferences, and comments, keep them in the margin or draw brackets around them in order to distinguish them from the raw data. This distinction is crucial, because of the tendency to make inferences based on selected perceptions or personal biases. If we are happy, we tend to see happy people; if tired, we see the teacher's and students' behavior through the filter of fatigue and interpret it accordingly. We may see relationships that don't actually exist and miss ones that do. Therefore, recognizing that complete objectivity is impossible, we should still aim to achieve it rather than relying on our own interpretations of events.

You will find that recording nonverbal behavior tends to be much more impressionistic than recording verbal behavior. If we observe a student fidgeting in his seat, picking his nose, and looking out the window, it is tempting to assert that he is bored; yet that is an inference. Keep checking on yourself to make sure you are distinguishing between actual behavior and inferences drawn from behavior.

It is much easier to be comprehensive in your note taking if you establish a standard format and abbreviations. For example, indenting student comments will help you distinguish them from teacher comments and will save you from repeatedly having to indicate who is talking. Abbreviating words by omitting vowels, employing homonyms and using phonetic representations will also allow you to record more efficiently and quickly.

Note taking has a number of advantages as a means of gathering data about classroom actions. It is relatively simple and very economical. You can flip back and forth in your notes easily when you begin to interpret the data. The notes can be cut up and juxtaposed in whatever fashion you want to help you discern patterns or repeated themes. Ideas and events can be assimilated rapidly by scanning written notes. The notes constitute a permanent record, which you can keep to compare with other observations and to develop, support, or reject hypotheses.

A major disadvantage of note taking is the difficulty of recording everything you see and hear. Even though you have selected limited objectives to guide your observations, action often develops so fast that you fall behind and miss some of what is said or done. Taking notes forces you to keep your eyes on the paper in front of you, and prevents you from observing the class uninterruptedly. In other words, your observation system tends to become overloaded with stimuli. Nevertheless, note taking is probably the most frequently used method of gathering data in the classroom.

STANDARDIZED OBSERVATION SYSTEMS   Standardized observation systems make use of lists of categories—as minuscule as sneezes or smiles or as broad as teacher-student rapport—to record the verbal or nonverbal interaction in the classroom.

Although many observation systems have been developed, only a few are in general use. Probably the best-known category system for observing teachers and pupils is Flanders's Interaction Analysis, described earlier in the chapter (pages 169–171). You will remember that Interaction Analysis is a technique for categorizing direct and indirect verbal behavior in the classroom.

Flanders identified ten different categories of verbal behavior; the first seven apply to teacher talk, the next two to student talk, and the final category records silence or confusion. The categories are: (1) accepting student feelings; (2) giving praise; (3) accepting, clarifying, or making use of a student's ideas; (4) asking a question; (5) lecturing, giving facts or opinions; (6) giving directions; (7) giving criticism; (8) student response; (9) student initiation; and (10) confusion or silence. Categories 1–4 represent indirect teacher influence, while categories 5–7 represent direct teacher influence. An observer using Flanders's system records every three seconds the category of verbal behavior occurring that instant; then an analysis is made of verbal interaction during the entire class period. Thus a profile of the teacher's direct or indirect influence can be obtained.

Flanders's system has limitations, but it can be a helpful and informative tool in analyzing a certain kind of verbal behavior in the classroom. It has been used extensively, and considerable research data has been collected. Instructional booklets and audiotapes are available to students interested in learning to use the system and interpret data. Many universities and colleges, as well as public schools, have used Interaction Analysis to help teachers analyze their teaching.

If you are interested in learning more about other observation systems, the following books and articles will be helpful:

Acheson, Keith A., and Meredith Damien Gall. *Techniques in the Clinical Supervision of Teachers.* New York: Longman Inc., 1980.
Simon, Anita, and E. Gil Boyer, eds. *Mirrors for Behavior: An Anthology of Classroom Observation Instruments.* Philadelphia: Research for Better Schools, Inc., 1967.
Hansen, John. "Observation Skills." In *Classroom Teaching Skills: A Handbook.* Ed. J. M. Cooper. Lexington, Mass.: D. C. Heath, 1977.

ANALYSIS OF ARTIFACTS   Much can be learned about life in the classroom without directly observing teachers and students. The textbooks and supplementary materials in use can reveal a lot to the careful observer. Similarly, the tests given, the placement of chairs and desks, the materials displayed on the bulletin board, and the audiovisual equipment used (or neglected) are clues about what activities take place and what kind of learning is valued. What kinds of questions are on the examinations? Do they emphasize the acquisition of facts to the exclusion of solving problems, analyzing or synthesizing ideas, making evaluations, comparing or contrasting different points of view, drawing inferences from limited data, or forming generalizations? Do the chairs and desks always face the teacher, the dominant person in the classroom? Or are they frequently grouped in small circles, indicating opportunities for pupil-pupil interaction? Is a multimedia approach used so that students may learn from a variety of sources?

You probably have the idea by now—clues about what a teacher thinks is important, whether students are involved in instruction as well as learning, and how the teacher views his or her role can be garnered by a careful analysis of materials used and produced in the classroom. Valuable inferences may be made from data available to the naked eye; it is crucial to remember that such inferences are only hypotheses and that additional data must be gathered to confirm or invalidate them.

INTERVIEWS   Interviewing teachers, students, administrators, counselors, librarians, and other school personnel is an excellent way to gather data about life in school. People who play different roles in the school, and thus see it from different vantage points, often have highly disparate views of it. The cook in the school kitchen may have a very different opinion of the food's quality than do the students or the teachers, and the administrator's view of detention hall is probably very unlike the students'. Questioning the students about what occupies most of their time in the classroom, what they think the school's purpose is, why they go to school, or how their good teachers differ from the poor ones can produce fascinating and highly valuable data. Some sample questions, the answers to which should help you better understand life in a particular school, are listed below:

1. Where is the school located in the community?
2. How old is the school?
3. Is it a parent-, teacher-, administration-, or student-centered school? What evidence leads you to your conclusion?
4. Does the school have an adjoining playground or recreational area? When is it used most—before, after, or during school?
5. Is there a school library? Where is it? How does a student gain access to it? What are the library procedures?
6. Where is the nurse's office? What are the major concerns of the health administrator in this school? What are the major complaints (types of illnesses)? What are the procedures for being sent home or remaining in the health office?

7. Where does physical education take place? What is the usual activity? Who participates? What do students do if they are not participating?

8. What is the procedure for tardy students?

9. Who administers this procedure?

10. Do students move from one classroom to another during the school day? How is this accomplished?

11. Is there a dress code? Who decided on its standards? How are infractions handled?

12. What are some frequent causes of disciplinary action against students?

13. What is the system for reinstating a student who has been suspended or expelled?

14. Is there a teachers' lounge? What is the function of this lounge?

15. Are teachers allowed to make educational decisions? If so, what kind?

16. How does a student make an appointment to see the principal or a counselor? What is the usual waiting period?

17. Does the student council have any real power to promote change in the school? If the answer is yes, ask for some examples.

18. Does the student council represent the entire student body, or is it a select group?

19. Do parents come to the school? If so, when and for what reasons?

20. Is there a lunchroom in the school? Describe the facility. Do students congregate in identifiable patterns during lunch?

21. Are there extracurricular activities? Music, sports, clubs, meetings?

22. Does the school empty faster at the end of the day or during a fire drill?

23. If you are investigating a secondary school, does it have a newspaper? Ask the editor or a staffer what its function is and how much freedom students have to print what they wish.

24. Is there an auditorium? How often is it used? Why?

25. Are students bussed to school? Ride a school bus one day to see what it's like. Is it different in the morning from the afternoon?

26. Listen to the students' language, in class and out. Any difference?

27. Ask an administrator, secretary, custodian, teacher, librarian, and nurse to describe the student population.

28. Are students trusted? What evidence can you find one way or the other?

29. Are teachers trusted? Must they sign in and out? In what areas of school life do they have decision-making power?

30. What is unusual about this school?

31. Which students are most popular with their peers? Which are most respected? If there is a difference, why?

32. Which teachers are most popular with students? Which are most respected? If there is a difference, why?

33. What do the school's administrators do? What are their major areas of responsibility? What are the major pressures on them?[22]

VIDEO- AND AUDIOTAPES   Public schools and colleges are making increasing use of mechanical recording devices as analytical and training tools. Audiotape recorders have been available for quite a while, but portable videotape recorders are a relatively recent innovation. Both devices, particularly videotape recorders, have enabled teachers and researchers to analyze what happens in the classroom more completely and objectively. Videotape recorders can register both the image and the sound of classroom interaction, and the resulting record is more accurate and comprehensive than either notes or an observation schedule. Videotapes have many other advantages: the tapes can be replayed without limit; they are reusable after erasing; the fast forward and rewind components make it possible to locate or repeat a particular passage quickly; and the data can be stored almost indefinitely.

The same criteria or objectives may be applied to taped data as to live observation. The advantage, of course, is that something that is missed in the first viewing can be repeated until the viewer has absorbed it—a luxury unavailable in live observation. You might wish to analyze verbal interactions using Flanders's Interaction Analysis, or to watch the behavior of a particular child, or to count the number of encouraging gestures the teacher makes towards students. The possibilities are endless.

Many teacher education programs are collecting videotapes to demonstrate particular classroom phenomena to prospective teachers, some showing only a single "critical incident." The tape can be stopped to allow speculation about how the teacher will or should respond, started again to view the teacher's actual actions, and stopped for further discussion.

We have not attempted to train you in the techniques, methods, and tools of classroom observation, believing that this is better and more appropriately accomplished as part of your teacher education program. Instead, we have tried to acquaint you with methods that have been and are currently being used by educators to gain a greater understanding of school environments.

[22]The authors are indebted to Professor Emma Cappelluzzo of the University of Massachusetts for many of these questions. Used by permission.

What Is Taught?

7

The curriculum of the schools is examined constantly by teachers, professors, textbook publishers, and parents. What should be taught in the schools? What is taught? What freedoms and constraints are placed on teachers regarding what they can teach? What freedoms and constraints should be placed on teachers? The 1960s was a decade of much new curriculum development in the sciences, mathematics, social studies, English, and foreign languages. In the 1970s many educators questioned the impact and relevance of these curricula for the needs of individual students and society. The 1980s will probably see the continuation of a search for the most appropriate curriculum for American students and schools.

This chapter emphasizes that:

▪ The school curriculum, which has evolved over time through the influence of several different motives, consists of all the organized and intended experiences of the student for which the school accepts responsibility.

▪ Major curriculum reforms occurred in the 1950s and 1960s in science, mathematics, social studies, language arts, and foreign languages. The impact of these curriculum reforms has diminished considerably since their heyday in the 1960s and early 1970s.

▪ The relevance of the schools' curricula to individual and societal problems is a continually debated issue. Three major trends today in the academic subject-matter curriculum are the structure-of-knowledge approach, an emphasis on integrated studies, and establishment of basic education schools.

▪ Textbooks have such a strong impact on what is taught in the classrooms that some people argue that texts represent a national curriculum.

▪ Major curricular and instructional practices currently utilized in the schools include individualized instruction, mastery learning techniques, and open education.

*B*ASEBALL, DEBATING, READING, BIOLOGY. . . . Yes, along with love, toler-ance, and independence. Frustration as well as mathematics and dra-matics. Values and ceramics, woodshop and poise, history and boredom, auto mechanics and leadership—all are learned in school, some intention-ally, and others in reaction to or in spite of the teachers' intentions.

We define the *curriculum* as all the organized and intended experi-ences of the student for which the school accepts responsibility. In other words, the curriculum is not just the intellectual content of the subjects taught, but also the methods used to teach it, the interactions that occur between people, and the school-sponsored activities that contribute to "life experience."

During your high school years, many daily activities organized under the auspices of the school were probably considered "extracurricular." The formal courses of study—history, science, mathematics, English—were cur-ricular, whereas participation on the football team, cheerleading, Future Teachers Club, or the band belonged to another, lesser, category. But, we ask, shouldn't all activities that are school sponsored and contribute to the growth and development of the students be considered part of the curric-ulum? We strongly suspect that informal learning experiences are at least as important to intellectual and social development as are the formal courses of study. Consider, for example, the following list of goals.[1] Choose the three or four you consider most important and decide whether each is best achieved in a context of formal courses, informal school experiences, or a combination of the two:

1. develop skills in reading, writing, speaking, and listening
2. develop pride in work and a feeling of self-worth
3. develop good character and self-respect
4. develop a desire for learning now and in the future
5. learn to respect and get along with people with whom we work and live
6. learn how to examine and use information
7. gain a general education
8. learn how to be a good citizen
9. learn about and try to understand the changes that take place in the world
10. understand and practice democratic ideas and ideals
11. learn how to respect and get along with people who think, dress, and act differently
12. understand and practice the skills of family living

[1]These eighteen goals were part of a questionnaire given to a sample of Phi Delta Kappans. The results of the questionnaire can be found in the September 1973 issue of *Phi Delta Kappan,* pp. 29–32.

13. gain information needed to make job selections
14. learn how to be a good manager of money, property, and resources
15. practice and understand the ideas of health and safety
16. develop skills to enter a specific field of work
17. learn how to use leisure time
18. appreciate culture and beauty in the world

A strong argument could be made that each of these goals is best attained by a combination of formal and informal learning experiences. Some, certainly, cannot be achieved through formal educational channels alone. Nevertheless, most of the efforts that go into curriculum development are still concentrated around traditional subject matter. The typical elementary or high school is organized according to subject-matter divisions. Some historical background may help explain the current strong emphasis on traditional subject-matter areas.

WHERE DOES THE EXISTING CURRICULUM COME FROM?

Curricula are always changing in one way or another. Nevertheless, we can distinguish between sweeping changes that represent new philosophies of learning and teaching and minor adjustments that leave the overall curriculum relatively intact. What follows is not a thorough history of American curriculum revision, but a brief overview of the educational philosophies that have prompted major curriculum change, to help you better understand the motives that molded today's curriculum.

Shifting Motives

Two curriculum writers have identified five major motives that have held sway more or less consecutively and have dominated the development of the curriculum in American schools: (1) religious motives, (2) political motives, (3) utilitarian motives, (4) the movement for mass education, and (5) the movement for excellence in education.[2]

The religious motive held sway from approximately 1635 to 1770, when the schools were expected to promulgate the religious beliefs of the community. The period 1770–1860 was characterized by a politically motivated desire to produce a literate populace in order to insure the preservation of liberty and the new democratic form of government. Utilitarian goals from 1860 to 1920 resulted from the pressure of a rapidly expanding economy for educated people to fill the new jobs that were being created. The mass education motive (1920 to the present) is a product of the belief that all children are entitled to equal educational opportunities. Although this principle is widely espoused, it has yet to be fully achieved. The movement for excellence in education (1957 to the late 1960s) was prepared for by the discovery during World War II that many high school graduates

[2]J. Minor Gwynn and John Chase, Jr., eds., *Curriculum Principles and Social Trends* (New York: Macmillan, 1969), pp. 1–29.

SCHOOLS: THE PRESENT

were virtually illiterate in mathematics and science, but concern and action lagged until 1957, when the Soviet Union's launching of Sputnik focused on the public schools the most critical attention they had received in decades. Sagging SAT scores have refocused attention during the past decade on the need for excellence in education.

Sputnik and the
Reaction
to Progressivism

When the Russians launched Sputnik, the American public—which had complacently believed American schools to be far superior to any other country's—reacted against what they considered the "softness" of the curriculum and demanded a return to the "meat and potatoes" of learning—the academic disciplines, with particular emphasis on science and mathematics. More students were competing for college entrance, and middle-class parents wanted to make sure their children were prepared for the increased competition. During the so-called progressive education era of the twenties, thirties, and forties, the schools had emphasized citizenship and self-adjustment. If the progressive curriculum can be seen as child-centered or society-centered, curriculum development during the fifties and sixties must be considered discipline-centered; this approach was characterized at the time as a return to excellence in education, though many critics today question the superiority of such a disciplinary approach.

Prosperity was a major factor in the extensive curricular change of the fifties and sixties. The middle class saw education as the path to a good life for their children. The more education one received, the more likely one was to earn a good income and enjoy the comforts of life. As a result, the public was willing to spend increasing amounts of money for education. As is so often the case, however, action lagged behind intentions until Sputnik's launching triggered intense awareness of the public school curriculum. Because of its concern for national defense and worldwide prestige, the federal government poured huge amounts of money into curriculum development projects, teacher-training workshops, and research. The influence of the federal government on the development of new curricula cannot be underestimated. Prior to this period the federal government had played a limited role in education, which was considered the exclusive responsibility of the individual states. During the 1950s the role of the federal government in public education was a hotly debated issue; the outcome is obvious in the fact that federal involvement in education is taken for granted today, although the form of involvement is currently in doubt as the Reagan administration attempts to implement its educational policies.

Another contributory factor was the tremendous postwar knowledge explosion, which was forcing new approaches to curriculum planning by making many areas of the existing curricula obsolete. In addition, a combination of social and political factors encouraged a new approach to the educational needs of the country, including new emphases in multicultural and bilingual education.

Curriculum Reform in the 1960s and 1970s

The curriculum reform movement was crystallized by the publication in 1960 of *The Process of Education,*[3] a short book by Jerome Bruner, a Harvard psychologist. Bruner's ideas, though by no means entirely original with him, were the most profound and elegant expression of the spirit and convictions behind the movement for curriculum change. Bruner's basic thesis was that any discipline could be and should be studied, at any level of complexity, in terms of its "structure." Bruner defined the structure of a discipline as the concepts and methods of inquiry that are its most basic

[3]Jerome S. Bruner, *The Process of Education* (New York: Random House, 1960).

JEROME BRUNER
(1915–   )

Jerome Bruner achieved a certain fame among Harvard psychology students for his imitations of babies, baboons, and slow lorises, and for his sparkling enthusiasm for knowledge and discovery. Outside the Harvard community, however, he is better known for his studies of child development and his important work in educational psychology and curricular reform.

Bruner grew up in Lawrence, Long Island, where he spent his childhood fishing, sailing, and reading voraciously. He remembers that school was no challenge—it was too easy—and that he was always looking for something new to read. His father, a German-Jewish watch manufacturer, died when Bruner was twelve. After high school, Bruner went to Duke University for his B.A., and received a Ph.D. in psychology from Harvard in 1941. He served in the Office of War Information and then returned to Harvard, where he remained until moving to Oxford University in England in 1972. He remained at Oxford until 1979 when he returned to Harvard as a Sloan Foundation Fellow.

Bruner joined the critics of American education twenty-five years ago, when he served as secretary of a conference of scientists, scholars, and educators at Woods Hole, Massachusetts, on the teaching of science. For years there had been a gulf between "serious" psychology and such mundane matters as pedagogy; scholars looked down their noses at what they considered the province of teachers' colleges. The only exception was B. F. Skinner, the renowned behaviorist, who has done pioneering work on teaching machines and programmed instruction. Bruner's report on the Woods Hole conference, *The Process of Education,* was hailed as a major contribution to curriculum reform and won him instant fame. It has since been translated into twenty-two languages and is studied by teachers all over the world. The most memorable statement in the report, and the gist of Bruner's argument, is quoted widely: "Any subject can be taught effectively in some intellectually honest form to any child at any stage of development." According to Bruner, a school subject is not something one "knows about," but something one "knows how to do." It is a way of thinking and doing, rather than a collection of facts.

In keeping with his famous statement of two decades ago, Bruner developed a fifth-grade social studies curriculum called *Man: A Course of Study,* which provides ten-year-olds with materials like those social scientists use and en-

components. Instead of studying random facts or incidental phenomena, students should learn the principles that constitute the heart of a discipline. A knowledge of fundamentals would enable the student to inquire into and solve problems in the discipline independently. Learning the structure of a discipline would equip the student to transfer useful concepts from one situation to another, or, in other words, to learn how to learn. This Bruner considered crucial, because the totality of knowledge in any discipline is too massive for anyone to acquire, and because knowledge changes so rapidly that what is current one year might be out of date the next. Bruner urged that students be provided opportunities to become problem solvers

courages them to investigate what is human about human beings. The course, which includes units on the life cycle of the salmon, on baboons, and on the Netsilik Eskimos, was adopted by many schools during the 1960s and 1970s.

In 1960 Bruner and psychologist George Miller organized Harvard's Center for Cognitive Studies, where they investigated the sensorimotor acts of infants—sucking, looking, reaching, grasping—as if they were observing the behavior of an unknown species. From these simple, innate activities, babies develop four crucial abilities: voluntary control of their behavior; internal control of their attention; the power to carry out several actions simultaneously; and the use of reciprocal codes that pave the way for speech. By studying infants long before they learn to talk, Bruner and others have concluded that

language competence is just one aspect of the infant's ability to systematize learning. They suggest that the human mind is equipped with programs for the development of finer and more adaptable skills, not only for language but also for the use of hands, eyes, and tools. If they succeed in decoding these mysteries of the mind, the implications for education will be profound.

Bruner advocates more problem seeking and problem solving for all learners, from infants to college students. He has proposed a dual curriculum for colleges that could satisfy both traditionalists and innovators. On Mondays, Wednesdays, and Fridays, students would continue to take traditional courses; on Tuesdays and Thursdays they would be free to govern their learning in experimental ways. This experimentation might include taking part in university budget decisions and teacher evaluation and, most important,

learning to deal rationally with their own problems.

One way to implement such a dual curriculum is to make basic changes in student living arrangements. Bruner acted on his interest in extracurricular learning by becoming master of Currier House, a Harvard-Radcliffe coed residence. He helped solicit private funds for a day care center at the house, and invited people from many spheres of life to dine with students. He and his students wanted Currier House to serve as an example of how a community can encourage and make use of its members' initiative to deal with its own problems, both simple ones like the care of babies and large ones like drug abuse. Rather than limiting the curriculum to course work, Bruner sees the dual curriculum as an opportunity for students to put knowledge to work in their own lives.

through direct and prolonged experience with objects or raw data, in the same way that a historian studies history or a biologist biology. Teachers were encouraged to let students discover meanings for themselves. This *discovery* (or inquiry) *method*, Bruner asserted, would make it possible to teach young children complex concepts in language they could understand. Having learned a concept on a simplified level, they could later return to it at a somewhat more advanced level. Thus the concepts fundamental to the discipline's structure would be studied over and over throughout the school years, but each time from an increasingly complex point of view. The curriculum of the discipline would resemble a spiral; as students moved along the spiral, they would re-encounter familiar concepts in more complex forms.

Bruner's ideas alone did not cause the tremendous curriculum reforms of the 1950s and 1960s; many forces for change were already in motion prior to the publication of *The Process of Education*. However, Bruner's concept of the structure of disciplines catalyzed the already widespread reaction to the fusion of disciplines that had occurred in the schools, and it was implemented in numerous curriculum development projects. These projects had considerable impact on the public schools' curricula, particularly in the areas of mathematics, biology, chemistry, physics, and foreign languages. Their influence on social studies and English was not so great, because there were so many different social studies projects that their impact was diffused, and because little agreement was reached regarding objectives and methods for teaching English.

The new projects generally had less impact at the elementary level than at the secondary level, with the notable exception of mathematics and, possibly, science. Many elementary educators considered the study of distinct disciplines inappropriate to the elementary school. They felt that the significant problems of humanity could not be studied through the disciplinary approach, and called instead for an integrating curriculum that would treat life as something whole rather than piecemeal. They also were concerned that emphasis on underlying concepts, abstractions, and intuitive behavior would lead to neglect of practical operations and applications. Since the new curricula were designed to reform disciplines already well established in the schools, it appeared to many that they would leave no room for emerging fields. But probably more than anything else, the elementary educators objected to planning from the top down, from the secondary to the elementary level, which failed to take into account sufficiently the developmental processes of young children as learners—their interests, their individual differences, and the irregularity of their growth. To them, curriculum reform seemed to be putting the discipline before the child.

At this point, it would probably be useful for you to examine briefly what is currently taught in elementary and secondary schools.

WHAT IS THE PRESENT CURRICULUM?

Looking at the courses of study prescribed by the fifty states, one discovers that the similarities far outweigh the differences. We will discuss some of the reasons for this phenomenon later, but in the meantime let's examine what is presently taught in elementary and secondary schools across the country.

At both levels the curriculum is organized into subject-matter areas, which ordinarily are science, mathematics, social studies, foreign languages, English, reading and language arts, the fine arts, and physical education; the latter three areas tend to emphasize developing skills rather than mastery of a particular body of knowledge.

In some elementary schools all subjects are taught by one teacher; other schools bring in specialists to teach the fine arts and physical education, and still others hire specialists to teach reading, science, and mathematics.

Science

Science instruction in elementary schools is, to put it simply, in a state of flux. In an effort to "catch up with the Russians," a number of science curriculum revision projects were funded by the National Science Foundation and other federal agencies after the launching of Sputnik in 1957. These projects—which were developed by people of diverse backgrounds, including leading scientists, science educators, teachers, psychologists, educational evaluators, and artists—differed in format and intention, but each called for new teaching roles. The teacher was no longer considered the fount of knowledge. Instead of dominating the learner, the teacher was to create an open, nonthreatening atmosphere that would offer the child numerous opportunities to manipulate scientific objects and materials. In addition, the teacher was discouraged from simply *telling* the students answers and encouraged to allow them to ask questions, face problems, and pose tentative solutions; he or she was to foster an environment that would encourage a discovery or inquiry approach. Since these teacher skills differ fundamentally from those demanded by more traditional programs in science, a number of workshops were funded by the National Science Foundation to train teachers in the new approaches.

In the late 1960s, the discipline approach to science instruction was criticized for overemphasizing theory and ignoring the need for practical application. Many of the science projects had been too specialized to be applied to anything other than scientific research. These curricula appealed to budding scientists, but they did not help the average student identify the role of science in solving problems of society, particularly such problems as air pollution, overpopulation, and depletion of natural resources. More recently, a new trend to humanize the sciences has emerged.

This trend to humanize the elementary science curriculum has resulted in a multidisciplinary approach to instruction. This approach applies

basic laws of science to seeking solutions to problems faced by society. In using this approach, science teachers are often called on to work with teachers from other disciplines to help students relate scientific principles to social, political, and economic problems.

Unlike the elementary science programs, the secondary programs are generally still organized around the disciplines of biology, chemistry, and physics. As such, they appeal to a minority of students. The secondary science programs, we believe, could profit from an approach similar to that of the elementary programs' efforts to humanize the science curriculum.

Despite all the curriculum development efforts of the 1960s, a recent National Science Foundation study reported that 90 percent of teachers have now returned to the traditional textbook approach.[4] Enrollment in high school science courses has been decreasing steadily. More than one-half of high school students today take no science at all after the tenth grade. Only 4 percent of classes in elementary school science are taught in

[4]Edward B. Fiske, "Science's Heyday in the Schools Is Past," *The New York Times*, section 12 (April 22, 1979): 1, 14.

special science rooms, and more than one-third of the instruction is done with no special science equipment. At both the elementary and secondary levels, lecturing and reading from a single textbook is the predominant method of teaching. Laboratory instruction, a basic part of the inquiry-based curriculum, is disappearing.[5]

Mathematics

Before the 1950s, schools emphasized student mastery of basic computational skills. In the 1960s, a new type of mathematics curriculum—known as the *new math*—was developed. It viewed mathematics as a language that both communicates ideas about numbers and describes the quantitative aspects of ideas and objects. As a result, the new math stressed *structure* rather than drill and computational skills. The new math tended toward being abstract, and for the average student its conceptual theories were of little practical use.

Although some die-hard traditionalists advocate returning to the teaching of good old 'rithmetic, this seems both unwise and unlikely. If a renewed emphasis on computational skills is needed, the emphasis should occur within the new curricular emphases of the past thirty years, not by a return to an outmoded content.

Several trends seem likely in mathematics education for the 1980s. First, mathematics programs will continue to seek a balanced curriculum by stressing the interdependence of skills, mathematical content, and application. No one of these three areas will receive an undue focus at the expense of the other two.

Second, mathematics will become more integrated with other subject areas. That is, mathematical skills will be applied in a variety of situations, from home economics to social studies. Rather than focusing on mathematics primarily as a separate discipline, distinct unto itself, schools will emphasize its practical uses in other subject areas, particularly personal finance and consumer mathematics.

Third, mathematics will be made more relevant by an increased use of technology, particularly the use of calculators and computers. The advent of the inexpensive pocket calculator has caused some people to worry that people might lose the ability to perform fundamental arithmetical computations. Schools will continue to teach arithmetical skills, but there is no denying the fact that pocket calculators are here for good. Whether the population will suffer a loss of computational skills as a result remains to be seen. The use of microcomputers and computer programming in mathematics classes has added a great deal of relevance for many students. Not only do the computers add interest to the curriculum, but students are receiving valuable experience that may prove useful as they seek jobs.

[5]"Inquiry-Based Science Studies Are Giving Way to Rote Learning, NRC Says," *Phi Delta Kappan* 61 (November 1979): 225.

Social studies—the study of people, their ideas, actions, and relationships—is not a discipline in the same sense as are mathematics or science, although it draws on the various social science disciplines (history, geography, political science, economics, psychology, sociology, and anthropology) for its content and methods of inquiry. (A *discipline* has been defined as an area of inquiry containing a distinctive body of concepts and principles, with techniques for exploring the area and for correcting and expanding the body of knowledge.[6]) In contrast to the sciences and mathematics, fundamental concepts and processes have not been identified and agreed on by curriculum builders in social studies. History has traditionally been the leading discipline of the social studies, at both the elementary and secondary levels, and, although some inroads have been made by other disciplines, history still remains dominant.

The pattern of courses taken in high school has also remained relatively standard for the past thirty or forty years. Civics and world history are traditionally taken in the ninth and tenth grades, although many students take no social studies courses then. American history is usually taken in the eleventh grade. Problems of democracy and elective courses such as

[6]Arthur W. Foshay, "Knowledge and the Structure of the Disciplines," in *The Nature of Knowledge: Implications for the Education of Teachers,* ed. William A. Jenkins (Milwaukee: University of Wisconsin, 1961).

LOGO: THE SIMPLE COMPUTER LANGUAGE FOR CHILDREN

Logo is a simple computer language created for use with young children, and is particularly suited for teaching mathematical and logical operations. The major tool of Logo is the turtle, a graphic symbol on the video screen that responds to commands to go forward, backward, right, or left. The turtle can leave a trail or line behind it as it moves. These turtle graphics make Logo an immediately interactive language.

Students learn important geometrical and mathematical concepts, as well as logic and problem solving. Rooted in the theory of Jean Piaget, Logo allows students to control both the learning environment and the technology in order to plan their work, develop a logical sequence, and then test it. Logo teaches programming, employs graphics, and promotes problem solving. Logo's math-ematical functions include basic arithmetic, algebra, trigonometry, and calculus.

The major appeal of Logo is that it is easy to learn, easy to use, and fun. The language is compatible with most microcomputers, and software packages are relatively inexpensive. More and more school districts are using Logo as the basic language for their computer-education programs, particularly in the elementary grades.

© 1970 United Feature Syndicate Inc.

economics, American government, and sociology are taken in the twelfth grade.

In the elementary schools, the social studies receive little attention, serving primarily as another opportunity to teach reading and writing skills. Where social studies is taught, history and geography are the dominant disciplines. The approach at all levels is a textbook-centered curriculum. This may not be bad, however, as a report commissioned by the National Science Foundation concludes that the most important contribution of the new social studies programs developed in the 1960s to the improvement of education was "their impact on the development of instructional materials by commercial publishers."[7]

In the 1960s over forty new social studies projects were developed. Some of these focused on individual disciplines, such as anthropology, geography, and political science, whereas others focused on interdisciplinary approaches. Like most of the other curriculum development projects of the 1960s, social studies projects stressed inductive teaching. Students were expected to find generalizations from data.

Today, the social studies curriculum is a hodgepodge of different approaches and is in a state of disarray. The "back-to-basics" movement has re-emphasized the need for history and government at the secondary levels, but the emphasis on reading and writing has relegated social studies programs at the elementary school level to a back seat. In Texas, for example, the state does not provide social studies textbooks to school districts for grades one through three. Because most districts cannot afford to buy their own textbooks, this has the effect of eliminating formal social studies curricula in those grades. Time formerly spent on social studies is now spent on reading and writing.

[7]BCMA Associates, "Commercial Curriculum Development and Implementation in the United States," *Pre-College Science Curriculum Activities of the National Science Foundation*, Vol. II and Appendix (Washington, D.C.: National Science Foundation, May 1975), pp. 166, 167.

Language Arts and English

The language arts program seeks to develop in children the skills of reading, writing, speaking, and listening, and a knowledge of culture as represented in English language literature. The importance of language arts cannot be overemphasized, since no subject can be successfully studied without adequate language skills. Most elementary language arts programs share the common goal of developing in the student the following abilities:

1. intelligent use of common modes of communication
2. the ability to talk formally and informally with and to a group and individuals, and to listen effectively and courteously
3. the ability to read analytically and critically for information

---

CURRICULUM USES OF THE COMPUTER AT ONE SCHOOL

In 1975 Milton Academy in Massachusetts bought a minicomputer. (Microcomputers were not available then.) Since that time, in addition to many administrative uses, the computer has been used by faculty and students in the following ways for curriculum and instructional purposes:

▪ in social studies, for students to simulate problems requiring social solutions, to develop puzzles related to European history, and to analyze survey data from questionnaires developed by students on topics such as teenagers' use of alcohol and tobacco

▪ in mathematics, to individualize assignments for students by developing more than two dozen programs, including drill-and-practice programs, calculus demonstra-tions, curve-fitting routines, and general-purpose graphing and square-root finding routines

▪ in physics, to simulate the Millikan oil drop experiment, which determines the unit charge of an electron, in lieu of the actual experiment

▪ in reading, in grades three through six, using a program called MAZE, to produce one-of-a-kind paper-and-pencil mazes that are useful as spatial-relations exercises for students with certain kinds of learning disabilities

In addition, students developed programs for a variety of purposes, including:

▪ correlating U.S. senators' voting records on civil rights with other variables

▪ solving simple equations in the manner of a geometry proof (winning, incidentally, first prize in a national programming contest for students)

▪ producing strings of large block letters in a variety of sizes, which teachers in the lower school found useful for posters

▪ maintaining memberships for several extracurricular clubs

▪ keeping the hockey team's statistics

▪ typing and justifying the margins of the student newspaper

These are only a few examples of the many and varied curriculum uses of the computer that were implemented at Milton Academy. These examples demonstrate what a powerful and useful instructional device the computer can be.

Andrew A. Zucker, "The Computer in the School: A Case Study," *Phi Delta Kappan* 63 (January 1982): 317–319.

4. enthusiasm for continued learning through communication

5. facility with the English language through awareness of language patterns and structure, and effective skills in writing including spelling and handwriting

6. ability to use the tools of the language arts, particularly the dictionary, encyclopedias, and other reference and resource materials[8]

Language arts curricula must be organized to foster continuous growth and increasing sophistication in the four major skill areas during the elementary years, and graded elementary schools ordinarily employ sequential curricula. As the other curriculum areas did, language arts and English underwent revision in the 1960s. One thrust of this revision was to make English more relevant and meaningful to disadvantaged students by shifting to using examples of contemporary writing, including selections by black authors. Standard English and traditional grammar gave way to exploring acceptable alternative grammatical structures, without prescribing proper and improper usage. English classes offered improvised drama, imaginative writing, personal response to literature, and informal classroom discussion.

Language arts and English education have drawn considerable criticism in recent years, as many graduating students find they do not possess the basic reading and writing skills needed for employment. Additionally, college entrance exam scores indicate that verbal skills have declined in recent years. Discontent with student verbal skills has led to a "back-to-basics" movement, which many parents, students, and teachers support. This emphasis on a return to the teaching of fundamental skills in more traditional ways has had considerable impact on the language arts curriculum in many school districts. The result has been a demand for more reading of classical literature and more learning of traditional grammar, and an increased emphasis on formal rather than personal writing. There is also a return to the workbook and the hard-cover anthology. Recently there has been a shift from "relevant" literature back to the classics. In addition, many religious fundamentalists have objected to the reading material taught in schools. The banning of books has risen in America over the last eight years, with such books as J. D. Salinger's *The Catcher In The Rye* and Mark Twain's *Huckleberry Finn* being removed from both school libraries and reading lists in a number of school districts.

With the strong emphasis on competency testing to insure that students who are promoted do possess minimum skills, language arts and English are placing strong emphasis on a grammar-dominated curriculum that lends itself to standardized testing. If legislators and certain elements of the public judge schools, and even teachers, on the basis of their students'

---

[8]William Vernon Hicks et al., *The New Elementary School Curriculum* (New York: Van Nostrand, 1970), p. 158.

scores on standardized tests, the curriculum will continue to respond to these pressure groups by emphasizing those aspects of English that constitute much of the testing. Raising the standardized test scores appears to be the name of the game during the 1980s.

Teaching writing skills to students has been a vexing problem for teachers for many years. A major breakthrough appears to be occurring as students learn to use microcomputers as word processors. The microcomputers allow students to receive feedback from the teacher, make multiple revisions of the manuscript, and even check their spelling before printing their papers. Teachers using this procedure with their students report excellent results and increased enthusiasm for writing among their students.

Foreign Languages The foreign language programs of our public schools have changed considerably over the last thirty to forty years. Prior to World War II, most foreign language instruction stressed reading and writing, to the virtual exclusion of listening and speaking. Furthermore, foreign language instruction was almost exclusively the domain of the secondary schools. With the 1950s came the introduction of a new kind of foreign language instruction to elementary as well as high schools. This new audiolingual approach was designed to develop competence in speaking and listening to others speak a foreign language. As evidence of this dramatic change, the number of language laboratories—rooms equipped with listening tapes, headsets, and machines that can monitor the pace of the students and allow them to respond to the tapes—in public schools nationwide grew from several dozen in 1957 to eight thousand by 1966. There is, however, evidence that their use is not so widespread as was once believed.

The adoption of the audiolingual approach necessitated the retraining of many foreign language teachers and, with support from the National Defense Education Act and the U.S. Office of Education, hundreds of summer workshops were held. In addition to French, German, Spanish, Italian, and Russian, new materials were developed for the study of Arabic, Chinese, Japanese, Portuguese, Greek, and Hebrew.

By the 1970s many foreign language instructors concluded, however, that the audiolingual approach of the early 1960s was not very successful.[9] Enrollments in college foreign language classes declined nearly 10 percent between 1965 and 1975. Budgets for foreign language instruction were cut as it was placed lower and lower on the scale of school priorities. Since many colleges dropped foreign language requirements, a corresponding decline in enrollments occurred in the elementary and secondary schools. There appears to be a trend toward reversing this decline in the 1980s as some universities implement core curricula requirements and increase admission standards for incoming freshmen. Two years of high school foreign language study are being required by the major universities in Texas, for example.

In 1976, a presidential commission reported that only 4 percent of pupils graduating from high school had studied a foreign language for as long as two years. One-fifth of the public high schools in the United States offered no courses at all in foreign language. Among those that did, Spanish, French, and German were the most popular, in that order.[10]

Foreign language departments in the public schools are trying to make the study of foreign languages more attractive by expanding their course offerings, integrating language study with other subject-matter areas, and encouraging students to participate in the planning of new language courses. With the new emphasis on bilingual programs, early introduction of foreign languages has gained considerable support. Nevertheless, the future of foreign language study is uncertain right now.

The Arts

Teachers of the fine and applied arts have been fighting an uphill battle to maintain a secure position in the regular school curriculum. During the 1960s budgetary cutbacks were made in the arts to finance enriched programs in mathematics and the sciences. During the 1970s, however, many public school art programs became sources of pride.

Art and music in the elementary school are ordinarily taught by regular classroom teachers, although some schools hire specialist teachers in one or both areas. Dance and drama are largely ignored in the elementary

[9]Gerald A. Hayn, "High School Language Instruction in the 1970s," *Hispania* 56 (March 1973): 98.
[10]John D. McNeil, *Curriculum: A Comprehensive Introduction*, 2nd ed. (Boston: Little, Brown, 1981), p. 286.

school, though children of this age are less inhibited and seem to enjoy these activities more than do students in the secondary schools. The small amount of instruction in the arts provided for elementary students is replaced in high school by drama clubs, orchestras, bands, and dance groups. In most instances, instruction in music or dance during a child's elementary school years takes the form of private instruction outside the public school.

Artistic learning has three essential elements: (1) the development of abilities to create art forms; (2) the development of powers of aesthetic perception; and (3) the development of the ability to understand art as a cultural phenomenon. As Elliot Eisner, a noted art educator, states: ". . . An understanding of artistic learning requires us to attend to how people learn to create visual forms having aesthetic and expressive character, to how people learn to see visual forms in art and in nature, and to how understanding of art occurs."[11] To achieve these three elements of artistic learning, students must develop an appreciation of art, as well as the ability to produce art. For most students, the former will probably be most useful.

Curriculum specialists in the arts are suggesting integration of the arts with other subject matter to show the usefulness of the arts. For example, in the case of music, the development of lyrics could be studied in English courses. Music could also be used to teach poetry (rhythm), history (songs of people in history), mathematics (patterns and frequencies), and science (the physics of sound).

There is little doubt that the arts play a crucial role in the development of cultured, educated individuals and respond to a deep instinct in humanity. The major concern for the 1980s is whether a cost-conscious public will consider art, music, dance, and drama as "frills" as it examines school budgets and pushes for a return to the basics.

Physical Education and Recreation

Physical education is education of, by, and through human movement. It contributes to several broad areas of personal development: (1) physical fitness, (2) skill and knowledge development, and (3) social and psychological development.

Physical fitness is often confused with physical education, but it represents only a part of physical education programs. Concern over the lack of physical fitness of American youth led to the establishment of the President's Council on Physical Fitness and Sports in 1968. This council recommended that children in kindergarten through twelfth grade be required to take part in daily physical education programs that emphasize the development of physical fitness.[12] Since that time, physical fitness has as-

---

[11]Elliot W. Eisner, *Educating Artistic Vision* (New York: Macmillan, 1972), p. 65.

[12]President's Council on Physical Fitness and Sports, *Suggestions for School Programs, Youth Physical Fitness* (Washington, D.C.: U.S. Government Printing Office, 1973), p. 3.

sumed a prominent position within the physical education curricula in our schools.

The development of useful skills, knowledge, and attitudes are an important part of a physical education curriculum. By emphasizing long-range outcomes, particularly those that can be practiced on a lifelong basis, the individual student receives more than training or conditioning.

The physical education curriculum also tries to meet various biological, psychological, social, and mental needs of students. Values such as cooperation, teamwork, respect for the rights of others, and the like are desired outcomes.

One can picture the physical education curriculum as a triangle, the base of which represents basic instructional classes or services. Nearly all students participate at this level. Higher up in the triangle, and involving fewer students, is the intramural program, which schedules various types of competition on an in-school basis. Still higher, and with still fewer participants, is the extramural program, which involves the best intramural teams from one school with those representing other schools. At the apex of the triangle is the interscholastic program, in which the most highly skilled students represent their schools in competition.

In the early 1960s, physical education curricula were guilty of stressing highly skilled, competitive activities to the detriment of other legitimate physical education activities. As a result, many children became frustrated and humiliated because they did not excel. During the 1970s and early 1980s, however, the programs placed emphasis on lifelong sports such as golf, tennis, swimming, and other individual sports. There is currently more of an emphasis on recreation and less on competition. Less rigid sex roles and federal legislation (Title IX) have also opened up more opportunities for girls to participate in a wider variety of recreational and sports activities.

Elective and Vocational Courses

Most high schools today offer their students a number of options regarding the courses they take. Whereas the average high school student graduates with sixteen to twenty units—a year-long course representing one unit—large high schools may offer as many as one hundred courses. The average student, then, will probably choose among optional courses according to individual interests and academic or career ambitions.

Although college preparation has been the major goal of many high schools, increased effort has been made recently to provide comprehensive programs for students not planning to attend college. This trend is especially evident in rural areas, where small local high schools are being replaced by comprehensive regional high schools. Some of the new courses—such as industrial education, distributive education, home economics, business education, and agriculture—are specifically vocational. Others—such as driver education, consumer education, and conservation—have been added to the curriculum because of an obvious societal need or in response to student interest.

IS THE EXISTING CURRICULUM RELEVANT TO TODAY'S SOCIETY?

Perhaps the most basic function of all education is to increase the survival chances of the group. When educational systems have not fulfilled this function, whole civilizations have been known to disappear. What happened in those civilizations is that environmental conditions changed, requiring the development of new skills, new ideas, and new concepts to survive, but the more conservative elements of society insisted on maintaining the traditional educational forms. As long as the environment remained stable or changed very slowly, the skills necessary for survival also remained constant. In such times, when a culture is proved able to insure the survival of the group, education can be content to transmit that culture. If, however, the dominant characteristic of the environment is change, concepts and skills useful for survival must be separated from what is useless or outmoded, the former retained and the latter discarded. In addition, new concepts and skills appropriate to the new demands of the environment have to be developed to replace those that are discarded.

Our society and our environment are presently undergoing change at a rate unprecedented in human history. The population of the world is expanding at an almost geometric rate and exerting severe pressure on the environment. We are consuming natural resources at such a rate that it is only a matter of time before many will be depleted. We are polluting the air we breathe and, at the same time, destroying huge tracts of vegetation that provide us with oxygen. We are fouling the water we drink and, as a consequence, must spend billions of dollars to try (not very successfully) to purify it. Racial and ethnic prejudices, which have gone unchallenged for decades, are no longer being endured by their victims. Nations now possess the power to annihilate one another at the push of a button. In short, we have reached a point at which many leading thinkers are questioning the ability of humans (note: not of the United States or of the Soviet Union, but of *humans*) to survive another century on this planet.

If we are to rely on education to increase our chances of survival, education must turn its attention to the concepts and skills—that is, survival strategies—necessary to cope with or control such environmental change. We must question the relevance of our curriculum.

The Saber-Tooth Curriculum

In his classic satire on curriculum irrelevance, *The Saber-Tooth Curriculum*,[13] Harold Benjamin—using the pseudonym J. Abner Peddiwell—describes how

[13]J. Abner Peddiwell [Harold Benjamin], *The Saber-Tooth Curriculum* (New York: McGraw-Hill, 1939). One chapter of this book is reproduced in *Kaleidoscope: Readings in Education,* the companion volume to this text.

the first school curriculum was developed in the Stone Age. The earliest educational theorist, according to Benjamin's book, was a man named New Fist, who hit on the idea of deliberate, systematic education.

Watching children at play, New Fist wondered how he could get them to do the things that would gain them more and better food, shelter, clothing, and security. He analyzed the activities that adults engaged in to maintain, life and came up with three subjects for his curriculum: (1) fish-grabbing-with-the-bare-hands, (2) woolly-horse-clubbing, and (3) saber-tooth-tiger-scaring-with-fire. Although the children trained in these subjects enjoyed obvious material benefits as a result, some conservative members of the tribe resisted the introduction of these new subjects on religious grounds. But, in due time, many people began to train their children in New Fist's curriculum and the tribe grew increasingly prosperous and secure.

Then conditions changed. An ice age began, and a glacier crept down over the land. The glacier brought with it dirt and gravel that muddied the creeks, and the waters became so dirty that no one could see the fish well enough to grab them. The melting waters from the approaching ice sheet also made the country wetter, and the little woolly horses migrated to drier land. They were replaced by antelopes, who were so shy and speedy that no one could get close enough to club them. Finally, the new dampness in the air caused the saber-tooth tigers to catch pneumonia and die. And the ferocious glacial bears who came down with the advancing ice sheet were not afraid of fire.

The thinkers of the tribe, descendants of New Fist, found a way out of the dilemma. One figured out how to catch fish with a net made from vines. Another invented traps for the antelopes, and a third discovered how to dig pits to catch the bears.

Some thoughtful people began to wonder why these new activities couldn't be taught in the schools. But the elders who controlled the schools claimed that the new skills did not qualify as *education*—they were merely a matter of *training*. Besides, the curriculum was too full of fish-grabbing, horse-clubbing, and tiger-scaring, the standard cultural subjects, to admit new ones. When some radicals argued that the traditional subjects were foolish, the elders said that they taught fish-grabbing not to catch fish but to develop agility; horse-clubbing to develop strength; and tiger-scaring to develop courage. "The essence of true education is timelessness," they announced. "It is something that endures through changing conditions like a solid rock standing squarely and firmly in the middle of a raging torrent. You must know that there are some eternal verities and the saber-tooth curriculum is one of them!"[14]

The Saber-Tooth Curriculum was written in 1939, but its continuing applicability seems to be one of the "eternal verities."

[14]Peddiwell, *The Saber-Tooth Curriculum*, pp. 43–44.

What's Relevance? Before one can determine whether a particular curriculum is relevant, some difficult questions must be asked: Relevant to what? To life in society as it is now, as it probably will be in the future, or as it ideally should be? Relevant for whom? For the intellectual elite or for everyone? For the individual learner, or for society and its needs? And who determines social needs—the adults who represent the "establishment," or some other group? The question of curriculum relevance is very complicated, for it draws on one's entire philosophy of education. Is education's primary purpose to help students develop their minds by exploring ideas of the past that have proved to have enduring meaning? Or is education's primary purpose to help students experience growth through interaction with their environment? Is there a particular body of knowledge or repertoire of skills that all members of our society should possess? Or should students be free to explore many different areas in accordance with their own needs, curiosities, and interests? Should education give priority to the study of immediate problems and to developing the processes, understandings, and skills necessary for

---

PHONY CURRICULUM

Imagine a unit of study, somewhere in the primary grades, on "The Family...." How is "family" generally represented in the early grades?

The houses in which families live never, as far as we are told, include toilets. Members of the family never scratch themselves, utter obscenities, cheat on their wives, fix traffic tickets, drink beer, play the horses, falsify their tax returns, strike one another, make love, use deodorants, gossip on the telephone, buy on credit, have ulcers, or manifest a million other signs of life that even the most culturally deprived child knows about in the most intimate detail....

Certainly, at their dinner tables, no textbook fathers talk about having outbargained that New York Jew, about the niggers who are trying to take over the neighborhood, the cops, the Birchers, the hippies, the war, and so on. On the contrary, one may safely expect the textbook family to be disembodied, apolitical, generally without a specific ethnic identity or religious affiliation, free of social prejudice, innocent of grief, economically secure, vocationally stable, antiseptic and law-abiding straight down the middle. It occupies a universe from which disaffection, divorce, cynicism, loneliness, neurosis, bastardy, atheism, tension, self-doubt, wrecked cars, and cockroaches are inevitably absent.

Unless he is downright dull, it is impossible to imagine that at some level of experience the child is not aware of the thundering disparity between the real world and the school's priggish, distorted, emasculated representations of that world. It seems reasonable to suspect that the child's knowledge almost certainly includes the realization that, in plain language, the curriculum is phony, at least in relation to the example we have considered.

From *Clinical Supervision—Special Methods for the Supervision of Teachers* by Robert Goldhammer. Copyright © 1969 by Holt, Rinehart and Winston, Inc. Reprinted by permission of Holt, Rinehart and Winston, CBS College Publishing.

Curriculum has been and is a field of shifting emphases, often excesses— from societal needs, to the whole child, to subject disciplines and back around the clock again. And it has been and is disappointingly noncumulative.

— JOHN GOODLAD —

their solution? Or should education concentrate on guiding behavior according to agreed-on standards, and on study of the past as a way of preparing for the future?

In a society as large and pluralistic as the United States, all these philosophical positions, and more, have committed supporters. How can the schools incorporate in their curricula such diverse philosophies? If a certain philosophy is dominant within a given community, the curriculum of its schools is likely to reflect that set of beliefs, and those who don't agree will remain dissatisfied. On the other hand, some communities are responding to these diverse philosophical conceptions of the curriculum by providing alternative schools, each with a different curriculum emphasis, from which parents may choose.

Mortimer Smith argues that all educational philosophies, however diverse, fall into two basic categories, and he characterizes them as follows:

> On this matter of priorities in education, the picture seems clear: One group believes that the school must maintain its historic role as the chief institution in charge of intellectual training; another group—and perhaps the dominant one in public education—maintains that intellectual training is only a part of the school's total program, and not necessarily the most important part.[15]

If one considers the school's primary objective to be the intellectual training of students, any curriculum that does not emphasize scholarship will be judged irrelevant. Conversely, if one believes that the school should emphasize the development of the "whole child"—the child's emotional and social, as well as intellectual, growth—a curriculum devoted exclusively to English, history, the sciences, mathematics, and foreign languages will be considered inappropriate for many students and thus irrelevant. What one considers to be relevant curriculum, then, depends on the philosophical position one takes. At the present time there are conflicting trends in the academic curriculum, each representative of a different philosophy of what the school's academic emphasis should be.

TRENDS IN ACADEMIC SUBJECT-MATTER CURRICULUM

There are three major trends today in the academic subject-matter curriculum.[16] One trend is the continuation of the *structure-of-knowledge* approach that characterized curriculum projects of the 1960s. In history, for example, one source estimates that 20 percent of the nation's school districts are using this approach, in which students judge conflicting evidence and compile their own versions of history.[17]

[15]Mortimer Smith, "Fundamental Differences Do Exist," *American Education Today*, ed. Paul Woodring and John Scanlon (New York: McGraw-Hill, 1964), p. 29.

[16]McNeil, *Curriculum*, pp. 61–64.

[17]McNeil, *Curriculum*, pp. 61–62.

The second trend is toward *integrated studies,* curriculum development efforts in which two or more separate subjects are combined. This trend is a response to the many changes in society and the need for unifying themes to bring together knowledge from different disciplines so that students will be able to understand their commonalities or to interpret a social problem. Organizing themes for instruction are major concepts, scientific processes, natural phenomena, and persistent problems.

An example of such a program is that of the Laboratory School, University of Florida, where high school students acquire interdisciplinary concepts and abilities to investigate scientific questions of social concern.[18] Certain concepts that are important in all sciences—such as order, change, equilibrium, models, and quantification—have become the basis for the selection and organization of subject matter. Instead of studying physics, chemistry, and biology as separate subjects, students are presented selected knowledge from each of these disciplines to help them understand a complex problem.

In studying equilibrium, for example, the students examine how the body maintains internal balance. In order to do this they may use Newton's laws (balance); center of gravity, rotational and linear equilibrium, forces, and torques; biomechanics (explanation of vertigo); body structure; anatomy; roles of body systems in maintaining homeostasis; and "feedback systems models" as applied to their own body functions. In addition, the students study the role of body chemistry in maintaining a stable body. This curriculum requires team teaching, with the result that teachers learn from one another. Student reactions have been positive, and course enrollments have risen dramatically.

A third trend in the academic curriculum is toward establishing more *basic education* schools as part of the "back-to-basics" movement. Teachers in these schools teach the traditional school subjects directly without attempting to make them relevant or to design interesting projects. They emphasize the acquisition of knowledge and the study of great books—the classics. These schools represent a return to the older view of liberal education, in which certain knowledge is deemed of greater or more lasting value than other knowledge. Supporters of basic education disapprove of courses that emphasize process and inquiry without imparting facts, and of courses that encourage students to express value preferences and opinions. They do not believe in a curriculum where "good" and "bad" are merely subjective opinions and all ideas are deemed equal in value.

Those favoring a return to basic education point to the declining standardized test scores as evidence that our educational system of the late 1960s and the 1970s was deficient. Further evidence, they argue, appears when one compares the academic emphasis of the curricula in the United

[18]McNeil, *Curriculum,* p. 63.

JIM: I have mixed feelings about the back-to-basics movement.

KEVIN: How so?

JIM: On the positive side, it may lead to a refocusing on the appropriate role of schools. The movement forces us to consider the very legitimate question "How much can a school do or be expected to do?"

KEVIN: I think I know what you mean. The schools have either assumed or been assigned the task of solving the social and political problems that other institutions have been unable to resolve. The school's agenda has been so full and complicated that the basic purposes of the school have been slighted. What do you see as the potential danger of the movement?

JIM: I see two potential problems. First, I'm worried that there might be an overemphasis on simple skills to the detriment of skills required for living in a complex, ever-changing society.

KEVIN: Sort of like our own Saber-Tooth curriculum?

JIM: Exactly. The other thing that concerns me is that the current emphasis on testing may lead to a narrow curriculum that stresses only that learning which can be measured by objectively scored, convergently oriented tests. There's a danger of relying on quantifiable evidence, of a rather simplistic nature, to represent broader, more complex abilities.

KEVIN: Still, though, it is hard to deny that in the late sixties and seventies, our schools made few academic demands on children and many basic subjects, like math and science, were somewhat soft-pedaled.

JIM: Yes, and it's that aspect of the back-to-basics movement which we need to support.

States with that of the Soviet Union. In mathematics, of the approximately four million Americans who reach the age of seventeen each year, three million have spent nine years studying arithmetic. By contrast, in the Soviet Union children complete arithmetic in the first three grades and start algebra in grades four and five. From the fourth grade on, mathematics is taught by a teacher whose training equals at least a Master's degree in mathematics in the United States. Only one-half of our population takes geometry, and for only one year at that. In the Soviet Union, all students study geometry for ten years: five years of intuitive geometry, three of semi-rigorous plane geometry, and two of solid geometry.[19]

Similar results pertain to secondary school science. Less than one-tenth of the high school students in the United States take one year of physics. In the U.S.S.R. secondary school students take five years of physics. Approximately 16 percent of American high school students take one year of chemistry. All Soviet secondary school students complete four years of chemistry, including a year of organic chemistry. Whereas one year of biology is typically offered in the United States, Soviet students receive six years of compulsory training in biology. Similar comparisons can be made in

[19]*Newsletter*, Boston's Museum of Science, October 1982, p. 2.

both foreign language training and geography.[20] Compared to people in the U.S.S.R., and in many other parts of the industrialized world, the majority of our population are scientific illiterates. Accordingly, supporters of basic education urge that American schools must return to a strong academic orientation, without the alleged frills of the 1970s, if we are to maintain a position of economic and technological superiority in the world.[21]

[20]*Newsletter,* p. 2.
[21]A leading advocate of the basic education position is Mortimer Adler. His recent book, *The Paideia Proposal,* eloquently presents the arguments for needing a strong academic curriculum.

COMMISSION CALLS FOR REFORM IN U.S. EDUCATION

In the spring of 1983, the National Commission on Excellence in Education issued a scathing report to the American people in which it asserted that " . . . the educational foundations of our society are presently being eroded by a rising tide of mediocrity that threatens our very future as a Nation and a people." Likening the situation to "an act of war," the commission charged that "we have, in effect, been committing an act of unthinking, unilateral educational disarmament."

After eighteen months of work the commission identified the following as examples of the problem the United States faces:

▪ International comparisons of student achievement reveal that on nineteen academic tests American students never ranked first or second and, in comparison with other industrialized nations, ranked last seven times.

▪ Twenty-three million American adults and about 13 percent of all seventeen-year-olds are functionally illiterate by the simplest tests of everyday reading, writing, and comprehension.

▪ There has been a steady decline in achievement test scores in recent years in such subjects as English, mathematics, and science.

The report notes that " . . . for the first time in the history of our country, the educational skills of one generation will not surpass, will not equal, will not

even approach, those of their parents." It concludes that "our society and its educational institutions seem to have lost sight of the basic purposes of schooling, and of the high expectations and disciplined effort needed to attain them."

Other major findings of the commission include:

▪ Secondary school curricula have been homogenized, diluted, and diffused to the point that they no longer have a central purpose.

▪ The amount of homework for high school seniors has decreased and grades have risen as average student achievement has declined.

▪ Only eight states require high schools to offer foreign language instruction, but none

HOW IS A NEW CURRICULUM DEVELOPED?

When you begin to teach, it is likely that the curriculum you use will already have been formulated. It may have been developed by a large national curriculum project such as SMSG or BSCS, or it may be the work of teachers within the school district. Your school may provide a curriculum guide—a compilation of objectives and activities for a particular course—whose purpose is to aid the teacher in planning and organizing the course for the year. These curriculum guides range in quality from being nearly worthless to acting as a source of helpful ideas, particularly for beginning teachers. When you begin to immerse yourself in the curriculum, you are likely to ask questions such as these: How do you develop a curriculum? Are there any guidelines? How do you choose what should be included

requires students to take the courses.

▪ Among requirements for a high school diploma, thirty-five states require only one year of mathematics and 36 require only one year of science.

▪ One-fifth of all four-year public colleges in the United States must accept every high school graduate within the state regardless of program followed or grades.

▪ Too many teachers are being drawn from the bottom quarter of graduating high school and college students.

▪ Teacher salaries are too low, with the average salary after twelve years of teaching being only $17,000 per year.

▪ There exists a shortage of mathematics and science

teachers that is becoming critical.

To remedy these problems the commission made the following recommendations:

▪ All high school students should take four years of English; three years of math, science, and social studies; and one-half year of computer science. College-bound students should take at least two years of a foreign language.

▪ Colleges should raise entrance requirements.

▪ Textbook content should be upgraded and updated.

▪ School districts should consider establishing a seven-hour school day and a school year of 200 to 220 days instead of the current six-hour day and 180-day year.

▪ Teachers should work eleven months a year, get paid more than the current $17,000

average after twelve years, be evaluated by their peers, and climb "career ladders" that lead to a "master teacher" rank.

▪ State and local officials should implement and fund the proposed reforms while the role of the federal government should be to identify the national interest in education and fund such programs as those for the gifted, the disadvantaged, and the handicapped.

The commission recognized that to achieve the desired results would require more than a series of "quick fixes." "Reform of our educational system," the report states, "will take time and unwavering commitment."

National Commission on Excellence in Education, *A Nation At Risk: The Imperative for Educational Reform* (Washington, D.C.: U.S. Govt. Printing Office, 1983).

"Boy, did I have trouble with that test! I couldn't tell
whether it was oral or written!"

© 1983; Reprinted courtesy of Bill Hoest and Parade Magazine.

and what should be omitted? Is it purely a matter of choice on the part of
the developers? Is the curriculum based on any particular philosophical
position? Will people with different philosophies of education develop different curricula, or will all curricula be basically the same?

These kinds of questions have been posed for years by curriculum
developers, and the result has been a number of curriculum development
models.[22] However, the unembellished facts of life about curriculum development are that very few curricula are developed according to clearly
articulated principles. Much of what is taught in the schools today is developed by teachers, either individually or in groups, and tends inevitably
to be influenced by such factors as what's available in texts, what other
teachers are doing, what guidelines have been established by the school
district or the state, what the department has done in the past, what the

[22]Two of the most recognized books on curriculum development are Ralph W. Tyler,
Basic Principles of Curriculum and Instruction (Chicago: University of Chicago Press, 1950),
and Hilda Taba, *Curriculum Development: Theory and Practice* (New York: Harcourt, Brace
& World, 1962).

SCHOOLS: THE PRESENT

teachers' own preferences are, seat-of-the-pants intuition, how former students have responded to certain topics and learning experiences, what's happening in the media, and what college courses the teachers have taken—the proportion differing for each teacher according to the phase of the moon and the number of days until Christmas. We do not mean to put down teacher-developed curricula. The important thing to remember is that *the curriculum is what happens to the kids, not what is in the curriculum guides or the resource units.* Any number of factors influence this "final," or "received," curriculum, including textbooks and curricular and instructional practices.

ADDITIONAL INFLUENCES ON CURRICULUM

Although we can examine what is taught in the schools independently in terms of the subjects offered, the curriculum as experienced by the students is affected by a number of factors. The individual teacher, of course, is a major variable in what students actually learn. The classroom and school context also affect the delivery of the curriculum. We have chosen to focus on two other major influences on the curriculum as actually delivered to students: textbooks and individualized instructional approaches.

Textbooks

Education in the United States is constitutionally the domain of the various individual states; that is, the states are empowered to establish a curriculum and organize and finance school systems. Unlike many countries in the world, we have no national curriculum that is established by the federal government and implemented throughout the country. Some educational observers assert, however, that we do possess a national curriculum of sorts, called textbooks. Several recent studies have concluded that most of what students do in classrooms is textbook-related. For many teachers, content ideas are derived solely from the text, and the materials used most frequently in their lessons are the textbook, workbook, teacher's guide ideas for boardwork, and accompanying dittoes and tests. The objectives and goals for student learning are defined by the textbook (even the text you are now reading), learning activities and materials are provided to teachers as part of the textbook package, and tests, geared to the textbook's objectives, are usually prepared for the teacher's use.

Two states—Florida and Texas—because of their single statewide adoption systems, seem to influence greatly what is contained in many elementary and secondary school texts.[23] Both of these states have open hearings, where citizens have the opportunity to examine textbooks that are being considered for statewide adoption and to express their objections

---

[23]Mike Bowler, "The Making of a Textbook," *Learning* 6–7 (March 1978): 38–42.

to particular books. Because textbook adoption is a multimillion-dollar business, publishing companies must be careful not to include material that might be found offensive by influential groups and factions. One can certainly question whether there is an inherent conflict between the notion of a pluralistic nation and the conservative forces that influence the textbook industry and, therefore, the curriculum of our nation. Should publishing companies and the values of two states control the curriculum to such a strong extent? If not, what are the alternatives? One thing appears certain: textbooks are one of the major determinants for the curriculum of our nation's elementary and secondary schools, and that situation does not appear likely to change in the near future.

Individualized Instruction

Individualizing instruction means different things to different people. Some people use the term to suggest that all the students proceed through the same curriculum but at different rates. To others, it means that the same curriculum is presented to all students but by different instructional methods, depending on the learning style of the students. For still others, it

means that different curricula are offered to meet individual needs, allowing each student to choose the instructional objectives that best fit his or her unique interests and needs. We will examine three major approaches to individualized instruction: (1) systematic programs as represented by Individually Prescribed Instruction (IPI) and Individually Guided Education (IGE); (2) mastery learning; and (3) open education.

IPI AND IGE   Individually Prescribed Instruction (IPI), originally developed at the University of Pittsburgh's Learning and Research Center, is one systematic approach to individualization for elementary school children. The essential characteristics of the IPI system are the student's freedom to move through the curriculum at her or his own rate of progress; behavioral objectives—that is, objectives stated in terms of what the learner should be able to *do* after mastering the lesson, arranged sequentially in order of complexity (see page 89 for further explanation of behavioral objectives); the intention that the student work on objectives until he or she achieves them, thus emphasizing accomplishment rather than failure; emphasis on self-direction, self-initiation, and self-evaluation on the part of the learner; individualized techniques and materials providing a variety of instructional alternatives; the organization and management of the total school environment to facilitate individual instruction; and provision for continuous feedback on the effectiveness of the program.

IPI is currently available in four areas: language arts, mathematics, social studies, and science. Because its objectives are so clearly stated, teacher direction is minimal. Instead, diagnosis is a crucial aspect of IPI; placement tests are administered to students to determine the instructional program appropriate for each child. Before each unit, a pretest is administered to determine the point within the unit where the child should begin, or whether he or she has already mastered the material. At the end of the unit, a post-test is administered to see if the child has in fact achieved the behavioral objectives. If the student has not done so, the teacher notes where he or she has fallen short and prescribes additional instruction. There are also curriculum-embedded tests, taken while the student is progressing through the curriculum, designed to provide data on the mastery of each behavioral objective and to determine whether the student needs additional work.

The instructional materials used in IPI programs include worksheets, tape and disc recordings, programmed materials, individual readers, manipulative devices, and computer-assisted instruction. Since no two students learn in quite the same way, IPI attempts to present a variety of instructional materials.

Another individualized program, with characteristics similar to those of IPI, is Individually Guided Education (IGE). However, IGE differs from IPI on several counts. First, IGE utilizes a multi-unit school organization within which the instruction of groups of different-aged children becomes the responsibility of units or teams of teachers. Second, IGE addresses itself to improving home/school communication to insure that the school's efforts are supported and reinforced by the parents. Third, IGE leaves most instructional decisions in the hands of the teachers, whereas the IPI materials are more prescriptive. Fourth, IGE has developed its system at the secondary as well as the elementary school level.

MASTERY LEARNING   Another approach to individualizing instruction and improving learning has been developed by Benjamin Bloom, a noted educational psychologist, and his associates. Calling his strategy "mastery learning," Bloom argues that approximately 90 percent of students can master the curriculum of the public schools if the kind and quality of instruction and the amount of time available for learning are made appropriate to the characteristics and needs of each student. The problem has been, he asserts, that most students are provided with the same instruction (same in terms of amount, quality, and time available for learning). When this occurs, students who possess more aptitude for given subjects will outperform students possessing less aptitude. On the other hand, accepting that students are normally distributed according to aptitude, if the kind and quality of instruction and the amount of time available for learning are made appropriate to the characteristics and needs of *each* student, the majority of students may be expected to achieve mastery of the subject.

Research on the effects of mastery learning strategies has been favorable and positive. Reviewing more than one hundred studies on mastery learning, one observer concluded that the results "indicate that mastery strategies do indeed have moderate to strong effects on student learning when compared to conventional methods of instruction."[24] Bloom reports that when students do master a subject and receive both objective and subjective evidence of the mastery, there are profound changes in their views of themselves and school. The students begin to like the subject and desire more of it. Students' self-concepts also increase as a result of exposure to successful learning experiences.

Implementing mastery learning is not easy, but successful techniques have been identified and are summarized as follows:

1. Define instructional objectives behaviorally so the teacher and learner know exactly where they are and what must be accomplished.

2. Teach the behavior or attitude sought in the objective directly rather than building to or around it.

3. Provide immediate feedback to all learner responses.

4. Set the level of instruction so that students are maximally successful.

[24]Robert B. Burns, "Mastery Learning: Does It Work?" *Educational Leadership* (November 1979): 112.

5. Divide instruction into small, self-contained modules.

6. Control the stimulus so the teacher knows exactly what the learner is responding to.

7. Provide positive feedback to reinforce the learner's "critical" response, that is, the response that corresponds to the desired behavior identified in the instructional objective.[25]

Bloom's basic message is that while differences in intelligence and aptitude do exist in every classroom, teachers can adjust the quality of instruction and the time allowed for each student so that more students can succeed. It should be noted that mastery learning strategies are especially critical during the early grades of school because if students do not acquire certain basic skills, catching up in the later grades becomes exceedingly difficult.

Open Education

Open education is a highly individualized, child-centered learning experience based on the assumption that learning will be more effective if it develops from what interests the learner rather than what interests the teacher. The teacher does not abdicate position and authority in the classroom, but instead facilitates learning by structuring the environment to respond optimally to each child's needs and interests. The child, rather than the teacher, is the source of learning.

There are four basic principles operating in an open classroom. First, the classroom is decentralized; open space is divided into flexible "interest areas" according to function. The room does not look like a classroom. Second, the children are free to explore the room and choose their own activities. Third, the environment is rich in learning resources—books, rulers, measuring tape, building toys, tape recorders, and dozens of other instructional materials. And, finally, the teacher and the aides spend most of their time with individual children or small groups; they rarely present the material to the class as a whole.[26]

Respect and trust in the child are perhaps the most basic underlying principles of open classrooms. A first-time visitor to an open classroom is usually surprised—the room has no identifiable front or back, the children are all doing different things at different times, and the teacher may be working with an individual child or observing. The class is a beehive of activity.

The theoretical rationale for the open classroom stems mainly from the work of the Swiss child psychologist Jean Piaget. Much of Piaget's

---

[25]Joan S. Hyman and S. Alan Cohen, "Learning for Mastery: Ten Conclusions After 15 Years and 3,000 Schools," *Educational Leadership* (November 1979): 104–109.

[26]Ronald Gross and Beatrice Gross, "A Little Bit of Chaos," *Saturday Review*, May 16, 1970, pp. 71–73, 84–85.

lifetime was spent studying children and their developmental stages. He believed that it is a waste of time to tell children things that they can't experience through their senses. They must be allowed to manipulate objects, try different experiments, pose questions, and test their findings against other children's perceptions. Communication and interaction among peers is an essential part of a child's learning. Only after children have had a great deal of sensory experience are they ready to comprehend abstract concepts. Piaget was critical of the traditional classroom approach for emphasizing conceptualization without offering children the opportunity to experience through their senses.

JEAN PIAGET
(1896–1980)

Jean Piaget's life work, which is reflected in over fifty books and several hundred articles, became the pivotal point upon which educational thought and the practice of schooling began to turn.

Born in Neuchâtel, Switzerland, in 1896, Piaget displayed his own scholarly promise at a very early age. As a small boy, he was intensely interested in nature. He was an active birdwatcher and a collector of fossils and seashells. At the age of ten, after spotting an albino sparrow in a local park, he immediately went home and wrote up his observations and sent them to a natural history journal. His report was published, and, as he later reported, "I was launched."

Once started on the path of investigation and study, he never wavered. When still a young boy, he became assistant to the curator of the local natural history museum. At the same time he became a widely published collector of and expert on mollusks. Upon entering the university, Piaget broadened his basic interest in biology and natural history to include philosophy and mathematics. His interest then expanded from these subjects to the still young field of human psychology. He went to the University of Paris and in the course of his study met Alfred Binet, who developed the first intelligence tests. Binet asked young Piaget to work for him. Piaget's job was to ask children of various ages questions in order to establish standards of responses to the questions. Instead of just recording their answers and going on to the next question, Piaget went further. He probed the students for the reasons behind their answers. This modification led to his major contribution to learning: stages of intellectual development. What Piaget observed was that children at different ages answer questions and seem to see the world in characteristic and predictable ways. Children at different ages seem to reason in strikingly different ways. From these observations Piaget developed his basic theory of cognitive or mental development. He saw the process of mental development for all people as one composed of four main stages: the sensorimotor (infancy or birth to two years), the preoperational stage (two to six), the period of concrete operations (seven to eleven), and the period of formal operations (eleven through adulthood). Individuals at each stage have a predictable way of thinking about things. Further, the development of each stage is a

Open classrooms do not require specialized teachers. But the teachers do need to be alert and ready to respond to and help individual students in their various activities. Since the curriculum is not restricted to teachers' lesson plans but is literally everything that is going on in the room, it can be as unpredictable and as broad as the children's interests. However, teachers need not be afraid to admit ignorance in certain areas. In fact, they can seize such opportunities to help the students by designing experiments or research problems themselves. In this way, they function as models and demonstrate to the children that ignorance is a problem to be solved rather than a source of shame.

necessity for advancement to the next stage. For instance, three-year-olds (having passed through the sensorimotor stage) are very busy learning language as a means of representing the environment in which they must function. Whereas a year or so earlier they could only interact directly with the immediate environment, they now can represent in their minds various elements in their world and store them there for later use. However, there are still many things they cannot do. For instance, when they see certain operations, such as water being poured from a tall, thin glass into a short, wide glass, the act of pouring seems to have an effect on the quantity of water. Older children immediately recognize that the amount has remained the same and only the appearance has been

changed. This is but one example of a thought process that is characteristic of a particular developmental stage.

Piaget used this basic theory to shed further light on the issue of heredity versus environment, particularly as it relates to learning. Rejecting the extreme positions that denigrate either heredity or environment, he steered a middle path. He saw nature providing each of us with a predetermined, genetically programmed mechanism that directs us to go through the specific stages of mental development. In a way, the child unfolds according to a schedule and in accord with a general plan. Environment plays a key role, in that the child needs a certain kind of environment at each stage of development. In order to progress mentally through the stages, the child needs to manipulate and interact with a variety of environmental elements. To learn

eventually to conceptualize the conservation of water as it goes from a tall, thin container into a short, wide one, the child needs to have had a variety of concrete experiences in which he or she sees this principle worked out in a familiar environment.

Jean Piaget made a startling impact on educational thinking. Specifically, he helped us see that the child is not a passive agent to be impressed with knowledge. Rather, the child is a stimulation-seeking being for whom action is a direct link to thought. Further, Piaget's ideas provided the intellectual underpinnings for the increased attention to the period of early childhood, as demonstrated by day care centers, preschools, and nursery schools, and the open, active learning environment of the British infant schools.

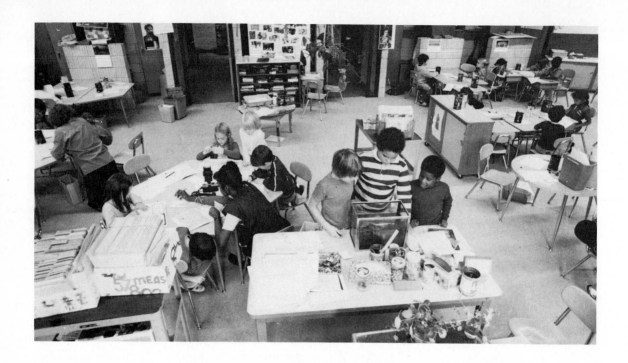

The open classroom approach received widespread publicity in Great Britain in 1967, when a parliamentary commission, now referred to as the Plowden Committee, urged its adoption by all English primary schools. In the early 1970s, many American schools adopted the open classroom approach, and it enjoyed great popularity and visibility during the 1970s. However, interest in this approach has waned recently. Parents, legislators, and some educators are concerned that essential skills such as reading and mathematics may be left up to chance in an open classroom. The back-to-basics movement discussed here and in Chapter 12 is a counterreaction to many of the ideas and practices of the open classroom approach. And, as discussed in Chapter 10, there is some research support that a direct instructional approach, rather than an indirect approach, is strongly related to increased academic engaged time, which in turn is related to increased pupil achievement in reading and mathematics in the elementary grades.

There is no doubt that the open classroom approach will continue to appeal to many parents, educators, and children. Although similar to IPI and IGE in its emphasis on individualized instruction, it differs in its openness and in the child's almost total responsibility for what and when he or she wants to learn. IPI's and IGE's behavioral objectives largely predetermine the scope of the curriculum, leaving the child free to move through it at his or her own rate. Whereas IPI and IGE gradually allow the student more responsibility for designing his or her own curriculum, the open classroom gives the child that responsibility at the outset. For those children who are able to assume this responsibility for their own learning, the open classroom approach seems appropriate. However, many children need more direction and guidance to develop basic reading and mathematics skills than is offered in the open classroom. We are at a stage in education when alternatives, not final answers, are needed. The answers will come only after extensive testing of the alternatives, and IPI, IGE, mastery learning, and the open classroom offer distinct choices among instructional approaches.

Discussion Questions

1. Which of the five motives identified by Gwynn and Chase as influencing curriculum development since 1635 do you think are still operative? What evidence can you marshal to support your views?

2. What is your view of the recent developments in your favorite subject field?

3. With which of the two basic philosophical stands summarized by Smith on page 219 are you most in sympathy? What evidence can you muster to support your position?

4. With which of the three major trends in academic subject-matter curriculum do you feel most comfortable? Why?

5. Should teachers be allowed to teach curricula of their own design? Where does professional autonomy and the teacher's freedom of choice come in? What should be its limits?

6. In your opinion, is the prevalent use of textbooks in the schools a positive or negative influence on teaching and learning? Can you see both the benefits and the dangers? If so, what are they?

7. What approaches to individualized instruction appeal to you and why?

8. What would you do to improve the curriculum of the public schools?

For Further Reading

Eisner, Elliot W. *The Educational Imagination.* New York: Macmillan, 1979.
    A stimulating, controversial book regarding forces influencing today's curriculum.

McNeil, John D. *Curriculum: A Comprehensive Introduction,* 2nd ed. Boston: Little, Brown, 1981.
    A comprehensive overview of major curriculum issues, as well as brief descriptions of new directions in the various subject fields.

Peddiwell, J. Abner [Harold Benjamin]. *The Saber-Tooth Curriculum*. New York: McGraw-Hill, 1939.

> A satirical spoof on the origins of schools, the inadequacies of the curriculum, and the reluctance of educators to keep the curriculum relevant to societal needs. Humorous and entertaining reading.

Tyler, Ralph W. *Basic Principles of Curriculum and Instruction*. Chicago: University of Chicago Press, 1950.

> A little booklet that is the classic rationale for curriculum development. Tyler stresses the need to use several data sources, including the learners' needs, to develop an adequate curriculum. Although developed in the fifties, Tyler's principles for curriculum development are still held to be valid.

The following journals contain many interesting and helpful articles for teachers in the respective subject-matter fields.

- science—*The Science Teacher; School Science and Mathematics*
- mathematics—*The Mathematics Teacher; School Science and Mathematics*
- social studies—*The Social Studies; Social Education*
- reading and language arts—*Language Arts; The Reading Teacher*
- English—*English Journal*
- foreign languages—*Modern Language Journal*
- physical education—*Journal of Health, Physical Education and Recreation*
- music—*Music Educators' Journal*
- art—*Art Education; Arts and Activities; School Arts*
- vocational education—*Industrial Education; Journal of Home Economics; Business Education Forum; Business Education Review*

How Are Schools Governed, Controlled, and Financed?

8

Very few beginning teachers are concerned about issues related to school governance and control. The topic seems remote to them; it is something administrators and teacher organization representatives care about but is not particularly vital for beginning teachers concerned with learning how to survive. We feel differently; we believe that beginning teachers must have some understanding of the way schools and school systems operate since they will be affected personally by control, governance, and financial decisions. If you do not understand how these decisions are made and how they might affect you as a teacher, your effectiveness as a professional will be diminished.

This chapter emphasizes that:

▪ Although the right to govern schools is delegated legally, control and influence over school operations are often exercised by people without legal authority.

▪ Legal responsibility for school governance belongs to the state, but policy decisions and administration are delegated to local boards of education. The school district superintendent is the educational leader and chief administrator of the school district.

▪ Professional educators, informal groups, parents, teachers, businesses, and the federal government all exert influence and some measure of control over educational decisions in the United States.

▪ The role of the federal government in education dramatically increased from 1965 to 1980, including the creation of a federal Education Department. Recently, however, the Reagan administration has been trying to reduce the role of the federal government in education.

▪ Because of court rulings, public school financing is becoming more of a state-wide responsibility and less dependent on local property taxes.

*S*OMETIMES SCHOOL-RELATED EVENTS occur that at first appearance may seem strange or illogical. A closer examination, however, may reveal answers that make sense when viewed from a political standpoint. For example, how do you explain the fact that:

- your favorite high school teacher was not given tenure?
- the multicultural curricula that everyone was talking about a couple of years ago never got off the ground?
- in some schools teachers are expected to police bathrooms and lunch yards?
- two years after the new elementary school opened it needed major repairs?
- the last school bond issue in your town or city was decisively defeated?
- a textbook with a fresh approach to some aspects of "the system" was removed from circulation after a year, even though the teachers favored its use?
- your high school student newspaper was heavily censored by faculty and administrators?
- purchasing or construction contracts don't always go to the lowest bidder or the most qualified firm?
- in many school districts teachers have little or no voice in the selection of textbooks or supplementary materials?
- schools have developed an image of being resistant to change?

It is quite likely that at least one of these questions applies to your local school district; all their answers reflect the disparity between governance and real control of the public schools, or problems related to school financing. The purpose of this chapter is to explore how schools are officially organized and governed and how they are actually controlled and financed. Although there is a legal authority for the schools and an organization established to exercise this authority, the school system is controlled in large part by informal forces that do not appear on any organizational chart. We will first examine the legal governing authority that exists in most school districts, and then discuss the influence of informal groups. We will then examine how schools are financed and look at the differences that exist among the various states.

We have tried to draw from literature and experience to describe how things really are, not how they're supposed to be. The result will, we hope, give you insight into school control that will help you be a better, more professional teacher.

HOW GOVERNANCE DIFFERS FROM CONTROL

How is controlling different from governing? The right to govern is delegated legally, but domination or command that results in "control" of people or of a situation is not necessarily officially sanctioned. Often, however, the governing person or group also exercises control, as in the case of a strong president or a monarch whose powers are not constitutionally restricted. In other instances, those who govern exercise little real control, as in the case of a figurehead monarch who is manipulated by someone else behind the scenes.[1] Such situations have occurred from time to time in monarchies when young children have succeeded to the throne and the real power and control have been wielded by advisers and guardians. Between these two extremes is the situation in which those who legally govern share power with persons or groups possessing no legal authority. This state of affairs is prevalent in public education. Considerable control over the operation of our schools is exercised by persons without legal authority, largely through personal connections and the exertion of pressure on legal officeholders.

WHO LEGALLY GOVERNS PUBLIC EDUCATION?

In most countries, the public schools are a branch of the central government, federally financed and administered and highly uniform in curricula and procedures. In the United States, however, responsibility for the public schools has evolved as a state function as a result of the Tenth Amendment to the U.S. Constitution. Each of the fifty states has legal responsibility for the operation and administration of public schools within its own boundaries. In most aspects of public education (we will discuss certain exceptions later), the authority of federal, county, and city education agencies is subject to the will of the state authorities.

Although legal responsibility for school governance belongs to the state, policy decisions and administration are ordinarily delegated to local boards of education, which exist because Americans have come to insist on control of schools at the local level. However, the state does not relinquish all its responsibilities, and it retains the power to revoke or countermand decisions made by the local units. One result of this delegation of authority to local units is that the efficiency and achievements of school systems vary widely across the nation, and even within individual states.

The State Authorities

THE STATE BOARD OF EDUCATION   The state's legal responsibility for public education requires it to establish an organizational framework within which the local units can function. The result is the establishment of state

[1]This situation reminds us of the governing husband who insisted that he made all the big decisions in his family while his wife made the small ones. He decided what the nation should do about the energy crisis, inflation, and foreign policy, while his wife made the decisions about the family budget, where they lived, and where he worked.

boards of education to exercise general control and supervision of schools within the state. The state board of education is the state's policy-making body. It typically will establish goals and priorities for education in the state; formulate education policy and curricular offerings; establish and enforce rules and regulations for the operation of educational programs; represent the public in matters regarding the governance of education and report to the public on accomplishments and needs; and make recommendations to the governor and/or state legislature for the improvement of education. The state board of education establishes and enforces minimum standards for the operation of all phases of elementary and secondary education from state to local school system level.

The procedure for selecting state board members varies from state to state. In most states, members are appointed by the governor, although in about one-third of the states members are elected by the people or by representatives of the people. Two states have ex-officio members who serve on the state board because of the positions or offices they already hold.

THE CHIEF STATE SCHOOL OFFICER   The executive officer of the state board of education—whose title may be, depending on the state, chief state school officer, superintendent of education, commissioner of education, secretary of the state board of education, or something else—usually is responsible to the state board of education for the administration of public education. Such responsibilities normally involve teacher and administrator certification, organization of the program of studies, curriculum revision, application of the state finance law, approval of school sites and buildings, collection of statistical data, and direct supervision of elementary and secondary educational programs. This officer exercises little direct administrative authority over local educational officers, but his or her indirect influence is widely felt on the local level. In some states the officer is elected by the voters, whereas in others he or she is appointed by the state board of education or the governor.

THE STATE DEPARTMENT OF EDUCATION   The chief state school officer, as well as being the executive officer of the state board of education, also serves as the administrative head of the state department of education (sometimes called the state department of public instruction). Whereas the state board of education is involved with policy making, the state department of education is responsible for the *operation* of school systems at the state level.

Originally organized to provide statistical reports, state departments of education have grown in size, power, and influence. Their primary responsibilities usually include administering and distributing state and federal funds, certifying teachers and other educational personnel, providing schools with technical assistance in improving curriculum and teaching, providing educational data and analyses, providing administration for special programs, and accrediting college and university educational certification programs. Most schools, school districts, and colleges of education are strongly affected by policies and actions of these state departments. School and college personnel, including public school teachers, actively serve on advisory committees and task forces to assist the chief state school officer and the state department of education in their decision-making processes.

The Local School District   To facilitate local control of education, the state creates local school districts for the purpose of carrying out the educational program in conformity with state educational policy. The school district is thus a unit of the state government and is usually distinct from the local municipal government.

THE SCHOOL BOARD   The policy-making body of the school district is the local school board of education, which represents the citizens of the district in setting up a school program, hiring school personnel to operate the schools, determining organizational and administrative policy, and evaluating the results of the program and the performance of personnel. Although school board members are usually elected by the citizens of the local district, they are officially state officers and not, as many people think, simply local representatives. Thus board members must operate the schools in conformity with the guidelines and policies established by the state board of education and the state department of education, and not on a strictly local perspective.

The responsibilities of local school boards in the United States are of critical importance, since these boards control and direct the public school systems. Their policy decisions directly affect the students, teachers, and taxpayers in the community. The success of America's program of public education is dependent upon the selection as board members of able men and women, who serve voluntarily, usually without pay, and who determine the broad policies under which the schools operate. Because school boards represent the community in establishing the school district's educational program, the selection of school board members is of great importance.

Methods of selecting school board members are usually prescribed by state law, with approximately 85 percent of the school boards being elected by popular vote and the remainder appointed. When appointments are made, the responsibility for making appointments falls most frequently to the mayor or city council.

What does the composite profile of school board members look like?[2] From 1972 to 1981 the proportion of women serving on boards increased

[2]Kenneth E. Underwood, James C. Fortune, and Harold W. Dodge, "Your Portrait: School Boards Have a Brand-New Look," *American School Board Journal* (January 1982):17–20.

Table 8.1 Selected Characteristics of School Board Membership, 1981

Characteristic	Percentage	Characteristic	Percentage
Sex		*Ethnic Group*	
Male	67.2	Afro-American	3.7
Female	32.8	Anglo-American	91.5
		Hispanic-American	2.1
Age		American Indian	0.6
Under 25	0.7	Other	2.1
26–35	10.9		
36–40	17.1	*Income*	
41–50	39.8	Less than $20,000	9.6
51–60	22.8	$20,000–$29,999	23.2
Over 60	8.7	$30,000–$39,999	24.1
		$40,000 +	43.1

Source: Kenneth E. Underwood, James C. Fortune, and Harold W. Dodge, "Your Portrait: School Boards Have a Brand-New Look," *American School Board Journal* (January 1982):17–20.

Reprinted, with permission, from The American School Board Journal, January. Copyright 1982, the National School Boards Association. All rights reserved.

from 12 to 32.8 percent (see Table 8.1). Anglo-Americans comprise the overwhelming majority of school board membership—91.5 percent.

Most school board members are middle-aged (nearly 40 percent are between 41–50 years old). The annual family income of 43.1 percent of the board members is more than $40,000. Board members are better educated than the general public, 65.9 percent having finished four or more years of college. Sixty-one percent are in professional or managerial occupations. These figures indicate that in many ways school board members are not always typical of the public they serve.

THE SUPERINTENDENT OF SCHOOLS   The superintendent, a professional educator selected by the local school board to act as its executive officer and as the educational leader and administrator of the school district, is undeniably the most powerful officer in the local school organization. Theoretically, the superintendent's role is administrative and executive—he or she keeps the schools functioning—whereas the board of education retains legislative and policy-making responsibilities. In practice, however, the superintendent has become the major policy maker in the public schools. Consider the following description of powers:

> . . . the administrator is in a position either to promote broad participation in decision-making and creativity on the part of individuals in the organization or to run a tight ship and discourage the

efforts of any of the participants to rock the boat. The administrator does more than set the climate for the participants of the organization. He establishes certain goals; he allocates resources; he develops the criteria for the selection of personnel; he is the bridge between the organization and the broader society from which he derives the resources with which it has to operate. He controls the use of sanctions, both positive and negative, within the organization, and by his use of them, he establishes the determinants for the behavior of subordinates.[3]

WHO CONTROLS AMERICAN PUBLIC EDUCATION?

There is no easy answer to this question. It is like asking who controls America. The president does—but so does Congress. The Supreme Court does—but so do the local police. The giant corporations do—but so does a small but influential group of political activists. Similarly, the formal, legally constituted bodies control or influence certain aspects of public education as a consequence of the authority invested in them. The federal government exerts influence on public education through the passage and enforcement of legislation. Professional educators—including superintendents, principals, university professors, and leaders of professional organizations—possess a major portion of the control and decision-making power over public education by virtue of the offices they hold and the organizations to which they belong (for example, the National Education Association or the Association of Supervision and Curriculum Development). These professional organizations, though they lack legal authority, have considerable influence.

It is not the intention of this chapter to examine the authority and power possessed by each of these groups that enable them to control certain aspects of public education. However, a brief look at the roles of the professional educator, informal group power, parent and teacher organizations, business, and the federal government yields some fascinating insights into how decisions about public education are actually made.

Professional Educators

One observer of American education, James D. Koerner, has charged that important decisions in education emerge from a "labyrinthine structure of forces and countervailing forces, but that the interests of professional educators tend to be dominant."[4] When Koerner refers to "professional educators," he does not mean classroom teachers. He is speaking of several organizations he considers to have disproportionate influence on the

[3]Keith Goldhammer et al., *Issues and Problems in Contemporary Educational Administration* (Eugene: University of Oregon Center for the Advanced Study of Educational Administration, 1967), pp. 3–4.

[4]James D. Koerner, *Who Controls American Education?* (Boston: Beacon Press, 1968), p. 155.

administration of the schools—the National Education Association (particularly its administrative branches), state departments of education, departments and schools of education in colleges and universities, educational accrediting organizations, and other groups such as school administrators. A more detailed discussion of the NEA and the American Federation of Teachers follows in Chapter 11.

Koerner argues that the people most directly involved—classroom teachers, parents and other laypersons, and academic specialists in departments other than education—have for too long been dominated by the professional education "fraternity." For instance, the state board of education is entitled to do nearly anything it chooses, within the limit of the law, affecting education in the state. However, Koerner asserts, it rarely governs in any but the most general way. The board of education usually allows the state department of education to make policy, or yields its power to local school authorities. State departments of education and the superintendencies of local school districts are staffed by professional educators, and as a result the influence and power wielded by this group is much greater than Koerner believes it should be.

Looking at the local scene, Koerner argues that the power of local school boards is greatly overestimated, and that local control is largely a myth. He attributes the school board's weakness to three sources: its preoccupation with housekeeping details, its failure to assert authority, and external controls forced on it by other bodies. The board's preoccupation with trivia instead of policy making and its failure to assert its authority is seen by Koerner as the result of the superintendent's increased power. Although in theory the servant of the board, the superintendent has increasingly become its leader.[5] Because local school boards often lack adequate staff to do their own research, they must rely on professional educators (primarily the superintendent and his or her staff) for such services. As a result the superintendent has become the major policy maker in the public schools.

In many school districts, for example, the school board agenda is prepared by the superintendent, with occasional suggestions from the board members. Matters relevant to the educational program are often conspicuously absent from the agenda. When someone remarked that the school board in one particular district seemed to devote very little time to education, the superintendent replied, "They don't know anything about it; but the things they know they talk about, like sidewalks, sites, and so forth. I let them go on sometimes because I don't want them to talk about curriculum."[6]

[5]Roscoe C. Martin, "School Government," in *Governing Education: A Reader on Politics, Power, and Public School Policy*, ed. Alan Rosenthal (New York: Doubleday, 1969), p. 270.
[6]Norman D. Kerr, "The School Board as an Agency of Legitimation," in *Governing Education: A Reader on Politics, Power, and Public School Policy*, ed. Alan Rosenthal (New York: Doubleday, 1969), p. 159.

The outside controls exerted on the local board are numerous and strong. Koerner cites a hypothetical example of a board that wishes to make changes in the vocational training curriculum. Realizing that vocational training no longer serves the needs of the students, the board decides to cut back on its programs. This is, theoretically, one of the local school board's sovereign rights, but a number of events are likely to occur to change the board's mind. First, the vocational education lobby might exert pressure on other members of the local government and on the state legislature or state department of education to protect the interests of vocational education teachers. Second, the regional accrediting association might come to the aid of the status quo, threatening possible disaccreditation of the schools involved if the board does not rescind its decision.[7] Third, the National Education Association state affiliate might "investigate," and through its power "persuade," the board to a different view. Does the board, then, in fact have the power to control the curriculum?

It should be noted that Koerner's views are but one interpretation of how school systems and education in general are controlled. There are many in education who do not support his view that education is overly dominated by the professional education "fraternity," or that the superintendent is so all-powerful. In fact, the high turnover of superintendents may be indicative that school boards are more influential than Koerner gives them credit for being.

Koerner's hypothetical example illustrates how various educational groups and associations protect vested interests in the continuation of, or opposition to, certain programs or practices, and can exert pressure on the legally constituted body responsible for making such decisions. It is appropriate at this point to discuss the role of superintendents, since they are quite often the direct recipients of these pressures.

Informal Group Power **OUTSIDE PRESSURES ON THE SUPERINTENDENT** In a study sponsored by the New York Board of Regents, Ralph B. Kimbrough interviewed a large number of school board members and superintendents in the state of New York. Among other questions, he asked: "In actual practice, whose views carry the greatest weight in the important decisions in each of these areas (such as the curriculum and staff selection)?" The responses indicated that the superintendent was allowed to make all such decisions.[8]

---

[7]Although accreditation does not bring distinction to a school, the lack of it is a stigma. Its graduates will have trouble gaining entrance to certain colleges and universities, and teacher organizations may discourage their members from teaching there.

[8]Ralph B. Kimbrough, *"School Boards and School Board Membership: Report of the New York State Regents Advisory Committee on Educational Leadership,"* 1965, pp. 58–59, as cited in James D. Koerner, *Who Controls American Education?* (Boston: Beacon Press, 1968), p. 141.

The superintendent thus has almost complete control over the internal operations of the school district, an area in which the informal power structure takes little interest. However, Kimbrough's findings indicate that decisions pertaining to economics, which might have great impact on the community, are not made by the superintendent but by the informal power structure in the community.

Neal Gross discovered that superintendents are subjected to pressure by a number of different groups and individuals, and this impinges on their decision-making power.[9] As might be expected, parents and PTAs were the most frequent source of pressure on superintendents and school board members.

Gross's survey indicates that parents, followed by teachers and school board members, are most likely to demand additional funding for the schools, and that the town finance committee or city council is most likely to apply pressure to reduce expenditures. Because local and municipal officials fear that the voters will consider them responsible for all local taxes, including school levies, they use whatever means they can to reduce taxes, including pressuring the superintendent and the school board to limit school expenditures.

Superintendents reveal that school board members and parents often apply pressure to have friends hired by the school district or to have teachers they dislike fired. Interestingly, although newspapers are not normally a source of pressure, they do at times try to promote greater emphasis on school athletics. Local businesspeople are likewise interested in promoting athletic competitions.[10]

One superintendent related an incident about the chairperson of the school board who called to inquire about the bus contract. The usual complaints had been received about the bus service, and the chairperson argued that a friend of his, the owner of a local taxi service, could do a better job. The superintendent replied that the company that presently held the contract cost less than would the friend's company, and also provided better equipment and more experienced drivers than could be obtained locally. "That's all very well and good," the chairperson responded, "but you've got to learn to support the local community if you're going to stick around."

One hour later the superintendent received a telephone call from another school board member, who usually supported him on crucial issues. The school board member explained that he knew what he was about to ask was against the rules, but that he thought he would ask anyway.

---

[9]Neal Gross, *Who Runs Our Schools?* (New York: John Wiley & Sons, 1958), pp. 49–50.

[10]Neal Gross, "Who Applies What Kind of Pressures," in *Governing Education: A Reader on Politics, Power, and Public School Policy*, ed. Alan Rosenthal (New York: Doubleday, 1969), pp. 91–99.

His niece had applied for a teaching job—was there anything the superintendent could do to help her? He knew that she didn't have as much experience as some of the other applicants, but he felt sure she would make a pretty good teacher. After all, he had known her all her life. The conversation ended with the board member asking the superintendent to do what he could.

SUPERINTENDENTS SPEAK OUT

Superintendents are under considerable pressure from individuals and groups to make decisions in their favor. Arthur Blumberg has compiled (from many superintendents) personal descriptions of those pressures and conflicts. We have included a few of their statements to bring you a better sense of the problems and frustrations associated with the job of superintendent.

One superintendent describes dealing with an array of groups and individuals:

Well, you always have superintendent-board conflict, particularly when there are factions on the board. The superintendent's in the middle trying to balance these. Then there is the administrative staff, whether it be principals, assistants or whatever. Obviously there's the union. Community groups all over the place. Sometimes student interest groups. . . . The news media is constant. TV, the local paper vs. the city paper. And there are support groups, booster clubs, for athletics, the band, even art. And special interest groups. For

the handicapped, for example. They're coming right off the walls of late. There are the Federal and State mandates. All the Titles and categorical aid programs. The PTAs, the businessmen, the clergy, real estate interests. Parents with kids with specific problems. I'm going 100 miles an hour all the time. You always have another mountain to climb.

Another superintendent describes in the following way the many different kinds of pressures he experienced:

I'm talking, for example, about problems with the community and with the kids. I'm talking about being involved in a lawsuit because of an insurance recovery. I'm talking about having to go to the state capital and speaking with legislators because bills under construction are very poor for education. I'm talking about dealing with curriculum matters—sex education, for example—and knowing all the ramifications of how the churches feel about it. Or knowing whether or not it's important to have the same reading series in a building for all grade levels. Or dealing with the intricacies of

budgeting or the overwhelming number of personnel issues we deal with. This is a human enterprise. All aspects of it. There are no material products that we deal with. They're all human. And this intensifies and magnifies the number of problems.

Because the superintendent interacts with so many different constituencies and has to make so many decisions, conflict is an inevitable part of the job. A third superintendent states:

It's all an indication, I guess, of the fact that no matter what you do, you immediately begin to infringe on people's territory. It is really an unbelievable job. The whole job is conflict-ridden. And sometimes the central character in that conflict—the superintendent—ends up being a casualty of it, no matter how rational and reasonable he thinks he's being. Eventually, I think it gets to everyone.

Arthur Blumberg, "Living With Conflict—Superintendents At Work," 1982. Prepublication manuscript. Used by permission of author.

The pressures brought to bear on both superintendents and school boards are tremendous. Superintendents' jobs are particularly vulnerable to pressure, since their livelihood depends on school board and community support, and inability to reconcile the conflicting pressures of different groups is a major reason for the short job span of the average superintendent. These pressures may also influence how the superintendent administers the public schools. As Gross says:

> If he must spend much of his time placating certain pressure groups, anticipating threats, and developing strategies to deal with them, he will not have much time left to administer the schools efficiently and work with his staff to develop and carry out an effective educational program. He may not have time to do these things at all.[11]

Thus, whereas superintendents possess considerable power, they maintain it only so long as they are effectively able to handle external pressures.

HOW IS SUCH PRESSURE EXERCISED? The influence of informal groups on decision making in school districts has only recently been explored, but data from a number of case studies indicate that an informal power structure exists in many, and probably most, school districts.[12] These data further indicate that the pressure of informal groups of power elites, such as middle-class business executives or key influentials, has a telling influence on decisions; this important power is exercised in most local school districts by a relatively few persons who hold top positions of influence in the informal power structure of the school district. In fact, these informal groups tend to exert far more influence than do formal organizations on basic decisions affecting the public schools.

Evidence from case studies of many school districts reveals that the composition of these power-wielding informal groups varies; however, businesspeople are the largest single occupational group represented. Kimbrough states that, "as a consequence of their superior status, businessmen exercise the greatest effect upon, and often dominate, educational policies in the nation."[13] In contrast to Koerner's assertions, Kimbrough found that educators are poorly represented at the top levels of the power structure, with the occasional exception of the superintendent. Kimbrough agrees with Koerner that most school board members are not part of the informal power structure.

How do these influential members of informal groups actually exercise their power? Kimbrough cites an example from a medium-sized district.

[11]Gross, "Who Applies What Kinds of Pressures," pp. 103–104.

[12]Ralph B. Kimbrough, "An Informal Arrangement for Influence Over Basic Policy," in *Governing Education: A Reader on Politics, Power, and Public School Policy*, ed. Alan Rosenthal (New York: Doubleday, 1969), pp. 105–136.

[13]Kimbrough, "An Informal Arrangement," p. 119.

First, let us assume that an educational project costing several million dollars is proposed for the local school system and that there exists an informal group of community leaders who will be positively affected by the project if it is approved. The project may have been proposed by one of the leaders of this group, by an organization or public official, or it may have evolved through some combination of circumstances. Kimbrough's studies indicate that the following activities may be expected:

There will be an increase in interactions among the leaders of the power group. These interactions to discuss the proposal may occur at civic occasions, on the telephone, or at social gatherings. Small groups of leaders may get together for personal discussions. Thus definite action is preceded by considerable informal talk.

Because of the project's importance, a meeting of the top power wielders in the group is held to resolve differences of opinion and to make a decision, for which the preliminary informal interaction has provided a framework. A decision is reached, and plans for action are drawn up.

A fanning-out process then occurs—key persons not at the meeting are drawn into the group and numerous others are alerted about the decision. This process involves the use of persuasion and reasoning to convince others of the logic of the decision. The public officials who will formalize the decision may, at this point, experience some form of subtle anticipatory coercion. The "Big People" rarely make direct threats but will, if necessary, later resort to threats, bribes, coercion, and political deals.

If for some reason formal action on the project does not proceed according to the wishes of the power brokers, key supporting personnel are induced to resort to parliamentary roadblocks, such as appointing a study committee or referring the issue to a standing committee established for such emergencies. This maneuver allows time to exert heavier pressure for a favorable decision.

Power or control is exercised on a different level by other individuals and groups outside the formal decision-making structure, including the parent-teacher association, taxpayers' associations, and teachers' organizations. Some individuals who influence decisions informally through group membership also occupy positions within the formal organization; teachers are a notable example.

Informal interpersonal relationships are often used to achieve desired objectives, as in the case of a certain principal who managed to get for his school materials and privileges denied other principals.[14] A casual observer might have attributed his success to his aggressive personality. However, the real explanation was that at Rotary Club meetings he usually sat by the assistant superintendent in charge of administration. Whenever he wanted

[14]Kimbrough, "An Informal Arrangement," p. 128–129.

something he simply told the assistant superintendent at the Rotary meeting. Try to trace that decision-making process on a formal organizational chart!

In many school districts there exist two administrative networks: one formal and legally recognized; the other informal, friendly, and, in many instances, far more efficient than the official one. Consider the situation that permits the following kinds of occurrences in one large school district: A teacher who does not believe in filing lesson plans is not rehired in spite of good reports from superiors. When the dismissal is announced, there is no dissent; the favorable reports have been forgotten. A principal who has refused to let a child transfer in under the open-enrollment regulation, because there is no more space, receives a call from a legislator or school board member and suddenly discovers an empty seat.

DIALOGUE

JIM: We haven't given much attention in this chapter to one of the key figures in the business of governing and controlling schools.

KEVIN: Who's that?

JIM: The principal. The principal's the one whose influence the teacher feels most. No other person influences school environment, faculty and student morale, curriculum, and instruction as much.

 KEVIN: I tend to agree, but one study I know of found that in the primary grades 63 percent of the students didn't know the principal's name, and 86 percent had never spoken to him. And the 14 percent who had spoken to him had done so in a nega-

tive situation. That study doesn't indicate much impact.

JIM: Oh, but it does! I would say that the principal was influencing the students tremendously. His absence from their daily life was having an impact on them.

KEVIN: Well, in a sense, yes.

JIM: The critical factor, as far as I'm concerned, is that principals see themselves as the school's leader rather than its administrator. If they are skillful and adept at human relations, decision making, and facilitating staff wishes, they can enhance the conditions in which they, their staff, and the students work.

KEVIN: I think that their attitude toward children is the

single most significant factor in determining or changing the school's climate. Principals can set the tone of the entire school by the way their attitudes are reflected in their actions.

JIM: My advice to young teachers who are looking for their first jobs is to find out as much as they can about their prospective principal's beliefs about children and about how learning should occur. I'd also talk to other teachers in the school about the principal's leadership ability. Does the school reflect his or her beliefs about children and learning? If the teachers can't tell what the principal's beliefs are, he or she can't be much of a leader.

Parents and Teachers   The local parent-teacher organization serves as a communications link between parents and the formal school organization, with teachers usually acting as representatives of the schools. The formal school system ordinarily operates by means of down-the-line communications. When the formal hierarchy does not respond to up-the-line communications from parents or teachers in a manner satisfactory to them, they can resort to the informal system in an attempt to get a more favorable response.

An instance of this occurred when the energetic principal of a New Haven, Connecticut, school in a low-income neighborhood organized the PTA in an attempt to improve the school's facilities. He began by going to an important neighborhood leader and persuading her that the children in the school needed help. Convinced, the woman and the principal went to work on the PTA. To arouse parent involvement, they convinced the PTA to endorse a hot lunch program; this required the PTA to raise funds and hire kitchen help. As the PTA became more active, the principal began a campaign for a new school to replace the old one. When the city administration raised obstacles, the principal called together the PTA members and other neighborhood leaders to ask their support for the construction of a new school. Within twenty-four hours they were exerting pressure on the administration. Needless to say, the problem was solved.

However, teachers have become increasingly frustrated by the impotence of most parent-teacher organizations and their ineffectiveness as a means of implementing teachers' educational aims. Consequently, the role of teachers' organizations in determining educational policy is ever increasing. Largely as a result of collective bargaining techniques, including strikes and the threat of strikes, teacher organizations are winning more and more power over educational policy.

Today many teacher organizations have won recognition as the official bargaining representatives of their members, whereas in the past, boards of education insisted on dealing with teachers as individuals. Teacher organizations are also demanding that issues previously considered the prerogatives of school boards and superintendents be subject to collective bargaining. Among these issues are teacher and paraprofessional salaries, clerical and secretarial assistance, curriculum development, fringe benefits, inservice training, class size determination, textbook selection, and even the appointment of department heads and other school administrators. As one commentator has put it, "They want to negotiate everything." In an increasing number of school districts, teacher organizations are winning the right to negotiate these issues with school boards. As another observer has remarked, "It is not at all difficult to foresee a time when virtually all American teachers will be employed under collective bargaining contracts that cover not only salaries but a long list of other items."[15]

Influence of Business

Collective bargaining is one of many procedures that educators are borrowing from the business world. But the impact of business on education is not a new phenomenon. Industrial growth in the United States was paralleled historically by the application of industrial principles in the schools. At the height of an industrially inspired "efficiency movement" in the 1920s, a number of business techniques of dubious educational merit were introduced into the schools. Schools were compared to factories whose products were students; dollar values were assigned to parts of the curriculum; the size of classes and teacher loads were increased for the sake of efficiency, and detailed clerical records were kept. Education was, in effect, confined to cost-saving and mechanical functions to reduce "overhead." The public then demanded a profitable return on money "invested" in schools. Some teachers and educators fought the trend, but so powerful and far-reaching was the movement that their voices were not heard. It was later recognized that educators had gone overboard in applying commercial principles, unscientifically, to a social institution. But the damage had been done, and many such practices of questionable educational value are still used in schools across the country.

[15]Koerner, *Who Controls American Education?*, p. 42. A more detailed discussion of teacher organizations follows in Chapter 11.

> *The most significant impact of business on education has been to give it a strong utilitarian and vocational flavor. In terms of a people's intellectual, aesthetic, moral, and emotional development, it narrows the leadership base for American civilization, reinforcing the utilitarian, consumptionist standard. . . . Thus, the corporation's effect on education has been to drain it of its moral quality and to fill it with functional utility. This is the basis for a strong economy, but not a great society.*
>
> — NEIL CHAMBERLAIN —

Increasing attention has been given in recent years to the amount of control business exercises over education. In one study, Grace Graham shows that the great prestige of the business world has enabled it to have significant influence on American education.[16] Today's schools by and large endorse and teach the values of business. The dominant theme of the "business creed" consciously and unconsciously disseminated by businesspeople is praise for the achievements of American capitalism; the fundamentals of this creed are being absorbed by most students throughout the school day. As Graham says, "In general, teachers seemingly stress many of the values that businessmen praise highly. For example, teachers struggle to inculcate respect for hard work, punctuality, neatness, a sense of duty, and acceptance of the sanctity of private property."[17]

Teachers usually grade their pupils at least partly on the basis of how hard they try. They emphasize the importance of education as preparation to get a job. "This emphasis by educators on the economic rather than on the intellectual and aesthetic contributions of education to a full life indicates the extent to which teachers themselves accept the businessmen's creed."[18]

Both the school board and the superintendent are influenced by the business community. In most school districts, the superintendent resembles an executive or business manager more than an educational philosopher. Knowledge of budgeting and finance is essential for hiring and success as a superintendent. Indeed, today school management and budgeting processes are being revitalized by the "systems" approach, which has been borrowed from private industry. Most school boards are also likely to have a business orientation, since businesspeople have continually been well represented on local boards. As a result, school boards tend to be economy minded and to stress the elimination of frills and the reduction of overhead—approaches that may be sound in business but are unlikely to encourage educational experimentation.

The National Association of Manufacturers (NAM), the public relations arm of the business community, runs a comprehensive and far-reaching public relations program directed at the schools, which consciously disseminates the "business creed."[19] The NAM exerts influence to try to eliminate from the curriculum and from textbooks any tendency toward "creeping collectivism," and promotes "pro-American" doctrines. Local manufacturers are urged to investigate what is being taught their own children and to find out how much money is being spent by taxpayers to spread

[16]Grace Graham, *The Public Schools in the New Society* (New York: Harper & Row, 1969), chs. 2, 6, and 8.

[17]Graham, *The Public Schools*, p. 27.

[18]Graham, *The Public Schools*, p. 28.

[19]Graham, *The Public Schools*, p. 18.

doctrines abhorrent to the business community.[20] Another NAM public relations project is Business Education Day, when teachers and local business leaders exchange roles. Its purpose is to show educators how our economic system functions, and the exchanges provide a channel of communication between schools and the community. However, the project also tends to promote a pro-management slant on business issues, and the American Federation of Teachers, a union organization, has taken a strong stand against closing the schools at taxpayers' expense for the advantage of a particular interest group.

Links between education and business also occur when corporations give the schools free products to promote their images. Most parents and teachers would agree that schools should be protected as neutral zones from commercial exploitation; however, consider what is already permitted. Commercial sponsors provide the schools with pencils, book covers, notebooks, posters, information and recruitment booths, field trips, a career day, billboards, scoreboards, benches, vending machines, school newspaper ads, yearbook patrons, service club sponsors, honor student prizes, graduation gifts, collection drives, essay contests, fund raisers, and candy sales. It should not be surprising that so many supplementary curriculum materials such as tapes, films, filmstrips, and print materials, sponsored by and carrying advertising messages for large corporations, find their way into the classrooms. As one teacher stated: "Teachers are not allowed to make students buy additional materials such as workbooks anymore and these industry materials sometimes fill a need which textbooks do not supply." The danger, of course, is that a form of subtle brainwashing may take place. Consider, for example, the following opening statement taken from a glossy, full-color, illustrated booklet available to teachers upon request from the American Tobacco Company: "Cigarettes and civilization—the two seem to go together." Later on in the same booklet we read: "Many of the common sailors were quick to learn that tobacco satisfies a human need."[21] Although these examples may represent an extreme propagandist position, whenever commercially sponsored and developed materials are offered to the public schools, the danger exists.

Businesses have also offered direct assistance to schools, particularly in the large cities; in some instances businesses have even "adopted" particular schools, offering technical, managerial, and financial aid.

The influence of business on education in America has been and continues to be strong. Another influencing and controlling force on education has been the federal government, to which we now turn.

[20]S. A. Rippa, *Education in a Free Society, An American History* (New York: David McKay, 1967), p. 156.

[21]Sheila Harty, *Hucksters in the Classroom* (Washington, D.C.: Center for Study of Responsive Law, 1979), p. 121.

Miss Peach by Mell Lazarus. Courtesy of Mell Lazarus and Field Newspaper Syndicate.

Control by the Federal Government

It could be argued that the most powerful educational decision-making body in the United States is the Supreme Court, several of whose decisions in recent years have had a profound effect on education. A prime example is *Ingraham* v. *Wright* (1977), in which the court ruled that corporal punishment (paddling and other similar forms of punishment) is not unconstitutional under the Eighth Amendment of the Constitution, which prohibits "cruel and unusual" punishment. Because some of the Court's decisions have reduced the power of state and local educational authorities, deep resentment has been generated among those who abhor this "federal intrusion" into state rights. Other people applaud the Court's decisions as steps to make American education more responsive to democratic principles.

The federal government also exerts powerful influence on education through legislation providing monetary aid to local and state authorities and through the administration of these funds by federal offices and departments. Congressional acts apportioning federal funds to education have provided funds to colleges, cities, states, and agencies to finance a wide variety of projects, including construction of buildings and other educational facilities; improvement of instruction or administration; development of educational personnel, including teachers and paraprofessionals, particularly for poverty areas; loans for prospective teachers; and educational research. Although the federal government may provide less money for public schools than do state or local governments, federal funds are strategically important and have a far greater impact than their proportion of school funding would suggest.

Because much federal aid is categorical—that is, the money must be spent for purposes that are stated generally in the legislation and more precisely by the federal agency administering the funds—the federal government is able to exert influence on school districts and institutions that accept or seek this aid. For example, to qualify for federal funds to improve its reading program, a school district must conform to the guidelines and restrictions that accompany the money. Many financially stricken school districts are grateful for additional funds regardless of the restrictions on use.

There is a danger inherent in this situation, and that is that a school district might be tempted to divert its own resources from a much-needed program to a less important project that the federal government would be willing to help finance. Thus, the prospect of federal money may encourage neglect of a local district's particular needs. Despite these potential dangers, the majority of educators support the federal government's role in education.

Since the early 1980s, a change in federal aid to education has been occurring. The Reagan administration proposed drastic reductions in the tightly targeted categorical programs, and instead provided no-strings aid to state and local education agencies in the form of block grants. (*Block grants* are sums of money that may be spent in ways [with some restrictions] determined by state and local governments.) If block grants to the states replace the federal categorical aid, then the federal role in education will be transformed. It is unclear at this writing what the new balance of power will be.

In 1979 the Carter administration and Congress split the Department of Health, Education, and Welfare into two parts, thus creating a federal Department of Education. Whereas some people viewed this as merely an attempt to consolidate federal education efforts, others believed that establishing a cabinet-level department was a backdoor way of creating a national education policy, thus breaking sharply with the long tradition of a limited federal involvement in education. Proponents of the Department of Education argued that its establishment would not lead to federal control, because the Tenth Amendment to the U.S. Constitution places the responsibility for education on the states, and existing federal law prohibits officials from exercising "any direction, supervision, or control over the curriculum, program of instruction, administration, or personnel of any educational institution, school or school system." Opponents of the department believed that it would lead to more federal influence over education, more bureaucratization, and the creation of a federal policy for education. It is unknown at this time how long the Department of Education will remain in existence. As of 1983 President Reagan was proposing to dismantle the Department of Education and replace it with a Foundation for Education Assistance that would oversee a reduced number of federal programs. If Congress does create such a foundation, then education no longer would be directly represented in the president's Cabinet.

*Sources of School
Revenue*

The total amount of money for education available to a school district is a sum of locally raised revenues, state aid, federal aid, and miscellaneous revenues. Historically, most of the money used to support public elementary and secondary schools has come from local revenue sources, primarily the property tax. Recently, for the first time in American history, the state's share of support for public education exceeded the local share (see Table 8.2). Reasons for this increase in state support are discussed in the following section.

How are these educational expenditures paid? By what systems of taxation? State revenue systems are as diverse as school finance plans, and reflect the socioeconomic makeup, the political climate, and the educational needs of each state. These systems rely on a wide variety of revenue sources. While local governments rely primarily on the property tax for income, state governments use a combination of sales, personal income, corporate income, and excise taxes to generate revenues. A majority of states require that citizens in a school district vote on either the property tax rate to support education or the school budget itself. In recent years passing school budgets and school tax referendums has become increasingly difficult. Taxpayers have been rejecting proposals to increase funds for education by repudiating the prevailing methods of raising local school revenue—the heavy reliance on local property taxes. The result has been efforts such as California's Proposition 13 and Massachusetts' Proposition 2½, which lowered local property taxes sharply. Although this revolt has not markedly slowed the rise in public school expenditure, which is expected to increase from 96.8 billion dollars in 1980–81 to 123 billion dollars by 1990–91 (in

Table 8.2 Percentage of Revenue Received from Federal, State, and Local Sources for Public Elementary and Secondary Schools

	PERCENTAGE OF REVENUE			
SCHOOL YEAR	*Federal*	*State*	*Local*	*Total*
1919–20	0.3	16.5	83.2	100
1929–30	0.4	16.9	82.7	100
1939–40	1.8	30.3	68.0	100
1949–50	2.9	39.8	57.3	100
1959–60	4.4	39.1	56.5	100
1969–70	8.0	39.9	52.1	100
1979–80	9.8	46.8	43.4	100
1981–82	8.6	47.7	43.4	100

Source: W. Vance Grant and Leo J. Eiden, *Digest of Education Statistics 1981,* National Center for Education Statistics (Washington, D.C.: U.S. Government Printing Office, 1982), pp. 21 and 75.

Table 8.3 Percentage of Revenue by Government Source for Public Elementary and Secondary Schools, for Selected States, 1979–80

STATE	PERCENTAGE OF REVENUE		
	Local	State	Federal
California	23.0	66.3	10.7
Hawaii	0	84.7	15.3
Mississippi	18.9	56.0	25.1
Nebraska	75.7	16.7	7.6
New Hampshire	85.1	8.2	6.6
New Mexico	16.6	63.6	19.9
New York	53.8	38.0	8.2
South Carolina	37.1	45.0	17.8
Texas	39.3	49.1	11.6
Wisconsin	57.0	37.3	5.6

Source: W. Vance Grant and Leo J. Eiden, *Digest of Education Statistics 1982,* National Center for Education Statistics (Washington, D.C.: U.S. Government Printing Office, 1982), p. 74.

1980–81 dollars), in some places it has resulted in shortened school years, reduced curricular offerings, teacher layoffs, and the abolition of extracurricular activities.[22]

There are considerable variations from state to state regarding the percentage of revenue received from federal, state, and local sources (see Table 8.3). Federal contributions to state revenue for public education range from a high of 25.1 percent for Mississippi to a low of 5.6 percent for Wisconsin. Local contributions to revenue range from a high of 85.1 percent for New Hampshire to a low of 0 percent for Hawaii, which has a statewide school district.

In an effort to reduce federal spending, the Reagan administration cut the federal budget in the area of education. This resulted in the elimination or reduction of many federally sponsored programs such as the national Teacher Corps, vocational and adult education, compensatory education, and block grants for improving school programs. The federal share of support for public education fell from 9.8 percent in 1979–80 to 8.6 percent in the school year 1981–82 (see Table 8.2). This decrease reflects the president's intent to reduce the role of the federal government in educational matters. How far this reduction will go remains to be seen. One thing is clear, however: the "golden" days of education, when money was readily

[22]Martin M. Frankel and Debra E. Gerald, *Projections of Education Statistics to 1990–91,* National Center for Education Statistics (Washington, D.C.: U.S. Government Printing Office, 1982), pp. 101–102.

available and flowed freely, are over for the time being. The American public is in a penny-pinching mood caused by so many demands for tax dollars to provide for an array of public services such as highways, prisons, mental institutions, as well as education.

SCHOOL FINANCE REFORM

Many knowledgeable educators and politicians argue that one of the greatest causes of unequal educational opportunity is the method used to finance school systems. School districts whose property values are high generate much more money to finance their schools than districts whose property values are low. Within the same state, for example, the average amount of money spent per child in one district may be more than twice the amount spent in a nearby district. Such spending differentials result in great educational disparities, as measured by pupil-teacher ratios, training and experience of staff, availability of facilities, equipment, and counseling services. This is particularly true for many large cities that have unusually heavy demands against their deteriorating tax bases for other municipal services, which make their problems of raising revenues substantial. In addition, these cities have high proportions of pupils with costly educational needs that require added spending. Poor children, low-achieving students, the non-English speaking, those in higher cost curricula, and the handicapped are among the pupils who impose high costs.

In 1971 a class action suit, *Serrano* v. *Priest*, was filed by pupils and their parents against California state and county officials concerned with financing public schools. The suit charged that the school financing scheme was unconstitutional. The Supreme Court of California supported the parents' claim that the quality of a child's education may not be a function of wealth other than the wealth of the state as a whole. The court also held that the California system of financing schools on the basis of local property taxes violates the Fourteenth Amendment to the U.S. Constitution.

In 1973 the Supreme Court of the United States reversed a similar decision (known as the *Rodriguez* case) involving the school finance system of the state of Texas by a 5-4 vote. The Court found that the Constitution was not violated because the right to an education is not guaranteed explicitly or implicitly by the Constitution. The Court did state that the finding should not be interpreted as a victory for the status quo but urged the states to solve obvious inequalities.

Many state constitutions contain equal protection clauses, unlike the U.S. Constitution, and education has been interpreted as a protected right in many states. Thus the precedent established by the *Serrano* case has led other state courts to rule that their school financing systems violate their state constitutions.

State governments continue to wrestle with the problems of equalizing educational opportunity and financial responsibility. Educators, parents, and public officials are greatly concerned that the quality of a child's education not depend on whether the child lives in a school district with high property values. Many of these concerned citizens are urging that the state government become responsible for raising educational revenue and for distributing the full costs of local schools to school districts. The school districts would continue to be in charge of the operation of the local schools, but they would no longer have to sponsor school bond elections to raise money.

The different states will probably try many different schemes for financing public schools. There is no doubt that the issue is complex and difficult to solve. The courts have provided the direction for school financial reform, but it will be the primary responsibility of state legislative bodies to develop school finance systems that may be expected to produce equal educational opportunities.

Discussion Questions

1. Can you offer any examples from your experience of the distinction between governance and control? How do you suppose the persons in control obtained their power? What were the advantages and disadvantages of this state of affairs in the situations you are familiar with?

2. What do you see as the advantages and disadvantages of the public schools being a branch of the federal government? Are you familiar with any country where this is the case? What is its school system like? How does it compare to the system of which you are a product?

3. From what you have read about the role of the superintendent, what impressions have you formed about the constraints on and power of the superintendent?

4. How were the interests and values of business reflected in your education? Were you aware of the influence of commercial values and methods on your schooling at the time? What is your opinion of this state of affairs?

5. Do you think the PTA is a potentially effective means of influencing school policy? Where do you think the interests of teachers and parents coincide? Where do they diverge? In what areas do you think informal influence might be more effective than collective bargaining?

6. How involved should the federal government be in public education? What are the advantages and dangers of a reduction of the federal government's involvement in public education?

7. Of the methods of school financing discussed in this chapter, which do you believe would be most equitable? Why?

8. In the light of what you have learned from this chapter, what do you think of Paul Woodring's statement that "education is too important to be left to the educators"?

For Further Reading   Berke, Joel, Michael Kirst, and Michael Usdan. *The New State Politics of Education.* Cambridge, Mass.: Ballinger, 1976.

> Good insights into state politics in education.

Campbell, Roald, et al. *The Organization and Control of American Schools.* 4th ed. Columbus, Ohio: Charles E. Merrill, 1980.

> A good overview of the American educational system, including both governance and control issues.

Garms, Walter I.; James W. Guthrie; and L. G. Pierce. *School Finance: The Economics and Politics of Public Education.* Englewood Cliffs, N.J.: Prentice-Hall, 1978.

> A good overview of school finance issues by leaders in the field.

Koerner, James D. *Who Controls American Education?* Boston: Beacon Press, 1968.

> States that professional educators and their organizations exert major control over American education. Koerner deplores this and urges that changes be made to reduce the power of superintendents, professors of education, state departments of education, and the professional organizations.

Mosher, Edith K., and Jennings L. Wagoner, Jr., eds. *The Changing Politics of Education: Prospects for the 1980's.* Berkeley, Calif.: McCutchan Publishing Corp., 1978.

> The proceedings of a symposium on the politics of education, including school finance, elementary and secondary education, and the exercise of power.

Rosenthal, Alan, ed. *Governing Education: A Reader on Politics, Power, and Public School Policy.* New York: Doubleday, 1969.

> A compilation of readings on the politics of education. Case studies, as well as expository articles, demonstrate how educational decisions are made and who makes them. The chapters by Kimbrough and Gross are particularly interesting.

Scribner, Jay D., ed. *The Politics of Education: The 76th Yearbook of the National Society for the Study of Education.* Part 2. Chicago: University of Chicago Press, 1977.

> An excellent volume by different contributing authors on various aspects of the politics of education.

Wirt, Frederick M., and Michael W. Kirst. *Schools in Conflict.* Berkeley, Calif.: McCutchan Publishing Corp., 1982.

> An up-to-date analysis of the politics of education by two leaders in the field.

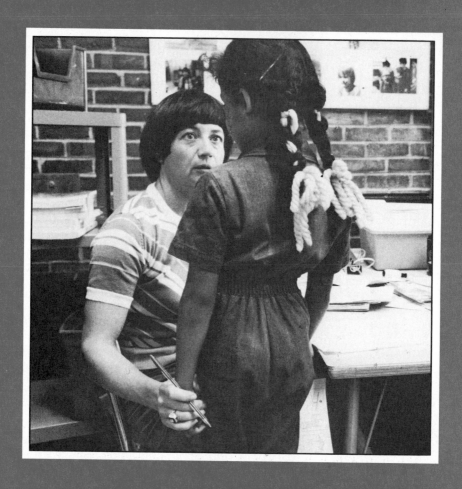

TEACHERS

IV

What Can
the New Teacher
Expect?

9

Although they have spent an enormous amount of time in schools, many new teachers are shocked and surprised by the actual experience of being a teacher. In this chapter we try to help prospective teachers anticipate some of the problems that lie ahead. Much of the material comes directly from the experience of beginning teachers.

This chapter emphasizes that:

■ Although prospective teachers may feel that schools will have few surprises for them, being on the other side of the desk is a very different experience and can cause a sense of culture shock.

■ Administrators play an important role in the life of the new teacher, but it is a role with many facets that can be very confusing to the beginning teacher.

■ Although fellow teachers are an enormous source of learning and support, they can also be a source of difficulty.

■ New teachers learn much about that in which they are supposed to be expert: instruction.

■ While the teacher's main purpose is to give service to children, students are a source of both satisfaction and dissatisfaction.

■ Working with parents can be surprisingly complex, and is rarely what the new teacher has anticipated.

*T*HE FIRST YEAR OF TEACHING has been described as an emotional roller-coaster, filled with peaks of exhilaration and dips of discouragement. The first year is a year of great intensity for the beginning teacher. It is intense because of the unexpected demands presented by teaching and because of the surprises that reside in what was thought to be a familiar world—the classroom. Some of the intensity comes from the problems confronted by the teacher; some comes from the satisfaction in solving those problems and in succeeding as a professional.

The surprises of the first year of teaching are wrapped in everyday boxes—some contain sweet treasures and others hold boobytraps. We have categorized these surprises in the following way:

- the school milieu: the shock of the familiar
- administrators: mixed bag and many hats
- peers: a mixed blessing
- instruction: so much to learn
- students: friends or fiends?
- parents: natural allies with different agendas

In this chapter we will look at each of these features of the initial year of teaching. Our purpose is not to take the surprise out of the first year. We hope, instead, to achieve three purposes. First, we want to alert you and to get you thinking about certain dimensions of teaching that now may not seem so important to you as they will when you teach. For example, we have known many preservice teachers who gave all their attention to mastery of subject matter and paid little attention to a whole range of issues relating to dealing with students. Second, in the case of certain problem areas, we are, quite frankly, trying to forewarn you. We are convinced that many of us are very good at kidding ourselves, and we have known too many students whose rose-colored vision of teaching has turned to disillusionment. Third, we wish to make you aware of certain aspects of teaching that may hold special, unexpected satisfactions.

THE SCHOOL MILIEU: THE SHOCK OF THE FAMILIAR

One of the oddest phenomena related to becoming a teacher is the new teacher's sense of strangeness in what is, after all, a very familiar setting. People who become insurance sales representatives, astronauts, or psychiatric social workers know they are moving into a strange environment, and they expect these new work worlds to present them with very different experiences from those they had as students. New teachers, however, are re-entering a familiar setting, even if it is not the same school in which they were taught. The school routine of classes, periods, bells, tests, homework, and report cards is in their blood. The hierarchical system of principals, teachers, and students is taken for granted. The rituals and pageants—assemblies, Thanksgiving class presentations, honor society induction, sports rivalries with other schools—are all instantly recognizable. The existence of cliques, in-groups, and out-groups among both students and faculty is no secret either. But despite all their experience and sophistication, beginning teachers are often overwhelmed by their initial exposures to school.

The beginning teacher's shock at the familiar is sometimes manifested in visible signs of mental and physical stress. In the early months of the school year it is not uncommon for the new teacher to experience depression and self-doubt, outbursts of crying, physical exhaustion, insomnia, crankiness, inability to control temper, and even fits of vomiting before going to school in the morning. The anthropologist Estelle Fuchs has studied the world of the beginning teacher. In her words,

> Most of us are aware of the tensions and strains accompanying unfamiliar routines or activities. However, the symptoms expressed

by beginning teachers . . . go far beyond the ordinary fatigue associated with a new mode of employment. They are surprisingly similar to the phenomenon described by anthropologists as "culture shock."[1]

Culture shock is the feeling of dislocation people experience when they initially encounter a foreign culture. Peace Corps volunteers, foreign students, tourists, and newly arrived immigrants frequently report that when first thrust into the strange life patterns of a foreign culture they feel numbingly disoriented, forced to assimilate too much too soon, and afraid they have made a drastic mistake to have gone to a strange country. It is easy to explain culture shock among Peace Corps volunteers and immigrants, but why teachers? Haven't we just said that teachers, as ex-students, are accustomed to the culture of school? It appears, though, that the new teacher's very familiarity with life in schools is a problem in itself. "School" is a very complicated series of structures, people, and interactions, and knowing part of it does not imply knowledge of the whole. Being one of twenty-five students sitting and listening to a teacher is very different from standing in front of twenty-five strange children and taking charge of their learning. People learn a great deal about teaching through years of teacher watching, but there is much that they do not learn. Also new teachers have to learn not only a new set of school routines for their particular school, but also how to administer them. They have to learn their way around a new building and find out how to requisition the supplies they need. They have to get acquainted with their administration, their fellow teachers, and especially their students. And on top of all this, first-year teachers have to develop lesson plans from scratch. They must build complete units, design bulletin boards, devise an evaluation system, and make up tests. The pressure of all this newness can cause strain.

The following account by a new second-grade teacher[2] speaks to the kinds of culture shock problems experienced by teachers in many situations.

JOAN CHEFFERS/SECOND GRADE   "The next time I hear someone say, 'Teaching is an easy job,' I think I'm going to slap their face . . . or cry! I can't believe how tired I am. I've been teaching for five weeks, and it seems as if it has been five months. I never realized that life on the teacher's side of the desk could be so different, so tiring. I remember seeing the old movie *Up the Down Staircase* and thinking it was exagger-

[1]Estelle Fuchs, *Teachers Talk: Views from Inside City Schools* (Garden City, N.Y.: Doubleday, 1969), p. 21.

[2]All the cases in this chapter that are not accompanied by specific citations are slightly altered or fictionalized accounts of situations and problems experienced by the authors or by beginning teachers with whom the authors have worked. The names have been changed to save us all from embarrassment.

ated. My kids are younger and don't have the kinds of problems those high school kids in the movie had, but they still have problems, and they are so demanding. They all want my attention, and they all seem to want it at the same time. 'Miss Cheffers, someone took my pencil! Did you do it?' 'Miss Cheffers, Ralph and Maxine put gum in my hair.' 'Miss Cheffers, my father doesn't think we're doing enough arithmetic in this class

WHAT WOULD YOU DO?

1. You are a woman, a beginning teacher in a ninth-grade English course. As the first semester proceeds, you realize that one of your students, Fred, has a crush on you. He is constantly volunteering to help you pass out papers, and he lingers after class each day to talk to you. He found out your home address and came to visit you one Saturday morning. His actions are becoming obvious to the other students, who are starting to kid him about his infatuation.

What would you do?

2. You are generally recognized as one of the most popular teachers on campus. The students look upon you as a friend who can be trusted, and you have told them that if they ever have problems, school-related or personal, they should feel free to come to you. One day Maryanne, a junior in one of your classes, seeks you out. She is close to hysteria, and tells you that she is ten weeks pregnant. You are the first person she has told. She begs you for advice, but insists you do not tell her parents.

What would you do?

3. You are a third-grade teacher. Until recently, you have been quite comfortable in your class of twenty-seven children. About three weeks ago, you had to speak to Debbie. Although she is the brightest student and the natural leader in your class, she was continually talking when you were trying to address the class. Since then she has been as cool as ice to you. But, more worrisome, she has turned the class against you. They seem hostile, and there are continued signs of lack of cooperation. The principal wants to talk with you because she has heard many complaints recently.

What would you do?

4. You are a white teacher in a recently integrated school. There are seven black students in one of your classes. Because you fear alienating the blacks and being accused of prejudice, you make special efforts to treat them fairly. One day three of your white students come to see you and accuse you of coddling the blacks and discriminating against whites.

What would you do?

5. You teach in a school that uses a letter grading system. You have assigned your students a term paper. You know that one of your students has spent hours and hours on his report, but its quality is quite poor. The student has already expressed his hope that you will take effort into account when grading the reports.

What would you do?

6. You are the same teacher described in case number five. When you assigned the term paper you distributed a sheet containing all the necessary information about the assignment, including the due date. All but two of the reports were handed in on time, and those were both a week late. Adequate time was allowed for the completion of the paper.

What would you do?

and says I can tell the kids to shut up if you won't.' 'Miss Cheffers, I need to go to the nurse. I have a terrible nosebleed coming on!' And on and on.

"And the forms! They never end. Forms for shots. For lockers. For parent volunteers. For books. And we have an attendance procedure here that must have been designed by a sadist! It consumes hours of time. The principal's office continually wants information. I keep filling out forms and sending them in, only to be greeted with more forms. I can't imagine what they do with all the information.

"On top of all this, I'm supposed to teach! I leave school in the afternoon—always the last one out of the building—and I'm numb from the hairline down. On some nights I can hardly unwrap a TV dinner. And I spend what little free time I do have staring at the TV set and having imaginary arguments with Sandra's know-it-all father (whom I have yet to meet) about why we actually are doing just the right amount of arithmetic. What is most discouraging is that Sandra's father wins the arguments.

"Clearly, this has been the most frustrating five weeks of my life. I feel as if I've been swimming in molasses. Student teaching was a breeze compared to this!"

But many of the surprises of school life are very pleasant ones. There is much love and human warmth in the classroom. The aspects of school life that one might have dreaded never actually materialized. The content that one felt unsure of turned out to be one's strength. Also, within the four walls of the classroom, some people find a new self whom they didn't know existed.

JOAN GEE/OFFICE MANAGEMENT "All through elementary and high school I was bashful. In my high school graduating class I won the 'Most Shy' award. I dreaded being called on, even when I knew I had the right answer! Part of it is that I blush so easily. So my approach was to be like the furniture or the wallpaper and hope that the teacher wouldn't see me. Still, I liked school and always liked my teachers, even the ones that had fun with my blushing. When I decided to become a teacher, I knew my shyness was going to be a problem, but I figured that I could pass my blushing off as a permanent sunburn.

"Something happened, though, when I became a teacher. I began to notice a change when I was student teaching, and once I had my own class, it was quite clear: I'm a different person in my class. I feel very outgoing, almost to the point of being aggressive. Also, I've discovered that I'm a ham actor. And what a stage my classroom is! I love it. And my students seem to love it, too. It seems so odd that after all these years of trying to be invisible, now I'm discovering a whole new side of myself."

ADMINISTRATORS: MIXED BAG AND MANY HATS

When we were elementary and secondary school students, most of us had pretty simplistic notions of administrators. The superintendent was a vague presence we occasionally glimpsed in the hall talking to one of the staff or in front of a microphone on ceremonial occasions. The principal was much more a part of our school lives as someone beloved or feared, and occasionally both. Even though the principal was near at hand, our student's-eye view was rather one-dimensional. The principal represented AUTHORITY. In all but the rarest instances the principal stood directly beyond the teacher, supporting the teacher and the system. When, as students, we went to the principal's office, it usually meant we were in trouble.

New teachers' relationships with their principals are not so simple, however. School principals loom quite large in the lives of beginning teachers, and the teacher-principal relationship (and, to a lesser degree, teachers' relationships with vice principals, department heads, and master teachers) are many-faceted. The principal is, first of all, a colleague, a fellow educator[3] joined with you in the common task of bringing civilization to the young. You are both professionals. You are part of a common tradition. You automatically share common goals (such as improving the educational opportunities of children) and attitudes (for example, that people engaged in the important work of educating the young need more support from the public than they get).

Principals are the official leaders. They make decisions, or act as the funnel for the decisions of higher authorities. Decisions made by teachers or students are normally checked with principals. Principals speak for the school community to the superintendent, the press, and the local citizens. Although they are not necessarily the de facto leaders, the most influential people in school communities, they frequently are. Nothing is ever quite "official" unless the principal has been involved.

Principals are helpers. They can dispense information and materials, and, as experienced teachers, they are sources of tips, short cuts, and helpful suggestions. Teachers can directly request their help. Principals also visit classrooms, and, ordinarily, hold conferences with teachers. They are there to aid beginning teachers who are encountering difficulties and confusion.

Principals are initiators. A school system is a bureaucracy whose long arm extends from the state commissioner of education to the local district superintendent of schools to the individual school principal. Principals, in effect, act in behalf of the bureaucracy by introducing teachers into the bureaucratic life of school and teaching them how to function in it.

[3]One of the little curiosities of educationese, the official language of schools, is that administrators refer to themselves as educators—as in "leading educator" and "innovative educator"—and teachers are simply called teachers. Occasionally, when the principal attempts to rally the teacher-troops, she or he broadens it to "we educators. . . ." Some few, guilty, perhaps, for having left the classroom, insist that they are still "just teachers." One thing you can count on, though: "educators" invariably make more money than teachers.

Principals are crisis managers. When something happens that a teacher cannot handle, the principal's office is where he or she naturally turns for help. Besides being a potential source of help, a principal needs to know about crises in the school in order to try to deal with them effectively.

Principals are facilitators. Schools run on things—pencils, books, paper, heat, hot lunches, sanitary toilets, lights, construction paper, petty cash, and keys. It is the principal's job to keep teachers supplied so that teachers, in turn, can carry out the aims of the school.

Principals are reward dispensers. Although it is the school board which actually hires teachers, the board typically acts on the recommendation of principals. Later, they can give or withhold compliments on teacher performance and give or withhold extracurricular duty assignments. Principals assign classes to teachers, deciding what kind of children they will teach and whether the children will be at the level or in the subject for which particular teachers are prepared.

Principals are judges. Theirs is the official view of a teacher's performance. First-year teachers are neither permanent members of the faculty nor permanently certified members of the teaching profession. Principals make decisions about a teacher's qualifications that can have a profound effect on his or her future in education. They can enhance or destroy people's reputations as teachers. They can write recommendations for or against teachers. They can insure that teachers are not rehired. They can block certification. And, of course, they can judge teachers positively and be very positive influences of teachers' entire careers. Obviously, principals derive a great deal of power from their roles as reward dispensers and judges.

Principals act as buffers between teachers and angry parents (or, occasionally, angry students). Teachers can be quite vulnerable to public attack. Parents hear tales from their children or from other parents and, if they have a question or a complaint to make against a teacher, go directly either to the principal or to the teacher. If they do not get satisfaction from the teacher, they then go to the principal. The principal is thus the official "complaint department." This is a delicate position, requiring the principal to be open and responsive to complaints and at the same time to support the position of the teacher involved. Such situations call for the skills of high diplomacy.

Principals are the sacrificial lambs. If the community, the teachers, or the school board become dissatisfied with what is going on in a particular school, the school's principal, who usually does not have tenure in that position, is vulnerable. The tenured staff cannot be dismissed (except under very special circumstances). The community cannot be substituted for another. Thus the principal, who may or may not be responsible for the reported problem, is likely to be chosen to pay the penalty. The ease with which the principal can be dismissed is, incidentally, a position shared with beginning teachers.

Having to wear all these hats and to perform all these roles makes for a complicated existence. The principal of a school today has a most difficult job, and to do the job well requires the strengths of a field general, a philosopher, a psychiatrist, and a saint. In light of the general shortage of these strengths, it is not surprising that new teachers often find themselves in conflict with their principals. Principals have to make many quick and difficult decisions, frequently with insufficient information or time, and they are sometimes wrong. A factor that contributes to conflict between administrators and beginning teachers is that administrators are often playing several roles at once. When they appear in teachers' classrooms to observe, they are both helpers and judges. They may say that they are there only as sources of aid, but some time in the future they must make recommendations about teachers to their superiors, and they obviously are influenced by what they have seen during their "helping" observations.

Another potential source of difficulty is that administrators must be like ships' captains, concerned with keeping the ship afloat, running, and moving in a particular direction, whereas teachers, who are there to stimulate learning and creativity, have a different set of concerns. Bizarre or random activity, questioning, and occasional chaos frequently play an important part in learning. And it is at this juncture that administrators who put too great a value on order most often collide with teachers.

Therefore, it is to be expected that there may be confusion and the potential for conflict between the administrator and the new teacher who is being initiated into the system. For one thing, beginning teachers often do not know how to work in a bureaucracy (that is, make it work for their ends) and sometimes are antibureaucratic. This can lead them into direct conflict with their administrators, whose job it is to train beginners in bureaucratic procedures, but whose primary responsibility is to make sure the school, as a totality, runs smoothly. Amidst these many roles and different hats worn by the administrator, there can be slippage and breakdown. The following account illustrates such a case.

STEVE MELLONWOOD/JUNIOR HIGH SOCIAL STUDIES "During the special orientation meeting for new teachers, the principal told us all that whenever we have a problem we should come and see him. He didn't expect us to be perfect and he felt his major job was to help new teachers. Later that week he stopped me in the hall and warmly repeated his offer of help. I really took him at his word. So in early October when I started having trouble planning and finding materials, I just went to see the principal. He was very cordial and, although he talked a lot about himself, he did give me some fairly helpful advice. I went to see him for three short visits. Just talking the problems out seemed to help. I started finding good materials and my classes really improved. I felt I was really doing well and I couldn't wait to get to school in the morning. Then in early December I started getting treated in an odd way by some of the senior teachers. They were always asking me whether or not they could help. Sort of like I had some incurable disease, and could they get me a glass of water. It was weird. Finally, I asked two of them in the lunch room, 'Why all the concern?' Well, it came out that the principal had told them that I was having big trouble and he had told a number of the senior teachers to do what they could for me. He had not been in to observe me once. Later in the year he came in for two brief observations (to conform to minimum standards in our district) and he never had time for a conference. He did, however, write up supervisor conference reports. They were lukewarmish and had no specifics. He did mention in both reports that I was improving and overcoming early problems. What improvement? What problems? All he had to go by was what I told him. I got so mad I wrote him a note to the effect that my self-reported problems had cleared up some time ago and that I felt my teaching was better than his report had indicated. I could see the handwriting on the wall, though. I started looking for another position, and got one without too much trouble. I liked the kids in my first school and many of the teachers. Somehow, though, I put myself in a box for the principal and he wasn't going to let me out.''

YOU KNOW YOU'RE IN TROUBLE WHEN

- you have threatened that if there is one more sound in the classroom you will personally call every parent to complain—and there is a sound.

- you walk into your usually noisy classroom and immediately all the students get in their seats and smile at you.

- the principal asks you what you plan to be doing next year.

- you have your students correct their own tests and the lowest mark in the class is 96 percent.

- it is 10:15 and the class has ripped through three-quarters of the work you have prepared for the day.

- you return after being sick for three days and the students chant, "We want the substitute!"

- it feels like February and it's only late September.

- the teacher across the hall comes in and offers to show your kids how to behave.

- the parents of eleven of your students ask to see the principal and you are not invited.

- unsolicited, your principal offers to write a recommendation for your placement file.

- you are convinced you have finally come up with challenging and interesting work for your class and when you present it they chorus, "We did that last year."

- after sitting in your class for five minutes, your supervisor starts to look at the clock.

An error of first impressions can also work the other way; the administrator who seems severe and distant can turn out to be warm and supportive.

MONA KLARFELD/FOURTH GRADE "Quite honestly, I was afraid of Mrs. Kelly when I first went for interviews. She seemed so businesslike and talked so much about high standards that I was sure that even if I got the job, I'd end up disappointing her. And after a few weeks with my fourth-grade wigglers, I was afraid I'd never get them settled down and working on tasks. I was wrong on both counts. The kids settled down— some too much, so that now my biggest problem is getting them excited and alive. And, boy, was I *really* way off on Mrs. Kelly. She is a jewel! She has so many ideas and gives them to me in the nicest way. I never feel I have to use her suggestions, but, in fact, I think I've used every one.

"But what has meant the most is that she has treated me like an adult, a professional. Here I am, right out of college and she is asking my advice about assembly programs and what to do about the cliques in our school. She has also made sure that the other teachers don't leave me out of things. I'm the only new teacher in the building this year, and they sometimes forget me. Mrs. Kelly has a great way of weaving me into things.

"I got very overtired and generally strung out after the Christmas vacation. I was depressed about my teaching and how little time or energy I had for any kind of social life. One day Mrs. Kelly intercepted me on my way to the lunchroom and took me around the corner to a sandwich shop. She knew exactly what was wrong with me and got right to the point, giving me super tips on how to organize my time and plan more efficiently. She even started me on a vitamin program that seems to give me much more energy. She has been terrific to me. She's made the year for me."

PEERS: A MIXED BLESSING

New teachers are vulnerable to many outside forces and also to their own insecurities. In the same way that a supportive administrator can turn a potentially disastrous year into a year of growth, a beginning teacher's professional peers can be even more influential in the process of learning how to teach and how to survive in the classroom. The following example is a case in point.

VICTORIA KESTER/SIXTH GRADE "I had a hard time finding a teaching job. I had hoped to teach in my hometown, but there were just no jobs in my subject. The best job was on the other side of the state, and when it became clear that there were no jobs on the local horizon, I took it. I was very excited about teaching; I really felt that I was starting out on an adventure. I was, however, also moving away from my parents. Being so far away from home meant that there were lots of things that were going to be new to me. I had to get a car, an apartment, establish a bank account and lots of other things, and all at once. It was literally like a crash course in being an adult. And that's what I felt like right from the beginning—an adult. It was so different from college and even student teaching. At my school people treated me like an adult, and they expected me to act like one. For the first months I felt as if I was play acting at being an adult. Well, now I guess the role is comfortable. Or maybe I just have my act down pat.

"Although I made friends with a few people in my apartment building, it was really very lonely at first. I don't think I would have made it without Joan Silver. Joan Silver teaches in the classroom next to mine. She's been as she says, 'in the trenches' for eighteen years, but she's got more ideas and energy and dedication than any of us fresh troops. Joan was a life saver for me. She took me under her wing even before school started. She has been a source of ideas and a source of great materials and a source of inspiration. And she has never made me feel like a taker or a leech. And, actually, I taught her some things. That's one of the reasons I admired her so much. She really wanted to know about the new ideas I had learned in my education courses, and she put a lot of them to work in her class.

"I guess we talked every day after school. A lot of the time we just spent the hour after school laughing. A couple of times the janitor came in thinking there was something wrong, but what he found was the two of us broken up with laughter. And about once a month she would drag me home for dinner. Joan always seemed to know when I was a little low, and that's when she'd insist that I come home with her for dinner.

"There is so much to learn in the first year and not just about subject matter. Important things—like how to get information from the school secretary and how to stay on the right side of the janitor—that you can never learn in education courses. Joan was my guide on everything from how to fill out my planbook, to which memos from the front office I had to pay attention to and which I could put in what she called 'the circular file.'

"It seems funny to say this, given the fact that Joan is twenty years older than I am, but I really think she's my best friend. She certainly has made this year a terrific one for me."

Although there are trends toward increasing cooperation among teachers, for the most part teachers work independently, in their own class-rooms and with their own students. When they are engaged in their profes-

sional work, they are isolated from one another. However, although administrators are the official source of support and help for beginners, fellow teachers are a much more accessible and less threatening source of support. As the case above illustrates, a teacher's colleagues can be a powerful influence, especially in the beginning of a career. This influence can, of course, be negative as well as positive. On the positive side, peers can be an ever ready source of ideas and teaching tips and can initiate the newcomer into the customs of the school. As Joan Silver was, a peer can be an inspiration to the new teacher seeking to gain mastery of a new role. A peer can demonstrate by example what the phrase "teacher as professional" means.

On the other hand, fellow teachers can have a negative influence, undermining a beginning teacher's idealism, lowering his or her standards, and offering no help at all. Perhaps some capsule portraits will clarify and illustrate this sad phenomenon. All organizations have people like the following. They are living witnesses to humanity's fall from the sublime.

Miss Pyrotechnics: She is a special-effects expert. She and her students spend most of their time decorating her classroom. The displays are beautiful and ever-changing. The desks and chairs are always just right! Even while the class is decorating, the room is spotless. The principal loves to bring visitors to her classroom. She has four special lessons (or routines) she can perform for these occasions.

The Mouth: His hobby is gossip. His arena is the teachers' lounge. He thrives on the trade of secrets, and no morsel is too small to be shared with his colleagues. Nothing is too personal not to be passed on. He should have gone into advertising . . . or broadcasting.

Mrs. Coaster: She has had twelve years of teaching experience. Or, to be more precise, she has had one year of teaching experience, which she has repeated twelve times. She still uses lesson plans from her first year of teaching. She knows not the words "outside preparations." She puts in time and nothing else. She has eighteen more years to go before retirement.

The Hoarder: His desk and cabinets are a veritable goldmine of goodies. He has chalk and paper enough to make it to the year 2000. He has materials that make the other teachers drool with envy. He is like a squirrel preparing for the long winter. Nothing is safe from his acquisitive hands. He is exceptionally nice to the office secretary and it pays off. He does not share.

The Big Planner: He is at his best in faculty meetings. He can create out of thin air the most exciting projects and is a champion for all innovative plans. He disappears when volunteers are requested.

The Sex Bomb: Appropriately, the Sex Bomb comes in two varieties. SHE: In the lunchroom with the women she is rather quiet, even dull. But when he—any "he"—comes within range, she is transformed. Her clothes suddenly look too tight. Her conversation becomes animated, to say nothing of her flashing eyes. As the situation dictates, she is in desperate need of help or the font of all succor. It seems that he and she need to meet after school for some more private discussion. HE: He begins to stop by a new woman teacher's classroom after school to check on "how things are goin'." He's helpful at first. He has a tendency to stand too close. His breath is hot, his hands moist. He knows a great deal about the proximity of intimate little cocktail bars where the two of them could talk about school in a more relaxing atmosphere. (Everyone on the faculty hopes that SHE and HE find each other soon.)

Mr. Up, Up, and Away: He dresses nicely. Carefully, that is. His shoes are shined. He volunteers for all committees. It is difficult to tell whether he is bright or dull. He is beautiful to watch. He never makes a false move. He never tells a joke. He never makes a wave—unless the tide is running in his favor. There is never any noise from his class. His students are always busy doing seatwork, but they seem a little glassy-eyed. He, obviously, is going someplace, but his students aren't.

The Ally Seeker: She courts new teachers. Shortly after you have met she tells you about The Great Injustice that was done her. She is telling you for your own good, she says. Although it happened to her seven (or was it eight) years ago, it could be happening to you now. It seems it would be better for everyone if you approach the injustice doer and slap him/her in the face before he/she does anything to you. Also, you would be proving that you are on the side of Justice. Avoid her. She bites.

Although we strongly believe that the teaching profession has a larger percentage of dedicated, selfless people than any other profession (excepting, perhaps, the ministry), it also has its share of rogues and fools. Beginners should pick their way carefully among this field of new colleagues.

INSTRUCTION: SO MUCH TO LEARN

Ultimately, a teacher's only real problem is his or her students' failure to learn and to develop. All other conflicts, triumphs, and defeats pale in significance if the children are learning and developing their human potential. The degree of the children's success as learners is the best measure of a teacher's success or failure. Although the closeness of the relationship between a teacher's instruction and a student's learning is frequently overstated, this relationship is crucial. As we said earlier, teacher effectiveness is an area in which there are few naturals. New teachers generally have much to learn in this area of instruction.

One major difficulty is the sheer newness of the role of teacher. Also, there is no such thing as a gradual immersion into that role. After a little student teaching, you suddenly find yourself in charge of your own class and responsible for taking it from the first day of school to the last. One of the particularly vexing problems for the beginning teacher is the search for effective curricular materials.

ROBERTA SWILLCUT/THIRD GRADE   "The overriding question of this year has been, 'What works?' I'm in a constant search for materials. It is never-ending. My kids aren't that bright, but they devour material and look at me as if to say, 'Well, what's next?' Our school has a curriculum guide that is only five years old, but it is terribly dated already. The students know a lot of the stuff already. They learned it in lower grades or just picked it up. They are bored by a good bit of the rest, too. I'm constantly squeezing ideas and tips from the other third-grade teachers. They are helpful, but they are in the same box I am. Then there is the problem of getting a big buildup on a particular workbook or special unit by a teacher who had had fabulous success with it. I try it and I fall on my face with it. Then there are the kids. They are so fickle. A couple of times I took their suggestion on things they wanted to study and work on. After much work and many late hours, I'd get these classes prepared and the very same kids who were so anxious to make the suggestions couldn't have cared less.

"My school district has curriculum specialists. Some of them are very good, too. Particularly the math specialist. He would give me *too* much material. I'd spend hours deciding about which approach to use to teach ten minutes' worth of material. The language arts specialist was a sweet lady, but very rarely available and most of her ideas were really out to lunch. I was on my own there. When you get right down to it, you have to make the curriculum and the materials *yours* before they are any good to you. Someone else's brilliant materials are nothing until you have made them your own. This is hard to do the first year."

The actual skills and strategies of instruction can be another problem area.

PAULA WARREN/ENGLISH   "I'm living proof that teaching is harder than it looks. I've always been a good student. I did very well in my education courses. In fact, I got an A in methods! However, I just about flunked once I had my own class. I really like working with the children independently and in small groups, but when I had to be up in front, before the entire class, I'd have trouble. Little things that I had taken for granted became quite difficult to do well. I'd always admired teachers who can ask a lot of good questions and keep things really moving without having to step in and monopolize. Admiring is not doing, believe me! I discovered that asking questions is a tricky business. First, it isn't that easy to come up with good questions. Then, you want to call on someone you think can answer or explore the question in an interesting way. Now, the really tricky part: listening carefully to what the student is saying and at the same time evaluating what he or she is saying and thinking of an appropriate response to those remarks *and* on top of that trying to figure out what the next move should be. Should I ask him or her another question? Should I call on Lois, who is falling asleep in the back? Should I try Charlie, who is so eager with that waving hand and always so painfully wrong with his answers? Where should I go? Should I correct what the first student said or get a student to . . . , meanwhile losing the train of thought I was trying to develop. It's very complex, this teaching game."

DIALOGUE

KEVIN: Are we in danger of giving the impression that all teachers struggle through an unhappy survival?

JIM: Come to think of it, we probably are.

KEVIN: Then we ought to correct it. Many teachers are quite skillful when they begin their careers. They have enough ability and training to perform at quite a high level of competence.

JIM: As a matter of fact, I have known a few.

KEVIN: Yes, so have I. The only problem for the ones I have known was that some of the older teachers become jealous.

JIM: Yes, teachers share human nature, too.

"I'm *not* an underachiever. You're an overexpecter."

Courtesy Randy Hall.

But while the instructional aspect of teaching can be a thicket of difficulty for many beginners, for others it is very exciting and inspiring.

MARVIN SHANN/JUNIOR HIGH SOCIAL STUDIES   "School has always been hard for me. But then again, if truth be known, I've always worked hard. In high school I really got turned on to history and I think it was then that I decided to become a teacher. In college I took every history course I could. I was way over the required number of history courses for certification. And I was lucky and taught at a very academic high school as a student teacher. I think I did well, too. At least, that's what everyone said. I was really disappointed that I couldn't get a job in that school and more disappointed when I couldn't find any openings as a history teacher. I was getting very discouraged until I was finally offered a junior high job in the same school district where I had student taught. My first thought was to let it go and wait for a "real" history job. What they wanted me to teach was social studies. There was some history involved, but there was also a lot of other social science material to teach. What I really wanted to teach were the intricacies of the British Parliamentary system and the rise and fall of Oliver Cromwell, and what they wanted was what seemed to me pretty low-level stuff. I was ready to hang it up. I could possibly work for the company my dad works for, or I could go back to school. Well, anyway, I decided I'd give junior high teaching a chance.

"The great surprise of teaching for me was not the kids or anything like that. It was, on the one hand, how little I knew about my strength, history, and how intellectually exciting teaching in general can be. I had taken dozens of history courses and considered myself a super buff, but I had missed the essential meaning of history. That's what I have been learning these first two years, and it has been as stimulating as anything in my life. Now I feel I'm just beginning to understand the purpose of history and what should be taught. I came to teach and probably ended up learning more than my students.

"Incidentally, I was offered the position I thought I really wanted, a position on the high school history faculty. I turned it down. I couldn't be happier than I am here."

RESEARCH ON TEACHER PLANNING

The Institute for Research on Teaching, Michigan State University, is conducting studies to describe elementary school teacher planning. Preliminary analysis of the data collected shows the following results:

- Teachers participating in the study reported spending an average of 12.8 hours per week in formal planning. However, the variety of settings and circumstances in which teachers report planning suggests that they are planning more or less continuously.

- Learning objectives are seldom the starting point for planning. Instead, teachers plan around their students and around activities.

- Teachers tend to limit their search for ideas to resources that are immediately available, such as teacher editions of textbooks, magazine articles, guest speakers, films, and suggestions from other teachers.

- Teachers indicated that most of their planning is done for reading and language arts (averaging 5 hours/week) followed by math (2.25 hours/week), social studies (1.7 hours/week), and science (1.4 hours/week).

- Teacher planning is more explicit and involves a longer lead time in team-teaching situations than in self-contained classrooms.

- The most common form of written plans was an outline or list of topics to be covered, although many teachers reported that the majority of planning was done mentally and never committed to paper.

- Planning seems to operate not only as a means of organizing instruction, but also as a source of psychological benefits for the teacher. Teachers reported that plans gave them direction, security, and confidence.

Communication Quarterly 1, no. 4 (Summer 1978): 1, The Institute for Research on Teaching, Michigan State University, East Lansing, Michigan.

STUDENTS: FRIENDS OR FIENDS?

Becoming comfortable and sensing that one is effective with children is a major concern for a new teacher. And well it should be. Students are the main event! They make the good days good and usually make the bad days bad. The relationship between teacher and students is multifaceted. An important aspect of the relationship is based on how well the students are achieving.

LOUISE AIKMAN/FIFTH GRADE "I have enjoyed my students this year, probably more than I should have. It was a tremendous kick to have my own class. And I was very worried about discipline. I think I jumped on the students so much in the first three weeks that they were shell-shocked until Thanksgiving. But I loosened up, and so did they. I've really liked the whole experience of being a teacher. And I've worked hard. It seems that my whole life this first year has been school.

"The one real down moment I had came right towards the end of the year. Something one of the sixth-grade teachers said really shook my confidence. She made some comment at lunch about how much fun-and-games was going on in my class. All of a sudden I began thinking that while I was having a great time—and maybe the kids were having a great time—they really weren't learning anything. I tried to think what I had taught them that was really important, and my mind was blank. I tried to think of particular students who I thought had really shown a lot of progress, and I couldn't think of anyone specific. I went around that way for a couple of days and I got sort of panicky. Finally, almost by accident, I came across one of the student's notebooks, which had all of his work from September, even his diagnostic tests. It was really enlightening. I could almost see the change from week to week in what he knew. The problems became more difficult, but he could master them. His compositions became more interesting, and the mechanics became sounder. His handwriting looked so much more mature. I figured, though, that maybe that was just one student. I asked to look at a few other students' notebooks, and there it was. They had changed. They were different. Not just different, but *better*. And I was an important part of that change."

There can be little doubt, however, that although students are the primary source of a teacher's success, they are also a source of his or her failure. There are three areas, in particular, that cause problems: discipline, social distance, and sex. Behind each of these areas of difficulty is an inaccurate set of expectations held by the teacher about children.

One indication of these out-of-line expectations is seen in the sharp change in attitudes experienced by people as they go through teacher education and into their first years of classroom teaching. Studies have shown that the longer college students stay in teacher-training programs, the more positive and warm their attitudes towards students become. But among beginning teachers there is a sharp drop in positive attitudes toward students. In fact, beginning teachers' scores are significantly lower than the scores of students just entering teacher education.[4]

Why does this happen? How can this phenomenon be explained? As we do at a number of other points throughout this book, we would like you to stop reading for a moment here and jot down some hypotheses about why beginning teachers' attitudes change in this way.

_____

_____

_____

What happens between the time one is a college student preparing to teach and the time one actually becomes a teacher is undoubtedly a complicated series of events. We would like to offer our own thoughts on the issue. College students alternate between being highly idealistic and extremely realistic in outlook. However, when they enter teacher training, most become very idealistic about children and education. They believe that as teachers they should have warm relations with students, and they want to make the classroom more relaxed and more responsive to the needs of students than it normally is. As college students take more education courses and observe in classrooms, their views of children become more idealistic and, as a result, more positive. By graduation, the rose-colored glasses are firmly affixed.[5] Also, college students have managed to completely shut out memories of many of the realities of their own childhood and adolescence. They forget things like the time they joined with the other seventh-graders to put four tacks on Miss Derriere's chair. They blot out all the juicy stories, most of which they knew were untrue, about the young

[4]N. L. Gage, ed., *Handbook of Research on Teaching* (Chicago: Rand-McNally, 1963), p. 509. The Minnesota Teacher Attitude Inventory, a test frequently given to college students planning to become teachers, is designed to measure attitudes that predict how well they will get along with students in interpersonal situations. Indirectly, it attempts to indicate how well satisfied the test taker will be with teaching as a vocation. The test has been a very popular instrument for research on teaching and has been used in over fifty research studies.

[5]This analysis does not, we fear, account for the Lundquist Effect, named after our good friend, Ernie Lundquist. Ernie deviated (as is his habit) from the normal. As Ernie progressed through teacher training he began to dislike children more and more. By the time he graduated he had a well-developed distaste for, as he called them, "the little creeps." So Ernie decided not to become a teacher. He became an administrator. However, Ernie found sitting in his office quite lonely. The only people who came to see him were the children. As Ernie talked to the children about what his school was really like, he gradually came to like, and eventually, to love children. But as for the teachers. . . .

home economics teacher. They forget about how they enjoyed reading (writing?) obscenities about their math teacher on the lavatory wall. They all forget how cruel kids can be to kids.

"Alice, we've decided that from now on we're going to call you Fatso Alice. . . . Why are you crying, Fatso Alice?"

"We started this club, Roger, and it's called the Red Devils. But you can't be part of it because you smell real bad, Roger."

"*Zits! Zits! Earl has lots of zits.* . . . Boy, look at old Earl run. And he's crying, too. What a sissy dope."

"My mother's a *what?!!*"

"I can always spot a gay. I can tell Paul's one just by the way he walks."

Need we say more? Just think back over your experiences with, and as, children, in and out of schools. Children are a mixed bag. So is the behavior of an individual child. One day the child is eligible for canonization and the next day should be shot by cannons. Somehow, though, the dark side of human nature recedes from view during teacher education. Fear not. It reappears. Beginning teachers rediscover human fallibility, in their children and in themselves, and the result is that their affirmative attitudes toward children plummet. Normally positive attitudes make a comeback, although they rarely regain the heights they reached during the latter stages of teacher training.

Nevertheless, it is the beginner's unrealistic expectations that are a great source of his or her problems. And, while there are many problems, as we said above, we are going to look at just three areas: discipline, social distance, and sex.

DISCIPLINE   Classroom control, classroom management, or discipline (pick your euphemism) is one of those problems that shouldn't exist. After all, school is an opportunity for children. The teacher works hard to help them. It's simple: the teacher is there to teach, and students are there to learn. Unfortunately, though, things do not work out this way.

The great majority of schools—whether kindergartens or high schools—are organized with the expectation that the teacher will be "in charge" of the class. You may not like this, and there are things you can do about it.[6] But it is still what is generally expected of a teacher by the children, the administration, and peers. (We will return to this matter of expectations in the section on social distance.) Few (and lucky) are the teachers who do not have to come to grips with their role as disciplinarian.

A discipline problem occurs when the expected pattern of classroom behavior is violated. Normally, a breach of discipline is an overt act by one or more students that distracts attention from or interrupts the performance

[6]See Herbert Kohl, *The Open Classroom: A Practical Guide to a New Way of Teaching* (New York: New York Review/Vintage Books, 1969).

DIALOGUE

JIM: I wish we could take care of this sticky topic of discipline with a few well-chosen clichés. For instance, "Well-planned and well-executed lessons are sure-fire insurance against discipline problems."

KEVIN: Or, "There is no such thing as a bad child, only bad teachers."

JIM: Or, "Be fair, firm, and consistent."

KEVIN: These sayings may be good advice, but this approach skirts the real problem. New teachers normally have discipline problems, and pretending they don't exist doesn't help.

JIM: The problem is that if we talk about discipline and control of students, we sound as if we're supporting the authoritarian-teacher model. On the other hand, we probably made our bias clear earlier.

KEVIN: I'm sure, too, that even teachers in open, more democratically run schools have discipline problems.

JIM: I think you're right. Let's get to it.

of the task at hand. Discipline problems are endemic to the first-year teacher. The basic explanation for this phenomenon is simply that first-year teachers have had little practice in being "in charge." Few college students have had much opportunity to give orders, coordinate the activities of a group of people, or tell others to do such things as "Quiet down," or "Stay in your seat!" In particular, young women are still somewhat unaccustomed to leadership roles (although this has been changing in recent years). Students, on the other hand, are accustomed to being taught by experienced teachers who know how to control them, usually rather effortlessly. Further, students can sense inexperience and hesitancy in a new teacher. Finally, school is not all fun and games for children, and they can get restless and bored. (Remember when you were in elementary and secondary school. Remember how long the school day was, how long you had to sit still at a stretch, and how much you had to do that didn't interest you.) These conditions, plus the potential for friction in any group of so many people, make it almost inevitable that first-year teachers will have some trouble establishing the kind of productive relationship with students that they seek.

WYLIE CRAWFORD/SCIENCE "In the beginning, my fears about discipline and class control were abated. Instead of finding students who were organized for an all-out, massed offensive, I found students who wished for the most part to be left alone; instead of finding students who were outspoken and arrogant, I found students who were yielding and eager not to 'make waves.' For the first week or two, the vast majority of my students just sat, seemed to listen attentively, and asked questions when called for. . . .

". . . my ideal classroom was one in which everyone was happy, where everyone felt free to speak out when he had something important to say, without fear of harsh criticism or ridicule from me or from his fellows. To create such a situation, it was only natural to smile, and so I did. And eventually, the class did too, but in a slightly different way. As the first month passed, the routine and boredom of even this school began to set in. Many of the students did not understand why they were required to take four years of science (or English, or physical education, for that matter). The happy, relaxed, loosely-disciplined class which I had seen developing began to take strange and subtle turns in the wrong directions. The students were not just happy and relaxed, they were content and almost asleep. I started to get the message: their natural curiosity had not been aroused. I tried to spice up my presentations and asked more questions of individuals in the class, but this seemed to no avail. The symptoms persisted—one student would be looking out the window; another student would be sitting on a table when there were chairs still available; two girls would be gossiping just a little too loud, and would continue even when I approached and finally stood right next to them.

THE FIRST DAY OF SCHOOL!! IT ALL SEEMS SO HOPELESS! —NEXT SUMMER IS JUST A SHIMMERING MIRAGE ON THE DESERT HORIZON!!

COME ON, SKYLER... IT CAN'T BE ALL THAT TERRIBLE.

DO YOU HAVE ANY IDEA HOW LONG IT TAKES TO BREAK IN A NEW TEACHER?

©Jefferson Communications, Inc. 1982
Distributed by Tribune Company Syndicate, Inc.

Reprinted by permission: Tribune Company Syndicate, Inc.

While these were noticeable changes, no one of them was objectionable enough to make a big fuss about. After all, my own concept of the ideal classroom atmosphere was broad enough to allow for occasional disinterested students. There would be days when they, too, would become involved and some other students would lose interest. Besides, in the cosmic view of things, the state of the world today was not going to hinge on the fact that a few minor infractions were tolerated occasionally. Treating the students as adults, I felt that they knew they were pushing my patience a bit and that a gentle reminder would be sufficient to set things straight. And it did, for a while. But soon I found myself giving mild admonishments more and more often, and always to the same small group of offenders. Now, instead of just looking out the window, they were waving to passing cars while my back was turned. Instead of just sitting on the tables, a few were sprawled out on them. My resolve was still not shaken. They would soon tire of such shenanigans, and I could win them back through my artfully designed presentations. After all, I had expected much worse, and we were still getting used to each other. When they saw the folly of it all, our little testing period would be over.

"In reality, as far as the students were concerned, the testing period was already over, and they had won the game. I was going to be a pushover. And, since the other students had been watching the events of the first month, my list of offenders got longer as my blood pressure got higher. The situation got to the point where I had to brace myself before walking into certain particularly 'liberated' classes."[7]

[7]Kevin Ryan, ed., *Don't Smile Until Christmas: Accounts of the First Year of Teaching* (Chicago: The University of Chicago Press, 1970), pp. 85–87. Copyright © 1970. Reprinted by permission.

SOCIAL DISTANCE   Establishing an appropriate social distance from students occupies a good deal of a beginning teacher's attention and energy. Like disciplinary techniques, a correct social distance does not come with a teaching certificate or one's first job. Beginning teachers frequently take refuge in the two extremes of behavior. Many hide their insecurities by acting strict and businesslike, sometimes bordering on being hostile. Others attempt to be completely "natural." They reject the stiff "teacherish" image and seek to break down all barriers between themselves and their students. The first extreme, the overly strict teacher, can give rise to long-term difficulties, whereas the "natural" teacher usually has short-term problems.

The problem with playing the role of the overly strict, aloof teacher is that it might become a permanent habit. Acting like a Prussian officer might appeal to a hidden need to make others submissive. Also, one might begin to believe that "a quiet class is a good class."

The problem confronting overly "natural" teachers is that their view of "natural behavior" is frequently not the same as the children's. The students expect their teacher to interact with them in certain recognizable ways—that is, they expect a certain degree of social distance. They are confused or put off when the teacher acts like "one of the gang." The crux of the problem, then, is that the beginning teacher often wants to be a friend or a pal, whereas the students expect and want the teacher to be an

---

TEACHERS BLAMED FOR ROWDY STUDENTS

Ann Landers

Dear Ann: I'll bet you are swamped with letters from teachers complaining about uncooperative, destructive, lazy, rotten students. I hope you will print just one letter from a student. Here's mine:

I'm 15, a freshman in high school (male) who usually makes the honor roll. I'm not an angel but I have never used foul language in class, hit a teacher, stolen or destroyed school property, drunk beer, wine or liquor on school premises or come to school stoned. There are plenty more like me.

I can cite two reasons students "act like animals." First, they learn fast if the teacher is afraid of the students. If the teacher is gutless and can't stand up to a loudmouth or a bully, the kids get the message. A teacher who has lost control of them can't teach. This is very unfair to those of us who are in school to learn.

The second reason for poor behavior is boredom. Some teachers are incompetent and lazy, plus they really don't like kids very much. Their classes are dull as dishwater—so the bored ones make trouble just to create excitement.

I have had some terrific teachers in my life, and I will never forget them. Most kids want to learn. I say give us more gutsy and competent teachers and there will be a lot less violence and goofing off in the classroom.—THE OTHER SIDE

Dear O.S.: Amen. You wrapped it up beautifully.

From *The Columbus Dispatch.* Reprinted by permission of Field Newspaper Syndicate.

---

adult. Students, because they are uncertain and striving to be adults themselves, seek to find strength and maturity in their teachers. Often they interpret the beginning teacher's efforts at naturalness and informality as weakness.

JOAN POSTER/SEVENTH GRADE   "Most of my year was spent alternating between being Wanda the Witch and sweet little Miss Muffet. I started out determined to be different from all those cold teachers I had had. I was going to be everyone's sweet Big Sister. I really was surprised when this didn't work. The children didn't respond. If anything, they seemed to be confused. Some of them started treating me like their big sister and I found myself getting annoyed. They became very familiar and started asking me all sorts of embarrassing questions—both in and out of class. The final straw came when one of my boys—one of my favorites, too—came up to me in the hall while I was talking to a senior teacher. Smiling, he patted me on the back and said, 'How's it goin', Miss Poster?' I was mortified.

"After that little incident, I became tough. I was all business. If anyone got close to being familiar, I cut them off at the knees. I really said some nasty things. I was just so uptight that I overreacted. I guess I was hurt that my Big Sister routine didn't work. Later I realized that one reason behind my wanting to be Big Sister was simply that I wanted to be loved . . . at any cost. I guess my insecurities led me to seek love from my students. Anyway, I spent most of the year going back and forth on this issue. One week Wanda and the next Miss Muffet. It was really a strain . . . for me and the kids. Finally, toward the end of the year things began to straighten out and I stopped playing a role. It was much more fun that way. I think everyone was relieved."

SEX   Sex is one of the great unacknowledged issues in the American school. Sexual attraction and romance between students, and even, believe it or not, between teachers, is recognized. But the idea that there might be sexual attraction or romance between a teacher and a student is taboo. It simply is not talked about. This doesn't mean it doesn't exist. Beginning teachers are more likely than others to be faced with this problem. For one thing, they are nearer in age to the students. Another factor that makes beginning teachers more vulnerable than experienced teachers is that they are often single, new to the community, and lonely. The strain of the new job may increase their need for affection, and this need may find expression in their relationships with students. In the same way, students often become attracted to their teachers. They sometimes attach themselves to young teachers, greeting them in the morning and walking them to their cars after school. This, too, can be a very awkward situation, in that the student wants to be treated as special and to feel that the affection is reciprocated. If the teacher rejects or embarrasses the student, the student can be hurt deeply.

Besides the platonic attachments teachers can have to young children, it is quite conceivable that a twenty-two-year-old teacher would find a sixteen-year-old student sexually attractive. As the following account indicates, high school teachers are particularly vulnerable to sexual attraction or manipulation. Our only advice in this area is *don't*.

GARY CORNOG/ENGLISH   "In one class there dwelt a fair young creature who found me to be an easily flustered appreciator of her many charms. She was a coquette and, to my way of thinking, a dangerous one. She had me at a great disadvantage. While she could liltingly ask special favors of me (such as my continued toleration of her misbehavior in class), I could not cope with her in anything like a spontaneous way. Unless I was in a phenomenally commanding mood, I could expect to hear such daily entreaties as 'Oh, Mr. Cornog! Mr. Cornog! Could you come here and help me?' 'Mr. Cornog, I just don't understand!' (All this spoken in a voice of tender urgency.) She would have her left arm raised, her right arm aiding it, and would be leaning forward and upward from her desk so that (I thought) I would not fail to notice her finer endowments (I didn't).

" 'What is it, Julie?' I would reply, hoping the fear in my heart would not be evident in my voice. It nearly always was.

" 'Mr. Cornog, there's something here I don't understand. Could you come here and look at it?'

"*Don't*, I tell myself. *Don't.*

" 'Read it to me and I'll explain it.' (*From here*, I almost added, but that would be too obvious.) No. She's getting up.

" 'I'll bring it up there.'

"She approaches. She arrives at my left side. I note a scent of lemony perfume; an attempt at make-up about the eyes. She leans over to place the book in front of me, and some of her long dark hair grazes my shoulder. By this time I feel thoroughly unwilling to answer any question regarding syntax. *What about private tutoring?* I hear my lecherous innards suggesting. Heaven forbid! My frustration causes me to blurt a response to her query, hoping that she'll return to her seat. The class by this time has observed me melting into a limpid pool behind the desk. She must be smiling triumphantly above me, her glory reflected in my devastation. If only she had been as innocent of malice in her manipulations as I had been tender in my innocence, then all would have been well. Alas, she was not. She thought it great sport to exercise her arts for the benefit of her friends, and I could think of no way to break the spell. I could not ignore her, because then the class would notice my attempt and think that she had really gotten to me. I could not allow her to continue to dominate me, for then the respect I sought would never appear. Who could respect a hen-pecked English teacher? The befuddled teacher doing battle with the temptress every day—what a tableau! What a cliché. It pained me to see myself in such a humiliating posture. It was so absurd."[8]

Some first-year teachers become terribly discouraged by their relationships with students. Most of us teach because we like young people and want to work with them. When we are rejected or make fools of ourselves, it is painful. Most problems with students are a result of inexperience, and the majority of second-year teachers find that most of their previous problems disappear and they feel very much at ease with their students. Developing satisfying relations with students usually involves some initial uncertainty. However, previous experience with children as a camp counselor, settlement house worker, or tutor can ease the transition. Contacts with children and adolescents before beginning teaching help you learn about how you relate best to children.

PARENTS: NATURAL ALLIES WITH DIFFERENT AGENDAS

The parent and the teacher are natural allies. Both are concerned about the child. They are both working to help the child become a more fully developed person, and both want the child to be happy, sensitive, intelligent, and well balanced. Frequently, though, the relationship between teacher and parent runs amuck and natural allies become antagonists. Instead of devoting their energies toward understanding and aiding the child, they waste them on conflict with one another.

For most prospective teachers, the parents of future students seem very remote. They do not seem particularly important in the light of all the more obvious issues and sources of difficulty. If you try to picture them, what probably comes to mind is a huge, undifferentiated mass of faces. Once you begin to teach, however, certain personalities and types come quite vividly to life. In an effort to speed the process of differentiation, we offer the following capsule portraits of some of the more troublesome types.

Mrs. Mysonthegenius: She has a nice boy. He seems to have average intelligence and he's rather nervous. After meeting her, you know why. If he doesn't make it to Harvard, she will be shattered. When she is not busy telling him to work harder, she is trying to convince you how lucky you are to have a future Supreme Court justice in your class.

---

[8]Kevin Ryan, ed., *Don't Smile Until Christmas: Accounts of the First Year of Teaching* (Chicago: The University of Chicago Press, 1970), pp. 18–19. Copyright © 1970. Reprinted by permission.

Mrs. Putdown: The first thing she tells you is that she was once a teacher. She then finds innumerable opportunities to indicate how much she knows and how good she was . . . and still is. She questions you about your "rationale" for teaching this content or using that procedure. When you answer her, she informs you that she prefers the old ways, the tried and true ways. She has dozens of ways of reminding you that this is only your first year of teaching. You wish she would go back to teaching.

Mrs. Latecomer: Her daughter has really been a problem. The girl is obviously unhappy and seems to have made little progress all year. You have looked for the mother at PTA meetings and Open House nights, but she has never shown up. You have written notes home, but they haven't been answered. You have called to make appointments, but she has missed them, having forgotten that she had to go to her Garden Club those days. You send home a failing report card. She complains to the principal that you don't like her daughter.

Mr. Heavyhands: You are at your wits' end with one student and you need help from his parents. He's picked three fights this week and his work is dropping off badly. Other teachers have been complaining about him. You call his father, who roars that he will be right over to school. He arrives breathing fire. You explain your concern, and he keeps socking his fist into the palm of his hand and describing what will happen when he gets his hands on "that no-goodnik." He is embarrassed and hurt by his son's behavior and he has a very old and simple solution. You are sorry you called him.

Mrs. Youthinkyouvegotproblems: She attends all the school functions. However, she never wants to talk about her daughter. She wants to share her own trials and tribulations with you. She heard you took a psychology course once and has chosen you as her therapist. She goes on and on and on. You get a tight feeling in the pit of your stomach.

Mrs. Specialhelp: Her son is doing very well in your class. She doesn't think so. He is always happy and carefree. She reports that he feels schoolwork is no challenge. She is convinced that he needs special attention. How about after-school tutoring? Maybe Saturday morning? All his other teachers gave him special attention. Aren't you "dedicated"?

The sources of teacher-parent problems are the same as those involved in any human relationship, but encounters are more highly charged than in most relationships. This is to be expected since a child and his or her future are at issue. The following account of Brenda's mother and a new teacher illustrates some of the dynamics that are usually hidden from view:

DONNA DAVIES/SIXTH GRADE   "It happened in late March. Ten days earlier Brenda's mother called me. She said she wanted to talk to me and asked if there was any day that I stayed late at school. She didn't get off work until 4:30 and couldn't make it to school until 5:15. I often worked late at school, and so I made an appointment for ten days later.

"I was curious about why she wanted to see me and I began to worry. Brenda had something of a reputation in the school. In September during the teachers' workshop before the opening day, two teachers 'sympathized' with me when they heard I had Brenda Carson. They didn't go into great detail why, and I didn't want to ask. However, I was watching Brenda out of the corner of my eye during those first months and, I guess I paid particular attention to her. However, in recent months I hadn't thought much about her. Until her mother called.

"Brenda's mother showed up right on time and after a few pleasantries she said, 'Well, I know you're busy, so I'll come right to the point. Three weeks after Brenda started kindergarten, Brenda's father and I separated. After a terrible on-again, off-again year, we decided to get a divorce. It was hard on both of us, but it was crushing for Brenda. She's an only child. Maybe she blamed herself for the breakup. I don't know, in any event she went into a kind of a tailspin. She was trouble at home and she's been a trouble in school almost from the moment of the breakup. She's no genius, but she's bright enough to do better than she's done. She just dug in her little heels and wouldn't try. She wouldn't bring books home. She wouldn't do assignments. Every time I asked her about school, her standard answer was, "I hate school." Once I got working and my life started to settle down, we were able to make a life together. But the school situation was still rotten. None of the other girls played with her. She was never invited to any parties. I even suggested that she invite one of her classmates to stay overnight one Friday night and the kid refused. We were both heartbroken.

" 'Then you came along. I don't know what you did to her but you certainly have turned her around. I sensed it the first day of school. She came home with a funny look in her eye and said, "This year is going to be different. I can just tell." She wouldn't say why, but after a few days I guessed. She was continually talking about you. From what you said to her to what kind of a car you drive. Honestly, one weekend when we were out grocery shopping she made me drive by your apartment, she was so curious to find out what it looked like.

" 'And, I guess you know how she's doing in school. I don't think she's missed her homework once. I'm sure she's not your best student, but I know she's doing pretty well, particularly considering the hole she was digging for herself. You look surprised at all this. I figured you might be. Brenda can really keep her feelings to herself when she wants to. But honestly, you have touched that girl in a special place. The difference in her is like night and day. And you can't imagine what all this has meant to me. Her pain was my pain and now it's gone away. And, Brenda even has friends now.

" 'Anyway, I just wanted you to know. I just wanted to see you and to thank you.'

"Brenda's mother was out the door before I could respond. It was so unexpected, I don't know what I could have said anyway. That one event has given me a great, great deal to think about."

A parent and a teacher are quite likely to perceive the same phenomenon in very different ways. The nerve-frazzled teacher perceives a child as a wild, undisciplined, raucous menace. The parents perceive their child as energetic, spontaneous, and sociable. Differences in perception are enhanced by the different circumstances under which they see the child. An apparently quiet, shy child is frequently a chatterbox in the security of home.

Evaluation is another area of difficulty. It is part of the teacher's job to make judgments about a child's performance, a process that can touch on some deep insecurities. It can wound the parents' hopes and aspirations. That this is the Age of Anxiety becomes very apparent to the teacher in her contacts with some parents who look to the school as the royal road to success for their children. In our competitive society, being average is taken by some as failure. If a child is average, something must be wrong with her. Or with you, her teacher. "How can she get over being 'average'?" The thought that their child could be *below* average is more than some parents can bear. For these reasons, the teacher needs to be especially sensitive when dealing with issues of evaluation, and would do well to stay away from what are, after all, meaningless terms like "above average" or "below average."

Social distance can be a source of difficulty in relations with parents as well as with students. Issues of social distance have been at the nub of much parent-teacher antagonism in recent years. Since most teachers are middle class or aspiring to the middle class, they normally have little trouble communicating with middle-class people. But when they deal with parents from a lower or higher class or a different ethnic group, or both, the potential for communications difficulties is heightened. Upper-class parents can look down on public schools and treat teachers condescendingly. Poor parents often have had unfortunate and unpleasant experiences with schools and, as a result, regard them with suspicion. Often these parents speak a different language or dialect than the teacher. They are put off by educational jargon. What the teacher sees as a humble classroom is to them part of a huge impersonal bureaucracy. In many urban areas this impression of the school as a cold, unfriendly, and impersonal institution is supported by the evidence: the school doors are locked, and parents have to pass by police officers and assorted hall guards before they are given a pass to see the head secretary in order to see the teacher. The fact that many lower-class parents have, as children, encountered prejudice in schools and found attendance at school more discouraging than helpful makes communication even more difficult. Since they have neither wealth nor connections, these same parents are forced to rely heavily on the schools to provide their children a way out of the deprivation and futility that characterizes so much of their own lives.

Another factor of more recent origin is an emerging negative attitude toward teachers in general. In recent years, all professionals, including lawyers and doctors, have received extensive public and private criticism. Teachers are no exception.

Still another factor in parent-teacher relations is the fact that going to school changes children. School exists to help children change in specified ways: to read, to speak a foreign language, to solve problems. And students do change. They master things. They acquire confidence. And they become increasingly independent of their parents. Some parents rejoice at the child's growing freedom from them. For others, this process of independence is painful. Hearing her little girl talk about how much she loves her teacher may arouse jealousy in a mother and cause her to act hostile when she meets the teacher. When a high school student comes home from school with political or social or religious views that conflict with those of his parents, it can cause resentment and confusion. Thus it is not uncommon for a parent to approach a conference with the teacher with a sincere mixture of appreciation and hostility.

The great majority of parent-teacher conferences are cordial, constructive, and characterized by mutual respect. Although there may be initial problems of perception or communication, the shared interest of parents and teacher in the child is enough to overcome these minor blocks. However, problems do develop—and they are not always the fault of the parents.

JOHN LUKE/HISTORY   "In the late winter we had our Annual Parents' Night. It was a big public relations show, timed about three weeks before the bond issue was to be voted on. All the teachers were to work with students on displays and projects. And, of course, we had to get lots of student work up on the board. The drab old school building looked like the Rose Bowl Parade by the big night. We met the parents in our rooms and gave them an overview of what we were doing for the year. I thought I would be nervous, but somehow I wasn't. I was so distracted and fascinated by their faces. I never suspected that they would look so much like their kids! Or vice versa. And the way some features from one parent and some from the other found their way into their child's face was so absorbing! In the midst of my opening soliloquy in bounced the principal with his flash camera to take a picture of all the fancy decorating I had done. Well, he just looked around the room, decided to save a flash bulb and headed for the door. My classroom had all the carnival atmosphere of a men's locker room. We 'chatted' about this a few days later.

"When I finished my talk, I handed out folders of their children's work and told the parents I would be happy to talk with them individually. Most of my students had been doing fairly well, so most of the evening went well. The parents of my two prize ding-a-lings didn't show,

AN INSTRUCTOR'S GUIDE TO MURPHY'S LAW

Murphy's law says, "If anything can go wrong, it will." There are many corollaries and related regularities. Among them:

1. Good students move away.
2. New students come from schools that do not teach anything.
3. The teachers' lounge will be in the worst room of the school. It will contain dusty furniture and one noisy mimeograph machine.
4. The shorter the working time, the more the mimeograph will malfunction.
5. The clock in the instructor's room will be wrong.
6. The school board will make a better pay offer *before* the teachers union negotiates.
7. When the instructor is late, he will meet the principal in the hall. If the instructor is late and does not meet the principal, the instructor is late to the faculty meeting.

8. Children who touch the instructor will have scabies or bubonic plague.
9. When speaking to the school psychologist, the teacher will say "weirdo" rather than "emotionally disturbed."
10. Disaster will occur when visitors are in the room.
11. The time a teacher takes in explaining is inversely proportional to the information retained by students.
12. Students who are blind, deaf, and/or behavioral problems will sit at the back of the room.
13. Extra-duty nights will occur when the best shows are on TV.
14. The problem child will be a school board member's son.
15. The instructor's study hall will be the largest in several years. The administration will view the study hall as the teacher's preparation time.
16. Students who are doing better are credited with working harder. If children start to do poorly, the teacher will be blamed.

17. Extracurricular duties will take more preparation time than classes.
18. Clocks will run more quickly during free time. (This is also known as the Law of Varying Time.)
19. A meeting's length will be directly proportional to the boredom the speaker produces.
20. On a test day, at least 15% of the class will be absent.
21. If the instructor teaches art, the principal will be an ex-coach and will dislike art. If the instructor is a coach, the principal will be an ex-coach who took a winning team to the state.
22. A subject interesting to the teacher will bore students.
23. Murphy's Law will go into effect at the beginning of an evaluation.

Duncan Long, "An Instructor's Guide to Murphy's Law," *Phi Delta Kappan* (January 1980): 336. Reprinted by permission.

an event I greeted with mixed emotions. Although I had been quite apprehensive about talking to these strangers, things were going well. I had been trying to be as direct and honest as possible. Looking back on it, I think I was especially intent on being honest because I felt the whole showboat atmosphere and intention of the Parents' Night was dishonest. My overreaction got me in trouble, though. One set of parents hung back. I hadn't met them yet, but I knew immediately who they were. They were Kenny Prewitt's parents. He, poor kid, had gotten the worst features of both parents. Kenny is a great big happy kid. He is not bright and he is quite lazy. All he likes to do is play his guitar, which he is pretty good with. The only time I have gotten any work from him was during a unit on the Civil War. I got him to look up the folk songs and marching chants of the Civil War. He gave a 'singing and strumming' report to the class. But, after that . . . nothing! I'm an easy grader and he was carrying about a C− at that time. Well, the Prewitts asked a lot of questions and I stayed with my straight-facts approach and avoided generalizations. Then Mr. Prewitt glanced anxiously at his wife, looked over his shoulder to see that none of the other parents was within earshot and said, 'Tell me, Mr. Luke. We're both college men. My son, Kenny. Is he . . . you know . . . college material?'

"I didn't know what to say, so I said, 'What do you mean?'

" 'We just want to know if we should be saving to send him to college. Does he have it for college?'

"All I thought of was that here was a guy who really wanted a straight answer, so I said, 'No.' Then I looked at Mrs. Prewitt. I should have looked at her before answering. Her calm face just seemed to break up, to dissolve before my eyes. After the tears came the hostility. 'How dare you prejudge my boy! Admit it, you don't like Kenny. You are trying to ruin his chances. We work hard to raise our only son and then some young know-it-all teacher ruins everything!' Underneath the hysteria, which subsided in about five long minutes, she was right. I had no right to make that judgment. Also, I didn't have enough data. Well, I made another appointment with them. During this I saw that frightening intensity behind their desire to get my class's number one guitar player into college. Some good things came out of this conference, though. Kenny's work picked up. I learned a good lesson, too. Somewhere T. S. Eliot says that human nature can stand just so much reality. I believe him."

A FINAL WORD

Most new teachers are very proud of themselves at the end of their first year. And they have learned an enormous amount in nine or ten months. This sense of personal growth has been captured well by one young teacher we know. She had an extremely difficult first year, but went on to become

an outstanding teacher. A week or so after the end of her initial year of teaching, she made the following statement:

> I could see myself as a teacher now. Before I was somebody pretending to be a teacher. I just couldn't believe that I was responsible for these children. I now realize that we can spend a whole period talking and things don't have to be so organized all the time. I now realize that I have the power to call a parent or send a note home or tell a child to stay in from recess. Now I know I should do what's best for me and not be afraid or fearful. I've liked giving of myself— it's something I've needed to do. I've learned to be more mature. I think I'm becoming grown up. The kids have helped me. At first I was trying to be what everyone at the school wanted me to be. Now I know that to make it as a teacher I need to be myself and accept myself for what I am. It took a whole year but now I am confident and relaxed. I am strong and tough when I need to be. I think I've made it.[9]

[9]Kevin Ryan, *Biting the Apple: Accounts of First Year Teachers* (New York: Longman, Inc., 1980), pp. 211–212.

Along with the trials captured so well in "An Instructor's Guide to Murphy's Law" (page 295), teaching has its pleasures and bright moments, too. And these pleasures are often what makes teaching a rewarding and fulfilling occupation. English novelist Joyce Carey has written that human joy is not in the great events but in the little everyday things, like a good cup of tea. Much joy can be found in the events it is easy for us to overlook. The joys and satisfactions of teaching can lie in everyday events and small surprises. As a teacher you may find joy in:

- experiencing those electric moments when you can *feel* the children thinking and *see* them making new connections.

- watching two lonely kids whom you brought together walking down the hall together, now friends.

- getting your planbook back from the supervisor with the comment, "These appear to be excellent lessons."

- finding, in your box on a rainy Friday afternoon, a note written in a childish scrawl, "You are my most favorite teacher. Guess who?"

- shopping downtown and meeting one of your students, who proudly introduces you to her mother as "my teacher," and being able to tell by the way the mother responds that you are respected in their household.

- having a former student call to tell you that he has a problem and needs to get your advice.

- turning in a plan for a new curriculum that you and five other teachers labored over and knowing that you did a good job and that it will make a major improvement.

- chaperoning a dance and having your most hostile student smilingly introduce his girl to you.

- hearing in the teachers' lunchroom that your supervisor called you "a real professional."

- dragging yourself back to school at the end of Christmas vacation and being greeted enthusiastically by your students as you enter your classroom.

- agonizing in advance over a conference with your most troublesome child's parents, only to have them back you up all the way.

- being observed by the principal and having your students make you look terrific.

- seeing the look of pride in a child's eyes as she brings her artwork for you to see.

- feeling the excitement as you move toward your classroom with what you know is going to be a knockout lesson.

- surviving until June, being bone-tired but proud of what you and your kids have been able to do.

Dear Mrs. Shulman,

   Hooray! It's the last day of school. You are as happy as we are, we bet. Being a teacher, you can't say so, can you??

   You probably hate us all. We were a bunch of rats a lot of this year. If you never teach again, we'll understand. We were not very nice. We would feel real bad if you decide that. You are the nicest teacher we ever had. You really tried and were always fair. Even when we weren't. Specially, the boys. We did lots of interesting things in class this year but the most interesting thing was you. Nice and interesting.

   We will all miss you. Have a nice summer. You deserve it. Keep teaching.

                                                    The Room 208 Gang

- cleaning out your desk on the last day of school after the kids have been dismissed and finding a box of candy with a card signed by the whole class.

- knowing all the time that what you are doing with your life *really does make a difference.*

Discussion Questions   **1.** Think of an occasion when you have experienced "culture shock"— when traveling abroad or in another part of this country, in an unfamiliar social milieu or, perhaps, on first entering college. Try to remember in as much detail as possible how it made you feel. Did you eventually overcome it? How? Can you trace the progression of your feelings and behavior from the first encounter to the final adjustment? What, if anything, does this suggest to you about ways to minimize the possible effects of culture shock when you begin teaching?

2. Can you remember or imagine any common types of teachers, like Mrs. Coaster or The Big Planner, whom we have not included in our descriptions? Try writing a short description of one or two.

3. How do you explain the attitudinal differences between prospective and first-year teachers revealed by the Minnesota Teacher Attitude Inventory?

4. Where do you stand on the issues of discipline and social distance? Do you believe the school should be concerned with discipline? What is your concept of an effective degree and method of discipline? How much social distance do you feel is appropriate for you? Is there anything about these topics that frightens you? What can you do to prepare yourself?

5. What do you believe is the primary reason many beginning teachers have rocky relationships with students' parents?

6. If you were to begin teaching tomorrow and were free to evaluate your students in any way you chose, or not to evaluate at all, what would you do? Be prepared to defend your position.

7. What do you expect to be the major problems you will encounter as a beginning teacher? What can you do now to begin solving them? What can you do after you begin teaching? What do you envision as the joys and satisfactions of a career in teaching?

For Further Reading

Cruickshank, Donald R., and Associates. *Teaching Is Tough.* Englewood Cliffs, N.J.: Prentice-Hall, 1980.

> A very practical book that addresses many of the core problems experienced by teachers and provides concrete approaches to solving these classroom problems.

Cuban, Larry. *To Make a Difference.* New York: Free Press, 1970.

> A candid view of the problems faced by teachers in inner-city schools. The book's major thesis is that the individual teacher must match to the student the methods and materials of instruction. The author discusses different learning styles, the teacher as liaison with the community and as curriculum developer, and specific problems such as race, discipline, and expectations.

Howey, Kenneth R., and Richard H. Bents, eds. *Toward Meeting the Needs of the Beginning Teachers.* Minneapolis, Minn.: Midwest Teacher Corps Network, 1979.

> An incisive book of essays that summarizes what is known about the induction into teaching. The authors look at the issues from the vantage point of the teacher, the administrator, and several others.

Kohl, Herbert. *36 Children.* New York: New American Library, 1968.

> A popular account of a Harvard graduate teacher's first-year experience in a ghetto school in Harlem. The students' initial hostility

to Kohl and the ways in which he overcomes their feelings are excellently described. The book also vividly describes the difficult conditions under which teaching is practiced in some sections of New York City.

Ryan, Kevin, et al. *Biting the Apple: Accounts of First Year Teachers.* New York: Longman, 1980.
> The accounts of twelve new teachers, based on a recent study of first-year teachers. Each account is a blending of what the teachers said was happening to them and what an observer saw during the first year of teaching.

Ryan, Kevin, ed. *Don't Smile Until Christmas: Accounts of the First Year of Teaching.* Chicago: University of Chicago Press, 1970.
> A collection of six exceedingly honest autobiographical statements by beginning high school teachers, with a concluding chapter by the editor on the first year of teaching.

What Makes
a Teacher Effective?

10

This chapter explores what we believe to be the essential attributes that distinguish teachers from other educated people. More specifically, the chapter examines what knowledge, skills, and attitudes are demonstrated by the effective teacher. Effective teaching is much more than an intuitive process. A teacher must continually make decisions and act on those decisions. To do this effectively, the teacher must have both theoretical knowledge about learning and human behavior and knowledge about the subject matter to be taught. A teacher also must demonstrate a repertoire of teaching skills that are believed to facilitate student learning, and must display attitudes that foster learning and genuine human relationships.

This chapter emphasizes that:

▪ Four major types of teacher attitudes affect teaching behavior: (1) attitude toward self; (2) attitude toward children; (3) attitude toward peers and parents; and (4) attitude toward the subject matter.

▪ A teacher should have an intimate knowledge of the subject matter being taught.

▪ A teacher should be familiar with theoretical knowledge and research about human behavior in order to recognize and interpret classroom events appropriately.

▪ Effective teachers demonstrate a repertoire of teaching skills that enable them to meet the different needs of their students.

▪ Recent research has indicated that academic engaged time, the time that a student spends engaged in academically relevant material that is of a moderate level of difficulty, is strongly related to student achievement in elementary school reading and mathematics.

▪ Certain teacher classroom management behaviors are strongly related to pupils' work involvement and freedom from deviance in the class.

*B*EFORE WE GET to the main issues of this chapter, we would like you to consider the case of Jenny Ferris. Jenny was beginning her first year of teaching. She prepared to be a high school art teacher, graduated, and was certified, but took a job as an illustrator for an advertising firm. After a year, she became disillusioned and decided to try teaching. She was offered a job in her own community, a small city in the Northwest. The school served students from a wide range of social backgrounds, from lower class to upper middle class. The bulk of the children came from solidly blue-collar working-class backgrounds. When she reviewed the records of her seventh-grade students before the school year began, she discovered that practically one-fourth of the students came from one-parent, or what she called broken, homes. Based on this observation, she expected to find children in her class who were starved for affection and suffering the effects of a family breakup.

Jenny was assigned five periods of seventh-grade art. During the first week she reviewed many of the basic principles of art, such as color, color perspective, and methods of construction. The lessons were not particularly exciting, but she wanted to set a foundation for what was to follow. The students were quiet and, in general, cooperative. She did not know whether this was because, as seventh-graders, they were new in the school or because they were serious students. After the initial weeks, however, Jenny wanted to see what their capabilities were. She believed that every student is capable of artistic production. One of her strongest views was that there is a spark of the divine in all of us and that a teacher's role is to help a student get at that spark and fan it into a flame. Jenny believed she was putting this view into action by allowing each of her students to create a piece of art of his or her own choosing. She supplied the materials for many different kinds of artistic productions, ranging from paintings to photography. Most of the students jumped at this opportunity and came in every day eager to get on with their projects. Among the few who were not responding to this opportunity was John Wilson.

John had seemed sullen to Jenny almost from the first day of class. She checked his record and found that he had been an average student in elementary school. Also, she discovered that his father was vice president of one of the big banks downtown. John was also reported to be quite athletic. But, for whatever reason, John had wasted three or four periods this week in what seemed to be idle activity.

John quickly had chosen a project involving clay. The first day he started on a very realistic replica of a baseball, but he lost interest along the way. Jenny couldn't recall what he did the second day, but on the third day she had trouble with John. Shortly after the class started, she noticed that he was getting a good deal of attention from some of the boys in class, and from the way they were acting she sensed something was amiss. John was shielding his creative efforts from view, but from a glimpse and also from the boys' reaction, she was sure it was an obscene statuette. She asked him to bring it up to the front, but he quickly twisted it beyond recognition and mumbled that it wasn't finished.

The next day she kept her eye on John. He was working by himself, but to no apparent purpose. After about twenty minutes he had a big mass of clay rolled into a shape a little larger than a softball. Then, out of nowhere, he started pounding the clay with his fist. Jenny let it go on for a minute or two, hoping that it would stop. John just kept pounding the clay harder and more and more students began paying attention to him. Finally, Jenny said, "John, stop that immediately! What are you doing?"

"I'm punching the clay. Whatta you think I'm doing?"

"Why? What for?" Jenny asked.

"I'm pretending it's my art teacher." The class hushed. Feeling herself flushed, Jenny said, "John Wilson, clean up your desk and come up here *immediately.*" John slammed the clay on the floor, picked up his books, and moved to the door. "You can't take a joke. The hell with you."

Jenny was stunned, but she became even more so when John walked out the door and slammed it loudly behind him. The class seemed as surprised as Jenny. They all looked dumbly at her. She took a deep breath and in a loud, serious voice said, "We've seen the last of John in this art class! Now let's get on with our projects."

The class went back to work quietly for the rest of the period. Jenny sat at her desk and pretended to look at some papers. Questions flooded her mind: "How did that happen? Why did he do that? Who does he think he is? Maybe he doesn't like art, but that's no way to behave! Can't he see that I'm trying? What will the principal think? What do the rest of the students think of me? What if John comes back?" She began to think about what she had done to provoke the incident. The more she thought about it, the madder she became. She had expected some trouble from the poorer element in the class but not from a boy whose father was a bank executive. She was tempted to go right to the phone and call his parents. But she didn't believe that she should get involved with parents. That was the principal's or counselor's job. Her job was to teach art. She was there to teach her students, and she wanted to keep parents at as much a distance as possible.

She reviewed what had happened this first month of school, particularly in terms of classroom control. She believed she had followed her plan, which was to show children that she was serious, to allow a little testing and fooling around, but to come down hard when students went too far. She thought she had followed that plan until the situation with John blew up. At that point in her reverie, the bell rang. The students began talking in groups, and she was sure they were talking about the incident with John Wilson. As they filed out of the room, many were looking in Jenny's direction.

Events like this are by no means an everyday occurrence in classrooms; in fact, teachers can go through their entire careers and never be confronted by such student behavior. We present it not for you to consider what you would do, but rather for you simply to think about it as an event, albeit a somewhat dramatic one, in a teacher's life. The incident illustrates the way human encounters can unfold in a classroom, and in particular how individuals think about them. The incident, nevertheless, contains examples of thinking, some concepts, some attitudes, and some teacher actions or behaviors. The primary concern of this chapter is teaching, especially the conceptions we hold about education and teaching.

We, along with many other educators, believe that elementary and secondary teachers require attitudes, knowledge, and skills unique to the teaching profession. Teachers must ask themselves not only "What am I going to teach?", but also "What should my students be learning?", "How can I help them learn it?", and "Why is it important?" To answer these questions, teachers must be familiar with children and their developmental stages. They must know something about events occurring outside the classroom and about what society needs and requires from the young. They must have enough command of the subject they teach to be able to distinguish what is peripheral from what is central. They must have a philosophy of education that guides them in their role as teacher. They must know something about how human beings learn and about how to create environments that facilitate learning.

What are the specialized skills and attributes of the effective teacher? The four areas of competence that we consider essential for a teacher are:

1. display of attitudes that foster learning and genuine human relationships

2. sureness and adequacy of knowledge in the subject matter to be taught

3. command of theoretical knowledge about learning and human behavior

4. control of skills of teaching that facilitate student learning

The rest of this chapter will examine in depth these four areas of competence.

WHAT ATTITUDES DOES THE EFFECTIVE TEACHER POSSESS?

Many people believe that the teacher's personality is the most critical factor in successful teaching. If teachers have warmth, empathy, sensitivity, enthusiasm, and humor, they are much more likely to be successful than if they lack these characteristics. In fact, many people argue that without these attributes an individual is unlikely to be a good teacher.

For years educational researchers have sought to isolate the characteristics essential to good teachers. In a massive study, David Ryans concluded that effective teachers are fair, democratic, responsive, understanding, kindly, stimulating, original, alert, attractive, responsible, steady, poised, and confident. Ineffective teachers were described as partial, autocratic, aloof, restricted, harsh, dull, stereotyped, apathetic, unimpressive, evasive, erratic, excitable, and uncertain.[1]

But this information is not very useful. After all, what human interaction wouldn't be improved if the participants possessed only positive traits? Getzels and Jackson, summarizing fifty years of research on teachers' personalities and characteristics, conclude: "Despite the critical importance of the problem and a half-century of prodigious research effort, very little is known for certain about the nature and measurement of teacher personality, or about the relation between teacher personality and teaching effectiveness."[2]

A person's *attitudes,* or predispositions to act in a positive or negative way, toward persons, ideas, and events, are a fundamental dimension of that person's personality. Almost all educators are convinced of the importance of teacher attitudes in the teaching process. Attitudes have a direct—though frequently unrecognized—effect on our behavior in that they determine the ways we view ourselves and interact with others.

We believe that there are four major categories of attitude that affect teaching behavior: (1) the teacher's attitude toward self; (2) the teacher's attitudes toward children and the relationship between them; (3) the teacher's attitudes toward peers and pupils' parents; and (4) the teacher's attitude toward the subject matter.

The Teacher's Attitude Toward Self: Self-understanding

If teachers are to help students have meaningful experiences, develop their aptitudes and abilities, face their inner difficulties, and accept themselves as people, they need to know and understand those students. But before teachers can do that, they must work at knowing and understanding themselves. Empirical evidence from psychology indicates that people who deny or are unable to cope with their own emotions are unlikely to be capable of respecting and dealing with others' feelings. A person who never admits to feelings of anger and hostility, for example, may overreact to, ignore, or deny the legitimacy of another person's anger, or may consider it "bad" to feel anger. The same is true of fear, feelings of inadequacy, and most other natural human emotions.

Thus if teachers are to understand and sympathize with students who are hostile, they must face hostile tendencies in themselves, and recognize the implications of these tendencies for their students and others with whom they have dealings. Unless teachers recognize their own anxieties, they will

[1]David Ryans, *Characteristics of Teachers* (Washington, D.C.: American Council on Education, 1960).

[2]J. W. Getzels and P. W. Jackson, "The Teacher's Personality and Characteristics," in *Handbook of Research on Teaching,* ed. N. L. Gage (Chicago: Rand McNally, 1963), p. 574.

be unlikely to understand and empathize with their students' expressions of anxiety. They may not recognize that students' inabilities to learn, inattentiveness, impudence, or irritability may be the result of anxiety. Teachers also need to recognize that their own anxieties may make them irritable, causing the students in turn to feel anxious and display similar symptoms. As Arthur Jersild has said, "A teacher's understanding of others can be only as deep as the wisdom he possesses when he looks inward upon himself. The more genuinely he seeks to face the problems of his own life, the more he will be able to realize his kinship with others."[3]

The question remains, "How can one achieve understanding of self and, after achieving it, accept it?" Jersild suggests that "to gain knowledge of self, one must have the courage to seek it and the humility to accept what one may find."[4]

There are a number of potential sources of increased self-understanding. Jersild suggests that books by sensitive and compassionate people who have made progress in their own struggles to know themselves can be a valuable aid in self-examination. For prospective teachers, such books might include Sylvia Ashton-Warner's *Teacher,* an account of her teaching experience in a Maori Infant School in New Zealand, and Herbert Kohl's *36 Children.* Another method Jersild suggests is *participant observation,* the process of observing a class and recording what you hear, see, and feel as you observe. Your record is then compared with the records of other observers. This experience may demonstrate to you that what you notice in any given situation is determined in large part by habits of thought that you take for granted. It may also illustrate that your "objective" perceptions are often projections of your own subjective state, and thus may tell you more about yourself than about the people you have observed.

Self-examination can also grow out of day-to-day relationships with others. The procedures by which you gain self-understanding are less important than the courage and desire to do so. We constantly find ourselves in new situations with new people who challenge us in new ways, and as a result self-understanding is a continuous process. Because teachers interact with and influence so many young children, they must work particularly hard to understand themselves and their actions in order to understand the children in their charge.

Your college years are likely to be a time of protracted self-examination. As you gain new independence from your family, examine values you may have taken for granted, test yourself against rigorous academic standards, encounter new ideas, and live in close quarters with others your

[3]Arthur Jersild, *When Teachers Face Themselves* (New York: Teachers College Press, 1955), p. 83.
[4]Jersild, *When Teachers Face Themselves,* p. 83.

own age, you probably find yourself experiencing new feelings and recognizing unfamiliar things about yourself. College is also likely to offer you more leisure than any future period of your life (believe it or not!) to explore and learn about yourself. Some colleges offer sessions run by trained leaders, as well as personal counseling sessions, to help you face and cope with feelings of limitation, insecurity, inferiority, or confusion, the need to be

---

EXCERPTS FROM A DIARY OF A BEGINNING TEACHER

As you read these excerpts try to identify what attitudes the teacher is manifesting toward self, children, peers, and subject matter.

September 7. I'm exhausted today. I gave them all back their papers which, thank goodness, took up part of the class time. I also assigned them four questions to do for homework. I didn't write the questions on the board, which was a mistake; I ended up repeating everything five or six times.

I feel so pushed, preparing and correcting papers; hope things calm down soon.

September 9. I tried playing a game with them in class today. It didn't go very well. One of the biggest problems was that I didn't have a firm enough control over the class to do it. I had them asking one another questions. They were divided into two teams and all that. I even set up a panel of judges who decided whether the answer to a question was right.

I also gave them a pop quiz at the beginning of the period. I tried it in one class at the end, but that didn't work as well; they were too excited from the game to settle down.

One real catastrophe today. The map fell on my head during fourth period. The class went wild, luckily the assistant principal was right outside the room and came in and rescued me.

September 13. I gave the quiz today and they did pretty well and then I finished up discussing geography—I hope. I only gave them twenty of the spelling words and left off the longest and most difficult. They were very upset because they said they had all learned that one.

The day has finally come. Despite all of the work and how tired I am, I think I am really going to like teaching.

September 26. I'm having a problem getting the classes to keep quiet now. For a while they were pretty good, but now they're beginning to get to me. Even the good students are starting to talk during class. I don't think it's because they're not interested because the talk is almost always about what I'm discussing, but still they're talking without permission. If it was only a little I wouldn't mind, but it's beginning to get to the point where I can't go on because of the talking.

September 27. The assistant principal came and visited one of my classes today. Before class I was talking at my desk with one student and all of a sudden I heard this deathly silence hit the class. (I guess that's not the right way to say it, but anyway.) I looked up and there he was. I started the class, I'd ask a question and there was absolute silence. Nothing. It was terrible! It's bad when they're all talking at once, but it's horrible when they're afraid to move.

September 29. I've been getting bored, teaching the same thing over and over and so today I

liked and approved of, lack of direction, and other problems. We urge you to regard self-examination as a serious commitment, and to undertake it *as a prospective teacher,* in an effort to make a good decision about whether to teach and to become the best teacher you are capable of becoming.

Consider for a moment a need basic to most people—the need to be liked. Teachers, too, especially beginners, need to be liked by their pupils

did different things in different classes. I discussed with some, gave some a quiz and had others writing. I tried discussing with my sixth-period class but they're just impossible after about ten minutes. I got really mad at them and told them to take out their books and study quietly for ten minutes and then I would give them a quiz. While they studied, I made up the quiz and it was a dilly—only four people passed. I suppose it isn't good educational psychology to do that but it made me feel much better, and at that point it was either them or me.

October 14. I have now firmly and purposely gotten my classes separated. That is, I am no longer doing the same thing five times a day. At first it was a big help being able to prepare only one lesson each night. But I realized that it was terribly boring for me, and my boredom would be reflected in the kids. Once I felt that I had my bearings, I decided to change all that. Well, it's taken me this long to carry out my plan. Al-

though I use much of the same material in all of my classes, I do not use it all at the same time or in the same manner. I can really see the difference in the classes.

October 19. Tonight was the PTA open house. I was pleased at how well it went. I guess that parents are not really ogres after all. But it was an awfully long day. I really do love teaching and I look forward to all of my classes, but I often feel that I am not doing my best for these kids. Teach and learn—and have I learned a lot in these seven weeks!

November 4. Teacher's Convention—WHAT A FARCE!

November 9. Every day I learn so much. I hope that the children are learning some too, but they couldn't possibly learn more than a fraction of what I have. I think there is hope for me yet. I already know so much more than I did in September. Sometimes I feel the huge mountain of things yet to learn pressing down on me but I

think I've made a significant dent in the mountain. I may live through the year. But then again, it seems overwhelming.

November 30. Beautiful day! Introducing a new unit and the kids were great—love it. Everything went well.

December 8. Ugliness! Nothing went well at all. Jabber, jabber, jabber—I don't know. Sometimes I get so upset and depressed it's horrible. They don't listen or follow instructions, or learn anything. I guess it's a normal feeling for new teachers.

December 12. Almost the end of the period before vacation. I guess not really but it seems like it must be. Happiness!! They announced that all evaluation meetings are cancelled until after Christmas. Hurray! Except for the faculty meeting Thursday.

Jean Morris, "Diary of a Beginning Teacher," *National Association of Secondary School Principals Bulletin* 52 (October 1968): 6–15. Reprinted by permission.

and their peers. Many teachers do not realize how strong their need for approval is; they may approve particular student actions not because they are in the student's best interests but for fear that if they disapproved they might lose the students' affection. Unfortunately, teachers rarely recognize their own motivations when such incidents occur. Unless they are aware of the strength of their own need, they will be in no position to examine and judge their actions correctly.

Another configuration of needs that can influence classroom behavior is represented by teachers who need to have students depend on them. These teachers feel pleasure when the students demonstrate that they need them. Thus such teachers habitually engineer situations in which the students have to depend on them in order to accomplish the assigned tasks. They usually behave like benevolent dictators in the classroom, kindly but relentlessly building a "cult of the individual." The novel, play, and movie of *The Prime of Miss Jean Brodie* depict this type of teacher very well. To be considered one of "Miss Brodie's girls," a student had to adhere to a code of Miss Brodie's invention. These teachers are potentially very damaging to students. Instead of producing students who are self-directed and who can make choices for themselves, such teachers inhibit growth. They may not behave consciously in this fashion; they are probably unaware of their own need for others to depend on them. These teachers need counseling to make them aware of their need and of its negative effect on students. The situation may even be serious enough to warrant therapy.

As we stated earlier, one's attitude toward oneself has a direct influence on one's attitudes toward others. Take, for example, a teacher who sees himself as friendly but is not considered friendly by his students and does not, by every objective criterion, behave in a friendly manner. He is not likely to change his behavior until he acquires some insight into his inaccurate self-image. He will be perplexed when his students do not respond warmly to what he considers friendly behavior, and will probably form negative attitudes toward them. If, on the other hand, he is able to adopt a more realistic self-concept—to recognize that he is not naturally friendly and that he will have to change his behavior patterns—he will be on the road to changing his attitudes toward his students and improving his relationship with them.

We hope that these examples illustrate vividly how one's personal needs and attitudes can influence one's behavior, and how self-knowledge can deepen insight and even change behavior in a positive direction.

The Teacher's Attitudes Toward Children

Children are sensitive observers of adult behavior, and they frequently recognize, and become preoccupied with, aspects of the teacher's attitude toward them of which the teacher may be unaware. A variety of attitudes or feelings toward students can decisively reduce the teacher's effectiveness; the teacher may have:

- strong dislikes for particular pupils and obvious fondness for others

- biases toward or against particular ethnic groups

- low learning expectations from poverty-level children or those with certain ethnic backgrounds

- a bias toward certain kinds of student behavior, such as docility or assertiveness.

Few teachers are entirely free of such attitudes at the outset, and self-awareness can be the crucial factor distinguishing a biased teacher from a fair one. Thus it is important that prospective teachers confront their own attitudes early, perhaps through group discussions, role playing, or simulated and real experiences. It is necessary to acknowledge one's attitudes in order to change them, but even then change is neither easy nor automatic. Any attempt to change attitudes must take into account both of their components: feelings and cognition. Attitudes may be based almost entirely on feelings, as when dislike for a particular student causes a teacher to refuse to let the student participate in a particular activity. Or, if a teacher feels strong rapport with a certain child, he or she may tend to let the child "get away with" more than other students are allowed. An example of cognition as the primary component of an attitude is the assessment of a student's needs causing a teacher to require the student to participate in particular activities, even those the child might dislike.

If an attitude is based on a negative feeling, it may be amenable to change through counseling or role-playing techniques. In a role-playing situation each of the participants is asked to portray as realistically as possible the behavior and feelings of another person, perhaps a member of a minority group. Rather than intellectualizing the feelings, the role player attempts to suspend her or his own feelings and to draw on the capacity to feel what the other person is experiencing. The result is that the individual playing the role begins to project herself or himself imaginatively into the identity of the other person. Role playing as a technique is based on the belief that one of the most effective ways to change attitudes is to participate in experiences in which one can observe the effect on others of attitudinal behavior; the process creates the content.

If, on the other hand, an attitude is primarily based on cognition, new information may be effective in producing attitude changes. An excellent illustration of this effect involves the notion of *teacher expectancy*. If a teacher expects a student or group of students to behave in a certain way, the teacher's attitude may serve as a *self-fulfilling prophecy*—that is, the students may behave in the predicted manner in response to the teacher's attitude and not as a result of the other factors on which the teacher's expectations are based. A teacher who is told that students are "slow" will have different expectations for their performance than if the students were said to be

WHY SHOULD I LOOK? I KNOW WHAT I GOT...

HEY, HOW ABOUT THAT?

I GOT AN "F" ON THE TEST, FRANKLIN...WHAT DID YOU GET?

I GOT A "B"! I'M VERY HAPPY...

I THINK I GOT AN "F" BECAUSE I HAVE A BIG NOSE...SOMETIMES A TEACHER JUST DOESN'T LIKE THE WAY A KID LOOKS...

"fast."[5] Regardless of their innate ability, students deemed "slow" may respond poorly precisely because of the teacher's low expectations. Many teachers have low expectations of poor children. Many educators cite this phenomenon as a major cause of low student performances in urban schools attended by poor children. The teachers' expectations can be changed if the teachers are provided proof that these students' abilities are not inherently inferior to those of other children. The teachers' attitudes toward these youngsters are likely to change somewhat as a result of their raised expectations.

At this point let us consider the position, most eloquently expressed by Carl Rogers, a noted counselor, psychologist, and therapist, that significant learning depends on certain attitudinal qualities that exist in the personal relationship between the facilitator and the learner. Note that Rogers uses the term *facilitator*, rather than *teacher*, because he believes it puts emphasis on what happens to the learner rather than on the performance of the teacher. The term *facilitator* also implies significantly different functions than does the term *teacher*.

The attitude most basic to the learning relationship, according to Rogers, is *realness* or genuineness. Instead of playing a role or presenting a front, the facilitator must enter into a relationship with the learner. The facilitator must be a real person, one who ". . . is *being* himself" and who is free to be enthusiastic, bored, interested, angry, sensitive, and sympathetic. As Rogers says,

> Because he accepts these feelings as his own he has no need to impose them on his students. He can like or dislike a student product without implying that it is objectively good or bad or that the student is good or bad. He is simply expressing a feeling for the product, a feeling which exists within himself. Thus, he is a person to his students, not a faceless embodiment of a curricular require-

[5]For further discussion of teacher expectations, see Thomas L. Good and Jere E. Brophy, *Looking in Classrooms*, 2nd ed. (New York: Harper & Row, 1978), pp. 65–108.

ment nor a sterile tube through which knowledge is passed from one generation to the next.[6]

Another essential attitude Rogers describes is valuing the learners—their feelings, their opinions, and their persons—as they are and as worthy in their own right, and accepting both their imperfections and their potentialities. The facilitator who possesses this attitude can accept students' occasional apathies, fears of failure, or hatred of authority, as well as their more positive characteristics. In short, this attitude is an expression of the facilitator's confidence and trust in the capacity of the human being.

A third attitude that Rogers considers essential to the establishment of a climate for self-initiated, experiential learning is *empathic understanding.* "When the teacher has the ability to understand the student's reactions from the inside, has a sensitive awareness of the way the process of education and learning seems *to the student,* then again the likelihood of significant learning is increased.[7] Empathic understanding implies that the facilitator understands the learner but does not judge or evaluate the learner. For example, a student might say to the teacher: "I don't like creative writing. I'm no good at writing." An empathic, nonevaluative response by the teacher might be: "You don't care for the writing assignments, and you don't feel you have much talent as a writer. What do you find the most difficult about writing?" Rogers urges that a teacher initially set the goal of making one nonevaluative, accepting, empathic response per day to a student's demonstrated or verbalized feelings. By doing so, he believes, the teacher will discover the potency of this approach.

Rogers's approach is intended to create classroom environments conducive to self-initiated learning. He maintains that the teacher's skills, knowledge of the field, curricular planning, lectures, and selection of books and other learning aids are all peripheral; the crux of the learning situation is the relationship between the facilitator and the learner, which should be

[6]Carl Rogers, *Freedom to Learn* (Columbus: Charles E. Merrill, 1969), p. 106.
[7]Rogers, *Freedom to Learn,* p. 10.

characterized by *realness, valuing,* and *empathy.* Unless the learning environment is characterized by those three attitudinal predispositions, according to Rogers, it is sterile and cannot produce significant learning.

There is little question that if you have empathy for your students, value them as unique individuals, and are secure enough to be yourself without playing a role, you will be a more successful teacher; and the atmosphere in your classroom will make possible for you and your students a joy, excitement, and closeness absent from many classrooms.

The Teacher's Attitudes Toward Peers and Parents

The teacher is not isolated in the classroom. He or she interacts daily with fellow teachers, administrators, and other school personnel, and must often have very sensitive dealings with parents. It can happen that a teacher who is very gifted in work with children has a disastrous professional life because of uncontrolled attitudes toward the adults he or she encounters. However, most teachers do not have significantly different attitudes toward adults than they would toward children possessing the same characteristics. Therefore, much of what we have already said about the teachers' attitudes toward themselves and toward children also applies to their attitudes toward peers and parents.

AUTHORITY   The teacher's attitude toward those who represent authority (ordinarily administrators, but for prospective teachers the university supervisor or the cooperating teacher) may be a source of conflict. Teachers may find it hard to be themselves while dealing with people who outrank them in position or prestige, though they may feel perfectly comfortable with people who are their equals or in a lesser position. Sometimes teachers find that they yield too readily to demands from others, especially those in positions of authority, and as a result feel guilty about complying rather than standing on their own convictions. When this occurs, the result is often a continuing undercurrent of resentment toward the person making a request.

These responses to authority are dysfunctional in that they impede communication and understanding. Teachers must examine their reactions to persons in authority positions and strive to overcome predispositions to hostility or anxiety unwarranted by reality.

COMPETITION   Some teachers develop a strong drive to compete with other teachers for recognition from both authority figures and students. They strive to have the best lesson plans, to be the "most popular teacher" or to maintain the friendliest relationship with the administration. Such persons are striving to be recognized and rewarded. As a result of this attitude, they sometimes cut themselves off from much-needed help and severely limit their ability to be of help to others. They are unable to recognize the need for cooperation and sharing of ideas for the benefit of both staff and students.

SUPERIORITY AND PREJUDICE   One attitude that never fails to cause trouble for teachers is a feeling of superiority to fellow teachers and the parents of students. They may feel intellectually superior to colleagues or socially superior to students' parents, or both. Some teachers simply have little tolerance for people who differ from them in values, cultural background, or economic status and, as a result, they treat others with disdain and contempt rather than patience and respect. Consider the following description of a teacher's meeting with lower-class black parents who have come to the school to lodge a complaint about their child's being teased:

> . . . The point was made by the Reading Teacher that this little girl actually was not so much teased by other kids as she was something of a troublemaker herself. It happened that this was not the truth. . . . The Reading Teacher then delivered an excellent and persuasive assessment of the little girl's incorrect behavior and she was so persuasive that the child ended up by apologizing to the Reading Teacher for all of the things that she had done wrong.
>
> The parents come up with a just and proper reason to place blame, and they *get* it instead. Up they come angry and with proper

outrage. Off they go, humbled, sad, and weakly, having as it were apologized for the stupid thing they've tried to obtain. The look of embarrassed humility.[8]

Had the girl's parents had high social standing, this scenario probably would not have taken place. Feelings of personal superiority can cause teachers to treat people in an offensive and humiliating manner.

The Teacher's Attitude Toward the Subject Matter

This section is short because our message is simple: it is most important that whatever subject matter you teach, you feel *enthusiasm* for it. Just as students can usually discern the teacher's attitude toward them, they are also very sensitive to the teacher's attitude toward the subject matter. One of the most striking characteristics of the excellent teacher is enthusiasm for what she or he is teaching, or "facilitating." The bored teacher conveys boredom to the students—and who can blame them for failing to get excited if the teacher, who knows more about the subject than they do, doesn't find it engaging?

Some teachers find it difficult to feel enthusiasm for a curriculum they haven't constructed themselves, or don't identify with, or don't want to teach. The surest way to guarantee that teachers are enthusiastic about what they are teaching is to allow them to teach what they are enthusiastic about. And we do not mean this as a mere play on words. We would rather see an enthusiastic teacher teaching Turkish military history or macramé than an uninspired teacher teaching Shakespeare. As one student put it, "There is nothing worse than sitting in a lesson knowing full well that the teacher is dying to get rid of you and rush back to the staff-room to have her cup of tea."[9]

Don't allow yourself to be pressured into teaching something you care little about. Make sure you have a positive attitude toward the subject you teach. Enthusiasm—if the teacher has it, life in the classroom can be exciting. If it is missing, there is little hope that the students will learn much of significance.

WHAT SUBJECT-MATTER KNOWLEDGE DOES THE EFFECTIVE TEACHER NEED?

The prospective teacher's subject-matter preparation can be seen as having two facets: study of the content of the discipline itself, and familiarity with the knowledge derived from it to be taught to the pupil.[10] In some fields, such as biology, the discipline is the same as the subject to be taught; other teaching fields, such as social studies, draw on many subject-area disci-

---

[8]Jonathan Kozol, *Death at an Early Age* (Boston: Houghton Mifflin, 1967), p. 92.

[9]Edward Blishen, ed., *The School That I'd Like* (Hardmondsworth, England: Penguin Books, 1969), pp. 141–143.

[10]The authors are indebted to B. O. Smith, author of *Teachers for the Real World,* for many of the ideas expressed in this section.

plines. In all fields, though, the knowledge to be taught is less extensive and advanced than the content of college disciplinary courses; the content of the school curriculum is selected from the available knowledge on the basis of the students' prior learning and the limitations of time. This is one reason expertise in a discipline is not a guarantee of success at teaching the same subject at the elementary or high school level. Another is that, in addition to the two kinds of subject-matter preparation just described, the teacher must have *knowledge about knowledge,* that is, sufficient perspective on a subject to be able to analyze and convey its elements, logic, possible uses, social biases, and relevance to the needs of the students. When a teacher can assert that a process for solving a particular problem is correct or incorrect, or identify a certain ethnic bias in a literary passage, the knowledge he or she draws on to make these assertions is what is meant by *knowledge about knowledge.*

We have assumed that the educated man is one who *knows;* yet *knowing* about literature may give one little sense of human tragedy or of belonging to humanity, little compassion. Knowing some science—let us say physics—may do little to help one sense the spirit of science. If we really believe in a liberal education, we must be more concerned with what students are and are becoming than with what they know and are learning in fact and skill. This does not mean that knowledge is unimportant but rather that the true teacher sees knowledge as a means, not as an end.[11]

It is precisely this concern for the uses of knowledge that many teachers lack.

Let's turn to the teacher's preparation in the disciplines that will constitute his or her teaching field. Most teacher education programs draw heavily on the disciplines. We consider training in specific disciplines as essential to a teacher's general education as it is to that of a doctor or a lawyer; and we are not advocating the total dissolution of disciplinary study. However, we believe that one of the major faults of existing teacher education programs is that the disciplinary approach fails to prepare teachers for the second facet of subject-matter preparation—the knowledge to be taught to the pupil. For instance, teachers who majored in mathematics might find that their college courses, however rigorous, simply didn't prepare them to teach elementary mathematics or algebra. The mathematics courses required of prospective teachers probably differ little from those prescribed for mathematics majors planning on careers in industry. As a rule—despite the involvement of many scholars in the curriculum reform movement—university professors are not concerned about preparing teachers to teach the subject matter that elementary and secondary school students are expected to learn. Most college courses are designed to prepare students for more advanced study within the discipline. The methods courses offered in schools of education represent an attempt—not always successful—to remedy this situation. In short, much of what prospective teachers learn from their study of the disciplines is not taught to children, and thus it is not directly applicable to teaching. This is particularly true for elementary school teachers, who are called on to teach content virtually ignored by the academic departments of the universities.

If a teacher's college education should include the study of various disciplines, and if the disciplines in themselves are inadequate preparation for teaching youngsters, what then do we propose? The teacher education program should offer opportunities for prospective teachers to develop curriculum units that are apt to be of interest to students, drawing on concepts and approaches from several disciplines. The mode of study should focus on problem solving, with the prospective teachers themselves assuming a major share of the responsibility for analyzing the problems, selecting and organizing the materials, and carrying on discussion. Through this process they would learn to think through problems on their own and would acquire the skills necessary to identify and locate relevant materials. By ex-

[11]Ernest O. Melby, "The Contagion of Liberal Education," *Journal of Teacher Education* 18 (Summer 1967): 135.

periencing the same kinds of difficulties that their own students will be likely to encounter, prospective teachers would be better prepared to deal with them effectively.

> To be prepared in the subject matter of instruction is to know the content to be taught and how the content can be related to the interest and experience of children and youths. To prepare the teacher in this subject matter will require courses oriented to the teacher's need for knowledge that can be tied in with the life of children and youths rather than discipline-oriented courses.[12]

Translating the content of discipline-oriented courses into a more appropriate mode of instruction will be a difficult undertaking. But we are convinced that allowing prospective teachers to organize materials to focus on meeting the students "where they're at" will make the job of translation easier.

We thus urge that prospective teachers know intimately the content they are to teach, and that this content be centered around human physical and social problems and issues relevant to the students' lives. It is equally important for teachers to be well versed in the disciplines from which the instructional subject matter is derived. In Smith's words, "The first is necessary for teaching anything at all. The second supplies a depth of knowledge essential to the teacher's feeling of intellectual security and his ability to handle instructional content with greater understanding."[13] Finally, teachers must have knowledge about knowledge as a whole, so that they can bring perspective and a command of the logical operations used in manipulating information to any subject-matter content. These three types of knowledge, we believe, are essential for effective teachers.

WHAT THEORETICAL KNOWLEDGE DOES THE EFFECTIVE TEACHER NEED?

Theories-in-Use

Let's return for a moment to the case of Jenny Ferris. In the incident described, Jenny operated from certain ideas or what some call theories-in-use, which are different from "pure" theories.[14] A *theory* is a still-unproved explanation of why something happens the way it does. In its simplest form, a theory is a hypothesis designed to bring generalizable facts, concepts, or scientific laws into systematic connection.

On the other hand, a *theory-in-use* is something people walk around with in their heads and apply in their dealings with people and the world. Theories-in-use are often quite different from the theories people come up

---

[12]B. O. Smith et al., *Teachers for the Real World* (Washington, D.C.: American Association of Colleges for Teacher Education, 1969), pp. 121–122. Reprinted by permission of the publisher.

[13]Smith, *Teachers for the Real World*, p. 122.

[14]C. Argyris and D. A. Schon, *Theory in Practice: Increasing Professional Effectiveness* (San Francisco: Jossey-Bass, 1974), pp. 3–19.

with when asked to justify doing this or that. Often, too, they are unexamined. We all have these theories-in-use, and they guide us as we make our way through our daily lives. You support a particular political party because you believe it advances sounder economic policies. You eat only certain foods because you have an idea that they have a healthy effect on the body. Or you decide to take a summer job in a public playground, believing that you'll get to know children better and that future employers might be pleased or impressed when they hear you've had that kind of experience.

Stop here and see if you can identify Jenny's theories-in-use:

1. _____

2. _____

3. _____

4. _____

5. _____

6. _____

7. _____

8. _____

As you probably discovered, Jenny has several theories-in-use. For example, Jenny has the theory that if you're from a broken home, you're probably starved for affection and suffering the effects of the breakup. She has a theory that we all contain a spark of the divine, and she used that theory to decide what she was going to teach and how. Jenny also has a theory that wealthy children behave better in schools than do children from poor homes, and, as a result, she expects certain behavior from certain kinds of students. She also has a classroom management theory that students should be given some leeway, but if they get out of line the teacher must come down hard on them. Jenny appears to have many theories-in-use, some of which are clearly questionable. A few seem to have contributed to her trouble, and some may get her into more trouble farther down the line. But notice that Jenny was not worried about her ideas or her theories-in-use. She was worried about what she did and what she will do. She didn't question some of her conceptions. Theories-in-use are the last things she had in mind.

Why Study Educational Theory?

The fact that Jenny did not reflect on the truth or falsity of her theories or try to recall some theories that she had learned during her teacher training is not uncommon. Indeed, many teachers question the basic usefulness of theory. It is not at all uncommon for beginning teachers to be told by a senior colleague, "Forget all that theory they've been giving you at the university. Here's what works in the real world. . . ." Further, preservice teachers often complain that courses are too theoretical. They want to get out to schools where the action is. This desire (perhaps it is your own desire) for things that work and ways to cope with real situations is important, and we do not want to diminish its importance. As a teacher you will need practical techniques and solutions to real problems. But to need practical tools does not mean that educational theory is less important. Theoretical knowledge about learning and human behavior equips the teacher to draw on concepts from psychology, anthropology, sociology, and related disciplines to interpret the complex reality of the classroom. The teacher who lacks theoretical background will be obliged to interpret classroom events according to commonly held beliefs or common sense, much of which is, unfortunately, based on outmoded notions of human behavior. The case of Jenny Ferris is an example of how lack of theoretical knowledge of classroom management can lead to inappropriate behavior on the part of the teacher.

First, although you, like Jenny, may have your own theories-in-use, these need to be challenged and tested. The best way to do this is to pit them against other theories and ideas. Jenny probably would not have become involved in such trouble if more of her ideas had been challenged.

Second, we believe that theoretical information *is* practical. The problem is not that theory is wrong or unworkable, but that many teacher education programs offer students few opportunities to apply theory to practical situations; it is usually up to the neophyte teacher to translate theory into practice on the job. But theory is extremely important, even if you occasionally fail to apply it effectively. As the great American educator John Dewey said, "Nothing is so practical as a good theory."[15]

Third, by giving attention to theoretical knowledge now, we are looking ahead to the future. In other words, even if it has limited interest to you at this point, we want you to know that at a later stage of your development you will encounter theories that will enlighten and enrich your work with the young.

Every teacher should be familiar with currently respected theoretical knowledge about human behavior and social systems. In addition to such general knowledge, there exists specialized theoretical knowledge, which is the unique province of the effective teacher. Teaching is neither static nor a matter of intuition; it has given rise to a body of theoretical knowledge that is constantly growing.

For these reasons, then, we think it is important for you to give attention to educational theory both now and throughout your training.

[15]For the moment we will downplay the fact that John Dewey was primarily an educational theorist.

Theoretical knowledge relevant to teaching is derived from courses such as educational psychology, educational sociology, educational anthropology, linguistics, foundations of education, tests and measurement, and classroom management. But because the relationship of theoretical knowledge to a given occupation is typically indirect, it is not enough for you simply to take the appropriate courses. Theory develops within a discipline and is formulated in terms suitable to that discipline but usually unsuitable or inadequate for a learning situation. For teachers, this means that principles derived from psychology must be adapted to a classroom before they become useful. A classroom is always subject to a number of variables that are absent in the experimental situation. In the late afternoon of a school day, for instance, both teacher and students are likely to be tired, and their behavior is likely to differ from their morning behavior. In contrast, the laboratory experiments from which theory is derived are controlled to eliminate such variables. Thus, in order to make the necessary adaptations, a teacher must have a command not only of the theoretical knowledge but also of the learning situation.

Perhaps going back to the case of Jenny Ferris will help clarify. Jenny knew from her educational psychology course that any behavior that is reinforced will be strengthened and any that is not rewarded or punished will be weakened. Nevertheless, she adopted a teaching practice in which she allowed "a little testing and fooling around" but planned to discipline offenders. Her past experiences should have told her that many students enjoy testing the teacher and "fooling around"; further, she should have realized that these activities do not contribute positively to learning outcomes or to a constructive classroom atmosphere. Somehow, though, the theoretical knowledge about reinforcement and punishment did not carry over to her professional practice—to her teaching. Jenny failed to grasp the concept that allowing the students to fool around and test her could possibly be reinforcing their behavior. Her failure to apply mild desists, stopping the behavior before it could escalate, indicates that she never quite internalized the theoretical knowledge she "learned" in her educational psychology course.

A teacher's theoretical knowledge can be used in two ways: to interpret situations and to solve problems. (Practical knowledge, on the other hand, is more limited in applicability and is used primarily to respond to familiar situations.)[16] For example, a teacher may see a child acting like a bully and interpret the child's aggression as a reaction to some frustration the child had experienced. In doing so the teacher would be drawing on theoretical knowledge about frustration and its possible consequences to interpret the child's behavior. To solve the problem, the teacher would avoid shaming

[16]Smith, *Teachers for the Real World*, p. 44.

the child but would seek the causes of her frustration and try to channel the child's energy in a more constructive direction. Adults lacking theoretical knowledge would be likely to attribute the child's aggression to "bad character" and be unable to deal with the situation.

Problem solving is a primary aspect of the role of the teacher. Teachers are constantly required to make diagnoses and decisions about problems related to learning and to human relations. In order to do this effectively teachers must possess a high degree of theoretical understanding. They apply this understanding by formulating hypotheses both about the interpretation of problems and about the actions they should undertake in response to them. But there should be no air of finality about their proposed solutions. If the actions a teacher has chosen do not solve the problem, the situation should be reinterpreted and alternative responses sought and tested.

Classroom problems are rarely entirely original, except in the case of the new teacher, to whom nearly all are unprecedented. As a result, once teachers have developed and incorporated a solution to a given problem, they will tend to use the same solution, with appropriate modifications, when confronted by similar situations; a solution that worked once in a particular situation is habitually relied on as the "correct" way to handle all related problems. One teacher's way to handle disruptive outbursts might be to separate the offending child from the others. This solution deals only with the symptom rather than with the problem itself, which might vary from insecurity because of parental neglect to dislike of the school environment. Single-solution behavior is dangerous because it fails to take into account all the variables of individual situations. Teachers must guard against the "single-solution rut."

Because of their insecurity and lack of theoretical knowledge, beginning teachers often seek "recipes" to solve certain categories of problems. "What do I do when one child hits another?" Questions of this type are

Miss Peach by Mell Lazarus. Courtesy of Mell Lazarus and Field Newspaper Syndicate.

requests for pat answers. Unfortunately, these plugged-in approaches rarely work. The reasons one child hits another are as numerous as are the possible and appropriate teacher responses.

As a teacher, you should not only refrain from using single solutions but also avoid seeking them; instead, you should acquire knowledge about learning, patterns of behavior, how children from different cultural backgrounds behave, and what values influence their values. You should also become familiar with such concepts as motivation, self-concept, feedback, reinforcement, attitude formation, perception, and peer approval.

Let's consider an example of how theoretical knowledge can help a teacher interpret classroom events and solve the problems arising from them. In psychology, *self-concept* is defined as the sum of a person's beliefs about and evaluations of himself or herself as a person. All people have images of the kind of people they are, derived from previous experiences, and they tend to behave in ways that are consistent with those images. A child's self-concept is an important factor both in ability to learn and in interaction with other children and his or her environment. For instance, if children view themselves as likable and outgoing, they are apt to respond in a friendly manner when meeting new children. If children are insecure because they view themselves as weak, ugly, or unwanted, they will not respond easily to a group of new children.

Suppose a teacher observes that a particular boy is doing poorly in science. The problem at issue is how to help this child improve his performance in that subject. A number of factors may be influencing his performance—he may possess inadequate or incorrect scientific concepts; he may not be interested in science; he may not be very intelligent; or he may view himself as inept in science and thus not try as hard as he might. Several of these factors may be interrelated in complex ways.[17]

A teacher who functions as a problem solver would hypothesize that the boy's poor performance could result from any of these factors and proceed to investigate further by collecting information about the child's previous performance in science, his intelligence level, and his self-concept. In this way the teacher can determine whether the child's self-concept is an important determinant in his poor science performance.

If the child's intelligence level is high and his previous experience indicates that he should be doing reasonably well in science, the teacher might hypothesize that the principal reason for the boy's poor performance is his conception of his own abilities. What can the teacher do? Can a teacher help change a child's self-concept? The answer is an unequivocal maybe. If the teacher is one of the child's major sources of self-information, he or she may be able to encourage a revised self-concept through a guid-

[17]The authors are indebted for this example to Frederick J. McDonald, *Educational Psychology* (Belmont, Calif.: Wadsworth, 1965), pp. 439–441.

ance program designed to help the child gather reliable information about himself. Sometimes children lack self-understanding to such an extent that they must be referred to specialized professional help before progress can be made. Again, the teacher may have to make that decision on the basis of his or her own observations and knowledge.

If the child's problem does not seem serious enough to require referral to a specialist, the teacher might try any of several approaches to improve the child's self-concept in science. Discussing his abilities with him, helping him view his abilities more realistically, and arranging for a successful experience are among the potential ways to change the child's self-perception. The teacher proceeds throughout as a hypothesis maker, forming tentative ideas about experiences that might improve the child's self-concept, and testing those ideas. The teacher's hypotheses will become more perceptive and accurate as his or her understanding of the variables influencing a child's self-concept increases.

A teacher needs much more than a common-sense understanding of human behavior. The capable and effective teacher uses theoretical knowledge drawn from various education-related disciplines to formulate and test hypotheses about human behavior in the classroom. In our opinion, the translation of theory into practice cannot be left to chance; you must constantly take advantage of opportunities that allow you to apply theoretical concepts to classroom situations and to receive guidance and feedback from your instructors about the application of these concepts.

WHAT TEACHING SKILLS ARE REQUIRED OF AN EFFECTIVE TEACHER?

Knowing Versus Doing

Simply knowing something does not guarantee the ability to act on that knowledge. There is a profound difference between *knowing* and *doing*. Teachers may know, for example, that they should provide prompt feedback to their students on their written assignments, but they are not always able to act on that knowledge. No teacher education program can afford to focus exclusively on theoretical knowledge at the expense of the practice, or "doing," dimension of teaching, just as no individual teacher can rely solely on knowledge of subject matter. All prospective teachers need to develop a repertoire of teaching skills to use as they see fit in varying classroom situations.

Research has not yet conclusively identified the teaching skills that have the most beneficial impact on student learning, but many educators have independently defined the skills they believe essential to effective teaching. Among them are the following:

- the ability to ask different kinds of questions, each of which requires different types of thought processes from the student
- the ability to reinforce certain kinds of student behavior
- the ability to diagnose student needs and learning difficulties

- the ability to vary the learning situation continually to keep the students involved

- the ability to recognize when students are paying attention and to use this information to vary behavior and, possibly, the direction of the lesson

- the ability to utilize technological equipment, such as motion picture projectors or microcomputers

- the ability to judge the appropriateness of instructional materials

- the ability to define the objectives of particular lessons and units in terms of student behaviors

- the ability to relate learning to the student's experience[18]

A Repertoire of Teaching Skills

This list is far from complete. It does make clear, however, that teachers need a large repertoire of skills to work effectively with students with varying backgrounds and different educational experiences. There is some evidence that the outstanding characteristic of an effective teacher is flexibil-

[18]Partially adapted from Smith, *Teachers for the Real World,* p. 71.

CHARACTERISTIC BEHAVIORS OF EFFECTIVE TEACHERS

Educational researcher Jere Brophy summarized research studies which indicate that teachers do have a significant effect on the learning rates of students in urban schools. His review emphasizes that instructionally effective teachers share common characteristics that are independent of such factors as students' prior achievement, class size, student body composition, group dynamics, and teacher health and welfare. He delineates eight behaviors shared by effective teachers in urban schools:

1. They hold and project high expectations for student success. A sense of personal efficacy is promoted.

2. They maximize opportunities for students to engage in learning experiences.

3. They manage their own time and organize the classroom efficiently.

4. They pace the curriculum to maximize student success experiences.

5. They engage in active teaching with all students whether individually or in groups of varying size.

6. They work toward mastery of knowledge and skills by systematically monitoring student progress and providing feedback.

7. They are sensitive to grade-level differences in rate of learning and type of teacher-student contact required.

8. They provide a supportive learning environment that is characterized by an emphasis on cognitive objectives within an ambiance of warmth and personal support.

Jere Brophy, "Successful Teaching Strategies for the Inner-City Child," *Phi Delta Kappan* 63 (April 1982): 527–530. Used with permission.

ity,[19] since varied approaches are necessary to meet the multiple needs of students.

We believe strongly that a teacher education program should train candidates in the performance of selected teaching skills. Many teachers and teacher educators, however, blanch at the term *teacher training*. They regard training as something one does with animals, not human beings; human beings, they say, should be educated, not trained. We don't agree. We believe that a teacher's preparation must consist of both education and training. The objection that training teachers makes them robots and prevents the release of their creative energies is contradicted by what we know of training in other occupations. Surgeons and pilots, for example, are trained to perform certain operations proficiently and even automatically. This level of mastery enables them to turn their attention and energy to tasks more worthy of their creativity. As B. O. Smith says, "A trained individual has relaxed control, which frees him from preoccupation with immediate acts so he can scan the new situation and respond to it constructively. Training and resourcefulness are complementary, not antithetical, elements of behavior."[20]

The skills in which a teacher is trained should depend on the age level and cultural background of the children to be taught, the subjects to be taught, research evidence on the effectiveness of certain skills, and other factors. Once the necessary skills have been selected, a training procedure is developed. Smith argues that the training process must have the following six components:

- establishment of the practice situation
- specification of the behavior
- performance of the specified behavior
- feedback of information about the performance
- modification of the performance in the light of the feedback
- performance-feedback-correction-practice schedule continued until desirable skillfulness is achieved[21]

Classroom Management Skills

There is no other dimension of teaching that causes more concern for beginning teachers than that of managing the classroom and maintaining discipline. "Will I be able to manage and control my class(es) so I can teach effectively?", is a question most beginning teachers ask themselves. Because there is such a great concern about this aspect of teaching, we have chosen

[19]Donald Hamachek, "Characteristics of Good Teachers and Implications for Teacher Education," *Phi Delta Kappan* 50 (February 1969): 341–344.
[20]Smith, *Teachers for the Real World*, p. 80. Reprinted by permission of the publisher.
[21]Smith, *Teachers for the Real World*, p. 71. Reprinted by permission of the publisher.

to spend considerable space on this one skill area, realizing that there are other skills, which are also deserving of time and space.

Let's start by examining what we mean by the term *classroom management*. Weber argues that teaching consists of two major sets of activities: instruction and management.[22] Instructional activities are designed to facilitate directly the student's achievement of specific educational objectives. Asking questions, evaluating learner progress, and presenting information are examples of instructional activities. Managerial activities are intended to create and maintain conditions in which instruction can take place efficiently and effectively. Developing teacher-student rapport, establishing productive group norms, and rewarding promptness are examples of managerial behavior. Oftentimes a particular teaching behavior may be viewed as serving both instructional and managerial purposes, but it is useful to distinguish between these two types of activities when one is faced with classroom problems. Trying to solve managerial problems by instructional means, and vice versa, will not produce very effective results. A definition of *classroom management*, then, might be: That set of teacher behaviors by which the teacher establishes and maintains conditions that facilitate effective and efficient instruction.

As with most complex teaching skills, classroom management requires a thorough understanding of theoretical knowledge and research findings, as well as an action, or performances, component. This knowledge or theory component comes primarily from educational, social, and humanistic psychology. As with many other areas of investigation, there is no consensus regarding the one most effective approach to classroom management. Instead, there are different philosophies, theories, and research findings, each tending to address particular dimensions or approaches to classroom management. A brief overview of some of these different approaches will be helpful.[23]

BEHAVIOR MODIFICATION   Of all the approaches, this approach to classroom management has the strongest base in theory and research. Its basis comes from behavioral and experimental psychology, particularly the work of B. F. Skinner, and views classroom management as the process of modifying student behavior. The teacher's role is to foster desirable student behavior and to eliminate undesirable behavior. This is accomplished primarily by consistently and systematically rewarding (reinforcing) appropriate student behavior and removing rewards or punishing for inappropriate student behavior.

[22]Wilford A. Weber, "Classroom Management," in *Classroom Teaching Skills*, 2nd ed., ed. J. M. Cooper (Lexington, Mass.: D. C. Heath Publishing Co., 1982), p. 283.

[23]These approaches are identified and described by Weber in "Classroom Management," pp. 304–335.

SOCIOEMOTIONAL CLIMATE   The roots of this approach stem from counseling and from clinical psychology, which places great importance on interpersonal relationships. Advocates of this approach believe that effective classroom management is largely a function of positive teacher-student relationships. The teacher's task, then, is to build positive interpersonal relationships and a positive socioemotional climate. Theorists who would be classified as proponents of this approach include Carl Rogers, who believes that attributes such as realness, accepting, and empathic understanding must be present if the teacher is going to be able to facilitate learning; Haim Ginott, who stresses the importance of effective communication in promoting good teacher-student relationships; and William Glasser, who argues that teachers must help students develop a sense of identity, worthiness, and success.

GROUP PROCESS   Social psychology and group dynamics form the base of this approach to classroom management, particularly in the work of Richard and Patricia Schmuck, and Lois V. Johnson and Mary Bany. The basic assumption is that learning takes place within a group context and, as a result, the nature and behavior of the classroom group affect each individual's learning. The teacher's role is to establish and maintain an effective, productive classroom group. To do this the teacher must help the group achieve unity and cooperation, establish standards and coordinate work procedures, use problem solving to improve conditions, and substitute appropriate goals for inappropriate goals.

AUTHORITARIAN   This approach views classroom management as basically a process of controlling student behavior. The role of the teacher is to establish and maintain order in the classroom, primarily through the use of discipline. This approach is not vindictive or mean, but can be very caring. There is no doubt, however, as to who has the authority in the classroom. The authoritarian approach advocates establishing and enforcing classroom rules, using soft reprimands and desists, and using commands and directives. One authoritarian system that is currently receiving considerable attention is *assertive discipline,* developed by Lee and Marlene Canter. They argue that the teacher has the right to establish clear limits and expectations, insist on acceptable behavior from the students, and follow through with appropriate consequences that are known in advance to the students when rules are broken.

Teachers should not perceive these different approaches as being mutually exclusive. In fact, Weber argues that the most effective classroom manager will be one who uses a pluralistic approach and applies the managerial strategy or strategies that appear to have the best potential to be effective in a particular situation. To do this requires that the teacher ultimately must become a decision maker who possesses a repertoire of different approaches.

Research Related to Classroom Management

ACADEMIC VERSUS BEHAVIOR TASKS   Walter Doyle's observations of the induction of student teachers into the classroom environment offer us some fascinating insights into the processes of classroom management.[24] Doyle analyzed the classrooms he observed in terms of *tasks,* which he defined as consisting of (1) a goal and (2) a set of operations necessary to achieve the goal. His model comprises two broad types of classroom tasks: academic tasks and behavior tasks. An academic task exists whenever student performance is exchanged for grades. That is, students are required to

---

[24]Walter Doyle, ''Task Structures and Student Roles in Classrooms,'' paper presented at the annual meeting of the American Educational Research Association, Toronto, Canada, March 1978.

perform certain kinds of academic operations that will influence the grades they receive. Behavior tasks can be viewed as disruptions, or "off-task," responses often thought to interfere with learning in classrooms. When a student accomplishes a behavior task, there is a violation of some known rule or rules of conduct. Students who are skillful at behavior tasks usually sustain the off-task behavior for a reasonable period, and they usually "get away with" the violation.

Doyle discovered that students initiated behavior tasks frequently over the course of the first day or so after the student teacher assumed the teaching role in the classroom. They were testing the student teacher's ability to manage classroom routines and rule systems. Rarely were verbalized rules accepted at face value. Rather, students sought evidence that the student teacher would actually follow routines and enforce rules. Behavior tasks were the way the students obtained such evidence.

Students tested managerial skills by requesting information the student teacher had little or no opportunity to know, such as details of an assignment given to the class several weeks before the student teacher arrived. Students would also ask questions about school policies that student teachers could seldom answer. When the student teacher could not provide the information requested, the students grumbled about the teacher's abilities, which was often unnerving to the student teacher.

Other behavior tasks involved more direct violations of school or teacher rules, such as talking and note passing, during lessons. If the student teacher became irritated and began to issue directives, the students often responded with comments such as "You're mean," in an attempt to soften up a student teacher who was sensitive to being liked by the students.

Doyle observed that in nearly all instances only a few students participated in behavior tasks, at least initially. It appeared that some students seemed to rely on others to test the rule system.

Doyle also noted that it seemed important for students to know their peers' behavior task skills in order to interpret tests of the teacher's managerial abilities. If a student was highly skilled at behavior tasks, then other students might either tolerate the student teacher's inability to manage or else be very impressed by successful management in these situations. On the other hand, if a student was not perceived as being skilled at behavior tasks, then failure to manage the situation reflected poorly on the student teacher. Doyle remarked that since teachers know considerably less about students than students know about each other, this places new teachers in a vulnerable position.

Students seemed to use two criteria to judge a teacher's ability to manage behavior tasks. First, students appeared to expect teachers to act when action by a teacher was required to stop disruptions and restore order. Second, students seemed to respect what Doyle calls "tactical superiority." Teachers who were able to anticipate possible consequences of student

Q: "Why are you fighting?"

A: "We're not fighting; we're just playing."

Q: "Why are you chewing gum in class?"

A: "Tastes good."

Q: "Why are you smoking?"

A: "I like to smoke."

Q: "Why didn't you have a pencil?"

A: "I forgot."

As a teacher or school administrator, would you like to decrease discipline problems in your school by 50%?

Teachers who are faced with the responsibility of disciplining students use the "Why?" question as a very natural, almost instinctive response to inappropriate behavior. In tracing the origins of a great number of serious discipline cases over the past five years, I have found that over half began with a relatively minor misbehavior on the part of the student, followed by a why from the teacher.

Asking why of a student who has misbehaved or performed incorrectly is not sensible. Most often, it invites a flippant response or even overt hostility. Instead of asking why, tell the student what he has done or is doing incorrectly and give the student direction. This can best be done in a calm, polite, serious, and firm manner, as in these examples:

"Tom, you're late. Go to your seat quietly."

"Betty, you're smoking on campus. See me at 3:05 today."

NEVER 'WHY?' NOR 'IF . . . , I'LL . . .' How to Cut Your Discipline Problems by 50%

"Dotty and Jane, I have reason to believe you cheated on your exam. Please see me five minutes before the end of the period."

There is no reason to ask why: the student will come and tell you why if he has a good reason for being late, or chewing gum, or fighting, or cheating, or being in the hall. If the student does not have a valid reason, we should not demand to hear it, nor should we place the student in a situation which demands covering up or being untruthful.

Another point: In many incidents where the why question is used, a threatening "If . . . , I'll" statement often follows the student's answer.

"Why are you late?"

"If you're late again, I'll have to keep you after school."

"Why are you fighting?"

"If I catch you two fighting again, I'll send you to the office."

"Why are you smoking on campus?"

"If I see you smoking again, I'll suspend you for five days."

What about this "If . . . , I'll" threat? Many teachers believe that students have the right to know the consequences for misbehavior beforehand. I

agree that every misbehavior must have a consequence. The consequence may be very minor—talking to the teacher after class—or it may be severe—a lengthy suspension or even expulsion. *But it must be given consistently, and it must follow an instance of misbehavior.* And there is no need to threaten if consequences are given consistently. Students soon learn what the consequences are from experience—their own or others.

Consider this: When a teacher says, "If I catch you cheating again, I'll have you stay after school," she is implying that it's O.K. to cheat this time but not the next time. This confuses students. The teacher should say, "You are cheating. Stay after school Tuesday." Here there is no threat. Both the offender and the other students learn the consequences of misbehavior, and a realistic chance to improve his behavior is offered to the misbehaving student.

These two concepts may sound simple, yet the leadership necessary to obtain a large majority of the teaching staff to implement the "Never 'why?' nor 'If . . . , I'll' " philosophy is not at all simple. However, the increase in teacher satisfaction and the improvement in student attitudes and behavior are worth it.

Marvin J. Woodstrup, *Phi Delta Kappan* (April 1977): 609. © 1977, Phi Delta Kappan, Inc. Reprinted by permission.

behavior and handle behavior tasks early were considered effective. One student described a student teacher as the best teacher he had ever had because "We never knew what he was going to do and he always knew what we were going to do." Respect, then, is earned through the responses teachers make to the behavior patterns and actions of students in their classrooms.

ACADEMIC ENGAGED TIME   During the 1970s the National Institute of Education (NIE) funded numerous research studies in an attempt to discover what the basic skills of teaching are. Because of the great concern with declining student achievement in reading and mathematics, most of the research efforts focused on the teaching of these subjects in the elementary grades. Early efforts in this research thrust attempted to identify those teaching behaviors (such as teacher talk, number of higher-order questions, clarity of presentation) that were related to student achievement. This line of research did not prove particularly productive for many reasons. However, by shifting the research focus from teacher behaviors to student behaviors—primarily *academic engaged time* (also known as *academic learning time*)—some interesting and relevant findings emerged.

Academic engaged time is the time a student spends engaged in academically relevant material that is of a moderate level of difficulty.[25] Several research studies indicate that academic engaged time in reading or mathematics, more than any other coded teacher or student behavior, is most strongly related to achievement in those respective subjects.[26] Simply put, the more time elementary students spend working on reading or mathematics activities, the more likely they are to achieve in those areas. Whereas this finding may not seem very startling, observations indicate that tremendous differences exist in the amount of time individual students spend engaged in academic activities, both across classrooms and within the same classroom.

The research on academic engaged time clearly indicates that a primary goal of elementary teachers (and possibly secondary teachers, although the research has been limited to elementary schools) should be to keep students on-task. Unfortunately, there has not been sufficient exploration of the teacher behaviors that help keep students on-task. We do know, however, that classes that are poorly managed usually have little academic engaged time. A major task of teachers is to learn how to manage their classes so students are productively engaged.

Numerous studies, including the BTES study mentioned in Chapter 6 (p. 166), indicate that the most efficient teachers are able to engage their students about thirty minutes a day longer than the average teacher. If the

[25]David Berliner et al., *Proposal for Phase III of Beginning Teacher Evaluation Study* (San Francisco: Far West Laboratory for Educational Research and Development, 1976).

[26]Barak Victor Rosenshine and David C. Berliner, "Academic Engaged Time," paper presented to the American Educational Research Association, New York City, April 1977.

most efficient teachers are compared with the least efficient, daily differences of an hour in academic engaged time appear. Spread out over 180 days, students of efficient teachers get 90 hours more of academic engaged time than students of average teachers, and 180 hours more than students of inefficient teachers! Differences of this magnitude may help explain why students in some classes learn more than students in other classes.

KOUNIN'S RESEARCH   Jacob Kounin's research on classroom management in the elementary school grades provides us with some insights about which skills can help teachers improve their classroom management and keep pupils on-task.[27] Of the concepts Kounin identified to describe teacher classroom management behavior, three seem particularly useful. The first concept he termed *withitness*. Teachers who are ''with it'' are ones who communicate to pupils, by their behavior, that they know what is going on. Teachers who are ''with it'' will pick up the first sign of deviancy, will deal with the proper pupil, will ignore a minor misbehavior to stop a major infraction, and so forth.

The second and third concepts are concerned with the problems of lesson flow and time management. *Smoothness* concerns the absence of behaviors initiated by teachers that interfere with the flow of academic events. Examples of teacher behavior that do not reflect smoothness are when a teacher bursts in on children's activities with an order, statement, or question; when a teacher starts, or is in, some activity and then leaves it ''hanging'' only to resume it after an interval; and when a teacher terminates one activity, starts another, and then initiates a return to the terminated activity.

[27]Jacob S. Kounin, *Discipline and Group Management in Classrooms* (New York: Holt, Rinehart & Winston, 1970).

The third concept, *momentum*, concerns the absence of teacher behaviors that slow down the pace of the lesson. Kounin conceptualized two types of slow-down behaviors: *overdwelling* (when a teacher dwells too much on pupil behavior, a subpoint rather than the main point, physical props rather than substance, or instructions or details to the point of boredom); and *fragmentation* (when a teacher deals with individual pupils one at a time rather than with the group, or props one at a time rather than *en masse*). Momentum is judged by the absence of such slow-down features.

Kounin found strong correlations between teachers' use of withitness, smoothness, and momentum and their pupils' work involvement and freedom from deviancy. That is, the pupils of teachers who demonstrated these three skills tended to be involved in their work and tended to stay on-task. It is our hope that future research efforts will provide us with more answers about how teachers can increase their effectiveness in keeping students academically engaged.

OTHER RESEARCH FINDINGS   Reviewing several studies on discipline, one researcher concluded that there are four important characteristics of effective classroom managers.[28]

1. *Teachers should be able to develop and implement a workable set of rules.* Effective classroom managers develop a clearly defined set of rules, usually small in number, and communicate these rules to their students. Students know what is expected of them. The rules are perceived by the students as being reasonable and necessary, and the rules are enforceable.

2. *Teachers should develop definitions of inappropriate behavior and be able to respond quickly and consistently to such behavior.* This characteristic is very similar to Kounin's concept of *withitness*, discussed in the preceding section. Several factors were identified in determining whether a behavior was inappropriate. First, the act itself; second, the person(s) involved; and, third, the timing of the behavior. Ineffective teachers are inconsistent in how they treat different students; some students are reprimanded for inappropriate behavior, while other students seem to be able to get away with the behavior. Teachers must also communicate to their students when certain behaviors are acceptable and when they are not. Some behaviors are appropriate during small group work but inappropriate during a lecture.

3. *Teachers should be able to structure classroom activities and monitor student work to minimize disruptive behaviors.* Several studies reviewed by Lasley stressed the importance of learning the skills necessary for organizing teacher-paced, small group, and multi-task instructional activities. Good classroom

[28]Thomas J. Lasley, "Research Perspectives on Classroom Management," *Journal of Teacher Education* 32 (March-April 1981): 14–17.

managers also keep track of students as they are working to ensure that they stay on-task. Circulating among the students during seatwork to monitor their work seemed to be important.

4. *Teachers must be able to respond to problem behavior without, at the same time, denigrating the student exhibiting the behavior.* Teachers sometimes become aggressive because of their inability to cope with the frustrations caused by student misbehavior. When this occurs they may lash out in anger at the offending student. Public censure may cause the student to lose face and may provoke student aggression. Responding to a student privately is more effective than scolding him or her publicly.

We are learning more about what constitutes effective classroom management behavior. Understanding the related theories and research, and practicing the skills which this body of knowledge has identified as being effective, will help you to establish and maintain the conditions that promote student learning.

DISCIPLINE SUGGESTIONS FOR CLASSROOM TEACHERS

---

1. On the first day, cooperatively develop classroom standards.

2. Incorporate school and district policies in the classroom list.

3. Establish consequences for good and poor behavior.

4. Expect good behavior from your students, and they will try to live up to your expectations.

5. Plan and motivate interesting, meaningful lessons. Show *your own enthusiasm* for lesson activities.

6. Prevent negative behavior by continuous emphasis upon *positive* achievement.

7. Develop student self-discipline as rapidly as possible. Lead each student to make his or her own decisions rather than to rely on yours.

8. If behavior problems cannot be solved in the classroom, seek the help of counselors and administrators.

9. Reinforce good behavior by rewarding students in public. Correct or punish in private.

10. Work closely with parents. Encourage them to send students to you with positive attitudes toward classroom learning.

11. Avoid useless rules, snap judgments, and loss of composure.

12. Be *consistent, fair,* and *firm.*

13. Refrain from threats or promises that you may not be able to carry out.

14. Recognize that children have limited attention spans and assign alternate activities.

15. Discipline *yourself* in manners, voice, disposition, honesty, punctuality, consistency, fairness, and love for your students, so that your own example inspires behavior at its best.

Emery Stoops and Joyce King-Stoops, *Phi Delta Kappan* 63, (September 1981):58. Reprinted by permission.

A FINAL WORD

You may have found this chapter to be a difficult one because of its theoretical emphasis. We think it is an important one, however, because it provides you with an overview of what a truly effective teacher needs to know and be able to do. It may have been a frustrating chapter if you concluded that there is no way that you can achieve the ideal that we described. We share that frustration, since we ourselves have not measured up to this ideal in our own teaching, and we're not certain that we ever will. Nevertheless, we continue to aspire toward being the type of teacher we have described in this chapter. If you, too, can fix your sights upon this conceptualization of what makes an effective teacher and can continually work toward this ideal, you are certain to observe the positive and rewarding results in your own classroom.

Discussion Questions

1. Do you agree that it is preferable for an enthusiastic teacher to teach an unimportant subject than for an uninspired teacher to teach a crucial subject? What implications do you see in this remark? On what assumptions about teachers, students, and subject matter is it based?

2. We say on page 312 that teachers' low expectations of poor children can be changed if the teachers are provided with proof that the children's abilities are not inherently inferior to those of other children. What do you think might constitute such proof?

3. Do you have negative feelings about any group or type of people? Can you identify the basis of those feelings? Do you want to change them? How might you try?

4. Carl Rogers argues for a teacher who "is *being* himself" and shows feelings. Do you agree? Have you known any teachers who did so? Do you think children can cope with any reaction from the teacher as long as it is honestly expressed? Do you think this kind of teaching requires any particular prior training?

5. Has reading about Jenny Ferris and her theories-in-use helped you identify any of your own theories-in-use or those of teachers you have known?

6. What is the difference between common sense and theoretical knowledge?

7. Can you give an example from your own experience to illustrate John Dewey's statement, "There is nothing as practical as a good theory"?

8. Which of the skills listed on pages 325–326 seem most important to you? What skills would you add to the list? subtract from it?

9. Do the research findings on academic engaged time surprise you at all? If the findings seem commonplace to you, why do you suppose teachers vary so much in their ability to keep students on-task?

10. Kounin's classroom management concepts seem to have great promise. How can you use these concepts?

For Further Reading

Charles, C. M. *Building Classroom Discipline.* New York: Longman, 1981.
> A practical, easy-to-use book that examines several different models and approaches to classroom management.

Cooper, James M., ed. *Classroom Teaching Skills.* 2nd ed. Lexington, Mass.: D.C. Heath, 1981.
> A self-instructional book designed to help teachers acquire basic teaching skills such as writing objectives, evaluation skills, classroom management skills, questioning skills, and inter-personal communication skills.

Ginott, Haim. *Teacher and Child.* New York: Macmillan, 1972.
> An application of Dr. Ginott's philosophy concerning children as applied to teachers and their relationships with children.

Good, Thomas L., and Jere E. Brophy. *Looking in Classrooms.* 2nd ed. New York: Harper & Row, 1978.
> An excellent book that provides teachers with concrete skills that enable them to observe and interpret classroom behavior of both teacher and student.

Joyce, Bruce, and Marsha Weill. *Models of Teaching,* 2nd ed. Englewood Cliffs, N.J.: Prentice-Hall, 1980.
> A useful book for both teachers and teacher educators. It describes numerous teaching models that are based on different assumptions about teaching and learning.

Smith, B. O., et al. *Teachers for the Real World.* Washington, D.C.: American Association of Colleges for Teacher Education, 1969.
> Focuses on the knowledge, skills, and attitudes teachers need.

Is Teaching a Profession?

11

This chapter focuses on the teacher as a professional, or member of an occupational group. We attempt to show how this rather abstract concept, *professionalism,* affects the daily life of the classroom teacher. In effect, we put the role of the individual teacher in the larger context of the profession.

This chapter emphasizes that:

- A teacher can become involved in different types of situations and conflicts in which he or she will need counsel or support.

- Teachers have become more powerful in recent years, but they don't have the same kinds of power that members of other professions have.

- The question of whether or not teaching is a profession can be judged by reference to specific criteria. Furthermore, there are cases both for and against teaching as being a profession.

- The current educational demands require the teacher to be a continuous learner. There are various ways for teachers to continue their professional growth.

- The National Education Association and the American Federation of Teachers, the most influential teacher organizations, have quite different origins and are competing for the support of classroom teachers.

- The teaching profession is still defining itself and much depends on its capacity to maintain the public's trust.

*T*HE ESSENCE OF A CAREER in teaching is work and involvement with the young. When people think about becoming a teacher, their thoughts and daydreams usually revolve around working with students. Rarely do they bother with hypothetical issues beyond the scope of the classroom. This is both natural and appropriate, since the teacher's success or failure depends on his or her effectiveness with children. Nevertheless, there is more to being a teacher than this. Teachers work within a system that exposes them to pressures from many quarters. Prospective teachers are frequently somewhat naïve about the pressures and forces that will impinge on them, and naïveté can be dangerous, in terms both of making a career decision and of making a successful career.

To help you see this point, we would like you to indulge in a set of daydreams for a few moments. We will offer you a series of brief scenarios and, after reading each one, you should reflect on how you might react. As you read each one, imagine yourself teaching in that ideal classroom you carry around in your head. Assume that all indications are that you are doing a fine job. You are really enjoying it. Your students are making nice progress. They seem to be interested in their work. A few parents have indicated that although they were initially worried that their precious child was to have a new (read "untested") teacher, they are thrilled with the child's progress in your class. Okay. Things are going very well, and . . .

1. Two mothers ask for a conference with you. You haven't met them, and you know only that they are parents of two girls who act very quiet and cliquish in class. At the conference, the mothers come right to the point. They claim you favor the boys in your class and systematically ignore the girls—not just their girls, but all the girls. They say you teach only to the boys. The mothers become quite emotional and suggest that since you are a young unmarried woman you are working out your preoccupation with boys on the class. [If you are a male, reverse the situation. The mothers are parents of boys and are accusing you of excessive interest in little girls. Fiend!!] They say they have talked to some of the other mothers of girls in the class and claim that these mothers agree. They came to warn you that they "intend to take action!" On that note, they raise eyebrows, pick up purses, and huff out.

2. Four days in a row representatives of the Yearbook Committee burst into your classroom unannounced and literally take over. They claim they are signing up subscribers for the yearbook, but they take a good ten minutes each time, most of which is devoted to wisecracking, showing off, and subtly putting you down in various ways. Their attitude is something on the order of, "Look, teach. You're new in this school and you've got a lot to learn. We've been here four years and we know our way around. Don't try to pull rank on us." When they finally leave, it takes a long time to get your students back in a mood to do some serious work. You complain to the principal (who happens to be a former yearbook adviser), who says,

"Yearbook is one of the biggest things in this school. It is a student-run activity in which everyone takes great pride. Last year the yearbook won honorable mention in the South-Southwestern Regional Yearbook Conference for high schools with over 2,000 and under 2,500 students with a lower-middle-class socioeconomic population. All of us who were here last year were very proud of the kids and what they did for the school. I know once you're here with us a little longer, you'll get into the swing of things. I'll send you a few copies of past yearbooks. I know you're going to help this year's yearbook staff in every way you can. They're really great, live-wire kids and come from some of our best families." You ask around and find out that you should expect visits from the yearbook staff three or four times a week for the next two months. They have pictures to take, workers to enlist, advertisements to sell . . . and new teachers to break in.

3. You get a special-delivery letter from a group called PAP (Patriotic American Parents). You have heard that they are very active in your area and are especially interested in schools. Their letter informs you that their lawyer is preparing a case against you for using books that are on their disapproved list. (You didn't know there was such a list but, sure enough, there is, and you have.) They claim they have evidence that you are waging a subtle but nevertheless vicious war against the cause of justice and liberty and have succeeded in temporarily deflecting the minds of some of your students from the truth. Furthermore, they want to know why you display the U.N. flag. Finally, you are said to recite the Pledge of Allegiance in a much too hasty fashion, which is clearly a sign of your disrespect for country. This is the first you have heard of these charges or even of the Patriots' interest in you. You think of yourself as patriotic and are shocked by the letter. They have requested that you respond in writing by next week or they will begin legal proceedings.

4. In late January, the superintendent—who holds a conference with each new teacher—told you she thought you were doing a fine job and that she wanted you to return next year. In passing, she remarked that she would be getting a contract to you in the spring. Toward the end of April, you got a little nervous and called her. You spoke to her executive secretary, who said not to worry, that you were on the list, and that a contract would be coming before long. You stopped worrying. Today is the last day of school, and you find a very nice personal note from the principal in your school mailbox. He thanks you for your fine work during the year and says he is sorry you will not be back next year. You call the superintendent's office. She is in conference, and her executive secretary says that they are not renewing your contract. She cannot remember speaking to you in April. She knows nothing about the case. She does know, however, that the board of education has put on a lot of pressure for cuts in next year's personnel budget. She ends by telling you, "You must be very disappointed, dear. I know how you feel."

5. You noticed something peculiar when you sat down at the faculty dining table one lunch hour. Conversations stopped, and you had the distinct impression your colleagues had been talking about you. A few days later, an older teacher stopped you in the hall after school and said, "I don't want to butt in, but you really are upsetting Mrs. Hilary and Mrs. Alexandra." Mrs. H. and Mrs. A. have the classrooms on either side of yours. Apparently, they claim your class makes so much noise that they can't get anything done. Both are very traditional in their approach to education. You believe in a more activity-oriented approach. Although your class is rather noisy occasionally, it is never chaotic, and its noise is usually a by-product of the students' involvement in the task. Twice Mrs. Alexandra has sent messengers with notes asking that your class be more quiet. You have always complied. You hardly know either teacher. You have never really talked to Mrs. Alexandra except to say hello. Mrs. Hilary, with whom you've chatted, prides herself on being a disciplinarian. What she means, you have inferred, is that she is able to keep the children quiet. You know Mrs. Alexandra is chummy with Mrs. Hilary. You go to the vice principal, who seems to know all about the case, but only from the Hilary-Alexandra angle. Inexplicably, the vice principal gets quite angry and claims that until you came along the faculty got along beautifully. Furthermore, you are being very unprofessional in making complaints against experienced teachers. You feel as if you are trapped in a Kurt Vonnegut novel.

6. You had been teaching industrial arts for two months when you met another new teacher at a faculty meeting. A few weeks later you both were assigned to chaperone a dance. Then you began going out on "real dates." By Christmas you knew you were over the edge. On New Year's Eve you became engaged. On Valentine's Day you both announced the news to your students (none of whom were surprised) and to your faculty colleagues (who didn't have a clue). You have both been doing well and want to stay on at your jobs next year. On April Fools' Day, you get a notice from the personnel director calling your attention to the board ruling against hiring couples. You know that there are no openings in any nearby schools. You plan to get married on the first Saturday in June after school ends.

Keep in mind that these little horror stories are not everyday occurrences. Also, it is important for you to know that entrance into any profession has its trials. These accounts were written to help you with the realization that you can be an effective teacher and still have trouble keeping your job. What is the common theme running through each of these anecdotes? You, the teacher, were succeeding in your work with children, but forces outside the classroom began to impinge on you. A parents' vigilante group accused you of prejudice: the Patriots wanted to make a target case of you. When the yearbook wiseacres started playing havoc with your class, the principal failed to back you up. On two occasions the school system bureaucracy was ready to put you on the unemployed rolls. Two of your colleagues damaged your reputation with the faculty and administration. Other than that, it's been a super year.

Although you may feel confident that you could handle some of these situations, it is doubtful that you could cope with all of them. In some cases you would be powerless to respond effectively to your adversaries, and you might end up a helpless victim of circumstances. Fortunately, a teacher is not alone. Like people in many other occupational groups, teachers have organizations that protect them from such indignities and injustices. These organizations function on several levels, from the local to the national, and their very existence can keep situations like those described from occurring, except in rare instances. But when they do occur, these organizations are committed to supporting the teacher.

In becoming a teacher, you are not just committing yourself to work with children. You are joining an occupational group composed of other individuals with similar responsibilities, concerns, and pressures, whose help you need and who in turn will need your help.

THE TEACHER AND POWER

As a society we are becoming increasingly aware of how our lives are affected by big institutions and power blocs. Policies and products of the giant corporations daily affect events and details of our lives. We are becoming increasingly aware of the power of labor unions to affect the nation's economic health. Further, we have a new appreciation for how the power of the American Medical Association affects the quality and nature of health service in our country. These groupings of men and women have power. They can affect the lives of those around them. People who have power can use it for good or for evil. Anyone who wants to effect major change in an institution must first have power.

For years, teachers wielded little influence in our society, except that which they wielded in their own classrooms. Until the 1960s teachers were considered a quiet and docile occupation group.

Beginning around 1960, teachers became better organized and more vocal. Whether the general public has liked it or not, teachers have gained power. Teachers seem to have extremes of power. On the one hand, through their professional organizations they have a great deal of political power in federal, state, and local elections. Politicians court the teachers' votes and listen to their views. Also, teachers can strike (or, as they euphemistically say, "withhold their professional services"). According to the 1980 Census, among couples with one or more children under eighteen, 60 percent of the wives did some kind of paid work away from the home. Therefore, when teachers strike not only do schools close, but many parents are forced to stay home from work to take care of their children. Being able to stop a school in its tracks means having power.

At the other extreme, teachers have immense power in their own classrooms. Although they are usually assigned a particular curriculum, they decide just how it will be taught. The teacher decides which child will be given special attention, which child will be rewarded, and which child will not be rewarded. As everyone who's ever been a student knows, the teacher has immense influence on the daily lives of students.

Nevertheless, teachers don't seem to have much power in the middle of those extremes. They have very little say over the conditions of their daily employment. They don't make decisions about what subjects are taught, which teachers are hired or fired, who the principal and other administrators are, what the school's grading policy is, how long the school day is, and so on and so on. If a new school is to be built, the teachers who will work in the new building are rarely, if ever, consulted about the kind of environment they would consider most suitable and conducive to learning. When a new principal is chosen, the teachers are not asked to participate in the decision making. Rarely are they even asked what they think the new principal's qualifications should be. As one Arkansas teacher stated, "I've been teaching in this same school and living in this same community for twenty-six years. I've had all sorts of commendations and good teaching awards. But in twenty-six years not once has anyone on the school board or any of the administrators asked my advice on an educational matter. I haven't been asked about one darned thing."

Discouraging as this picture may seem to some of you, not all teachers are dissatisfied with the existing state of affairs. Some are quite content to simply teach and leave all the squabbling to those they call "the activists." They think that teachers have come a long way in recent years and that they should be satisfied with what they have gained. They would agree with the statement "Education is too important to be left in the hands of the educators." The more activist teachers, however, feel that this attitude is itself the problem, and that this kind of passivity has kept teachers oppressed and the quality of their service low. They assert that teaching will not truly become a profession until their colleagues take a more vigorous, independent position. And this leads us directly to the question "Is teaching a profession?"

WHAT IS A PROFESSION?

A profession is more than a group of individuals all engaged in the same line of work. Professions have a more-or-less recognizable set of characteristics that distinguish them from nonprofessions.[1] As you read the list of

[1]We have drawn heavily on two excellent books: Myron Lieberman, *Education as a Profession* (Englewood Cliffs, N.J.: Prentice-Hall, 1956), and Robert B. Howsam et al., *Educating a Profession*, Report of the Bicentennial Commission of Education for the Profession of Teaching (Washington, D.C.: American Association of Colleges for Teacher Education, 1976).

Yes ☐   No ☐

Yes ☐   No ☐

Yes ☐   No ☐

Yes ☐   No ☐

Yes ☐   No ☐

Yes ☐   No ☐

Yes ☐   No ☐

Yes ☐   No ☐

characteristics of a profession, check whether or not you think teaching qualifies on each premise.

First, a profession renders a unique, definite, and essential social service. Only the people in the particular profession render the service. For instance, only lawyers practice law. The service rendered must be considered so important that it is available to all the people in a society.

Second, a profession relies on intellectual skills in the performance of its service. This does not mean that physical actions and skills are not needed, but rather that the emphasis in carrying on the work is on intellectual skills and techniques.

Third, a profession has a long period of specialized training. Because professional work requires special intellectual skills, specialized intellectual training is needed. General education, such as that represented by a bachelor's degree, is valued, but not considered adequate. The specialized training must cover a substantial period and not be obtained in cram courses or correspondence schools.

Fourth, both individual members of the profession and the professional group enjoy a considerable degree of autonomy and decision-making authority. Professional groups regulate their own activities rather than having outsiders set policies and enforce adherence to standards. Whereas factory workers have very limited decision-making power and are closely supervised in the performance of their work, professionals are expected to make most of their own decisions and be free of close supervision by supervisors.

Fifth, a profession requires its members to accept personal responsibility for their actions and decisions. Along with having a high degree of freedom and autonomy, the professional must shoulder a large measure of responsibility for his or her performance. Since the professional's service is usually related to the human welfare of individuals, this responsibility is an especially serious one.

Sixth, a profession emphasizes the services rendered by its practitioners more than their financial rewards. Although the personal motives of any individual professional are not necessarily any higher than any other worker's, the professional group's public emphasis is on service.

Seventh, a profession is self-governing and responsible for policing its own ranks. This means there are professional groups who perform a number of activities aimed at keeping the quality of their services high and looking out for the social and economic well-being of the professional members. Also, these self-governing organizations set standards of admission and exclusion to the profession.

Eighth, a profession has a code of ethics that sets out the acceptable standards of conduct of its members. For a professional group to regulate the quality and standards of service, it needs a code of ethics to aid it in enforcing these high standards.

These, then, are the major requirements of a profession. Few professions satisfy all of them fully. However, the list does serve as a benchmark by which occupational groups can measure themselves and direct their development if they wish to enjoy professional status.

The question "Is teaching a profession?" probably arouses little interest in many of you. Most people thinking about a career in teaching are more interested in whether it will be a personally rewarding way to spend their time than in whether or not it is a profession. Will teaching bring me personal satisfactions? Will it provide an outlet for my talents and energies? Will I be effective with kids? These questions are, we suspect, closer to your skin. Nevertheless, the professionalism of the teacher and the related issues are important to teachers and have an effect on the *quality of education*. They will also affect the quality of your life as a teacher.

TWO SIDES OF THE ISSUE

The Case FOR Teaching as a Profession

The very nobility of the teacher's work is evidence in favor of its status as a profession. Society has entrusted teachers with its most important responsibility—the education of the young. Although teachers have never received the respect that is their due, through the course of history great minds have acknowledged their worth. Martin Luther asserted that the teacher's vocation was second only to that of the ministry. Thomas Carlyle in *Sartor Resartus* calls teachers "fashioners of souls," who ought to be "world-honored dignitaries" like generals and field marshals. As more and more people recognize how crucial education is to the fulfillment of our personal and national goals, the opportunities and rewards for the teacher will improve, as they have improved rather steadily throughout the last three centuries in this country, and particularly in the last fifty years.

Although children learn from many people—from parents to television personalities—teachers are the specialists who pass on to the young the key skills necessary to participate effectively in the culture. They aid the young in acquiring the most difficult, if not the most important, skills: those that involve thinking and manipulating ideas. Neither reading nor geometry is often learned on the street. Although teachers do not undergo a particularly lengthy period of specialized training, they are in a sense continually training. Teachers are expected (and, in some states, required by law) to upgrade their teaching skills continually.

The autonomy of the teacher, like that of every professional, is somewhat limited. Unlike lawyers and doctors, who can reject clients, teachers' students are assigned to them. They also have a supervisor, their principal or department head. They teach a curriculum that has been chosen or developed largely by others. However, within these limits, teachers have an immense area of personal control. They normally determine the method of instruction. They decide which aspects of the curriculum they will highlight and which they will cover quickly. The limits on their creativity are

few or nonexistent. After the initial few years of teaching, they are seldom observed and evaluated. Teachers' classrooms are their castles. And if teachers feel that they do not have enough autonomy or do not agree with their administrators, they are free to move to another school. However, a teacher's autonomy is accompanied by a responsibility to teach effectively. Like any professionals, teachers must be able to justify the manner in which they render their social services. They must be able to justify their grading policy and evaluations of student work. Teachers are expected to claim responsibility for their actions and to be open to criticisms of their teaching performance.

Teachers are represented by organizations, such as the National Education Association and the American Federation of Teachers, whose major function is improving education by improving the teaching profession. They provide information and aid to classroom teachers; they support them against unjust pressures from members of the public or the school board; they set standards and censor teachers who violate these standards; they provide ancillary economic services, such as travel programs, group insurance policies, investment programs, and professional book clubs; and, finally, they attempt to influence the laws and regulations that govern schooling and the teaching profession.

Some argue that teaching is not a profession because teachers lack the autonomy of, say, a small-town lawyer, or because they have not achieved the economic status of dentists and doctors. These arguments are superficial. So, too, is the assertion that teaching is not a profession because many teachers do not act like professionals. Neither do many ministers, architects, or lawyers. Certainly the crucial nature of the teacher's work and the selfless spirit of service of the best teachers raises teaching to the level of a profession.

The Case AGAINST Teaching as a Profession

The roots of the teaching "profession" go back to ancient Greece, where slaves called *paidagogos,* or pedagogues, taught children to read and write and helped them memorize passages of poetic history. Recently teachers, along with such other occupational groups as barbers, beauticians, taxidermists, athletes and—according to a recent commercial—even dishwashers, have latched on to the term *professional* in an attempt to raise their salaries and their status. But a careful look at current practices reveals that teaching does not qualify as a profession. If education is a teacher's unique

Ten forty-three.
In exactly TWO MINUTES
I'll ring the
FIRST BELL and
they'll all
stand still!

All, that is, except
your potential DEVIATE!
Your fledgling REBEL!
Your incipient BOAT-
ROCKER! THEY'LL try
to move alright!
THEY'LL have to
learn the HARD
way not to move!

So I'll SCREAM at 'em
and take their NAMES
and give them FIVE
DETENTIONS and EXTRA
HOMEWORK! NEXT time
they won't move
after the first
bell!

Cartoon by Barry Base.

function, the teacher has a great deal of competition. Ignoring for a moment the mounting criticism of compulsory miseducation (such as forcing children to attend school even when education is inferior), let us admit that teachers have no monopoly on education. Children today learn a tremendous amount from the media: "Sesame Street," public affairs specials, *Time*, Dan Rather, films, novels, Steve Martin, *Seventeen,* and *Popular Mechanics*. Then there are the nonteacher educators: parents, ministers, older friends, neighbors, employers, best friends, coaches, scout leaders, playground and camp counselors, grandparents. The world is bursting with teachers, and those who hold forth in school buildings have only a small piece of the action.

Although teaching has intellectual and theoretical foundations and requires a rather short period of specialized training (considerably less than some of the skilled trades), entrance into the profession is not particularly competitive, particularly on intellectual grounds. If it is a profession, it is one composed of a large percentage of college graduates of only average intellectual ability.

Although there is a good deal of talk about teachers' autonomy and decision-making power, both exist at a very low level. Teachers are the second rung from the bottom (superior only to students) of the hierarchy commanded by the board of education. They teach whom they are told, what they are told, and when they are told. If their supervisors do not like the results, teachers are only rarely protected by their professional group

Because when they've learned not to question the FIRST BELL, they'll learn not to question their TEXTS! Their TEACHERS! Their COURSES! EXAMINATIONS!

They'll grow up to accept TAXES! HOUSING DEVELOPMENTS! INSURANCE! WAR! MEN ON THE MOON! LIQUOR LAWS! POLITICAL SPEECHES! PARKING METERS! TELEVISION! FUNERALS!

Non-movement after the first bell is the backbone of Western Civilization!

from being fired (or, more gently, "not rehired") by the board of education. Most of the important decisions that affect teachers' daily lives, even those that bear directly on the standards of their own profession, are made by nonteachers. Teachers do not formally evaluate other teachers. Administrators do that. Teachers, typically, do not have much to do with and very little say in the preservice training of teachers.

In only a few states do teachers have a say in the licensing and certification of teachers. Laypeople and bureaucrats do that. Some teachers, like factory workers, even have to punch a timeclock (more genteelly, they "sign in and sign out" . . . to the same effect). In sum, they have very little to say about what goes on in their "shop."

The same is true of the teacher's responsibility. Teachers rarely lose their jobs because Johnnie can't read or Samantha failed calculus. After a teacher achieves tenure, it takes some form of gross negligence, clear incompetency or serious sexual offense for him or her to be fired. As for the professional organizations policing their own ranks, there is much rhetoric but next to no action. The professional organizations for teachers are just like other self-serving organizations, whether composed of teamsters or dentists; their primary energies go to their own survival and growth. Secondarily, they attempt to protect their members, increase their salaries, and expand their welfare benefits. Most teachers, however, are minimally involved and interested in professional organizations and their activities, except when they call a strike—an odd activity for a "profession." Most teachers claim they are too busy to take an active role in professional affairs. This lack of real involvement in professional activities might stem from the fact that so many teachers have second jobs, either as homemakers or in the labor market. They are unenthusiastic about working for higher standards because one of the first sacrifices to professionalism would be their second jobs. In actual fact, teachers work in circumstances very different from those of other professionals. They are hired, like other public servants, rather than operating as independent agents. They are on a fixed salary schedule and protected by tenure laws, rather than independently having to find a market for their services. Teaching is a low-pay, relatively high-security job, rather than a high-pay, low-security profession. Seniority as a teacher may be more important than competence. Talk about professionalism may be personally satisfying to teachers, but it does not conform to the reality of the teacher's occupational life.

A Third Possibility

Like most important questions, "Is teaching a profession?" cannot be answered satisfactorily with simple pro-and-con arguments such as those just offered. Also, teachers differ so much in the conditions under which they work, and possess such varying degrees of knowledge, commitment, and expertise that it is difficult to come up with a definitive answer. In some schools, teachers fulfill many of the criteria of professionals. In other schools, they seem to function as clerks and technicians. Our view, however, is that teaching for most is a semiprofession. In certain ways teaching is clearly eligible for professional status, and in certain others it deviates sharply from accepted canons of professionalism. On the one hand, teachers provide an intellectual service to the community. They undergo specialized training to master the theoretical basis of their work. Ethical standards guide their work with students. On the other hand, they function too often like many other lower-level white-collar workers and civil servants. Too often seniority and security are the rule, rather than excellence and independence. Like many other occupational groups that are called professional, teachers, at this moment in history, only partially qualify.

Another way to look at the issue, and one we favor, is to think of teaching as being in the process of becoming a profession. As shown by the historical descriptions of the work and living conditions of teachers discussed in Chapter 4, the life and the status of teachers has changed dramatically.

Whether teaching becomes a profession in your career lifetime will depend on some of the following factors. First, teachers must take on a larger role in the governing of their career affairs. Whereas the direction of education and the schools should be in the hands of many groups (parents, community leaders, students, and teachers), control over the teaching profession per se should be in the hands of teachers. Up to now, the great majority of teachers has taken the attitude of "Let George do it." As a result, outsiders make the major decisions about who should teach, how teachers should be trained, and under what conditions they should render their services. Although teachers are eating better these days, they still lack self-determination.

Second, teachers must demand better training. As long as the public feels that any college graduate with a smattering of education courses can walk in off the street and do a teacher's job, people will not treat teachers as professionals. We do not for a moment mean to imply that teachers should adopt artificial trappings, like a doctor's smock or a general's uniform, to seem more distinctive and impressive. Rather, teachers must appear better because they are better. Like architects and surgeons, teachers must know their work, and it must be imbued with a sense of high purpose. Also, they must know a great deal about what they are teaching and how it can be taught most effectively. When that happens, the public will decide whether or not teachers should be treated as professionals.

Third, we may simply have to recognize that all of the two-and-a-half million people working in the American schools are not interested in and, in some cases, not capable of measuring up to the standards of professionalism. At present, what we are calling (and, incidentally, will continue to call) the *teaching profession* is a mixed bag, with a great many transients "just passing through," a great many rather uncommitted teachers, and a great many truly excellent, dedicated career teachers.

More than twenty years ago, Walter Beggs captured what we believe to be the essence of the professional teacher:

> Let us define a career teacher as one who plans to, and actually does, make a life occupation of teaching; one who is philosophically, emotionally, and spiritually committed, that is never satisfied with what he does and how well he's doing it, and who fully intends to keep on growing for the rest of his life.[2]

Beggs goes on to estimate that only about one out of four presently practicing teachers fits his definition. And herein lies the difficulty. Until the great majority of teachers qualifies by Beggs's definition, or until there is a qualitative regrouping of those presently identified as "teachers," teaching will not be called a profession.

PROFESSIONALISM AND CONTINUING EDUCATION

Much of the debate over the status or professional standing of teachers hinges on the competence of teachers: "Are they up to the task?" Public polls over the last decade show that public faith in public education is declining. People are concerned about the performance of school children and seem to be saying that teachers are not getting the results that the public wants and expects. Part of this concern over the performance of the American student is a result of the pressures from abroad; there is worry that American students will not be able to meet either the economic challenges provided by their Japanese counterparts or the military challenges provided by their Russian counterparts.

A related aspect of this concern for the level of teacher competence has to do with social change. At one time it was considered adequate for a teacher to have obtained an undergraduate education and a teaching license and then to have no further training; however, forces both inside and outside the teaching profession now have adopted the stance that the teacher must be a continuous learner. Many states have legislated continuing education for teachers. In fact, in more than one-half of the states, "the days of permanent certification are over."[3]

Central to this drive for continuing education of teachers is the existence of new knowledge and the demand for new skills. A dramatic example of this is the rise in interest in computer literacy. As the American society has become increasingly dependent on mechanized information

[2]Quoted at 1963–1964 convention of the National Commission on Teacher Education and Professional Standards (NEA), in Myron Brenton, *What's Happened to Teacher?* (New York: Coward-McCann, 1970), p. 242.
[3]Marge Scherer, "Who's Afraid of Teacher Competency Tests?," *Instructor* (February 1983): 48.

Types of Continuous Learning Opportunities

services, the needs and advantages of being comfortable and competent with computers have become clearer. Therefore, elementary and secondary schools and colleges are rushing to provide students with this new competency. In 1983 there are a number of colleges that all but require computer literacy for admission. For example, beginning in September 1983, Clarkson College required each incoming student to pay an extra fee for the use of a personal computer.[4] For these college students the personal computer has become as important as the pen and the library card. Movements such as the computer revolution require teachers, if they are to prepare students for the demands of the world, to think of themselves as—and in fact be—continuous learners.

One of the aims of education, according to school constitutions and college catalogues, is to develop the ability to engage in independent study. *Independent study* is jargon for being able to go it alone. Although this approach is much discussed by educators, students seem to get little actual practice in choosing their own areas of interest and systematically investigating them. Independent study, though, is one of the most important means available to the teacher for continual self-renewal. Teachers are confronted daily with things they do not understand about children and knowledge and their interaction. "What are children really doing when they yell out answers to homework problems?" "What are the fundamental skills of composition that children should know?" "How can I help my students use history for their own benefit?" Such questions are daily grist for the teacher's independent study mill. Of course, the teacher's study should not be confined to professional problems. His or her own interests may lead into such areas as organic gardening, physical fitness, old movies, politics in colonial America, or the humanizing of the corporate state. Not by professional problems alone doth the teacher live!

Group study is another common mode of continuing learning for the teacher. It frequently takes the form of committee work. Problems arise in the school for which there are no apparent solutions, so a group of people take on themselves the task of exploring the problem with a view toward recommending an enlightened course of action. In recent years, teachers and administrators have begun inviting community residents to these study groups in order to obtain opinions from outside the school. Typical issues these study groups might take on are, "Alternatives to the present second-grade reading program," "An analysis of the unused educational resources in a particular community," and "The potential benefits and cost of using paraprofessionals in our high schools."

A third way to continue to learn is to take courses or work toward an *advanced degree*. Most colleges and universities offer courses suitable and

---

[4]*The New York Times*, April 5, 1983, p. C1.

interesting to teachers. Special and regular courses are offered in the evening and during the summer vacation. These courses and degree programs not only allow teachers to gain a deeper understanding of their work but also make it possible for some teachers to train for other jobs in education, such as guidance counseling, administration, or college teaching.

A fourth means of continuous growth and learning is the *inservice program* sponsored by the school or school district. These inservice programs are often targeted at school- or district-wide problems or issues. For instance, if students in a particular school are getting unsatisfactory grades on standardized achievement tests, the district may choose to provide special inservice training for the faculty, or it might decide to switch to a new, supposedly better mathematics program. Such a change would require special training for the faculty and would thus become the focus of the inservice program. Inservice training often takes place weekly or monthly, before or after school. Also, special days are sometimes set aside on which school is cancelled or the students are dismissed early so the teachers can participate in inservice training.

A fifth method of continuous training comes through *supervision*. During a teacher's early years in the profession, school districts provide her or him with professional advice in what amounts to one-to-one help. For instance, if you are a new industrial arts teacher, your department head will observe your classes regularly and discuss the observations with you. Or, if you are an elementary school teacher, your building principal may make regular visits and follow them with feedback sessions. Although supervision can sometimes be quite threatening, particularly to nontenured teachers, it offers an opportunity to obtain valuable information about your teaching techniques and skills. And it is worthwhile for a teacher to try to change it from a threatening situation to a learning situation.

Table 11.1 gives some additional types of continuing education activities and suggests just how widespread this movement towards professional education is. Although the table indicates a drop in the percentages of teachers involving themselves in a number of categories of advanced training over the ten-year period, this change may very well be explained by other factors. For instance, the number of new teachers declined sharply between 1971 and 1981. Fewer new teachers meant that fewer teachers would be returning to universities for master's degree programs and course work for specialized certification areas.

Continuing Education: A Final Word

Great athletes and great musicians do not become great by accident. Nor do they simply turn themselves over to a coach or mentor and soon reach excellence. Individual athletes and musicians work hard for their achievements. They consciously set out to discipline their minds and bodies and to master the needed skills and knowledge. Once they reach a level of mastery, they continuously work to maintain their skills and acquire new

Table 11.1 Percentages of All Teachers Participating in Professional Growth Activities, 1971–81

Activities	1971	1976	1981
Workshops sponsored by school system during school year	58.6	68.3	67.4
Workshops sponsored by school system during summer	20.5	21.9	13.4
College courses in education during school year	40.1	45.4	21.3
College courses in education during summer	30.4	33.8	13.3
College courses in fields other than education during school year	26.1	25.9	12.7
College courses in fields other than education during summer	21.5	16.2	5.7
University extension courses	32.6	33.8	18.7
Association-sponsored activities	24.5	23.3	27.1
Curriculum committee	40.8	44.7	34.2
Committee other than curriculum	35.3	38.6	32.6
Educational TV	11.3	12.2	13.4
Educational travel, not sabbatical	26.4	23.0	14.7
Sabbatical leave–travel	3.8	7.2	2.4
Sabbatical leave—full-time college	2.4	3.7	0.6

Source: "The Status of the American Public School Teacher, 1980–81" (conducted by the National Education Association). Used with permission.

ones. To achieve and maintain a degree of excellence, the individual *must* take an active role; in this respect, what is true for tennis and the piano is true for teaching.

Becoming a teacher may be compared to sculpting a work of art from a piece of stone. The difference is that the teacher is both the sculptor and the stone. The teacher begins with a vision of what he or she wants to be and then sets to work transforming the vision into a reality. The process requires an understanding of the material with which one is working—the self—and of the tools one can use. It also requires a vision of what one needs to become. Finally, it takes long hours of chipping away at and smoothing surfaces. To be a teacher, particularly a teacher who is continuously moving forward, is a lifelong commitment.

THE PROFESSIONAL ASSOCIATIONS

The protection of teachers' rights and the improvement of their working conditions and rewards will not just happen. In the words of Ernie Lundquist, the distinguished educational theorist and taxidermist, "Nobody gives you nothin' for nothin'."[5] Whatever advances teachers make will occur largely as a result of their hard work and readiness to stand up for what they believe.

Teacher salaries (which are the major cost of schooling) and other educational expenses come out of the taxpayers' pockets. Tax revenues are used for many purposes and are heavily competed for by groups attempting to fight crime and delinquency, increase aid to the elderly and the poor, and increase our military preparedness. In the rough-and-tumble of a democracy, teachers need someone or something to look out for their interests and the interests of the recipients of their services—children. This is the function of the teachers' associations. At present, there are two national organizations, the National Education Association (NEA) and the American Federation of Teachers (AFT), that claim to speak for teachers. They represent teachers to the federal, state, and local governments, to educational authorities at the state and local level, and, finally, to the general public. It is important to know something about them, because if you become a teacher, they will claim to be speaking for you.

Before discussing the two major organizations, we should point out that there are many different teacher organizations operating at a multiplicity of levels. Normally, each school district has professional associations that are linked to county, regional, and state organizations. Of perhaps greater importance to the beginning teacher are organizations of teachers in particular specialties at these different levels. There are active organizations for teachers of reading, English, mathematics, home economics, and all the established curricular areas. They play an important part in keeping the teacher informed about developments in their fields through journals, inservice training institutes, and conferences and conventions. Because there are so many of these organizations and their activities are so varied, we will restrict our attention to the large umbrella organizations—the National Education Association and the American Federation of Teachers.

The National Education Association

The National Education Association is a complex institution that is difficult to describe briefly. It operates on the national, state, and local school district levels and serves a very diverse clientele. Despite that diversity, the NEA

---

[5]Ernie Lundquist's contributions to society are too numerous to list and are assuredly well known to the reader. Nevertheless, we would be remiss if we did not mention the famed Lundquist theory of child development ("All work and no play makes Pierre a dull boy") and the Lundquist Metaphysic ("Everything is related to everything else, except for pepperoni and the designated hitter rule, neither of which are related to anything and both of which are offenses against God and man"). Finally, there is the famed Lundquist Dictum to teachers ("Sticks and stones will break their bones, but names will lead to libel suits and the loss of big bucks").

has grown to 1.7 million members in 1983 accounting for three out of four of the elementary and secondary public school teachers in the United States. To serve the special needs of members within the association, there are many program-related standing committees (such as Human Relations, Teacher Benefits, Teacher Rights, and Instructional and Professional Development) and several special committees (Minority Affairs, Teacher Retirement, Resolutions Study, and National Public Relations). In 1982–1983, the NEA had an operating budget of nearly $83 million and served 12,000 local-level affiliate organizations.

To serve the needs of its members, the NEA has three types of support services: communication, research, and Uniserv. A number of publications and other communication media are used to disseminate information about NEA's policies and programs internally to the profession and externally to the public. Furthermore, the communications provide support for NEA governance, administration, program units, and affiliates.

NEA research is designed to provide information necessary to the achievement of NEA goals and objectives. Research and information services compile data in areas such as negotiations, salaries, school finance, teacher retirement systems, and surveys.

The Uniserv program is a cooperative effort by which local, state, and national associations provide professional staff at the local level to improve the service programs at all levels of the association. Uniserv is designed to coordinate rather than duplicate the service programs at the local, state, and national levels and to create equitable distribution of association services regardless of geography or density of membership. Since the first year of its existence, 1970, the Uniserv program has expanded dramatically; it now requires one-fifth of the NEA budget.

In addition to the three types of support services, a number of special services are available to members, such as travel programs, insurance policies, mutual fund programs, and book club programs. Also, the NEA aids teachers (like those in the vignettes which began this chapter), teachers whose legal rights are being violated or who are being treated unethically.

The goals of the NEA, as declared in its charter, are "to elevate the character and advance the interests of the profession of teaching and to promote the cause of education in the United States." In the 1950s and 1960s the NEA was influential in improving the preservice training of teachers and raising the entrance qualifications for teaching, largely through the activities of the now-defunct National Commission on Teacher Education and Professional Standards. More recently, however, the great bulk of NEA's energies and monies are expended on service for its membership, practicing teachers.

Beginning in the 1970s, the association became much more politically oriented. For example, in 1976 the NEA for the first time endorsed and vocally supported a presidential candidate, Jimmy Carter. Carter's campaign manager said at the time, "the massive support from teachers was critical to our winning this very close election. All over the nation we turned to the NEA for assistance. We asked for help and they delivered." In the same election year, the NEA endorsed and assisted 272 successful candidates for election in the House of Representatives, a majority of the house. Teachers had flexed their muscles and politicians all over the country took notice. The grateful president showed his appreciation by bringing into realization a long time NEA dream: the establishment of a cabinet-level Department of Education.

NEA CODE OF ETHICS

Preamble

The educator, believing in the worth and dignity of each human being, recognizes the supreme importance of the pursuit of truth, devotion to excellence, and the nurture of democratic principles. Essential to these goals is the protection of freedom to learn and to teach and the guarantee of equal educational opportunity for all. The educator accepts the responsibility to adhere to the highest ethical standards.

The educator recognizes the magnitude of the responsibility inherent in the teaching process. The desire for the respect and confidence of one's colleagues, of students, of parents, and of the members of the community provides the incentive to attain and maintain the highest possible degree of ethical conduct. The Code of Ethics of the Education Profes-

sion indicates the aspiration of all educators and provides standards by which to judge conduct.

The remedies specified by the NEA and/or its affiliates for the violation of any provision of this Code shall be exclusive and no such provision shall be enforceable in any form other than one specifically designated by the NEA or its affiliates.

Principle I—Commitment to the Student

The educator strives to help each student realize his or her potential as a worthy and effective member of society. The educator therefore works to stimulate the spirit of inquiry, the acquisition of knowledge and understanding, and the thoughtful formulation of worthy goals.

In fulfillment of the obligation to the student, the educator—

1. Shall not unreasonably restrain the student from independent action in the pursuit of learning.

2. Shall not unreasonably deny the student access to varying points of view.

3. Shall not deliberately suppress or distort subject matter relevant to the student's progress.

4. Shall make reasonable effort to protect the student from conditions harmful to learning or to health and safety.

5. Shall not intentionally expose the student to embarrassment or disparagement.

6. Shall not on the basis of race, color, creed, sex, national origin, marital status, political or religious beliefs, family, social or cultural background, or sexual orientation, unfairly:

a. Exclude any student from participation in any program;

However, the next election told a very different story and dramatically underscored the limitations of the NEA's political strength and strategies. The White House was lost to Ronald Reagan, who campaigned across the nation saying that he would eliminate the Department of Education. And, although NEA congressional candidates won in 209 of 278 house races, the NEA did not fare so well in the Senate campaign. Of the thirty-one Senate candidates the NEA supported, sixteen lost. The new, more politically aggressive strategy of the NEA was put to a second national test, and it clearly failed.

The verdict is still out on the political potency of teachers. On the one

---

b. Deny benefits to any student;

c. Grant any advantage to any student.

7. Shall not use professional relationships with students for private advantage.

8. Shall not disclose information about students obtained in the course of professional service, unless disclosure serves a compelling professional purpose or is required by law.

Principle II—Commitment to the Profession

The education profession is vested by the public with a trust and responsibility requiring the highest ideals of professional service.

In the belief that the quality of the services of the education profession directly influences the nation and its citizens, the educator shall ex-

ert every effort to raise professional standards, to promote a climate that encourages the exercise of professional judgment, to achieve conditions which attract persons worthy of the trust to careers in education, and to assist in preventing the practice of the profession by unqualified persons.

In fulfillment of the obligation to the profession, the educator—

1. Shall not in an application for a professional position deliberately make a false statement or fail to disclose a material fact related to competency and qualifications.

2. Shall not misrepresent his/her professional qualifications.

3. Shall not assist entry into the profession of a person known to be unqualified in respect to character, education, or other relevant attribute.

4. Shall not knowingly make a false statement concerning

the qualifications of a candidate for a professional position.

5. Shall not assist a noneducator in the unauthorized practice of teaching.

6. Shall not disclose information about colleagues obtained in the course of professional service unless disclosure serves a compelling professional purpose or is required by law.

7. Shall not knowingly make false or malicious statements about a colleague.

8. Shall not accept any gratuity, gift, or favor that might impair or appear to influence professional decisions or actions.

National Education Association, *Code of Ethics of the Education Profession,* adopted by the NEA Representative Assembly, 1975. Reprinted by permission of the Association.

hand, one political commentator referred to teachers as, "Bright, articulate, and reasonably well informed making them naturals for political activism."[6] Also, teachers as an occupational group have the best record of registering in voting: well over 70 percent.[7] On the other hand, teachers do not have the huge financial coffers to pour into elections that other political pressure groups, such as labor or a conservative business interest, have. More fundamental, though, is the fact that teachers don't appear to have deep attachments to either the political left or the political right, to either the Democratic Party or the Republican Party. They tend to reflect the political attitudes of their home communities. As a result, the NEA was unable in the close presidential election of 1980 to deliver an overwhelming majority of teachers to the party of its choice. In fact, only 52 percent of the teachers voted for Carter.

Over the years the NEA has had its victories and made its share of mistakes. In the past it was frequently criticized for its slowness to take action on important issues and problems. For example, it avoided taking a stand on the Supreme Court's important school segregation decision in 1954. Recently, however, it has championed the rights of black teachers in some Southern states who have lost their jobs as a result of the consolidation of black and white schools. In fact, in 1977 Louisiana became the last of the NEA's seventeen Southern and border states to merge racially segregated teachers' associations. The development of the Uniserv program in 1970 was a vigorous reaction to criticism from association memberships concerning adequacy of attention to teacher problems.

On the other hand, the political activism of recent years seems to be a mixed success. The NEA leadership may well have lost touch with the bulk of its membership. Stanley Elam has suggested that the leadership miscalculated, thinking that the power base for education was teachers. Elam says, "the power base of education is the public's faith in schooling as the key to success for the younger generation."[8] Many teachers and many of the public have looked upon teacher political activism in recent years as too narrowly self-serving. Shortly after the founding of the NEA, in 1859, one of its great leaders, Horace Mann, said, "Be ashamed to die before you have won some victory for humanity." That statement, for many years a motto of the NEA, reflects an altruistic spirit that many inside and outside the profession find lacking in the current agenda of the NEA.

The fact that the NEA has become more aggressive and has adopted new policies in the last few decades is the result of many factors, not

[6]Steven Chaffman, "The NEA Seizes Power: The Teachers' Coup." *The New Republic,* 11 October 1980, pp. 9–11.

[7]Stanley Elam, "The National Education Association: Political Powerhouse or Paper Tiger," *Phi Delta Kappan* 63, No. 3 (November 1981): 169–174.

[8]Elam, "National Education Association," p. 173.

the least of which is the competition from the American Federation of Teachers.

The American Federation of Teachers

If the NEA can be compared to a large department store, then the American Federation of Teachers, or AFT, more closely resembles a small specialty store that aggressively promotes a few items. In contrast to the NEA, the AFT has traditionally been interested exclusively in representing teachers and other nonsupervisory school personnel.

John Dewey, the great American philosopher and educator, took out the first AFT membership card in 1916 and remained an active member throughout his life. Dewey thought there ought to be an organization exclusively for teachers. As we have indicated, this "teachers-only" emphasis has been a major instrument in the AFT's struggle with the NEA for the allegiance of teachers. The AFT contends that in the NEA's broad efforts to improve education little has been done to improve the lot of the classroom teacher.

> In the structure and successful operation of schools, the teacher is central. Good teachers make good schools. The professional teacher not only knows how to direct the educational and personal development of children in the classroom, he also joins with his colleagues in an effective organization to advance the interest of teachers, pupils, and the schools through collective bargaining.[9]

The AFT has a membership of over 600,000, making it approximately one-third the size of the NEA. Although the AFT has fewer than 2,000 local affiliates throughout the country, in the 1960s and 1970s it built up great strength in major urban centers. The AFT won a major victory in 1960, when its affiliate, the United Federation of Teachers (UFT), became the sole bargaining agent for all New York City teachers. At present, the AFT represents teachers in New York City, Chicago, Philadelphia, Washington, D.C., Cleveland, Pittsburgh, Kansas City, St. Louis, Detroit, and Boston.

The leadership of the American Federation of Teachers thinks of the organization as a part of the American labor movement. The AFT itself is affiliated with the AFL-CIO, which in turn has a membershp of over 14 million. Much of the AFT's growth has been due to success in introducing the collective bargaining process into the annual salary negotiations of teachers. The NEA was, at first, opposed to such an approach. Perhaps because of the success of the AFT, the NEA has dropped its opposition, and supports what it calls "work stoppages." Through the use of the strike, and the threat of strikes, the AFT has been responsible for raising starting salaries

Other workers are teachers' natural allies because they share patterns of organization, tactics, strategies and goals. If teachers want higher salaries and better pensions, so do factory workers, airplane pilots, and the musicians of the New York Philharmonic. The taxes of these other workers help pay teachers' salaries and help make educational improvements possible. Over the past decade teachers have won as much as they can on their own; they cannot make further gains without the active support of the American workers.
— ALBERT SHANKER —

[9]American Federation of Teachers, *Goals of the American Federation of Teachers AFL-CIO* (Washington, D.C., n.d.), p. 3.

of beginning teachers to well over $14,000 in some major cities. In Boston in 1983 a teacher with nine years' experience and still only a Bachelor's degree now receives just under $24,700 a year. Although the AFT is noted for hard bargaining on bread-and-butter issues—such as salaries, benefits, and retirement after twenty-five years of service—it has also been a defender of academic freedom and of greater participation in decision making by teachers. In the early 1970s it formed an internal group to continually

AFT BILL OF RIGHTS

The teacher is entitled to a life of dignity equal to the high standard of service that is justly demanded of that profession. Therefore, we hold these truths to be self-evident:

I. Teachers have the right to think freely and to express themselves openly and without fear. This includes the right to hold views contrary to the majority.

II. They shall be entitled to the free exercise of their religion. No restraint shall be put upon them in the manner, time or place of their worship.

III. They shall have the right to take part in social, civil, and political affairs. They shall have the right, outside the classroom, to participate in political campaigns and to hold office. They may assemble peaceably and may petition any government agency, including their employ-

ers, for a redress of grievances. They shall have the same freedom in all things as other citizens.

IV. The right of teachers to live in places of their own choosing, to be free of restraints in their mode of living and the use of their leisure time shall not be abridged.

V. Teaching is a profession, the right to practice which is not subject to the surrender of other human rights. No one shall be deprived of professional status, or the right to practice it, or the practice thereof in any particular position, without due process of law.

VI. The right of teachers to be secure in their jobs, free from political influence or public clamor, shall be established by law. The right to teach after qualification in the manner prescribed by

law is a property right, based upon the inalienable rights to life, liberty, and the pursuit of happiness.

VII. In all cases affecting the teacher's employment or professional status a full hearing by an impartial tribunal shall be afforded with the right to full judicial review. No teacher shall be deprived of employment or professional status but for specific causes established by law having a clear relation to the competence or qualification to teach, proved by the weight of the evidence. In all such cases the teacher shall enjoy the right to a speedy and public trial, to be informed of the nature and cause of the accusation, to be confronted with the accusing witnesses, to subpoena witnesses and papers, and to the assistance of

study questions of educational policy. The organization is called QuEST (Quality Education Standards in Teaching). QuEST operates as an ongoing study group, investigating such questions as teacher education and certification, the use of paraprofessionals, and the effect of federal money on local education.

Although the AFT has been considered the more liberal of the two major teachers' organizations, it has recently been criticized for an increas-

counsel. No teacher shall be called upon to answer any charge affecting his employment or professional status but upon probable cause, supported by oath or affirmation.

VIII. It shall be the duty of the employer to provide culturally adequate salaries, security in illness and adequate retirement income. The teacher has the right to such a salary as will: a) Afford a family standard of living comparable to that enjoyed by other professional people in the community; b) To make possible freely chosen professional study; c) Afford the opportunity for leisure and recreation common to our heritage.

IX. Teachers shall not be required under penalty of reduction of salary to pursue studies beyond those required to obtain professional status. After serving a reasonable probationary period a teacher shall be entitled to permanent tenure terminable only for just cause. They shall be free as in other professions in the use of their own time. They shall not be required to perform extracurricular work against their will or without added compensation.

X. To equip people for modern life requires the most advanced educational methods. Therefore, the teacher is entitled to good classrooms, adequate teaching materials, teachable class size and administrative protection and assistance in maintaining discipline.

XI. These rights are based upon the proposition that the culture of a people can rise only as its teachers improve. A teaching force accorded the highest possible professional dignity is the surest guarantee that blessings of liberty will be preserved. Therefore, the possession of these rights imposes the challenge to be worthy of their enjoyment.

XII. Since teachers must be free in order to teach freedom, the right to be members of organizations of their own choosing must be guaranteed. In all matters pertaining to their salaries and working conditions they shall be entitled to bargain collectively through representatives of their own choosing. They are entitled to have the schools administered by superintendents, boards or committees which function in a democratic manner.

American Federation of Teachers, *Bill of Rights*. Reprinted by permission.

ing protectionism. It has appeared to be the foe of the attempts of urban communities to put the control of the schools into the hands of neighborhood people. Also, AFT's strong commitment to win more autonomy for classroom teachers in dismissing and disciplining disruptive children has been interpreted by some poor and minority-group people as working against the interests of their children.

In addition, the shrinking student enrollments in our major cities, which are the real power base of the AFT, has both preoccupied the AFT's time and sapped its energies. And, finally, the more conservative mood of the 1980s and the growing unwillingness of taxpayers to be pressured into support for schools has left the AFT in an increasingly defensive position.

For over ten years there has been among the leadership of both the NEA and the AFT discussion of merger: merger into one teacher organization-union that would represent the entire teaching force. At various times during the 1970s, this merger seemed to be right around the corner.

The most important concern of a beginning teacher is his or her job, *and* being able to keep it for a second or third year. While, theoretically, the professional associations are advocates for every teacher who joins and pays dues, in reality they serve as a support system only for those teachers with seniority and tenure. Therefore, the "best" teacher becomes the one who has more "years-in" rather than the one with superior skills, abilities and achievement. In a situation where two teachers are hired in the same year, "experience" can mean the difference in the dates and times on their signed contracts. Do our professional associations support this practice? YES. As a beginning teacher, who will support *me*?

A DISSENTING VOICE: THE PROFESSION AS ENEMY

Professional growth is not encouraged through this type of hiring and firing. In a capitalistic society, the incentive to do a better job through hard work and self-sacrifice is removed when teachers are evaluated according to their years "in-service" and advanced college hours rather than on criteria such as professional successes and classroom achievements. Yet, through the power of collective bargaining, the poor teacher is rewarded, the average teacher is appeased, and the outstanding teacher is overlooked. Do our professional associations support this practice? YES. As an outstanding, but beginning, teacher, these are not *my* associations.

In cases such as teacher strikes, individual teachers must suffer the consequences if they take an action contrary to an Association vote. When board negotiations have otherwise failed and the Association members have voted to strike, this "unlawful" resistance can lead to personal fine, imprisonment, and loss of job. In this case, individual human rights become secondary to what de Tocqueville referred to as the "tyranny of the majority." Do *our* professional organizations have such little regard for individual preferences among teachers? As a "rookie" who is dedicated to her job, *no* professional organization is there to help *me*!

Debra Hallock Phillips. Used with permission.

The advantages of one giant organization being able to speak authoritatively for all the nation's teachers was very attractive to many people. It was suggested that the teachers' political strength in national elections and their ability to call a nationwide school shutdown would give teachers enormous power. The leadership of the two organizations, however, has been unable to bring about this amalgamation. Presently the NEA and the AFT remain two organizations competing with each other and at the same time trying to attract the attention and support of a public that is becoming less and less interested.

PROFESSIONALISM AT THE CROSSROADS

In the last decade there has been a great deal written and said about teacher power. The basis for this new power of teachers is said to have two elements: work stoppage and politics. As an occupational group, teachers have made substantial gains in the last thirty years in both their salaries and in the purchasing power of their salaries. However, in the school districts where teachers and boards of education have engaged in collective bargaining or teachers have engaged in strikes and other militant activities, teachers have received more money than in districts where teachers have been less active. On the other hand, this new activism has done little to enhance the role of teachers in determining educational policies, and there have been only marginal improvements in the teachers' working conditions.

Although there has been great enthusiasm for active participation in the political process by the leadership of the teacher organization in the recent past, that fervor seems to be cooling. Undoubtedly, there will be substantial involvement of teachers in forthcoming local, state, and national elections, but the strategies will no doubt vary. And, still, many cling to the dream of one professional association of teachers that has two million plus dues-paying members who are ready to be a major force on the American political scene and flex their muscles for education.

As we mentioned earlier, the teachers' capacity to close down schools through strikes and work stoppages is another source of their power. At present, over half of the married women in America are working. The large majority of them have children of school age. When the schools close, many mothers or fathers must stay home to tend to their children. Besides the educational strikes or work stoppages, these actions could have severe economic impact on the states and even on the nation. Therefore, between politics and work stoppages, the teachers' organizations will wield a great deal of power.

This new power could be used, of course, to the direct benefit of children. It could be used to improve teacher education, to give teachers a greater say in their own professional affairs, to divert more funds to edu-

I ask for philosophy from my union and it gives me politics, partisanship and public relations. Teachers learn to be pragmatists or they don't survive. Underneath their veneer of practicality, they are dreamers. Truckdrivers and longshoremen might not need a philosophical guiding light from their union leaders, but teachers do. Teachers yearn for commitment, for caring and for conscience.

— SUSAN OHANIAN —

cational research and innovative projects and, in general, to improve the professional services available to the public.

The new power and autonomy of teachers is not necessarily good, however. Nor is professionalism in itself desirable. Professionalism may, indeed, work against the highest goals of education. When all the rhetoric is pruned away, professional groups—whether they be the American Medical Association, the American Bar Association, or the National Education Association—appear to exist primarily for the benefit of their members. In the interest of protecting and expanding the rights of its members, a professional group may ride roughshod over the needs and rights of the client group. For instance, insisting on tenure rights for all teachers who have taught for three years or more makes it difficult to get rid of those teachers who turn out to be genuine incompetents. In the big cities, basing eligibility for transfer to more congenial schools on seniority may be robbing the most difficult schools of exactly the experienced teacher talent those schools need. Behind the never-never-land jargon of professionalism, one often finds naked self-interest. Occasionally, teachers use their "professional status" as a barrier to protect themselves from criticism by children and parents. "How dare you question what I have done. *I am a professional!*" The question of professionalism is a tricky one. It seems that ultimately it reduces to a need for balance. The teachers' right to be rewarded and safeguarded against unfair practices must be carefully balanced against the students' and the taxpayers' right to be served justly and well by the teacher. It is a constant struggle to strike an even balance. As Myron Brenton has said,

> Every professional group closes ranks to protect its own; teachers are no exception. But teachers are the exception in that they seem to want—at this juncture, at least—the best of both worlds: the security of the civil servant and the prestige and rewards of the professional. More than that, they want a major say in matters of educational policy while getting tenure protection. In other words, they want power without accountability, which is basically an anti-democratic stance.[10]

At this moment the direction the teaching profession will take is unclear. There is still muted talk of merger between the NEA and the AFT and talks of renewed political clout in the upcoming elections. On the other hand, there seems to be an erosion of support for teachers among the general public. Much will depend on the actions taken by teachers and the public's judgment of those actions.

Discussion Questions   **1.** How do people react when you tell them you are thinking of becoming a teacher? Why?

2. Do you know of a situation in which a teacher needed protection or in which a teacher's rights were violated?

3. Do you think that teachers should devote themselves to becoming professionals? If so, what must they do? Are you willing to do it? How do you feel about Walter Beggs's description of the "career teacher" on page 352?

4. How do you, personally, react to the idea of the teacher being a continuous learner? Which of the forms of continuing professional education has the most appeal to you? the least appeal?

5. Do teachers need a professional organization? What are the essential functions performed by such a group?

6. Compare the NEA Code of Ethics and the AFT Bill of Rights. How do the assumptions and attitudes about teaching represented by the two documents differ? What seem to be the overriding concerns of the two organi-

---

[10]Brenton, *What's Happened to Teacher?*, p. 255.

zations? How do the images of teachers they project differ? To what extent do you think a merger of the NEA and the AFT would solve the problems of each and end the competition between them? What new problems might such a merger create?

7. Do you think there is any kind of behavior outside the classroom that should be forbidden to teachers, or that should be cause for dismissal? To what extent is the teacher's personal life still subject to scrutiny by school officials?

8. What dangers or weaknesses seem to be endemic to professional organizations? Would you be willing to sacrifice security for professionalism? Will you be a professional? Why?

9. What is your opinion of tenure for teachers? What arguments for or against it can you suggest? Would you be willing to work in a school system that does not offer tenure?

10. For you, right now, what seem the most important issues for teachers to concern themselves with—increased power? higher salaries? better training? something else? Be prepared to defend your choice. What can you do to work for the changes you consider most important?

For Further Reading   Finn, Chester E. "Teacher Politics." *Commentary* (February 1983): 29–41.
   An analysis of recent political activities of both the NEA and the
   AFT. The author suggests that the NEA has moved toward a politically left social position and has abandoned the core concerns of
   education.

Howsam, Robert B., et al. *Educating a Profession*. Report of the Bicentennial
Commission of Education for the Profession of Teaching. Washington, D.C.:
American Association of Colleges for Teacher Education, 1976.
   Examines the problem of training teachers and proposes new steps
   to restructure teacher education in America.

Lieberman, Myron. *Education as a Profession*. Englewood Cliffs, N.J.: Prentice-Hall, 1956.
   Carefully analyzes the occupation of teaching to determine how it
   does and does not "fit" the standard qualifications of a profession.

Lortie, Dan C. *Schoolteacher: A Sociological Study*. Chicago: University of Chicago Press, 1975.
   A sociological view of the ethnos of the teaching profession, that
   pattern of orientations and sentiments that are peculiar to teachers.

McDaniel, Thomas R. *The Teacher's Profession: Essays on Becoming an Educator*. Washington, D.C.: University Press of America, 1982.
   A collection of essays on an array of concerns of the teacher, including many that deal directly with the issue of professionalization.

Sterling, Philip. *The Real Teachers*. New York: Vintage Books, 1972.
> Draws directly on the experience of a variety of teachers. Major topics are addressed by these teachers, and the fact that they speak in their own voices gives the book a strong sense of realism.

Waller, Willard. *The Sociology of Teaching*. New York: John Wiley & Sons, 1965.
> Originally written in 1932, this survey of what students and citizens thought of teachers and education over forty years ago still contains much of value. It is rich in incisive analyses of the teacher's role and suggestions for prospective teachers.

SOCIAL ISSUES AND THE CURRENT SCENE

V

What Are the Social Issues that Affect American Education?

12

Rarely does a day go by on which educational issues fail to make headlines in newspapers across the country. Violence in schools, teacher strikes, inequality of educational opportunity, prayer in the schools, declining student performance, and drug use are only a few of the issues that we read about daily. Underlying these issues are problems that complicate the efforts of young people to get an education—problems such as chaotic family lives and crippling poverty. This chapter explores some of the most sensitive and controversial issues in American education. Naturally, in such a short space we are able to treat each topic only briefly. However, we urge you to pursue additional reading on each of the issues.

This chapter emphasizes that:

▪ There are some critical problems affecting many school-age children that very directly influence the lives of the children involved and frequently spill over into the classroom. Among these problems are severe poverty, broken homes, child abuse, and various forms of escapism.

▪ The issue of public school desegregation and integration has been and continues to be a major controversy in American education. Much of the controversy involves issues such as de jure and de facto segregation, the meaning of "equality of educational opportunity," compensatory education, magnet school programs, and forced busing.

▪ Sexism and sex-role stereotyping affect students, especially females. Particularly noteworthy are how the public school curriculum reinforces sex-role stereotyping and how Title IX of the Education Amendments Act of 1972 is affecting the operation of schools.

▪ Violence and vandalism, which are not confined to urban schools, continue to be major problems in the schools.

▪ The American public's concern over declining student performance has led to an emphasis on making the school more accountable, which has spawned the back-to-basics, competency testing, and accountability movements.

▪ Other major tension points are religion in public schools and the school's role in moral education.

A HALF CENTURY AGO, the social philosopher George Counts challenged American teachers with the question, ''Dare the schools change the social order?'' This question suggests, first, that all is not perfect with the way in which we live together, and, second, that teachers should do something about it. The bulk of this chapter explores the first part of the question, but we also try to provide the reader with the kind of information that can be the basis for action.

But the topic of social issues, including under its umbrella problems ranging from birth defects to the sense of uselessness experienced by so many of our elderly citizens, is too large to discuss fully in one chapter. Our focus in this chapter is on the major problems facing the young and on the larger issues that affect the schools.

SOCIAL PROBLEMS AFFECTING THE YOUNG

Teaching is said to be a middle-class occupation that recruits middle-class people or people desirous of becoming middle-class. More to the point, most teachers come from relatively stable backgrounds. Whereas this is a potential source of strength, it has its drawbacks. One difficulty is that many teachers do not recognize the depth of the problems that some children bring with them into the classroom. The ways a child behaves and what the teacher takes to be the student's attitude may be thought to be the child's response to a particular class. For instance, a teacher may see a child acting very withdrawn and, after attempting to involve the child, may discover in the child a set of negative attitudes toward school, fellow classmates, and the teacher herself. At this point, the teacher might tend to personalize the situation, seeing the student's behavior and attitudes as a rejection of her efforts and of her classroom.

The children that stream into a teacher's classroom each September bring with them their own personal histories. Although they may wish to start afresh with the beginning of the new school year, much of who they are is wrapped up in their past and their current out-of-school lives. It is likely that some of these students bear deep scars from their past experiences and that some are currently caught in desperate problems. Painful pasts, of course, are common; problems, too, are a part of life. Few of us get through life without encountering some pain or misfortune: an alcoholic parent, a serious accident, a long sickness, a disability. Individuals, including young people, are often better and stronger for these troubles. That issue is not what we are addressing here. We wish to direct your attention to larger problems, widespread social problems. Our intention is not to suggest that the teacher should be a Mr. or Ms. Fix-It, taking in troubled children and, with a few quick adjustments to their psyches, sending them out into the world cured. Rather, we wish to make you more fully aware and more deeply sensitive to the sorts of problems that will come into your classroom with your students.

*The Poor and
Disadvantaged*

America is the richest large nation in the history of the world. The average citizen has material comforts that would make Louis XIV, France's seventeenth-century Sun King, beside himself with envy. In relation to seventeenth-century France and many modern Third World countries, the bottom of America's socioeconomic ladder does not look too bad. But if you are living in rural Maine in a tarpaper shack without plumbing or in a Cincinnati slum and your children have never slept in their own beds or seen a doctor, or if you are a migrant worker, with no permanent home for your children but only a dreary series of barracks, then the word *poor* has special meaning. And it is not simply the squalor of the living conditions but the psychological pain of American poverty that has an effect on the poor. To live in a rich land and to be viewed by others as "losers" has a deadening impact. To be able to afford a television set but not the goods that are advertised on TV nor the rich life that comes pouring through the tube is a special kind of impoverishment.

Fifteen or twenty years ago the American government and many of its people undertook a "War on Poverty." A major part of this effort was to upgrade the education of children, thus breaking the cycle of poverty in which so many children are trapped. There were a large number of federal, state, and local efforts (for example, Project Head Start) to provide special teachers, special curriculum, and special resources for the children of the poor. It was a time of high hopes and high ideals. The history of that period is captured well in a recent report of a major American foundation.

> As federal and state laws were passed to protect the rights of all children to equal educational opportunities, many people confidently assumed that the educational system would use the dollars allocated for special assistance to students who historically have been under-served for their intended purposes, and the effects show up in improved academic achievement. The facts told a disappointing story. Studies of the implementation of these programs revealed that the new ideas and extra resources that were supposed to benefit children frequently never reached them in the form of better services. Important educational innovations did not result in the improvement of student skills because the programs were never seriously carried out. Making things work, it appeared, required a complex network of related actions, and this network was constantly breaking down, whether because of insufficient resources, bureaucratic inertia, political pressure, inadequate training and supportive assistance to educators, or a combination of all of these factors.[1]

Said more succinctly, freeing children from the culture of poverty has turned out to be much tougher than anticipated.

[1]The Carnegie Corporation of New York, *Carnegie Corporation in a Changing Society: 1961–1981* (New York: Carnegie Corporation, 1982), p. 13.

One of the problems is that schools are not designed to serve poor children. Sociologists point out to us that the schools in this country were created and continue to be supported by the middle class to perpetuate middle-class values. There is nothing particularly startling about this. Middle-class people want their children to be like themselves, or possibly somewhat better. Therefore, they have built and continue to pay for a school system that reflects their values and supports the way of life with which they feel comfortable. Two groups in our society, however, feel rather alien to the middle-class dominated public school system: the upper class (the rich) and the lower class (the poor). It's hard to be too concerned about upper-class people. They traditionally have had the option of private education. They have always been able to send their children to a rather elaborate network of day schools, academies, and prep schools.

The poor, too, have been uncomfortable with the public schools, but they have had no alternatives. The poor are uncomfortable with the public schools for a complex set of reasons. Perhaps the point can best be made by an example.

Imagine yourself as someone thirty-five years old who left school at sixteen. Although you went to school longer than anyone else in your family, you never succeeded in school. In actual fact, if you hadn't left, you would have been thrown out. Your teachers always made you feel as if you were disappointing them. On the other hand, you always felt ill at ease in school, particularly around the kids who had more than the one or two sets of clothes that you had. You had to show up every day in pretty much the same outfit. By the time you left school you could hardly look the teachers in the eye for embarrassment and anger.

Now you have your own children. Although you personally can't see how staying in school till you were sixteen really helped you very much, you try to encourage them. However, you hate to go to school for parent-teacher conferences. You feel awkward talking to teachers, and it's still hard to look them in the eye. And then, going to visit school is expensive for you. You have to get off work, and that means losing even more money, and the foreman doesn't understand that very well. Your kids are in junior high, and you can hardly read their books—that is, when they bring their books home. You don't understand any of the math homework they are supposed to do (and rarely do), and to try to help them is just to make a fool of yourself. Besides, when you come home you have too much to do yourself, and you're too tired to fight with them about doing homework.

The last time you went to school, this nice shiny-faced teacher asked you if your kids had their own rooms to study in, away from the TV and with good lights. You wanted to laugh, and you wanted to cry. Somehow you know that school is the answer, but you can see it isn't helping with your kids. School just isn't "taking" for them and you don't know why, and they can't seem to explain it, and you feel like your own past is being repeated in them. They are beginning to question. They gripe about school all the time. They have started to cut school and complain that the teachers have it in for them. They may end up not going even as far as you went in school. They'd like nothing more than to quit now. At the same time, you keep on hearing and reading in the newspaper that education is becoming more important all the time and that only people with real skills are going to get jobs and make it in the future. It just doesn't seem right. And, somehow, it just doesn't seem fair.

As we said before, many people in our society thought they could eliminate poverty through education and that, through schooling, it would be relatively easy to free people from the chains of impoverishment. The efforts were well intentioned but, in retrospect, naive. On the other hand,

FROM HERBERT KOHL'S
36 Children

My alarm clock rang at seven thirty, but I was up and dressed at seven. It was only a fifteen-minute bus ride from my apartment on 90th Street and Madison Avenue to the school on 119th Street and Madison.

There had been an orientation session the day before. I remembered the principal's words. "In times like these, this is the most exciting place to be, in the midst of ferment and creative activity. Never has teaching offered such opportunities . . . we are together here in a difficult situation. They are not the easiest children, yet the rewards are so great—a smile, loving concern, what an inspiration, a felicitous experience."

I remembered my barren classroom, no books, a bat-

tered piano, broken windows and desks, falling plaster, and an oppressive darkness.

I was handed a roll book with thirty-six names and thirty-six cumulative record cards, years of judgments already passed upon the children, their official personalities. I read through the names, twenty girls and sixteen boys, the 6-1 class, though I was supposed to be teaching the fifth grade and had planned for it all summer. Then I locked the record cards away in the closet. The children would tell me who they were. Each child, each new school year, is potentially many things, only one of which the cumulative record card documents. It is amazing how "emotional" problems can disappear, how the dullest child can be transformed into the keenest and the brightest into

the most ordinary when the prefabricated judgments of other teachers are forgotten.

The children entered at nine and filled up the seats. They were silent and stared at me. It was a shock to see thirty-six black faces before me. No preparation helped. It is one thing to be liberal and talk, another to face something and learn that you're afraid.

The children sat quietly, expectant. Everything must go well; we must like each other.

Hands went up as I called the roll. Anxious faces, hostile, indifferent, weary of the ritual, confident of its outcome.

critics see our schools as part of the enslavement system. They claim that the schools not only do not help to develop the individuality and the talents of poor children, but also make these children believe themselves to be "losers." As a result of eight to ten or eleven years of schooling, these young people see themselves as unable to fit into the middle class and as people who, at best, will do society's menial work. And although some of these critics see this as a conscious plan, we do not. Such a scenario suggests that the teachers who are toiling in the urban and rural slums are either people of evil intentions or simply dupes. In our view, many of the teachers who are most heroic and alive are struggling valiantly to aid people oppressed by poverty.

Our past and present inadequacies and failures at educating the children of the poor tempt some to turn away and devote their energies to more solvable problems. We cannot do this. Ours is an evolving society. As a people, we are not finished with our own development. Eradicating the ravages of poverty and its withering effect on children should be on the top of our agenda as citizens of this nation and as educators. Although there are many important and solvable problems to work on, we cannot afford—in justice—to ignore this one.

The Family Under Pressure

The comic poet Ogden Nash once wrote, "A family is a unit composed not only of children but of men, women, an occasional animal and the common cold." What has been troubling the American family for the last twenty years is much more serious than a common cold. As a society we have undergone an enormous number of changes, from how we work to where we live, from what we do with our free time to how we get ideas. One of the major changes has been in the structure of the family. A key development has been the growing number of families in which both parents work. In 1970, the U.S. Census showed that 40 percent of the married women worked outside the home. In 1980 the figure had increased to 51 percent. The U.S. Labor Department estimates that by 1990 two out of three married women will be working outside the home. Part of this trend is that married women with children are now going to work or returning to work when their children are much younger than was true in the past. A result of this changing status of the mother is that she is not so involved as she traditionally has been in raising the children—that is, in attending daily to the child's social, intellectual, and moral development. Mom just isn't so available today as she used to be. Now, when many children return home from school, rather than talk with their mothers, they watch "General Hospital." Coming home to an empty apartment after school is standard for a large percentage of the children in our country.

But that is not the only change, nor the most important one, that seems to be affecting the American family. In the United States, the rate of divorce, particularly between couples who have children, has increased dramatically since 1965. The psychologist E. Mavis Hetherington, of the University of Virginia, has described the situation as follows:

> It is estimated that 40% of the current marriages of young adults will end in divorce and that 40%–50% of children born in the 1970s will spend some time living in a single-parent family. The average length of time spent by children in a single-parent home as the result of marital disruption is about six years. The majority of these children reside with their mothers, with only 10% living with their fathers even though this proportion has tripled since 1960.[2]

Being a child in a family where the parents' marriage is conflict ridden and unhappy may be less preferable than being part of an amiable separation in a family, but single-parent families, nevertheless, have one major disadvantage. In the 1980 census a single comparison stood out and spoke volumes: the average married woman with two children shared with her husband a combined salary of $23,000; her counterpart, a divorced woman with two children, had to live and support her children on a salary of $8,342. These single-parent families have been called "the new poor." It is not only the lack of a father figure, but the loss of a father's income that puts a special burden on these families.

Both of these trends, the two-career family and the single-parent family, have similar impacts on children, although in varying degrees. They both limit the amount of time the children spend in close contact with parents. The implication of these trends for teachers is well captured by the distinguished educator Ralph W. Tyler. A few years ago Tyler wrote:

> In the past, experiences in the home, the work situation, and the school made somewhat different contributions to the development of American youth. Most young people acquired their basic habits of orderliness, punctuality, and attention to work primarily in the home and the work setting. With the helpful supplementation of the school's regime, they came to recognize the meaning and importance of the productive work through participating in family chores and through holding part-time jobs that often involved the close supervision and critical appraisal of their efforts.[3]

Whereas in the past young people were actively involved in family and community, today the school is being urged to play a larger role in expanding the limited experiences of children. Also, schools are required to

---

[2]E. Mavis Hetherington, "Divorce: A Child's Perspective," *The American Psychologist* (October 1979): 851.

[3]Ralph W. Tyler, "The New Emphasis in Curriculum Development," *Educational Leadership* (October 1976): 65. We need to acknowledge the fact that the children of many working mothers and separated or divorced parents are extremely well cared for and come to school with positive attitudes and solid work habits. The issues to which we are addressing ourselves are the trends, not specific situations.

"We certainly should—especially since so few kids learn it at home anymore"

Courtesy, Houston Chronicle

deal with the new problems being brought to them by these new facts of family life. In the past, teachers could count on sure support from families; now teachers often find it difficult even to get in contact with many parents.

Abused and Battered Children

One of the authors, as an undergraduate in a social psychology class, had the following experience.

I was assigned to work for fifteen weeks in a settlement house for boys. So every Tuesday afternoon I went to a rather seedy part of the city and worked from 1 to 5. The first day the director assigned me to work with Pauly, who, he said, "needed special attention." I was told to try to get him to read, solve simple arithmetic problems, and, in general, to keep him out of trouble. He then took me to the playground and separated Pauly out from a crowd of young boys. I was shocked when I first saw him. Although Pauly was only seven, he was large and strong, and his hooded eyes told me instantly that he didn't like what he knew was in store for him. I can remember thinking that Pauly had taken an instant dislike to me. I took Pauly to a small room, where I discovered that he not only acted disagreeably but also smelled disagreeable. It was almost impossible to talk with Pauly. One minute he would be hyperactive, trying to get out of the room or throwing the books around. The next minute he would be withdrawn to the point of not responding to questions. In the three hours or so we were together, he read a few sentences and, through trial and error, solved a few simple addition problems. At the end I was exhausted and convinced that I had failed completely.

The next two-week period was pretty much a repeat of my first encounter with Pauly. So, before the fourth session I asked to talk with the director. I told him that I felt I was getting nowhere, but he disagreed. He told me that Pauly talked about me all the time. Although it didn't show in Pauly's behavior, I was buoyed by that slim compliment. Then I noticed that Pauly would be waiting at an upper window when I came on Tuesdays, and he complained bitterly if I were three or four minutes late. Things became easier in the sessions. Somewhere midway in the term I caught the director just as I was leaving and asked him something I had been wondering about. "How come Pauly has those little cut marks on his face and head and those seven or eight odd scars on his arms and legs?"

"Oh, that was a little present from his parents. The face and head marks are from blows, but the burn marks are from cigarettes."

I was stunned. In a clinical and almost casual way, he recounted how a social worker had taken Pauly away from his parents at age three and how the boy began screaming or crying every time an adult came near him. The director reported how pleased he was by the progress Pauly had made during those four years, and he ended by saying, "The shame is for every Pauly we rescue from one of those wretched homes, there are a dozen kids who are being tortured whom we never hear about."

As a field, the education of the young brings us in contact with the best impulses of humanity. Occasionally, however, we see the wreckage of its darkest and most vicious impulses. For many years this phenomenon, called the *battered child syndrome*, was one of society's dirty little secrets, a truth known only to a small percentage of social workers and law enforcement people. In recent years, in an effort to get stiffer laws and more effective prevention, the problem of child abuse has received national attention. We have become more aware of the magnitude of this problem—although it is difficult for many of us to comprehend it fully. Papalia and Olds report:

> Children known as "battered babies" are kicked, beaten, burned, thrown against walls and radiators, strangled, suffocated and even burned alive. Their bones are broken, their teeth are knocked out, their eyesight is destroyed, and their internal organs are injured. Many battered babies who live suffer mental, physical and emotional damage that can never be fully repaired.[4]

Because of the hidden nature of the battered child syndrome, reliable figures on it are somewhat difficult to obtain. Most professionals in the field acknowledge that a majority of cases are unreported. However, R. J. Gelles surveyed a random sample of households on the incidence of violence between family members.[5] Approximately 3.5 percent of the parents in his sample acknowledged that during the year prior to the survey they had acted in such a violent manner toward one of their children that the violence could have caused injury. When these figures are projected to the total population, they indicate that each year between 1.4 and 1.9 million children are subjected to forms of violence that could potentially cause injury. Given the fact that this study is based on self-admission of violent acts, and that all of the children were more than three years old (of a less vulnerable age), there is the strong suggestion that child abuse is even more widespread than supposed.

There has also been an increase in reported cases of sexual abuse of children. Although the number of reported cases of this most heinous crime is high, often the actual number of such cases is ten times the number reported. C. H. Kempe, who has written about sexual abuse of children, suggests that the actual figures may be fifty thousand cases per year.[6]

Recent reports on child abuse suggest that it is correlated with grinding poverty, unemployment, and depressing living conditions. However, it may very well be that the poor are more exposed, while the rest of us are able to afford private medical services and, therefore, are not so vulnerable to being reported. But whatever the conditions that bring people to the brink of frustration or anger at their children, it hardly justifies an adult's torturing a child. Sadly too, child abuse is more common with handicapped children, children who already need special care and affection.

[4]D. Papalia and S. Olds, *Human Development,* 2nd ed. (New York: McGraw-Hill, 1981), p. 193.

[5]R. J. Gelles, "Problems in Defining and Labeling Child Abuse," paper presented at study group Problems in the Prediction of Child Abuse, Wilmington, Del., June 1977.

[6]C. Kempe, "Sexual Abuse, Another Hidden Pediatric Problem." *Pediatrics* (1978): 382–389.

One of the particularly unfortunate aspects of child abuse is that people who were abused themselves as children are much more likely than other people to abuse their own children. Experts say that although the cause of child abuse is unclear, a culture such as ours that condones the use of force with children contributes to the climate that would let abuse happen.

The classroom teacher will not often directly encounter the problem of the abused child. However, if children come to school with welts and black and blue marks and unusual sores, the teacher should immediately bring this to the attention of the school nurse or the principal. On the other hand, teachers may find it difficult to understand why a child is so immensely hostile to them, particularly when they attempt to be friendly. The possibility that this negative reaction to adults is a learned behavior may help the teacher put the situation in perspective.

The abused child syndrome is not something that we can always do something about directly. Nor should we despair for those unfortunate children who are tortured. Many of these scarred children make good adjustments to life. As teachers, we need to make sure that school is part of life's healing process.

Escapism

One result of the enormous social changes in twentieth-century America is that the role of children has been altered radically. There has been a significant shift in what children do and how they spend their out-of-school time. Instead of coming home to chores, such as helping with the milking or putting up wood, children now come home to houses or apartments where there is little that needs to be done by them—and they do little. One of the effects of this, as James Coleman has pointed out, is that children today have little opportunity to gain a sense of responsibility through contributing to the economic well-being of the family.[7] In the past, children's labor was needed to help run the family farm or small business. Few children make a similar contribution to a family's income today. Some young people have paper routes or babysit or work in restaurants, but most jobs in which the young can learn skills and learn to take on responsibilities have all but disappeared. Further, in the last twenty years of relative affluence, the child, and particularly the teenager, has become a major consumer of the family's financial resources. Youth support the record and tape industries and contribute heavily as consumers to the car, clothing, and fast food industries.

The new age has transformed the out-of-school life of young people. Bruno Bettelheim has spoken of the students' "long wait for real life to begin." Many of today's students do commit themselves fully to school work, to sports, to hobbies, and to volunteer or paid work. They use their

[7]James Coleman, *Youth: Transition to Adulthood* (Chicago: University of Chicago Press, 1974).

time to confront life. There are, however, significant numbers of students that do not. They use their leisure time not to confront life but to escape from it. The escapism of youth takes many forms. Among the ones that are most widespread are alcohol and drugs, television and video games, and sex.

ALCOHOL AND DRUGS   Americans are characterized by a widespread use of alcohol and drugs. We use drugs for many purposes, from mood altering to mind expanding. Alcohol, which acts as a depressant, is a major problem in American society. According to the World Health Organization, in 1976 there were five million adult alcoholics in the United States. Estimates of teenage alcoholics vary. Grace J. Craig estimates that 2 percent, or one out of fifty of U.S. teenagers are alcoholics.[8] On the other hand, Kenneth Kenniston reports that one out of every twenty teenagers has a "drinking problem."[9] That means that a high school teacher should expect to have at least one alcoholic in each of his or her five or six periods every day. There is apparently a tendency for the greatest number of alcoholic teenagers to be among male students, especially among male students with low grades. Also, there is a higher proportion of alcoholism in cities than in suburbs or rural areas. Nevertheless, the problem of alcoholism among high school students is universal.

In her book *Human Development,* Grace J. Craig talks about some of the characteristics of high school alcoholics:

> [They] tend to have friends who also drink, and they tend to take a variety of other drugs. Many have serious psychological problems such as a poor sense of identity, a lack of inner goals, and a personality oriented toward the constant search for new sensations and experiences.[10]

Marijuana and the other, harder drugs have taken a strong hold among youth in this country since the late 1960s. Studies by the National Institute on Drug Abuse (1977) tell us that almost half (47 percent) of the sixteen- or seventeen-year-olds have used marijuana at least once. Twenty-nine percent report having used marijuana within the last month. Although marijuana causes some health hazard to lung and throat tissue, its primary danger comes from the fact that it alters perception and impedes motor coordination. Thus, there is growing evidence that marijuana "interferes with short term memory, reading comprehension, problem-solving ability, and general mental functioning."[11]

[8]Grace J. Craig, *Human Development.* (Englewood Cliffs, N.J.: Prentice-Hall, 1980), p. 379.

[9]Kenneth Kenniston and the Carnegie Council on Children, *All Our Children: The American Family Under Pressure* (New York: Harcourt, Brace, Jovanovich, 1977).

[10]Craig, *Human Development,* p. 380.

[11]Craig, *Human Development,* p. 85.

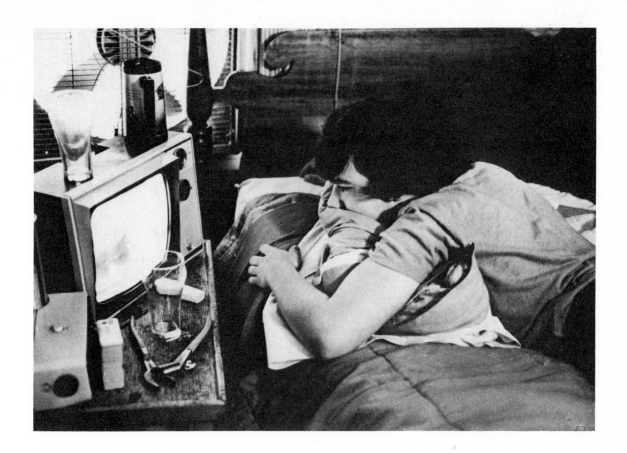

For many young people the use of alcohol and marijuana may be simple pleasure seeking; on the other hand, using these drugs can be viewed as escapist behavior, a way to keep from confronting one's responsibilities as a student, as a member of a family, and as a member of the community. Also, the fact that the use of both alcohol and marijuana by teenagers is illegal means that the use of these drugs is accompanied by an additional set of potentially destructive personal and social consequences.

TELEVISION There is an old wisecrack that if fish were scientists, the last thing they would discover would be water. Perhaps the same thing can be said about another omnipresent fact of modern life: the glowing tube. Social scientists have only recently begun to investigate television. In a way it sneaked up on us and was a part of our lives before we really knew it. Also, it is hard to study what the effect of television is, because there is such a variety in usage and in content. Some students may only occasionally watch "Little House on the Prairie," while other "regulars" watch as much as seven or eight hours a day and watch anything. What is the effect of watching a baseball game as compared with watching programs built around sadistic violence and sex? More and more experts are becoming concerned about what they see as the plug-in quality of television. The students come home, plop down in front of the set, and let it wash over them. They almost literally submerge themselves in television.

Whereas there are strong suggestions that television has negative physiological effects, inhibiting the proper development of the imagination, making it difficult for students to sit quietly and read, and interfering in other learning processes, there is one clear matter for concern. Kate Moody, in her recent book *Growing Up on Television,* states: "Growing up on television is a new human condition. Never before has an entire generation been weaned by an electronic box and raised while spending so much of its waking time *watching.*"[12] She goes on to report that the typical American child now watches television for more than thirty hours a week, which is more time than he spends with his parents, playing with peers, attending school or reading books. In the typical American household there is a TV set on for six and a half hours a day, and the projections are that figures will increase during the 1980s. Moody states that "by the time the child finishes high school, he will have spent 18,000 hours with the 'TV curriculum' and only 12,000 with school curriculum."[13] And, whatever may be the side effects of watching thirty hours a week—of passively viewing commercials and the canned world of TV—this is simply a great deal of time to *take away* from mental and physical development, from building a mind, a body, and character.

VIDEOGAMES   Not many years ago a new form of escapism burst on the scene—videogames. Overnight Pac Man became a national celebrity. Malls, arcades, and those homes affluent enough to afford videogames are now crowded with young people lining up to beat the newest games. Pac Man was quickly followed by a host of imitators, and the youth of the country are off on a new craze.

To date there is little hard evidence about the effects of extensive involvement with videogames on school performance and other mental learning. On the other hand, the case can be made that videogames are just another intellectual opiate, another something to keep the child's mind amused, rather than engaged in disciplined learning. Further, the very fast-paced, blinking-lights intensity of the videogames makes it more difficult for the student to sit quietly and work through a math problem or make sense out of a Shakespearean sonnet. But while we wait to find out the

[12]Kate Moody, *Growing Up on Television* (New York: New York Times Books, 1980), p. 3.
[13]Moody, *Growing Up on Television,* p. 5.

effects of this new craze, millions of young people are turning videogames into one of America's most quickly growing enterprises.

THE NEW SEXUALITY   The new, more relaxed attitudes toward sex have had their effect on the young. Clearly, today's youth are much more sexually active than any generation of the past. A 1973 study of premarital intercourse among high school students showed that about 25 percent of both male and female students were nonvirgins by the ages of sixteen or seventeen.[14] A later study by Planned Parenthood (1977) reported that the percentage of white adolescents who experienced intercourse had doubled between the years 1971 and 1977. Whereas widespread premarital sexuality was once considered the deviant behavior of the urban poor, it is now seen to be as suburban as the cookout and the two-car garage. Keeping up with these statistics are the growing numbers of teenage pregnancies. In Massachusetts, 20 thousand of the state's 300 thousand teenage girls (or one out of fifteen) gets pregnant every year. Only about one in ten of the pregnancies is planned.[15] The situation in the rest of the country is quite similar.

Just five years ago people were taking a somewhat relaxed attitude towards the new sexuality. However, that is all changing, largely because of the return of much more resistant strains of syphilis and gonorrhea and the emergence on the scene of Herpes Two. Herpes Two, which today is incurable and barely controllable, is said to be spreading by 600 thousand people each year. Many of these victims are teenagers.

Hans Sebald suggests that there are six motives for sex:[16]

1. the need for intimacy
2. the need for belonging
3. the desire for power
4. the desire for submission
5. curiosity
6. the desire for passion and ecstasy

A number of these motives, particularly the needs for intimacy and belonging, are motives that youth are apt to use for early sexuality. The student who is having difficulty at school or at home, who does not succeed in academic work, in sports or in other extracurricular activities, is tempted to find escape in sex. The psychologist Grace G. Craig states, "academic success or failure in high school may also be related to sexual behavior,

[14]Craig, *Human Development*, p. 359.

[15]John S. Dacey, *Adolescents Today* (Santa Monica, Calif.: Good Year Publishing Co., 1979), p. 225.

[16]Hans Sebald, *Adolescence: A Social Psychological Analysis*, 2nd ed. (Englewood Cliffs, N.J.: Prentice-Hall, 1977), pp. 130–131.

with failure-oriented adolescents turning to sexual behavior to gratify their need for success.''[17]

In addition to all of these forms of escape—alcohol, drugs, television, videogames, and sex—there is a more ultimate form of escape that is on the rise. That is suicide, the third most common cause of death in young people. Currently, more than four thousand young people kill themselves annually. This number shows a tripling of the suicide rate in a short, twenty-year period.

The problems that we've discussed in this section, then, are problems students bring with them when they enter the classroom. Many of the dismal statistics reported here together represent cries of help from troubled youth. Although teachers may not be able to solve these problems, they need to be aware of them and take them into consideration. There is, in addition, a group of problems in which the school is not so much the recipient of the problem, but is intimately entangled in the problem. These problems, which we shall discuss now, are ones for which teachers must actively and often directly seek solutions.

[17]Craig, *Human Development*, p. 359.

WHERE DO YOU STAND?

Before you launch into the rest of the chapter, take a few moments to answer the following questions about controversial topics in American education in order to assess your own position. You may wish to compare your responses with those of your classmates.

▪ Do you believe the public schools should be desegregated? Do you favor the use of busing to achieve desegregation? What means of desegregation, if any, do you favor?

▪ Are violence and vandalism problems in the schools with which you are acquainted? How do you think these problems ought to be handled?

▪ Do you favor or oppose a system that would hold teachers and administrators accountable for students' progress?

▪ What is your explanation for the declining test scores of students in our public schools?

▪ Do schools perpetuate sexism, thereby limiting the human potential of both boys and girls, but primarily of girls?

Opinion on these issues is extremely diverse. Whatever your views, however, you and your classmates are probably short on data to support your opinions. This is not unusual, since even people who feel strongly about these topics have often not really investigated the arguments for the other side and weighed the issues in order to arrive at a reasoned, logical position. Because these topics touch on our religious, political, or philosophical convictions, we usually respond to them emotionally rather than rationally.

TENSION POINTS IN AMERICAN EDUCATION

The goal of this section of the chapter is simple: to explore opposing positions on some of the most controversial topics in American education today in order to equip you, as a teacher, with understanding of and sensitivity to, the exposed nerve endings of American education. Keep in mind the significance of these tension points: they are the result of an attempt to educate children in a pluralistic society. That is, our society is made up of diverse individuals and groups, each with different axes to grind and different ideas about what a school should be, what it should teach, and what life in school should be like. Tension points are inevitable when diverse groups and individuals with different objectives for the schools attempt to achieve their objectives. As a teacher, you will certainly be involved. Since teachers have a deep responsibility to the schools, it is important that they provide leadership in seeking enlightened solutions to these complex and touchy issues.

One warning: our coverage of these tension points is not very deep. We only skim the surface of these issues; you should not be satisfied to stop here. It is your responsibility to dig below the surface if you want to find out what these issues really involve.

Inequality of Educational Opportunity

America is a multiracial society. It is considered by many people to be one of the most successful multiracial societies the world has ever seen. However, it is far from perfect, and many children born into the families of minority groups face severe disadvantages in their attempts to live decent lives and to go up the ladder of success. Schooling is, by design, intended to help individuals in this process. Whether or not the schools have been helping or hindering the progress of minority children—relative to majority children—has been a source of raging debate for over two decades.

According to the National Assessment of Education Progress, the source of our most comprehensive longitudinal measures of pupil performance, aggregate black performance (at ages nine, thirteen, seventeen) ranges between ten and seventeen points below the national averages in reading and math.[18] Among black secondary students, close to 20 percent fail to graduate, whereas for whites the comparable figure is 12.4 percent.[19]

These recent data support findings in one of the landmark studies in this area, the so-called Coleman Report. Completed two decades ago, the Coleman Report found that massive inequalities existed in public school achievement along social class and racial lines.[20] Coleman's research reveals, for instance, that twelfth-grade black students in the urban Northeast

[18]R. Edmonds, "Making Public Schools Effective," *Social Policy* (September/October, 1981): 56.

[19]Edmonds, "Making Public Schools Effective," p. 56.

[20]James Coleman et al., *Equality of Educational Opportunity* (Washington, D.C.: U.S. Government Printing Office, 1966).

read at the ninth-grade level and do mathematics at the seventh-grade level, and that Southern blacks, Mexican-Americans, Puerto Ricans, and Native Americans achieve at even lower levels. Dropout statistics attest to an even greater difference between the education of white middle-class children and that received by children of the poor and minority groups. In other words, students of low socioeconomic status and minority-group backgrounds score much lower than white middle-class students on a variety of verbal and numerical tests.

Whatever the reasons, large numbers of poor and minority-group students are leaving school without the verbal and computational skills necessary to function effectively in American society. Who, if anyone, is to blame for this situation? The schools? Teachers and administrators? Or is the responsibility that of society as a whole, and are the schools merely a scapegoat? Talk to five different people and you will probably hear five different opinions about where blame should be affixed. But assessing blame is not our function here. One can ask better questions, such as: What is meant by equality of educational opportunity? How is it measured? What are the responsibilities of the school system for providing equal educational opportunity? How can the achievement of poor and minority-group students be improved? Simple enough questions, but their answers are guaranteed to be controversial.

Equality of educational opportunity is hardly a new concept in American education, but its components have changed dramatically in the last two decades. For a long period in our history, the idea of equal educational opportunity involved the following elements:

1. providing a *free education* up to the time when the majority of students entered the labor force
2. providing a *common curriculum* for all children, regardless of background
3. providing that children from diverse backgrounds attend the *same school*
4. providing equality within a given *locality*, since local taxes supported the school system[21]

As a result of *Brown* v. *Board of Education,* the 1954 Supreme Court decision that held that segregated schools are inherently unequal because the *effects* of such separate schools are likely to be different, a new component was introduced into the concept of educational opportunity: that equality of educational opportunity is defined in terms of the effect, rather than the provisions, of schooling. In the *Brown* decision, the Supreme Court found that, even when facilities and teacher salaries were identical, "equality of educational opportunity" did not exist.

[21]James Coleman, "The Concept of Equality of Educational Opportunity," *Harvard Educational Review* 38 (Winter, 1968): 11.

Prior to *Brown*, the community and educational institutions were expected only to provide equal resources—teachers, facilities, materials—and responsibility for advantageous use of those resources lay with the child and his or her family. Today many people have come to consider it the responsibility of the educational institution, not the child, to create achievement. As James Coleman states:

> The difference in achievement at grade 12 between the average Negro and the average white is, in effect, the degree of inequality of opportunity, and the reduction of the inequality is a responsibility of the school. This shift in responsibility follows logically from the change in the concept of equality of educational opportunity from school resource inputs to effects of schooling.[22]

Others do not accept Coleman's assertion, arguing that the school should do its best to provide equal educational resources to all its students, but that it cannot be held accountable for differences in student learning. Although it is agreed that many poor minority children are not learning at a rate comparable to white middle-class children in our schools, opinions vary considerably as to the locus and the cause of the problem. At one extreme are those who think that the problem resides in the deficiencies of minority children. Their impoverished home life, their limited cultural milieu, or even mental capacities are cited as the sources of unequal results in school. At the other extreme are those who claim that the problem is in the schools, which neither stimulate nor instruct the child with the intensity that is needed. Teachers expect minority children to do poorly, and this becomes a self-fulfilling prophecy. This position assumes it is the school's obligation to diagnose the learner's needs, concerns, and cognitive and affective style, and to adjust its program accordingly. As with most issues, the answer probably lies somewhere in between—the students do have certain deficiencies, but the school needs to learn how to overcome them.

It is undeniable that the achievement of white middle-class children and poor lower-class minority children is unequal—the important question is how the achievement of poor and minority-group children can be improved. As you are probably already aware, solutions to this problem are proposed from many quarters, and considerable friction exists between groups who advocate different approaches. Three widely advocated approaches to the reform of public education are compensatory education, desegregation and integration, and magnet school programs.

COMPENSATORY EDUCATION   Compensatory education is an attempt to overcome deficiencies in the learner by grafting extra education onto the regular school program, or to avert potential learning problems through

---

[22]Coleman, "Concept of Equality," p. 22.

preschool programs such as Project Head Start. Programs such as the Ford Foundation–supported Great Cities School Improvement Programs, Chapter I of the Elementary and Secondary Education Act, New York City's early Higher Horizons Program, and the More Effective Schools Program were aimed at remedying specific learner defects, such as verbal retardation, lack of motivation, and experiential and sensory deprivation, which prevent the student from participating effectively in the learning process.

A tremendous amount of money and energy has been spent in the attempt to develop special programs to improve the academic achievement of poor children. Chapter I of the ESEA, for example, spent more than $2.4 billion in 1976.[23] This amount constituted approximately 4 percent of total national expenditures for public elementary and secondary education; of the public school children enrolled in kindergarten through eighth grade, 19.5 percent were compensatory education students; of the nation's school districts, 90 percent received Chapter I funds.[24] Thus, although compensatory education involves most of the nation's public school districts and many of its students and teachers, it constitutes only a small percentage of national expenditures for education.

Unfortunately, evidence indicates that little headway has been made in most of the programs. Studies that indicate that gains have been made in some programs are often contradicted by other studies. At this time there is little evidence to suggest that the roughly $2 billion per year invested in Chapter I has had much effect on significantly increasing the basic skills of poor and minority children. The parents of children enrolled in these compensatory programs, whose expectations were initially very high, have become increasingly dissatisfied with their results.

Some observers of compensatory education programs criticize them for simply offering massive doses of methods that have not worked previously. They see little point in strengthening programs that have failed in the past. Proponents of this approach argue that, considering the enormity of the problem, expenditures thus far are a mere drop in the bucket. They also argue that a simultaneous attack must be made on external factors that contribute to low achievement, such as poor housing, family instability, and low income. Because of its equivocal results, in the 1980s the compensatory education route to achieve equal educational opportunity is not nearly so popular among educators, parents, and politicians as it was in the 1960s and early 1970s.

DESEGREGATION AND INTEGRATION   In *Brown* v. *Board of Education*, the Supreme Court ruled that laws that require white and nonwhite students

---

[23]National Institute of Education, *Evaluating Compensatory Education, An Interim Report on the NIE Compensatory Education Study* (Washington, D.C., 1976).

[24]National Institute of Education, *Evaluating Compensatory Education.*

to go to different schools were illegal. The Court concluded that de jure school segregation, or segregation by law, violated the Fourteenth Amendment of the Constitution. Early desegregation efforts were aimed at eliminating de jure segregation.

Throughout the 1960s and into the 1970s, some school systems attempted to reduce or eliminate their de facto school segregation, that is, segregation resulting primarily from residential patterns. In many cases de facto desegregation efforts have been court ordered because the courts have ruled that racially segregated schools in numerous northern and western cities were purposely created over a long period by the official acts of local school boards and state governments. Thus the courts have concluded that what appeared to be de facto segregation in numerous cases is in fact a form of illegal de jure school segregation. As a result of these court orders, many school districts in the North and West have undergone desegregation efforts.

What have been the results of these desegregation efforts? In 1976 the U.S. Commission on Civil Rights issued a report[25] that evaluated school desegregation in a variety of school districts throughout the country. Among the report's findings are the following:

1. In 82 percent of the school districts examined, students desegregated peacefully without any serious disruptions.

2. Mandatory busing plans have worked in many areas where voluntary plans have failed. There has been only a minor increase in busing as a result of desegregation. Whereas slightly more than 50 percent of the nation's students ride buses to school, less than 7 percent of these riders are bused for desegregation purposes. Only 3.6 percent of public school students are bused for desegregation purposes.

3. Desegregation works best where volunteer community groups have organized to help implement the plans.

4. Resistance and disruption occur when local officials refuse to cooperate.

5. Desegregation works even where some citizens and leaders try to prevent its progress.

6. Desegregation has produced more positive attitudes toward schools and little change in the quality of education.[26]

Although the report of the U.S. Commission on Civil Rights is quite positive, there are some negative results of the desegregation efforts. One

[25]U.S. Commission on Civil Rights, *Fulfilling the Letter and Spirit of the Law: Desegregation of the Nation's Public Schools* (Washington, D.C., 1976).

[26]"Desegregation and Equality—Much Remains to Be Done," *Today's Education* 66 (January–February 1977): 24.

of the major problems concerns busing. Busing students to integrate schools is one of the most controversial and inflammatory issues in education today. Emotions on the topic run very high—so high, in fact, that white parents have slashed bus tires, burned buses, and physically prevented buses from running in order to avoid having their children bused to other schools.

The federal court system has been the prime mover in ordering school districts to employ busing in the desegregation process. The United States Supreme Court, in *Swan* v. *Charlotte-Mecklenburg* (1971), for example, found that the school authorities had an obligation to prepare students for a pluralistic world by having a ratio of black and white students in each school reflecting the ratio for the district as a whole. The Court concluded that the need to hasten desegregation was great, and busing was deemed an appropriate measure, provided that the distance of travel was not so great as to either risk the health of the children or impinge significantly on the educational process.

Busing to achieve desegregation has had mixed success. One of the most successful busing plans was that initiated in Berkeley, California, in 1968. Berkeley desegregated its elementary schools by two-way, cross-town busing. A later survey found that the whites did not leave the community, that there was no high teacher turnover rate, and that the SAT reading scores indicated that white, black, and Asian students all made better progress after desegregation.[27] On the other hand, in many other communities attempts to desegregate the schools by busing have met with tremendous community resistance. In fall 1974, in Boston, for example, violence occurred when school opened. Black students who were bused into white neighborhood schools faced jeering mobs. Crowds of angry white parents fought with police while attempting to block the buses carrying black students. Fighting erupted between black and white students inside some schools. Stabbings occurred. In addition, many white students assigned to be bused to schools in minority neighborhoods were kept out of school altogether by their parents. Now, approximately ten years later, the Boston public schools are much quieter. But although the schools are better integrated, the number of students in the schools is down dramatically. There has been a great exodus among white students whose parents have chosen to move to the suburbs or place their children in private schools. James Coleman, whose report we cited earlier and who, in 1966, was responsible for much of the public interest in the question of school integration, reported twelve years later that busing was a major cause for much of the white flight from our cities that has characterized the recent past.

A major obstacle to desegregating big-city schools is the fact that the minority population has increased dramatically as more and more white families move to the suburbs. With this population shift, the number of minority students in big-city school systems has also increased. Today, cities such as New York, Baltimore, Chicago, and Detroit have school minority enrollments of 70 percent or more. How can the schools in these cities be desegregated when there are so many minority and so few white students?

One solution is to take the emerging residential segregation as given— minority cities and white suburbs—and to attempt to overcome its effects on school segregation by metropolitan area-wide school desegregation. This

---

[27]Howard Ozmon and Sam Craver, *Busing: A Moral Issue* (Bloomington, Ind.: Phi Delta Kappa Educational Foundation, 1972), pp. 33–34.

approach would use the strategy of busing children to bring about racial balance over the metropolitan area. When this solution was attempted in the Detroit area, the Supreme Court, in a 5–4 verdict, rejected the plan. The Court seemed to say that the metro solution would be acceptable if acts by state officials leading to big-city school segregation could be proved. Since this was not proved in the Detroit instance, the suburban school districts could not be forced to integrate with the Detroit city school system. In the case of Wilmington, Delaware, however, the metro solution was upheld by the Supreme Court.

Another solution is to try to stop the white "flight" to the suburbs by making the inner-city schools so attractive and of such high quality that white parents would want their children to attend them. The magnet school programs (discussed in the next section) are examples of this attempt.

Busing, of course, is not the real issue. Busing is only one means of integrating society. Polls indicate that even those who are opposed to busing agree that our society needs to be integrated. The real problem is that existing housing patterns function to segregate our society and our schools. As long as existing housing patterns continue, desegregation of the schools will continue to be problematic.

There is another point that needs to be made: desegregation does not necessarily lead to integration. True integration is a very human process that can occur only after desegregation has gone into effect. It happens when people from different racial and ethnic backgrounds learn to be comfortable with one another and to get along together. It means ending racial prejudice and respecting ethnic differences. Anyone who has spent time in racially mixed schools, especially high schools, knows that black and white students who attend the same school can still be extremely distant from one another. Blacks may sit in one part of the cafeteria, whites in another. In many social situations, such as assemblies and athletic events, the same

DIALOGUE

KEVIN: I think you and I are like a lot of folks who want an integrated society but have been asked to "do it" with one tool, the schools.

JIM: Not only that, but the general solution, busing, has aroused such opposition that it has become a major factor in the erosion of support for education.

KEVIN: It seems highly unlikely to me that our goal, an integrated society, is likely to be achieved by focusing primarily on the schools.

JIM: The basic problem will not be solved by focusing on results of segregated residential patterns rather than on the residential patterns themselves. I really think that unless we integrate our neighborhoods we will not achieve an integrated society.

SOCIAL ISSUES AND THE CURRENT SCENE

scene often unfolds. There is no evidence that bringing together students from different racial groups, social classes, and neighborhood backgrounds will automatically lead to friendship, understanding, and appreciation for one another. Until our society becomes integrated, attempts to integrate our schools are likely to continue to produce tension. Whether the schools can be used successfully to help our society become integrated remains to be seen.

MAGNET SCHOOL PROGRAMS   One alternative to forced busing that has become popular in large school districts is the development of magnet school programs. Magnet schools are alternative schools that provide high-quality instruction in specified areas as well as in the basic skills. They are designed to attract (like a magnet) students of all racial and ethnic groups from all areas of the school district; thus they offer quality education in integrated classrooms.

Magnet school programs have been established with considerable success in such large cities as Houston, Boston, and Dallas. In Houston, for example, forty-six alternative educational programs, representing pre-kindergarten through twelfth grades, were in operation from 1975 to 1977. Total enrollment in the magnet schools was over 12,000 students. The ethnic makeup of this enrollment was 38.2 percent black, 28.4 percent Mexican-American, and 33.3 percent others. The program, along with other district efforts, reduced the number and percentage of ethnically isolated schools in the Houston Independent School District. In 1974–1975, there were 121 racially isolated schools, representing 52.8 percent of the total schools in the district. By 1977–1978, the number and percentage had been reduced to 98 and 41.7 percent, respectively.[28]

At the elementary school level, programs in Houston include a bilingual, multicultural school; a science careers academy; math and science academies; music academies; a literature and art academy; a fine arts academy; and ecology and outdoor education programs. At the junior high level there are three vanguard programs for gifted and talented students, as well as a contemporary learning center and a fine arts academy. Senior high magnet programs specialize in such areas as engineering professions; petrochemical careers; aerodynamics; foreign languages; contemporary or alternative learning; emphasis on fundamental or basic skills; and liberal arts, with special emphasis on preparation for college.

Evaluation reports on Boston's magnet school program indicate that the magnetic options are more effective if they aggressively attempt to integrate students by increasing appreciation of the rights of individuals and

[28]Claude H. Cunningham, "An Evaluation of Houston's Magnet School Program," paper presented to the Annual Meeting of the American Educational Research Association, Toronto, Canada, 1978, pp. 5, 19.

groups, by breaking down stereotypes, and by teaching respect for differences and similarities among racial and ethnic groups. The programs where this was accomplished best were those that "1) grouped students to accomplish tasks requiring interdependence, cooperation, group achievement, and decision making and 2) used curriculum materials that were sensitive to and made use of the multicultural experiences of the students."[29]

Magnet schools are likely to continue and flourish in the 1980s. Big-city school districts may even attract students from outlying suburban dis-

[29]Charles B. McMillan, "Magnet Education in Boston," *Phi Delta Kappan* 59 (November 1977): 162.

MARIA MONTESSORI
(1870–1952)

Maria Montessori became a proponent of preschool education, an urban educational reformer, and a believer in equal opportunities for women sixty years before any of these issues were matters of widespread concern.

As a child, Maria Montessori excelled in mathematics and thought of becoming an engineer. Later she developed an interest in medicine, and she overcame tremendous criticism to become the first woman to enroll in the University of Rome's medical school. After graduating, she lectured on anthropology at the university and became associated with the psychiatric clinic. She developed an interest in retarded children and, suspecting that they were far more capable of learning than was commonly believed, founded and headed the Orthophrenic School,

where she achieved remarkable results with mentally deficient children.

But it was not until she was thirty-six years old that Montessori found her life work. Believing her methods could be even more effective with normal children, she opened her first school, the Casa del Bambini (Children's House), to the preschool-age street urchins of Rome. Montessori's school was run on the principle of allowing children freedom within a carefully designed environment and under the sensitive guidance of a trained director. The materials and toys available in the school were prescribed, but the children were allowed freedom to handle or ignore them as they wished. Self-learning and individualization were stressed, but there were definite limits on freedom: students were required to come to school clean, and

even their free play was structured. However, a child was never forced either to play or to learn. The teachers were instructed simply to wait until the child became interested in a particular game or project. A child who was concentrating deeply on a ritual with a toy was not aided or corrected by a teacher unless she or he asked for help.

Montessori discovered that certain simple and precise educational materials evoked sustained interest and attention in the young child. Children under five years old would concentrate on a single task, oblivious to distraction, for periods of from fifteen minutes to an hour, and afterward seem refreshed rather than tired. Montessori's close observations of children led her to conclude that, from birth to age six, all children possess "ab-

tricts by their quality magnet schools. As gasoline and energy shortages become realities, many suburban residents would like to relocate inside city limits to reduce commuting and take advantage of the cities' cultural events. If city schools can be made more attractive by plans such as the magnet school programs, voluntary integration may occur. In the long run, voluntary integration is the only kind likely to succeed.

Sexism and Sex-Role Stereotyping

In the preceding section of this chapter, we made the point that racial and ethnic groups have been denied equal educational opportunities throughout our country's history. There is another social group that has suffered discrimination and denial of educational opportunities: women. Many women

sorbent minds," which equip them to learn more quickly and easily than at any subsequent period in their lives. Throughout these years, she found, children experience periods of specialized sensitivity, during which their interest and mental capacity are particularly suited to the acquisition of particular knowledge, such as colors, language, and textures. Montessori recognized that small children learn through their senses, and she developed methods of stimulating the child's senses in ways that would enhance learning. For instance, children were taught the alphabet with sandpaper letters that they could manipulate with their fingers. Montessori was the first to use flashcards as a sensory stimulus, and she even introduced the hula hoop, which became a fad in the United States in the

fifties. She was severely criticized for ignoring discipline; she replied that, in the conventional schools she had visited, children were "not disciplined, but annihilated."

Montessori's teaching methods have aroused considerable interest in the United States as a result of recent psychological research verifying many of her theories. Psychologists and educators have come to agree with her that the period of early childhood is critical in determining a person's intellectual potential.

Before her death, Montessori traveled widely, establishing schools, teaching teachers, and promoting her still-unconventional ideas. A typical Montessori classroom today is a beehive of activity, each child pursuing an independent task at his or her own speed. A two-and-a-half-year-old carries a tray holding a jug of water and two glasses across the room. On reaching the other side he be-

gins to fill the glasses with dry grains of rice. He is joined by a little girl who sweeps the spilled rice into a pile. A third child appears with a brush and dustpan to collect the deposit. A group of children is busy using colored pencils to shade designs they have made themselves with geometric forms cut out of metal. The teacher dictates words to some boys, who compose them on a mat with large movable letters.

New Montessori schools have recently sprung up in this country in response to parents' demands. Teachers of underprivileged or minority children, in particular, claim great success with Montessori techniques. The day care center movement, day care programs, and the early childhood movement, in general, have been significantly influenced by her views.

assert, and rightfully so, that societal values and mores have discriminated against them as a class and have significantly limited the development of their human potential. There is strong evidence indeed to support the contention that women in our society have been denied educational and employment opportunities that have been extended to men.

A major part of this issue is that women and men have very different socialization in our society. Constantina Safilios-Rothschild, who has reviewed studies of parents' socialization of boys and girls, has written the following:

> Mothers maintain physically close and affectionate relationships with girls for a longer period of time. Mothers expect girls to be more dependent and give them more physical attention. On the other hand, boys are given more independence training, more punishment and are encouraged more in intellectual curiosity. Mothers place a greater degree of pressure for achievement and punish dependency more in boys than in girls of pre-school age. In addition, boys' aggression is rewarded as appropriate masculine behavior while girls' aggression is never rewarded, though indirect expressions are tolerated. Mothers place pressures on girls for "feminine" neatness, obedience and conformity, while pressure on boys is for independence and achievement.[30]

This situation is not confined to the home, however. Many of us were educated in classrooms where teachers, as a matter of course, pitted the boys against the girls in spelling bees and other academic contests. These same teachers would frown at a girl who was seriously interested in competing in sports such as basketball or hockey. Deeper frowns still would be reserved for the young man who took home economics. Although preparing children for the major roles associated with their gender is natural and important for a society, some teachers carry this to an extreme, imposing rigid and stereotypic roles on the children. Carried to such an extreme, this is called *sexism.* Sexism has been defined as "all attitudes and actions which relegate women to a secondary or inferior status in society."[31]

Feminist researchers have leveled the charge that the schools are primary institutions where sexism abounds and is even taught informally in the curriculum. They argue that along with the home environment, the schools are where girls learn that a certain set of interests and behaviors are expected of them and that very little deviance is encouraged or even tolerated. Similarly, boys learn what interests and behaviors are expected of both them and the girls. It is the active encouragement in schools of such

---

[30]Advisory Committee on the Rights and Responsibilities of Women, *The Vocational Preparation of Women* (Washington, D.C.: U.S. Department of Health, Education and Welfare, 1975), p. 34.

[31]*Guidelines for Improving the Image of Women in Textbooks* (Glenview, Ill.: Scott, Foresman, 1972).

sex-role stereotyping that feminists find so objectionable. Although sex-role stereotyping is damaging to both sexes, it is particularly so for females since the occupational roles assigned to them are less prestigious than those assigned to males (e.g., nurse instead of doctor, secretary instead of lawyer).

How do schools contribute to and perpetuate sex-role stereotyping? Certainly one way is through the textbooks and other reading materials that are used in instruction. One study, conducted by a group called the Women on Words and Images, examined 134 books used in New Jersey schools.[32] The books represented eighteen major textbook companies. Boys and men are present in the books overwhelmingly more often than girls and women, with a 6-to-1 discrepancy between male and female biographies. Women appear in 25 different occupations, men in 147. The men's jobs represent a wide range of possibilities, whereas the women's are limited to traditionally female pursuits such as telephone operator, secretary, nurse, and teacher. A content analysis of the ''active mastery'' stories, in which the main character exhibited cleverness, problem-solving ability, bravery, acquisition of skills, and adventurousness, indicated males were portrayed four times as often as females. In contrast, girls were more often portrayed as passive and dependent, restricting their goals, practicing domesticity, being incompetent, and being victimized or humiliated by the opposite sex. Other similar studies tend to support these findings.

Feminists are concerned not only with how the curricular materials transmit sex-role stereotypes but also with the fact that many teachers and counselors do the same thing in their interactions with students. For example, female high school students are often advised that certain professions are ''appropriate'' for men, whereas others are ''appropriate'' for women. One study discovered that, in fact, counselors respond more positively to female clients who hold traditionally feminine career goals than to those who wish to prepare for professions usually reserved for men.[33] One woman reports, ''Women have frequently told me that their high school counselors had advised them to become legal secretaries when they wanted to become lawyers, nurses when they wanted to become doctors.''[34]

In 1972 Congress passed Title IX of the Education Amendments Act, which states, ''No person in the United States shall, on the basis of sex, be excluded from participation in, be denied the benefits of, or be subjected to discrimination under any education program or activity receiving Federal financial assistance.'' A great deal of confusion arose over which circumstances Title IX applied to and which ones it did not. Although the fine

[32]Betty Levy and Judith Stacey, ''Sexism in the Elementary School: A Backward and Forward Look,'' *Phi Delta Kappan* 55 (October 1973): 106.

[33]Nancy Frazier and Myra Sadker, *Sexism in School and Society* (New York: Harper & Row, 1973), p. 138.

[34]Frazier and Sadker, *Sexism in School and Society*, p. 138.

print required interpretation, the large print was at least clear: sex discrimination in educational programs receiving federal financing is against the law.

In 1975 the regulations regarding Title IX became effective. Title IX forbids sex discrimination in any educational institution receiving federal financial assistance—that is, sixteen thousand public school systems and nearly twenty-seven hundred postsecondary institutions. The law bans sex discrimination in physical education, athletics, financial aid, pension benefits, employment and compensation of staff, facilities, and counseling. In addition, Title IX regulations require that equal opportunity be provided in areas in physical education and athletics such as facilities, game and practice schedules, coaching, travel and per diem allowances, equipment, and supplies. Separate teams are permissible in contact sports, such as boxing, football, and ice hockey. Whenever a school has a team in a given non-contact sport for one sex only, and athletic opportunities for the other sex have been limited, members of the other sex must be allowed to try out for the team. Title IX regulations are greatly helping to correct inequities resulting from sex discrimination.

The following letter was written by an elementary school girl and appeared in a book called *Children's Letters to God.* Eric Marshall and Stuart Hample, comp. (New York: Simon and Schuster [Pocket Books], 1966). Reprinted by permission of The Sterling Lord Agency, Inc. Copyright © 1966 by Eric Marshall and Stuart Hample.

Do you think this little girl has been the victim of sexist practices or attitudes?

Dear god,
Are boys better than girls? I know you are one but please try to be fair.
Love
Silvia

The elimination of sexism and sex-role stereotyping in schools will be a complex procedure that will require the cooperation of teachers, administrators, school boards, counselors, educational publishers, and parents. Your role as a teacher will be especially important. As you interact with your pupils and as you select and use instructional materials, your sensitivity to this problem will help determine the attitudes of our future generations. It is to be hoped that educators will lead in efforts to evaluate school policies, curricula, and practices with regard to sex bias and will eliminate sex discrimination (along with racial and ethnic discrimination) in our schools. Why, for example, are the majority of teachers women and the large majority of principals and superintendents men? Remember, as in all these issues, if you're not part of the solution, you're part of the problem.

School Violence and Vandalism

Public attention in recent years has been drawn to the issue of crime and violence in schools. Parents, teachers, administrators, and politicians have all expressed concern. How serious a problem is school violence and crime? Where is it most likely to occur? What are the damage costs to repair school vandalism? How can school crime be prevented? The National Institute of Education (NIE) was charged by Congress to conduct a study to answer these questions. The findings are shocking. Consider the following facts from that report:[35]

- Although teenage youth may spend at most 25 percent of their waking hours in school, in the school districts surveyed 40 percent of the robberies and 36 percent of the assaults on urban teenagers occurred in schools. The risks are especially high for youths aged twelve to fifteen: a remarkable 68 percent of the assaults on youngsters of this age occurred at school.

- Eight percent of all schools surveyed indicated that vandalism, personal attacks, and thefts were serious problems. This figure represents approximately 6,700 schools in the nation.

- Although cities have the largest proportions of seriously affected schools, suburbs and rural areas have the largest numbers of such schools.

- During an average month, 282,000 secondary students are attacked and 112,000 are robbed, and 5,200 teachers are attacked and 6,000 are robbed.

- Estimates for the yearly replacement and repair costs due to school crime are around $200 million.

The study indicates that one of the most dangerous places for teenagers to be is in school, since they run a greater risk of personal violence

[35]The statistics reported in this section are from National Institute of Education, *Violent Schools—Safe Schools, The Safe School Study Report to the Congress,* Executive Summary (Washington, D.C., 1978).

in schools than on the street. It is comforting, at least, that classrooms are the safest spot in schools. The places with the greatest risks are the hallways and stairs during the between-class rush. Other risky areas are restrooms, cafeterias, locker rooms, and gyms.

Those committing violent acts are not dropouts hanging around the school but students who are supposed to be there. In fact, most victims recognize their attackers. The risks of violence are greater in schools whose student compositions are less than 40 percent white. However, there is no relation between a school's racial and ethnic composition and the risks of violence there, once factors such as the amount of crime in the neighborhood are taken into account. The majority of attacks on and robberies of students at school involve victims and offenders of the same race. However, a substantial proportion is interracial (42 percent of the attacks and 46 percent of the robberies).

While hardly confined to big-city schools, violence and vandalism are more pronounced in large urban centers. The severe violence is often associated with urban gangs. In 1976, Marvin reported that vandalism is related to the size of the school district. Looking at the amounts of money

If you heap upon the school all of the problems that the family, the church, the political system, and the economy cannot solve, the school becomes a kind of well-financed garbage dump, from which very little can be expected except the unsweet odor of failure.

— NEIL POSTMAN —

spent to repair the effects of vandalism, Marvin found that small school districts (10,000 students or less) paid slightly over $1.50 per pupil, medium-sized districts (25,000 to 10,000 students) paid $3.18, and the large school districts had a per-pupil cost fully three times that of small districts.[36]

Speaking about the problem of violence and vandalism in the urban schools, Manford Byrd, an experienced Chicago school administrator, stated the problem in the following way:

> The losses . . . cannot be measured in terms of dollars. No one has measured the immediate and long term effects on the education of children resulting from the climate of fear generated by the conditions. Many hours of education are lost because of false alarms and bomb threats. Much harm is done to educational programs when classroom windows are shattered, teaching materials destroyed or stolen, and schools damaged by fire and other acts of vandalism. When students and teachers are fearful of going to school . . . a healthy environment for learning is lost.[37]

Some of the other factors associated with school violence are impersonality and alienation, incentive structures, and school governance. Larger schools, and schools with larger classes, tend to experience more violence and vandalism. When teachers and administrators can establish personal relationships with students, thus reducing feelings of impersonality, the risks of violence decrease.

Academic competition seems inversely related to a school's risk of violence and positively correlated to the amount of vandalism. Competition for leadership positions also seems to increase the amount of vandalism. Although these findings may seem contradictory, they actually are not. The violent students are more likely to be those who have given up on school, don't care about grades, find the courses irrelevant, and feel that nothing they do makes any difference. These students are apt to take out their aggression in acts of violence against other students and teachers. Caring about grades can be an important step toward commitment to the school and to one's own future, bringing with it a reduction in personal violence. Vandalism, on the other hand, is more likely to occur when students feel that grades have been given unfairly or as a disciplinary procedure. Students who engage in vandalism tend to accept the school's values but feel they are losing out or are being cheated out of the competition for rewards. They therefore take out their aggression against the school rather than other students.

[36]M. Marvin et al., *Planning Assistance Programs to Reduce School Violence and Disruption* (Washington, D.C.: U.S. Department of Justice National Institute for Juvenile Justice and Delinquency Prevention, 1976), pp. 215–217.

[37]U.S. Senate Subcommittee to Investigate Juvenile Delinquency, *Challenge for the Third Century: Education in a Safe Environment—Final Report on the Prevention of School Violence and Vandalism* (Washington, D.C.: U.S. Government Printing Office, 1977), p. 17.

A firm, fair, and consistent system for running the school seems to be a critical factor in reducing violence. The rules need to be known, and firmly and fairly enforced. Good coordination between faculty and administration also promotes a better school atmosphere. If teachers have hostile and authoritarian attitudes toward students, more vandalism can result.

A major conclusion of the NIE study was that strong and effective school governance, particularly by the principal, can help greatly in reducing school crime and misbehavior. The principal must be visible and available to students and staff. Of equal importance to the principal's personal style of leadership is the ability to initiate a structure of order in the school. Schools also need to assure a structure of incentives, such as grades and honors, that recognize students for their efforts and achievements.

Security measures were also found to be helpful in reducing violence and property loss in schools, provided they are not used as a substitute for effective governance. School systems with serious problems were found to benefit from hiring additional security personnel with training in interpersonal skills as well as security functions.

NEW TEACHER POLL DOCUMENTS ASSAULTS

Violence continues to plague the nation's public schools, according to the results of the latest Teacher Opinion Poll conducted by the Washington-based National Education Association (NEA).

The survey found that 113,000 public school teachers were physically attacked by students during a recent 12-month period. Of those attacked, 2,500 were seriously injured, NEA said. Another 45,000 suffered emotionally as a result of the attacks.

Although the assaults occurred more often in large urban districts, NEA added, "significant numbers of teachers were also attacked in suburban, small-town, and rural areas."

Another finding of special interest: A majority of teachers believe their school's disciplinary policy is not strict enough.

The survey also revealed that:

- Teachers think 60% of the attacks were intentional.

- Eighty-five percent of those assaulted reported the incident to school officials, but only 15% reported the attack to law enforcement officials.

- In 90% of the cases, neither school personnel nor police filed charges.

- Of those who did not report the incident to anyone,

many said that they feared being seen as a failure.

- In 25% of the cases, no one took disciplinary action against the students, even though the teachers involved thought someone should have. In another 25% of the cases, teachers thought the action taken was insufficient.

NEA said a nationwide sample of public school teachers participated in the survey, which was completed in May 1980.

George Neill, "New Teacher Poll Documents Assaults," *Phi Delta Kappan* (December 1980): 238. Reprinted by permission.

The encouraging news is that although school violence and vandalism are bad, they still affect a relatively small percentage of teachers and students in the public schools, and they do not seem to have worsened since the early 1970s. The problem is probably as much a reflection on societal malaise as on the schools. Boredom, frustration, alienation, despair, and low self-concept are characteristics that teenagers may experience in their homes and society in general, as well as in schools. With high crime and vandalism rates prevalent in society, why should we expect anything different in our schools?

Teachers and administrators need not be helpless in dealing with this problem. In addition to those actions already cited, other steps can be taken. Intensive training in classroom management can increase a teacher's skills and effectiveness in preventing and handling violence. Communities and school districts can reduce violence in those schools that have serious problems with crime and disruption by increasing the number of teachers in the schools. One pilot program designed to reduce school crime discovered the following approaches to be successful: the use of peer counseling; the development of alternative programs for disruptive students; conferences among school officials, parents, and probation officers; increased student decision making in policy areas such as finding methods to handle offenders; and training school faculty and students in problem solving and communications.

Be aware that the problem does exist and that it may affect you personally, and work as hard as you can to alleviate the factors that contribute to its existence.

Declining Student Performance

Americans have always placed a high value on education. We have championed universal education and built a vast network of elementary and secondary schools and community colleges and universities. Our per capita public expenditure for education is more than twice as high as in Europe or the Soviet Union, and ten times as high as in Latin America. Also, we send more of our children to school for longer periods of time than any other nation does.[38] As a people, we believe in the power of an education. In recent years, however, the public's faith in public education has begun to erode. Across the country, local communities are turning down bond issues and other methods of taxation for financing schools. In a recent Gallup poll, the public was asked to grade the public schools: only 8 percent gave the schools an A.[39] Since the mid-sixties newspapers have been an-

[38]R. Bjork and S. Fraser, *Population, Education, and Children's Futures* (Bloomington, Ind.: Phi Delta Kappa, 1980), p. 32.

[39]George Gallup, "The 14th Annual Gallup Poll of the Public's Attitudes Toward the Public Schools," *Phi Delta Kappan* 64, no. 1 (September 1982): 39. In addition to the 8 percent giving the schools an A, 29 percent gave them a B, 33 percent a C, and 14 percent D, and 5 percent an F. Eleven percent responded, "Don't know."

nouncing regular drops in the scores of high school students' achievement tests, such as the Scholastic Aptitude Test (SAT) and the American College Testing (ACT). The public seems to be saying to their local schools, "Why should we put more money into public education if we are so dissatisfied with your performance?"

Until 1982, when there was a slight stabilizing of the scores, SAT scores fell steadily for twenty years. The average verbal ability fell by 10 percent, and average mathematics skills declined by 6 percent. Even the scores of high achievers declined. And it is true that many high school graduates are unable to read at elementary school levels. Some high school graduates can't read the instructions on a fire extinguisher or understand the printing on credit agreements. In one disastrous example, a navy engineman was rebuilding a diesel engine as part of a routine maintenance schedule. He could not read well, so he went about the process by looking at the pictures in a technical manual. When he tried to install the cylinder liners, there was no picture, so he installed them the way he thought they should be. The result was that he installed them upside down. It cost $250,000 to repair the engine.

Many reasons have been given to explain the illiteracy and the declining test scores. Since the high school dropout rate has declined to about 25 percent, down from 31 percent in 1960 and 37 percent in 1950, one explanation is that poorer students are remaining in school.[40] Some people blame the problem on the amount of television that children watch. Because so many hours a day are spent in watching television, the hypothesis goes, children have less time for reading and therefore are reading less and learning less academic material. Another explanation is that the vaunted educational innovations of the 1960s and early 1970s—open classrooms, flexible scheduling, elective courses, minicourses, individualized learning, and the like—detract from an emphasis on basic skills. Still another explanation is that schools demand less and less hard work from students. Books are less intellectually challenging and more student centered. Students are assigned less homework and, consequently, do less out-of-school studying. Regardless of the explanation that you choose to accept, the decline in quality of education has led to three controversial movements in education: the back-to-basics, competency testing, and accountability movements.

BACK-TO-BASICS MOVEMENT   The back-to-basics movement is difficult to describe. To the degree that it has spokespersons, they are among both the very best educated and the least educated people in the country. Although what they are striving to achieve is not always clear, their disenchantment with today's public schools and their desire to return to a more rigorous, more traditional curriculum is evident and often stated quite sharply.

[40]"High Schools Under Fire," *Time,* November 14, 1977, p. 62.

Proponents urge more emphasis on basic subjects, particularly reading, writing, and arithmetic, but also science, history, geography, and grammar. Rather than having schools provide more electives for students to choose from, back-to-basics supporters want students to take more traditional academic courses, such as history and foreign languages, and more courses with rigorous demands and standards. They want the schools not only to teach content, but also to help children acquire the capacity to engage in hard work. They believe that in order to have a society made up of strong individuals, our schools must turn out individuals able to take on difficult tasks which they can see through to completion. Back-to-basics proponents see the schools as catering to the students' desire for entertainment and escapism. They also would like the schools to demand more orderly and disciplined student behavior. They want the authority and centrality of the teacher to be reasserted, and desire a more structured teaching style. As we saw in Chapter 10, direct instructional approaches are effective in producing academic engaged time, which in turn is related to higher reading and mathematics scores in the elementary grades. Finally, back-to-basics advocates frequently want the schools to return to the teaching of basic morality and, in particular, the virtue of patriotism.[41]

In 1983, the back-to-basics movement received important support with the publication and wide dissemination of *A Nation at Risk: The Imperative for Educational Reform.*[42] Written by the National Commission on Excellence in Education, a blue-ribbon presidential committee, the report sharply criticizes our educational system and its recent performance. The report states, "We have been committing an act of unthinking, unilateral educational disarmament." It goes on to outline how the well-being of the nation and its citizens has been weakened by our current school practices, and it assails the relaxed school curricula and the deterioration of student preparedness and teacher preparation. It urges more and stiffer required courses for high school graduation, more homework, a longer school day (from six hours to seven hours), a school year extended from the current 180 days to 200–220 days, and increased salaries for teachers. The essence of the message, though, is for the schools to adopt a more rigorous and fundamental way of operation, an idea that has been welcomed by many back-to-basics advocates.

Many educators have reacted negatively to what they charge are the pressure tactics and hostile language of some back-to-basics spokespersons. They also distrust the deep strain of nostalgia and the desire to return to a simpler society that characterize the back-to-basics advocates. However, behind much of the emotion and rhetoric of the back-to-basics movement

[41]Other dimensions of the back-to-basics movement are discussed in Chapter 7.
[42]The National Commission on Educational Excellence, *A Nation At Risk: The Imperative for Educational Reform* (Washington, D.C.: U.S. Department of Education, 1983).

are ideas and aspirations that most educators believe in, too. For years, the schools have been expected to add more and more subjects to the curriculum. Each time a social priority or societal ill has surfaced, the schools have been expected to add a new subject to the curriculum and, thus, solve the problem. Many people inside and outside the schools believe that the schools have attempted to be ''all things to all people'' and that it shows. If nothing else, then, the back-to-basics movement will refocus the public and educators on the primary mission of the schools—to help children develop the necessary skills to live good lives and contribute to the well-being of society.

COMPETENCY TESTING MOVEMENT   This movement was generated by a public belief that the schools have certified incompetents as competent by passing them from grade to grade, graduating them, and giving them diplomas. The demand that students be required to pass certain minimum-level competency tests before being graduated has come from disappointed employers, parents, students, and legislators. In fact, as of 1983, thirty-eight states had taken some type of action to mandate the setting of minimum competency standards for elementary and secondary students. All the remaining states either have legislation pending or legislative or state board of education studies under way. It is clear that the minimum competency testing movement is being led, or pushed, by noneducators. The speed with which the movement has spread is both startling and unparalleled in American education. What started as an interesting idea in several states in 1975 had become law in thirty-eight states by 1983.

A number of basic questions must be answered within each state. First, what competencies should be measured? Should the competency areas be limited to the basic skills, or should they include school subjects like

© King Features.

SOCIAL ISSUES AND THE CURRENT SCENE

biology, Spanish, and history? Second, how are the competencies to be measured? Will the tests be limited to paper-and-pencil measures, or will on-the-job performances and school products such as paintings, experiments, and speeches be permitted? Still another issue is when to measure. Should students be tested during the year or at the end? Yet another question is what the minimum level should be and whether it will be the same for all students. If the same level is expected of all students, is a statewide testing program implied? And, finally, what should the schools do with students who fail the competency tests? Give them several more chances? Refuse to promote and graduate them until they do pass? Few of these questions have been answered at this point.

Educators are divided regarding the wisdom of minimum competency testing. Some, like Robert L. Ebel, former president of the American Educational Research Association, believe that the movement will do much to restore concern for cognitive development as the first mission of the school, thus motivating teachers to teach more purposefully and students to work harder.[43] Other educators believe minimum competency testing will lead teachers to focus instruction on the specific test items rather than on the broader concepts and ideas that the specific items are designed to test, will exclude the school from emphasizing aesthetic endeavors, and will lead to labeling students as successes or failures on the basis of imperfect tests.[44] It remains to be seen whether minimum competency testing will prove to be just another educational fad or a more permanent part of the scene.

ACCOUNTABILITY MOVEMENT Both the back-to-basics movement and the competency testing movement are part of a larger movement to hold the schools accountable for their failures. The accountability movement is insisting that the public schools can no longer measure success in terms of the number of dollars spent on each child's education, the teacher-pupil ratio, or the educational level of the teachers. Advocates of accountability argue that these measures are at best indirect, and that the only real test of a school is its students' achievement of knowledge, skills, and attitudes the school is attempting to teach. Only by looking at the results of students' schooling, they argue, can we ascertain the worth of the schools.

Another source of support for accountability is primarily financial. As schools become increasingly expensive to operate, inflation erodes the buying power of the dollar, and property taxes—which support much of public education—reach their tolerable limits, the public is demanding that the schools demonstrate what they are accomplishing. The public is no longer

---

[43]Robert L. Ebel, "The Case for Minimum Competency Testing," *Phi Delta Kappan* 59 (April 1978): 546–549.

[44]One article that reflects some of these concerns is Merle Steven McClung, "Are Competency Testing Programs Fair? Legal?" *Phi Delta Kappan* 59 (February 1978): 397–400.

willing to vote for increased taxes until they see what they are getting for their money.

Few would deny that the schools should be held accountable for their performance, but the definition and nature of accountability are matters of controversy. The notion of accountability is appealing to many people, but several fundamental questions must be answered before it can be put into practice:

- Who is to be held accountable for any given child's progress? the superintendent? the principal? the teacher? To what extent? How reasonable is it, for example, to hold a given teacher accountable for the progress of students if he or she is teaching in a dilapidated building, using books that are fifteen years out of date, and trying to cope with 50 percent more children than should be there? How fair would it be to allow teachers no control over the standards to which they are expected to perform?

- If school personnel are to be held accountable, to whom should they be answerable? the school board? the community? And how are results to be defined and measured?

- How will each participant's contribution to a child's learning be determined and distinguished from that of other participants?

- Should the schools be held accountable only for improvement in reading and arithmetic, skills that are easily measured? Or are the schools also responsible for the personal and humane outcomes of education, which are not so easily measured? If school personnel are held accountable only for improving easily measurable skills, might they not neglect other equally important educational outcomes? In any given year, is the student's improvement in reading more important than the strengthening of his or her self-concept and ability to work and play with other children?

Clearly, there are no pat answers to these questions. Many public school personnel who support accountability in theory are concerned about how it might work in practice.

The issue of accountability is one of the most complicated problems facing education in the near future. One thing appears certain: the debate over its merits and drawbacks is bound to help school personnel think more precisely about their goals, methods, and measures of achievement.

Religion and the Schools

- May public tax money be spent for the support of parochial schools?

- What religious observances, if any, are permitted in public school classrooms?

- May religious holidays be observed in public schools, and if so, which ones?

- From what public school activities may an individual be excused for religious reasons?

- May public school authorities rent or lease space to or from religious institutions for school purposes?

"Congress shall make no law respecting an establishment of religion, or prohibiting the free exercise thereof. . . ." During the past two centuries, the American judicial system has interpreted the First Amendment to the Constitution inconsistently with respect to religion and the public schools. The controversy surrounding this issue is not new; it has been a bone of contention since the beginning of public education in the United States. Where do we stand today?

Until the middle of the twentieth century, religious observances, including Bible reading and prayers, were common in the public schools. In fact, Bible reading and the recitation of the Lord's Prayer were required by the constitutions or by statutes in a number of states. In *Abington School District* v. *Schemp* (1963), however, the Supreme Court ruled both unconstitutional. In a 1962 decision (*Engle* v. *Vitale*), the Court had ruled against the recitation of a nondenominational prayer, holding that Bible reading and prayer violate both clauses of the First Amendment. The Court recognized that the schools did not compel a child to join in religious activities if his or her parents objected, but held that the social pressures exerted on pupils to participate were excessive. In essence, no distinction was felt to exist between voluntary and compulsory participation in religious activities.

The Court did note in its 1963 decision that the study of comparative religion, the history of religion, and the relationship of religion to civilization were not prohibited by this decision. It would also appear that, although the Bible may not be used to teach religion, it may, if objectively presented, be used in such areas of study as history, civics, and literature.

In another recent case, the Supreme Court approved the right of public school pupils who so desire to say prayers and read scriptures of their choice in the morning before school starts or after the regular school day has terminated. If prayers are said during lunch period, they must be silent. Needless to say, the Court has also ruled that direct religious instruction is not permitted in the public schools. Nor may public school teachers place religious pamphlets in schoolrooms.

A related issue is "released time." In a series of decisions, the Court ruled that a state could not allow teachers employed by specific denominations to conduct religion classes in public school buildings during the regular school day. However, the Court did rule constitutional a New York City program that permitted students to leave the school grounds during the school day to receive religious instruction elsewhere. Its reasoning was that the state must be neutral in regard to religion and, since no public funds were involved, the schools should cooperate with religious institutions by adjusting students' schedules.

The real controversy, however, revolves around the use of public tax revenues to aid private and parochial schools. The Supreme Court has already ruled that public money can be used to provide textbooks to private school students; but what other kinds of aid can, or should, the public provide? This question is currently generating considerable heat, smoke, and even fire.

The major breakthrough for private and religious schools was the passage of the Elementary-Secondary Education Act of 1965, which funneled millions of dollars into parochial schools through federal programs. In addition, parochial schools in many states have been receiving assistance ranging from pupil transportation, textbooks, health services, and general auxiliary services to salary supplements for teachers. In general, state assistance in areas other than transportation, milk, school lunch programs, and textbooks is attacked in the courts. People oppose the use of tax money to support nonpublic or parochial schools for reasons ranging from outright prejudice to fear that such assistance will undermine the public school system. The National Education Association and the American Federation of Teachers have consistently opposed the allocation of public money to private schools on the grounds that the public schools are not adequately funded now and that the situation would worsen if tax money were to go to private schools.

The other side of the argument is that the private schools, which provide education for approximately 5 million students a year, are lightening the burden of the public schools. For financial reasons, many of these schools are being forced to close. If, for example, the Catholic school system should collapse, 3 million new students would enroll in the public schools, creating a massive shortage of space, teachers, and money. Advocates of private school aid argue that by partially subsidizing private schools to keep them in operation, the public schools can avoid a deluge of students whom they would be unable to assimilate readily. Some sources estimate that if the Catholic schools were shut down the public school system would cost an additional $4 billion a year to operate.

Although strict separationists and opponents to public aid of private education have had the support of the courts in recent decades, the controversy over public and private schooling is hardly over. In a national survey in 1982, 74 percent of Americans defined themselves as "religious"; 26 percent defined themselves as "highly religious."[45] And because of this deep religious feeling in the country, many parents are concerned about the religious neutrality of the public schools. The fact that religious ques-

[45]Connecticut Mutual Life Insurance, *The Connecticut Mutual Life Report on American Values in the '80's: The Impact of Belief* (Hartford: CMLI, 1981), pp. 17–18.

tions, like the nature of humanity, can be dealt with comfortably in public schools from every perspective but a religious one strikes many people as unfair and simply wrong. They believe that by ignoring in the public school classroom the religious dimension of life, a distorted, and ultimately dangerous, view of humankind emerges—a view labeled the *secular humanist's view*. Speaking to this issue, Stephen Arons recently wrote, "When government imposes the content of schooling, it becomes the same deadening agent of repression from which the framers of the Constitution sought to free themselves."[46] Many parents are not only voting with their pocketbooks by turning down school budgets and tax requests, but they are also voting with their feet. In 1980 over eleven hundred private schools were opened. The overwhelming majority of these schools are Christian schools, related to a Protestant church and supported by parents who are removing their children from the public schools. Private education has always been costly, but in recent years the cost has gone up dramatically. In spite of costs, Catholic schools are able to maintain themselves; also, that the new Christian schools are in such an expansive period is a strong indication that the issue of church and state and the support for education will not slip away.

Moral Education

As we've discussed earlier in this chapter, there are frightening signs that young people today face special problems and obstacles. Many children are being exposed during early elementary school to illegal and damaging drugs. Many of our communities are awash with pornography. The use of alcohol among teenagers is soaring. Teenage crime continues at a high level. On the other hand, the church and the family, the two social institutions traditionally associated with helping youth develop a moral perspective, have lost much of their teaching power. The family is more fragile. Many families break apart when children are still at very formative stages. Also, the authority of parents to decide what standards a child should live by is diminishing. The decline of regular church attendance over the last twenty-five years is mute testimony to the church's weakened capacity to instill moral values. Presently, only four out of ten adult Americans attend church weekly.[47]

We live in a world of much change. Not only have our values changed, but many people believe that the former value consensus in the society seems to have fragmented. It is not uncommon to hear remarks such as, "My roommates and I have very different values." Or, "Of course, I have my own values, but who am I to impose them on others?" We exist in an atmosphere of value uncertainty and moral confusion. It would appear that

[46]Stephen Arons, "Separation of School and State," *Education Week* 2 (November 17, 1982): 24.

[47]Connecticut Mutual Life Insurance, *The Connecticut Mutual Life Report on American Values in the '80's*, p. 17.

amidst this atmosphere of doubt and concern people are turning to the schools, hoping that the teachers will assume a more vigorous role.

HISTORY OF MORAL EDUCATION   The idea of education as having a positive impact on morality has a long, long history in Western culture. Socrates believed that the purpose of education is to make humans both smart and good. The author Robinson Davies mirrored this belief but used more religious language: "The purpose of learning is to save the soul and enlarge the mind." Nor is this idea of education as having the dual purpose of intellectual and moral development new to public education. The concern for moral education has deep roots in the American schools. The founding fathers were convinced that if their experiment in democracy were to flourish, it would require an educated populace. This was a major reason why they insisted on the establishment of public schools. They also knew that self-government requires the development of an ethical sense and a set of civic virtues, such as respect for property and the willingness to put aside force for reason. They expected the public schools to carry on this moral education.

For many years the public schools in this country explicitly taught children how to behave according to a particular set of values and moral precepts. This teaching usually reflected the views of the dominant group: white Anglo-Saxon Protestants. The explicit teaching of morals and values, and occasionally religious doctrine, was a major cause for the establishment of private parochial schools in America. In the nineteenth century, newly arrived immigrants felt threatened by the values their children were being exposed to in the schools. Religious groups, such as the Roman Catholics, felt compelled to establish their own schools to insure the transmission of their values and religious traditions to the young. Other groups, religious and nonreligious, followed.

During the twentieth century a major effort has been made to make public education pluralistic. Educators have sought to make public schools open and hospitable to Americans of all ethnic and religious backgrounds. Although the schools often failed, a spirit of pluralism still is a dominant theme in American education. But the success of pluralism has sometimes been at the cost of moral education. One reason for this is that for many people religion and morality are closely intertwined. To raise issues of morality in the classroom is often to bring people's religious views into the classroom, and probably to bring them into question. Although skillful teachers are able to do this fairly and effectively, many teachers are fearful of dealing with issues that have religious overtones. As a result, as our sense of pluralism has been heightened, our public schools have become more and more hesitant to deal with value issues, especially those issues that involve religious aspects.

discussions. In the same general way that a basketball team needs practice and action to learn the game, so, too, does the child who is trying to become a moral person. The schools, of course, give children some training in how to behave toward one another. However, there is little stress on helping others and few opportunities built into school life to act on our commitments. If the schools are to be the positive force in the moral lives of youth that most people want them to be, teachers will have to give children a more flesh-and-blood approach to moral education.

THE TEACHER'S ROLE IN MORAL EDUCATION   The role of the teacher in moral education perhaps may best be seen through examining the "four Es" of moral education.[51] They are moral education through exhortation, example, expectations, and experience.

Exhortation. The first E, exhortation, involves teachers urging students to live good lives. Also, the teacher directly tells children and young people what is right and what is wrong. It involves urging people to behave in this way and not in that way, and, in general, instructing them to live by a certain set of standards. Much of the reason for students to encounter real and fictional human events through the study of literature and history is that this is a form of exhorting them to live their lives by high standards. However, this approach is not without its critics. Some are uneasy with the question, "Who is exhorting whom to do what?"

Example. The second E, example, refers to the moral model provided by the teacher, and, for that matter, by the students. In psychology, this phenomenon is referred to as *modeling.* The students see a certain type of behavior, either words or actions or both, and then imitate it. For instance, a teacher responds to a crisis situation calmly and with fairness to all the students. The students admire that way of responding and will try to imitate it. Or, the teacher controls students and intimidates them through sarcasm, and students try that behavior out on one another. If the students have a positive regard for the teacher, the probability that they will respond in a like manner in a similar situation is higher than if there is little regard for the teacher.

Long before psychologists gave us the term *modeling*, we spoke of the power of good example. Although it is an old truth, it is easy for many of us to forget that whether we are teaching long division, or geography, or keeping order in the lunchroom, we are modeling all sorts of things for

---

[51]Kevin Ryan, *Questions and Answers on Moral Education,* P.D.K. Fastback No. 153 (Bloomington, Ind.: Phi Delta Kappa, 1981). Many of the issues addressed here are more fully developed in this P.D.K. Fastback. In particular, the various approaches such as values clarification and cognitive developmental moral education are discussed.

children, and primary among them is moral behavior. Whether or not we are comfortable with this fact, as teachers we are moral examples. This of course can cut two ways. We can be examples of moral excellence or of moral weakness.

Expectations. The third E is expectations, by which we mean what the teacher and the school expect or call forth from the child. Expectations of what is demanded of students are often written down in school codes. More often, expectations simply exist in the social fabric of the school. People know what is expected of them in different situations; they know what they *ought* to do. In your own school experience or as part of your field experience in teacher education, you have been exposed to and will continue to encounter schools with very different sets of expectations for children. The climate or environment of certain schools is slightly hostile: from the front office to the gym, people treat one another rudely; disrespect is seen in the interactions between teachers and students and is very clearly expressed in graffiti scrawled across the walls. On the other hand, other schools call forth more civil behavior: there is respect for the individual. The principal treats teachers with warmth and cordiality. Teachers treat one another in that same manner. They treat students with respect. That same respect is expected among students. Expectations, then, are a significant part of a child's moral education.

Experience. The fourth and final E, experience, refers to those situations that involve students in activities in which they can respond with ethical or moral behavior. There are different types of moral experience. One example is a student's becoming involved in a debate over the American use of the atomic bomb on Japan in World War II. Here the experience, as it might be, using Kohlberg's method or values clarification, is primarily intellectual or verbal. Another example: suppose the teacher asks the students to give up a Saturday morning to pick up the debris around the playground. Students are involved in a very different experience, one that includes both mind and body. They are doing something with moral content, rather than just talking about what is right or correct. The fourth E, then, is much more concerned with moral actions than with moral words. The teacher provides experiences in which students can do service or be morally involved in a task.

Some people might respond that there is a fifth E or option: exclude. Some are concerned that the schools cannot teach moral education well or that they are already overburdened. Some might take this position out of sheer humility ("Who am I to be a moral model!"). Although the fifth E may be attractive, to exclude moral education from the schools is an impossibility. The simple fact of having children in school for six hours a day, 180 days a year, for twelve or thirteen of the very formative years in their lives, assures that they will learn a good deal about human values and what is right and wrong. Furthermore, schools are filled with moral content. It is not only the stories and history textbooks students read, but the ways in which teachers treat children: whether teachers are fair or unfair, kind or cruel; whether they allow children to bully one another or whether they promote a warm, community spirit. All of these are part of the schools' teaching of values and morals.

Even if schools claim not to be involved in moral education, moral education is going on. Certain behaviors and activities of students are consistently rewarded by teachers and, in turn, come to be valued by the students. The students learn that certain kinds of behavior, such as punching each other out, are "bad," whereas other kinds of behavior, such as beating everyone in the class on a test, are very "good." Coming to school every day and on time is rewarded behavior; thus regularity and punctuality become valued. Working hard and getting answers is rewarded; thus industriousness and certain kinds of achievement become valued by students. Students are quick to pick up these school values. They learn what particular intellectual and social behavior the teacher wants from them. They usually can tell which students the teacher likes and does not like. Although this learning may not be part of the conscious or overt curriculum of the school, it is, nevertheless, a strong part of the invisible, hidden curriculum. One of the major messages of schooling is an answer to the question, "What does it mean to be a good person?" Teachers, by their words and actions, by the content they select and even the way they teach it, answer that question for the students.

Discussion Questions

1. How does poverty affect the lives of students from poor families? What is the teacher's responsibility to children particularly burdened with poverty?

2. What should be the response of the schools to the issue of youthful escapism? Should the schools educate children about or ignore the areas of alcohol, drugs, television and videogames, and sex?

3. How does the current instability of the American family affect the schools?

4. Do you agree that equality of educational opportunity should be defined by its effects rather than its provisions? Can you think of an analogy to support your case for or against this position?

5. In view of compensatory education's lack of success at combatting the problems of inequality in educational opportunity, why do you suppose the schools continue to be seen as the means to a solution?

6. Why do you believe it is so difficult to integrate public schools?

7. What are your views about busing to achieve integrated schools?

8. Do you agree with our prognosis that magnet schools are likely to continue and flourish in the 1980s? Have you ever attended or visited a magnet school? If so, what is your evaluation?

9. Can you recall any sexist behavior that you have observed in schools? Do you think sexism and sex-role stereotyping are problems in our schools?

10. Were you aware of the extensiveness of school violence and vandalism before you read this chapter? Will it be a major factor in your decision regarding whether or not to teach?

11. Why do you think that standardized test scores have been dropping in the last decade? What are your reactions to the back-to-basics and minimum competency testing movements? How is the accountability movement related to these issues?

12. Where do you stand on the issue of public support for private schools? If your view prevails, what will be the effects on private education—and on society as a whole?

13. What do you think of the methods or approaches to moral education discussed in the chapter? How do you feel about being a "moral educator?"

For Further Reading   Brodinsky, Ben. "Back to the Basics: The Movement and Its Meaning." *Phi Delta Kappan* 58 (March 1977): 522–527.
> A short article explaining the composite demands espoused by supporters of the back-to-basics movement.

Craig, Grace J. *Human Development.* 2nd ed. Englewood Cliffs, N.J.: Prentice-Hall, 1980.
> A thorough description of the stages of human development from infancy to old age and a discussion of the issues related to each stage.

Havighurst, Robert, and Daniel Levine. *Society and Education.* 5th ed. Boston: Allyn and Bacon, 1979.
> An examination of many of the social issues touched on in this chapter. The authors summarize much recent research.

Lerner, Barbara. "American Education: How Are We Doing?" *The Public Interest* (Fall 1982).
> A comparison of American schools with others in both developed and underdeveloped nations. The author draws on data from recent studies by the International Association for the Evaluation of Educational Achievement (IEA).

National Institute of Education. *Violent Schools—Safe Schools, The Safe School Study Report to the Congress,* Executive Summary. Washington, D.C., 1978.
> A summary of a national study on crime in the schools. The Executive Summary synthesizes the major findings in fourteen pages.

Purpel, David, and Kevin Ryan, eds. *Moral Education . . . It Comes with the Territory.* Berkeley, Calif.: McCutchan, 1976.
> A comprehensive overview of the major issues and positions in the field of moral education, written by many different experts in the field.

What's New in Education?

13

Although Americans are living in a relatively conservative period of United States educational history, there are still some new and exciting developments and programs currently in effect in American schools.

This chapter emphasizes that:

▪ Alternative schools have emerged as a powerful reform strategy to improve the public schools by addressing such educational problems as desegregation, vandalism and violence, and disparate educational philosophies.

▪ School systems are organizing volunteer programs to take advantage of the many human resources that are available in a community.

▪ Microcomputers are being used in the schools to develop computer literacy among elementary and secondary school students and to aid teachers in monitoring instruction.

▪ Through multicultural and bilingual education, schools help students come to value cultural differences. These programs are an attempt to cope with the problems and opportunities created by a pluralistic society.

▪ Handicapped children have long suffered from social isolation. The federal government has spearheaded the attempt to integrate handicapped children with normal peers in regular classrooms. This effort, called *mainstreaming,* is one of the most significant new developments in education.

▪ More and more programs for gifted and talented children are being developed by school systems. This long-neglected group of students is finally beginning to receive appropriate services and special attention.

*C*HANGE, INNOVATE, REFORM. . . . James Cass of *The Saturday Review*, commenting on the 1960s and 1970s, has said that the most notable aspect of American education has been the preoccupation with change. The large majority of educational innovations, however, have had little lasting impact on the schools of our nation. Whereas the word *innovation* had positive connotations during the last two decades, today it is perceived negatively by many lay people and educators alike. These people believe that our emphasis in the past on innovations such as open education, new curriculum programs, and pass-fail grading systems has contributed to the decline of academic achievement by watering down the curriculum. Our efforts at innovative changes, they argue, have led us astray from the traditional values and approaches of the past. This rationale, coupled with times of fiscal austerity, has resulted in fewer attempts to change the schools in new and radical ways. We are at present living in a much more conservative era than has been true of the last twenty years.

Despite this conservative mood, there are important changes occurring in the schools. No social system ever stands still; it is always evolving and being altered in some way. Let's examine some of the new directions and emphases that are affecting schooling and education today.

ALTERNATIVE SCHOOLS

During the past decade the concept of alternative schools has emerged as a powerful reform strategy to improve the public schools. Alternative schools have been used successfully to assist in the desegregation of urban schools (see the discussion of magnet schools in Chapter 12), to increase parent and community involvement in public education, to support traditional or basic education schools as part of the demand for effective learning and accountability, and to meet distinct instructional needs for a wide variety of students. Probably no other strategy has been used so effectively over the last ten years to address so many different problems in education.

During the late 1960s and early 1970s, the alternative school movement was essentially a counterculture effort aimed against the public schools, which were viewed as stifling and oppressive. Since that time public school systems have responded to the challenges and pressures to change their traditional schools by creating alternative schools within the public school system. Because different parents want different types of schooling for their children, why not offer schools with different educational philosophies, curricula, and instructional procedures? By doing this the public school system can be responsive to the many different elements of the public to which it is responsible. Through the establishment of qualitatively unique schools, some of the pressures on school systems caused by forcing everyone to adjust to the one-school model can be alleviated.

Over 150 different types of schools have been identified as alternatives, including schools labeled as open education, schools without walls,

It's easier to start a new
school than to change an
existing one.
— SEYMOUR SARASON —

schools whose focus is on a particular subject matter such as mathematics or science, and schools for particular students such as dropouts. Recently, several large school systems have incorporated Montessori education in elementary schools. The fastest-growing alternative school has been the traditional or basic education program, which relies heavily on traditional curriculum and instructional strategies such as drill, recitation, and rote learning. The large demand for these traditional schools is indicative of the growing conservative nature of our society (see Chapter 7 for a further discussion of basic education schools).

The concept of alternative schools within the public school system has become very popular, having grown from one hundred or so schools in 1970 to more than ten thousand today. Alternative schools can be found in 80 percent of the nation's large school districts. An estimated three million students are currently enrolled in alternative programs in public schools.[1] Parents seem to like the idea of alternative schools because it provides them with options regarding the type of education their children can receive. Students like the idea because the schools seem more interesting to them, particularly at the secondary level, when more diversification among the schools is possible. Teachers like the idea because the students seem happier, and the teachers have the opportunity to work in curriculum areas that are of special interest to them. Administrators favor the concept because parents, teachers, and students all seem more content, even though alternative schools place more of a burden on administrators, who must develop and implement plans for school selection and operation.

Although only a few research studies have been conducted to assess the effectiveness of alternative schools, these studies indicate that students in those schools learn at a rate consistent with or higher than the district norm.[2] There is also evidence that alternative public schools contribute to a decrease in school vandalism and violence.[3] Because of their small size, emphasis on interpersonal relations and student success, and involvement of students in decision-making processes, alternative schools have fewer cases of violence and vandalism than traditional schools. We think that alternative schools are an innovation that will be around for a long time.

SCHOOL VOLUNTEER PROGRAMS

What do a successful engineer from a major oil company, undergraduate students at a local university, senior citizens from a retirement home, and a women's church group have in common? They are all among the hundreds of thousands of school volunteers who have contributed their time and

[1]Mary Anne Raywid, "The First Decade of Public School Alternatives," *Phi Delta Kappan* 62 (April 1981): 552.

[2]Robert D. Barr, "Alternatives for the Eighties: A Second Decade of Development," *Phi Delta Kappan* 62 (April 1981): 573.

[3]Barr, "Alternatives for the Eighties," p. 571.

skills to assist schools in a variety of tasks. Getting occasional help from interested persons is something schools have been doing since they were founded. So what is new about this? What's new is that now, instead of informal and ad hoc arrangements being made, school systems are making concerted efforts to organize and support volunteer involvement in the schools. In fact, there now exists a National School Volunteer Program, a nonprofit education association that provides leadership for thousands of school volunteers. Founded in 1956, its members build partnerships between public education and the private sector by working from their positions within the schools and communities. Its members are parents, professional educators, community organizers, and business leaders throughout the United States.

School volunteer programs provide Americans with the opportunity to contribute their time and expertise as individuals to help schools achieve various goals and objectives. In many school districts program coordinators recruit, train, and place volunteers in classrooms and school district offices. These trained volunteers, be they retirees, college students, or company employees, contribute in many ways: tutoring children in basic skills, providing management advice, serving as library aides, assisting with handicapped students, guiding students in career exploration, and raising community support, to name a few. In short, they supplement and enrich the efforts of professional educators by building a bridge between the school and the community. They become a human resource to assist the schools in times of pressing economic and educational need.

The Houston Independent School District (HISD) has been operating a Volunteers In Public Schools (VIPS) program since 1970 with great success. In 1981–82 over 13,000 volunteers donated over 391,000 hours of time. The district figured that the money value of this time was worth approximately $2.7 million.[4] HISD uses these volunteers in a variety of projects. Over 2,000 volunteers have participated in the kindergarten screening program to assess kindergarteners in areas of vision, hearing, language-learning, and motor performance. The business/school partnerships program seeks to pair at least one business with each of the twelve secondary vocational magnet schools to provide people, funds, and information to enrich programs. Some senior citizens serve as "living historians," speaking to classes about their personal experiences and remembrances of days gone by. In all, thirteen different volunteer programs exist.

The benefits of volunteer programs appear to be great. Students benefit from the assistance that volunteers provide the professional staff. Having more caring adults in the school to work with the children can personalize part of the educative process. Teachers benefit by having extra help in accomplishing the many tasks they are expected to perform. Volunteers benefit by experiencing a sense of fulfillment in knowing that they are contributing something valuable to youth. As one senior volunteer states, "To help a little girl or boy's eyes brighten up and say I can do that after trying and failed makes my day. I look forward to this day every day of the week." The school district benefits through the sense of good will and communication that such programs generate. We anticipate that these volunteer programs will continue to develop and expand during this decade.

MICROCOMPUTERS IN EDUCATION

Computers have been used in education since the 1960s, but the first commercially feasible microcomputer became available in 1975. Heralded as being as revolutionary as Gutenberg's movable print, microcomputers are taking education and schooling by storm. A recent survey discovered that students had access to some 96,000 microcomputers and 24,000 computer terminals in the spring of 1982.[5] The same survey also revealed that 29,000 of the 82,000 U.S. public schools now have at least one computer. During

[4]*VIPS 1981–82 Annual Report,* Houston Independent School District, Department of Volunteer Services, 1982, p. 5.

[5]"School Microcomputers Triple Since 1980, NCES Survey Shows," *Phi Delta Kappan* 64 (December 1982): 294.

"Yes, I'll tell you what could replace this wonderful education I'm receiving: a silicon chip!"

Courtesy of Martha Campbell.

the 1981–82 school year, these computers were used by approximately 4.7 million students, who averaged nine hours of access time each. Improved technology and lowered costs are the primary reasons that computer usage in the schools has increased so dramatically and is projected to continue at an unparalleled pace.[6] (See Chapter 7 for examples of curriculum and instructional uses of computers.)

A microcomputer is a small computer built around a microprocessor, which is a tiny electronic computer engraved on a silicon chip. These chips, smaller than a postage stamp, are used for a variety of machines, including video games, microwave ovens, and home computers. These microprocessors are so efficient and contain so much information that, in comparison, a 1945 vacuum-tube computer would have to be the size of New York City and would require more power than the city's subway system to do the work of the present-day table-top computer.

[6]At the time of this writing, the U.S. Congress was considering new legislation, known informally as the "Apple Bill," which would provide major tax benefits to companies who donate microcomputers to schools. It is known as the "Apple Bill," because the idea was proposed by the founder of Apple computers.

Table 13.1 A Teachers' Guide to Computer Terminology

byte	The computer space needed to store one character of information (a letter, symbol, number, etc.).
chip	Logic unit of computer; circuitry is put on this rectangular silicon piece.
CAI	Computer assisted instruction.
CMI	Computer managed instruction.
debug	To correct "bugs" or errors in a computer program.
floppy disc	Information storage device that resembles a 45 rpm record.
hardware	The computer components including all its nuts, bolts, cables, central processing unit (CPU), printer, disk drives, etc.
language	A code used by a programmer to organize the circuits for specific functions. Four languages are as follows:
	BASIC: Beginners All Purpose Symbolic Instruction Code is compact, easy to use, and popular with microcomputer users.
	PASCAL: An inexpensive, logically structured language, designed for more efficient programming, fewer errors and easier revision.
	PILOT: A dialog oriented language, quickly and easily learned, deals nicely with words and text.
	LOGO: Specially designed for children, LOGO includes a robot turtle that students can program.
memory	The storage area in the computer for the program and data, the RAM and ROM chips.
	RAM: *Random Access Memory* is used for programs and data, varies with each application, lost when power is turned off.
	ROM: *Read Only Memory* is a program built into the computer's memory by the manufacturer and cannot be changed.
program	Sequence of instructions that a computer follows to perform a specific task.
software	The computer programs; courseware refers to programs designed specifically for the classroom.

Source: Practical Applications of Research 4 (June 1982): 4. Bloomington, Indiana: Phi Delta Kappa. Reprinted by permission.

In many schools today, the phrase "computer-aided instruction" means making the computer teach the child. One might say the computer is being used to program the child. In my version, the child programs the computer and, in doing so, both acquires a sense of mastery over a piece of the modern and powerful technology and establishes an intimate contact with some of the deepest ideas from science, from mathematics, and from the art of intellectual model building.

— SEYMOUR PAPERT —

School administrators are using computers for various managerial and organizational purposes, such as class scheduling, payroll accounting, personnel reporting, and student attendance record keeping. These uses of microcomputers in school systems are very similar to the uses made in business. Of important significance, however, is the use of computers for instruction.

The two major functions of computer-based instruction (CBI) are: *computer-assisted instruction* (CAI) and *computer-managed instruction* (CMI). In CAI the student receives direct instructional help from the computer. Because of their data storage capacity, patience, and branching capability, microcomputers lend themselves to individualizing instruction. For drill and practice sessions, computers can be programmed to provide students with immediate feedback regarding the correctness of their responses to problems and exercises. Microcomputers can also help students develop problem-solving skills by immersing them in environments (called *simulations*), where they are required to solve complex problems and immediately learn the consequences of their decisions. Students who learn better pictorially can be helped by the graphic display capabilities of the computer. Writing skills can be improved by use of the computer as a word processor; the student can add, delete, or modify expressions more easily and can concentrate on intellectual content rather than the mechanical recording of thoughts on paper. Other examples of CAI applications include tutorials, information retrieval, and inquiry/dialogue.

CMI helps the teacher plan for and monitor student learning experiences. Individual learning plans can be stored in the microcomputer and retrieved as needed. Student testing and assessment can be programmed and the results filed. Additional CMI applications include record keeping, scheduling of student activities, and time and resource management.

Teachers and students who regularly use microcomputers seem to be very enthusiastic about the results. Teachers report that students seem motivated to use the microcomputer. A commonly reported phenomenon is that students' knowledge of the machines soon surpasses teachers' knowledge. Many teachers see this as positive. As one third-grade teacher states, "I think it is nice at that age to be able to tell an adult something and be right." One fourteen-year-old ninth-grader, who is a year and a half below grade level in reading, excels when it comes to computers. He recently designed a complex electronic football game that involves seventy-five subprograms, and he often finds that faculty members call upon him for help with computer problems. "It's sort of funny, in a way, to teach the teachers," he said. "But I realize that on some things I'm smarter than they are."[7]

[7]Edward B. Fiske, "Computers Alter Lives of Pupils and Teachers," *The New York Times*, April 4, 1982, p. 42.

Some educators are not quite so wholehearted in their endorsement of microcomputers. Some are concerned that an overemphasis on problems and ideas that lend themselves to quantification may detract from other forms of thinking. As one professor of computer science states, "To him who has only a computer, the world looks like a computable domain. You introduce a new symbolic system, and one begins to interpret the world in such terms. The danger is that we will end up thinking like a computer and that the only things we will recognize as legitimate problems are those where quantification and calculation play a big role." Others express concern that, like television, computers appear to be both addictive and alienating. The world of electronics, they assert, can be hypnotic and isolating, taking time away from such human experiences as going on family outings, telling stories, and constructing things.[8]

[8]Fiske, "Computers Alter Lives," p. 42.

Finally, we ought to keep in mind that one of the major goals of schools is to prepare students for the world of work. The new information technologies—computers, microprocessors, video devices, and inexpensive means of storing and transmitting information—are creating a revolution comparable to the invention of printing. Already this revolution is causing profound changes in the way business and industry are conducted. "Smart machines" now perform jobs formerly done by humans. The field of robotics, pioneered by Japanese industry and made possible by the microprocessor, is becoming a major element in industry. There will be less demand for industrial workers and more demand for workers who can program computers to perform mechanical tasks. As the computer changes the work place, schools will find themselves under pressure to modify their vocational education programs. Business and industry will place new demands on schools to produce graduates with greater knowledge of science and technology and with the thinking skills to make the best use of constantly developing information techniques.

What do we see as the future of microcomputers and schooling? In the next five to ten years there will be continued expansion of microcomputer usage in the schools, but it is unlikely that it will result in any radical or startling changes in schooling. Budgetary and fiscal problems will impede really major investments in computers. Even if the hardware were available, software producers still would have a long way to go to develop programs of sufficient quality and variety to satisfy teachers. Another problem that must be overcome before computers will be used commonly in classrooms is teachers' fears: fear of the unknown; fear of obsolescence or replacement; and a fear of "math anxiety," based on the assumption that computer work is primarily mathematics. Colleges of education and school districts have a tremendous task ahead of them if one of their goals is computer literacy of teachers. If prospective teachers graduate from college with little or no experience in using microcomputers, they are likely to resist using them in their classrooms. On the other hand, if new teachers have had extensive experience with microcomputers as part of their teacher preparation, they will more likely demand access to computers as part of their instructional activities.

MULTICULTURAL EDUCATION

We live in a pluralistic society, one with many different cultures. At one time in our history, the United States was considered a "melting pot" of many different kinds of people. Immigrants to the United States were expected to give up the language and customs of their old country and to adopt the language and customs of their new country. During the nineteenth and early twentieth centuries, the schools of this country contributed to the melting pot by socializing and acculturating immigrant children to American ways while discouraging them from maintaining the ways of their old countries. In fact, many states passed laws forbidding instruction in any language but English. Consciously or unconsciously, the basic idea was to produce a society with one dominant culture.

Today the concept of the melting pot has generally been rejected in favor of the concept of cultural pluralism. Cultural pluralism calls for the understanding and appreciation of the differences that exist among the nation's citizens. It aims toward a sense of being and wholeness of the entire society based on the unique strengths of each of its parts. It rejects both assimilation and separatism as goals of society. Instead, cultural pluralism seeks a healthy interaction among the diverse groups constituting our society; each subculture maintains its own individuality yet contributes to our society as a whole.

Multicultural education is education that values cultural pluralism and seeks the cultural enrichment of all children and youth through programs dedicated to the preservation and extension of cultural alternatives. Multicultural education goes beyond the goal of reaching awareness and understanding of cultural differences by recognizing the right of these different cultures to exist. Multicultural education values differences and individuality rather than similarity and imitation. Education for cultural pluralism includes four major thrusts:[9] (1) the teaching of values that support cultural diversity and individual uniqueness; (2) the encouragement of the qualitative expansion of existing ethnic cultures and their incorporation into the mainstream of American socioeconomic and political life; (3) the support of explorations in alternative and emerging lifestyles; and (4) the encouragement of multiculturalism, multilingualism, and multiple dialects.

Many school districts are attempting to permeate their curricula with a multicultural emphasis, believing that an emphasis on cultural pluralism is our society's best way to combat the prejudice and divisiveness that exist among the different subcultures of our nation. By developing mutual respect and appreciation of different lifestyles, languages, religious beliefs, and family structures, students may help shape a better future society for all its members.

Some educators, however, are concerned about what they believe are potential dangers of cultural pluralism in the schools. Their concerns about pluralism include the fears that it may destroy any sense of common traditions, values, purposes, and obligations; it may divert the schools' attention from their basic purpose to educate for civic, economic, and personal effectiveness; and it may lead to a deterioration of a sense of morality because no universal moral positions are considered acceptable to all elements of our society. These critics do not argue against the need to preserve

[9]"No One Model American," a statement on multicultural education issued by the AACTE Commission on Multicultural Education, *Journal of Teacher Education* 24 (Winter 1973): 264.

and to value the achievements of the diverse ethnic and racial groups of our country, but they reject the position that everything is of equal value, that the schools have a responsibility for teaching every possible belief and value, and that behavior is moral if it is believed to be so by any group.[10] These critics assert that there are limits to pluralism, and those limits must be articulated by schools and school leaders.

As with any attempt to redress social ills, excesses and overexuberance can occur. Nevertheless, we do believe that the basic goals and purposes of cultural pluralism are sound and warrant inclusion in the schools. Yet we must be wary not to detract from the schools' basic purposes by overemphasizing or distorting the goals of multicultural education.

BILINGUAL EDUCATION

A recent study shows that whereas 67 percent of the adult non-Hispanic population has completed high school education, only 41 percent of Hispanic adults hold a high school diploma. Hispanics aged fourteen to nineteen are twice as likely not to have completed high school as non-Hispanics in the same age group.[11] Moreover, National Assessment of Educational Progress data reveal that Hispanic students are significantly below the national average for every age group in each of the five subject-matter areas in which they were tested.[12]

Students whose native language is not English constitute one of the most conspicuous failure groups in the American educational system. Because of their difficulty in speaking, writing, and understanding English, these students fall farther and farther behind in school, with overwhelming numbers of them dropping out before finishing high school.

To cope with this problem, Congress passed the Bilingual Education Act in 1968 and amended it in 1974 to make it more explicit in intent and design. The 1974 act provided a definition of what constitutes a bilingual education program:

> [It is] instruction given in, and study of, English and to the extent necessary to allow a child to progress effectively through the educational system, the native language of the children of limited English-speaking ability, and such instruction is given with appreciation for the cultural heritage of such children, and, with respect to elementary school instruction, such instruction shall, to the extent necessary be in all courses or subjects of study which will allow a child to progress effectively through the educational system.

[10]M. Donald Thomas, "The Limits of Pluralism," *Phi Delta Kappan* 62 (April 1981): 589, 591–592.

[11]Flora Ida Ortiz, "Hispanic-American Education," ed. Harold E. Mitzel in *Encyclopedia of Educational Research*, 5th ed. (New York: The Free Press, 1982), II, p. 788.

[12]Ortiz, "Hispanic-American Education," p. 788.

By 1982 federal bilingual education programs cost about $160 million. This outlay of federal funds is more than matched by state and local expenditures. In Illinois, New York, and California, for example, state funds for bilingual education are more than double the federal funds.[13]

Much of the recent expansion of bilingual programs can be attributed to a series of court cases, the most notable of which is the 1974 U.S. Supreme Court case of *Lau* v. *Nichols.* The case involved a class action suit on the behalf of Chinese-speaking students in San Francisco, but it has implications for all the nation's non-English-speaking children. The Court found, "There is no equality of treatment merely by providing students with the same facilities, textbooks, teachers, and curriculum; for students who do not understand English are effectively foreclosed from any meaningful education." Basing its ruling on the Civil Rights Act of 1964, the Court held that the San Francisco school system unlawfully discriminated on the basis of national origin when it failed to cope with these children's language problems. Although the *Lau* case did not mandate bilingual education as the means by which to solve the problem, subsequent state cases have ordered bilingual education programs.

[13]Charles R. Foster, "Defusing the Issues in Bilingualism and Bilingual Education," *Phi Delta Kappan* 63 (January 1982): 343.

There are two primary models of bilingual education programs. The *transitional model* uses the child's native tongue only as an interim medium of instruction until the child develops fluency in English. These programs typically enroll students for three to four years. The transitional model is the one used in the majority of bilingual programs. The *maintenance model* seeks to maintain the child's native language by giving it equal emphasis with English as a medium of instruction. The goal is to continue the development of linguistic skills in both languages. This approach has greater support among educators and ethnic groups who seek to maintain the native language in face of strong social pressure to abandon it.

Considerable controversy surrounds the whole issue of bilingual education. There exists very little research to support the effectiveness of bilingual programs. In the absence of such evidence, the topic provokes much emotion and elicits many different philosophies about it. Whereas ethnic groups lobby strongly for expanded support for bilingual programs, in 1981 President Reagan charged bilingual programs with deliberately impeding the acquisition of English skills among minority groups.[14] His view is representative of a conservative philosophy that envisions many of our social innovations to be at the root of the country's problems. Until such time that research evidence on the effectiveness of bilingual programs is forthcoming, we can expect the debate to continue.

In the meantime, most school districts are in desperate need of bilingual teachers, particularly those who speak Spanish. If you speak Spanish, or still have time to include learning this language in your college program, you could help solve a serious educational problem and at the same time greatly enhance your employment opportunities.

HANDICAPPED CHILDREN AND MAINSTREAMING

In Chapter 12 we discuss the effects of segregation on minority children and describe legal and educational attempts to integrate differing racial and ethnic groups. The 1970s and 1980s have also been a time when another major integration effort has been attempted—the integration of handicapped children with normal peers in regular classrooms. This integration, called *mainstreaming*, is one of the most significant new developments in education.

During the nineteenth century, handicapped children—such as those who were blind, deaf, crippled, or mentally retarded—were taken from their homes and communities and segregated full time in state or private special schools. Consequently, education for the handicapped became known as *special education*. In the latter part of the nineteenth century and the beginning of the twentieth century, a movement developed to integrate mildly handicapped children into the community through the establishment

---

[14]Foster, "Defusing the Issues," p. 342.

of special classes for them in the public schools. If these mildly handicapped persons were going to live in the community as adults, the reasoning went, it was important that they not be segregated from the community during their childhood. However, even though these children attended public schools, they were still segregated from other more normal children by virtue of the fact that they attended special classes for the handicapped. The mainstreaming movement is a logical continuation of the effort to integrate handicapped children into the mainstream of society.

Federal and state courts and legislatures have ruled that equal educational opportunity for all dictates that physically and mentally different children have the right to share with others in education in an environment that least restricts them. Instead of being confined to special classes, handicapped children have the right to attend school with normal children so that they can learn to make adjustments, play and work with all types of people, and gain self-confidence. Many people also believe that the normal children will benefit from exposure to handicapped children by learning of their humanity and by reducing prejudices that they might have toward those different from themselves.

In 1975 Congress passed and President Ford signed the federal Education for All Handicapped Children Act (Public Law 94–142), which guarantees to the handicapped the right to a free and appropriate public education. It also guarantees due process procedures to insure that handicapped children in the United States will be treated equally with normal children with regard to identification, placement, and educational services. Between fiscal years 1978 and 1981, the federal government increased its spending for educating the handicapped from $294 million to $915 million.[15]

Even though the federal government is committing large sums of money to educate the handicapped, most states report that they are unable to fulfill all the special education needs of their schools. Some state education agencies estimate that "full service" for needy students would require a doubling or tripling of currently available resources. Thus, while the federal government is paying more money than originally allocated to help service the needs of handicapped children, the passage of legislation such as P.L. 94–142 also commits state and local resources to this purpose. The source of the money is a concern of most state education agencies.

The successful implementation of the mainstreaming concept is a challenge confronting public school educators. Many problems need to be overcome for mainstreaming to work successfully. Regular classroom teachers must be made aware of what kinds of disabilities some of their students will possess, and how these disabilities will affect instruction and learning. Public Law 94–142 defines handicapped children as those who are mentally

[15]W. Vance Grant and Leo J. Eiden, *Digest of Education Statistics 1982* (Washington, D.C.: National Center for Education Statistics, 1982), p. 173.

Table 13.2 Handicapped Population Three- to Twenty-one Years Old Receiving Special Education and Related Services, as Reported to Agencies under P.L. 94–142 and P.L. 89–313, by Type of Handicap, School Year 1979–80

TYPE OF HANDICAP	TOTAL	COMBINED	
		Percent of 3- to 21-year-old population	Percentage distribution of handicapped
Total	4,035,685	8.25	100.0
Specific learning disabled	1,281,395	2.62	31.7
Speech impaired	1,188,973	2.43	29.4
Mentally retarded	881,739	1.80	21.8
Seriously emotionally disturbed	330,999	.67	8.2
Other health impaired	106,287	.21	2.6
Orthopedically impaired	66,243	.13	1.6
Multihandicapped	61,923	.12	1.5
Deaf	41,489	.08	1.0
Hard of hearing	41,383	.08	1.0
Visually handicapped	32,676	.06	.8
Deaf/blind	2,578	.00	.0

Source: The Condition of Education, 1981 Edition, National Center for Education Statistics (Washington, D.C.: U.S. Government Printing Office, 1981), p. 278.

retarded, hard of hearing, deaf, speech impaired, visually handicapped, seriously emotionally disturbed, orthopedically impaired, or other health impaired, or children with specific learning disabilities who require special education and related services. Table 13.2 shows the approximate number and percentage of handicapped students between the ages of three and twenty-one who receive special education and related services under P.L. 94–142 and P.L. 89–313, another federal law pertaining to the education of handicapped children. As the table indicates, 8.25 percent, or over four million, of the three- to twenty-one-year-old population in the United States suffer from one or more of the listed types of handicaps and receive special education and related services. Obviously, some of these disabilities require that teachers tailor their instruction to meet the children's individual needs. In fact, P.L. 94–142 requires that the instruction for handicapped be based on an individualized education program (IEP). The state education agency must guarantee that there is a written IEP for each and every handicapped child in the state, developed jointly with the parents or guardian of each child, reviewed at least annually, and revised when necessary. This means that regular classroom teachers, in conjunction with special educators, must develop IEPs for each handicapped child based on that child's special needs. Many teachers have never developed such plans, nor have they imple-

MAJOR POINTS OF
P.L. 94–142

- insures that each *identified* handicapped child will receive a *free, appropriate* education

- requires that handicapped children be educated in the *least restrictive environment* and with nonhandicapped peers when appropriate

- identifies the handicapped children that the local education agency must serve

- defines special education

- requires that the instruction for handicapped children be based on an individualized education program (IEP)

- specifies the components of the individualized educational program

- sets up a timetable for local education agencies to follow in meeting the educational needs of their school-age handicapped youth

- sets up guidelines and specifications to be met by each state in meeting educational needs of handicapped children

- provides state education agencies the opportunity to apply for incentive grants for

preschool handicapped education

- insures that the handicapped child and his or her parents will be afforded general and specific procedural safeguards that will cover identification, placement, and evaluation of handicapped children

- sets up guidelines to be followed during due process procedures that involve a handicapped child's education rights

- requires that a comprehensive system of personnel development be developed and that it include both inservice and preservice training of general and special education instructional and support personnel

- sets up policies and procedures for the state's expenditures of federal funds in the education of handicapped children

- requires that states have an advisory panel composed of handicapped individuals, teachers, and parents of the handicapped

- specifies procedures for handling noncompliance situations

- requires that an active "child find" program be maintained by both state and local education agencies

- requires that local education agency plans coincide with approved state plans

- outlines the roles of the Commissioner of the U.S. Office of Education

- establishes a formula for gradual escalating cost sharing by federal government in educating handicapped children

- specifies that no more than 12 percent of school-aged children may be counted as handicapped

- insures that federal funds will be used for the excess cost of educating handicapped children and that state or local funds will not be supplanted in that effort

- provides policies and procedures to protect confidentiality of data and/or information regarding a handicapped child

mented them. Many educators expect that parents of normal children will soon demand that IEPs be developed for their children as well. If IEPs are thought to enhance learning and instruction, why shouldn't all children have their own plans?

Mainstreaming also requires that regular classroom teachers work as members of teams in planning and implementing the IEPs. Special educators play more of a support role, that is, teaming up with regular teachers to consult about individual children's needs. In many cases it is necessary to provide special instructional and/or support services to handicapped children who are in regular classes. Such help may require tutoring, small

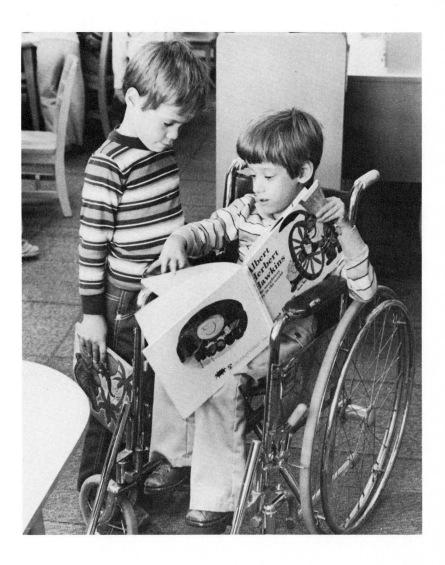

group instruction within a resource room, and counseling. Working as a team member invariably requires more time and effort than working alone. Although the quality of instruction may improve, the regular classroom teacher has to be willing and able to follow through with all the extra work that mainstreaming requires—diagnostic/prescriptive teaching, IEP development, new instructional strategies, and coping with such difficulties as having emotionally disturbed children in the classroom. As a regular classroom teacher you may want to take a course or two in special education to help you succeed with mainstreamed children. As with most new educational ideas, the success of mainstreaming will be determined in the classroom. At this point the philosophical commitment to mainstreaming is ahead of research and practice. We will not know for years whether mainstreaming is successful.

Your success in working with handicapped children will be greatly influenced by the attitude you have toward these youngsters. If you have positive expectations, provide the children with opportunities to learn, and reinforce their efforts, they can and will learn. They should participate in both independent and cooperative activities and be given accurate and continuous assessment. Involving the parents of handicapped children in both classroom and home activities can be very helpful. Most important, however, is the need for you to accept the differences that these children bring to your classroom, and to help them become an integral part of the class.

PROGRAMS FOR THE GIFTED AND TALENTED

One of the most challenging types of student a teacher can have in the classroom is the gifted or talented child. The gifted child is extremely bright, quickly grasping ideas and concepts you are teaching, and making interpretations or extrapolations that you may not even have considered. Gifted children may also display a creativity that manifests itself in original thinking or artistic creations. These children also exhibit a tremendous energy when working on a particular problem or performance area in which they are interested.

Sidney Marland, former U.S. commissioner of education, proposed the following definition of gifted and talented which has been used in federal legislation:

> Gifted and talented children are those identified by professionally qualified persons who, by virtue of outstanding abilities, are capable of high performance. These are children who require differentiated educational programs and services beyond those normally provided by the regular program in order to realize their contribution to self and society.
>
> Children capable of high performance include those with demonstrated achievement and/or potential ability in any of the following areas:

1. General intellectual ability
2. Specific academic aptitude
3. Creative or productive thinking
4. Leadership ability
5. Visual and performing arts[16]

The term *talented* refers to a specific dimension of skill (musical or artistic talent, for example) that may not be matched by the child's more general abilities, while the term *gifted* usually includes intellectual ability. Gifted and talented children are sufficiently different from most other children in intellectual and creative abilities that adaptations and adjustments in the usual curricula are required if they are to attain maximum personal development. Although special educational care and services for handicapped children have long been recognized and accepted, American education has been very slow to accept the notion that gifted children require special adaptations in both curricula and teaching methods. Because the idea of giftedness implies an elitism to many Americans, it seems undemocratic in their opinion to provide special services to children who already enjoy an intellectual advantage.

In 1971 Marland, who was then U.S. Commissioner of Education, estimated the gifted and talented student population at between 3 and 5 percent of the total student population. During the 1979–80 school year, a total of 766,759 gifted and talented students were served in special programs in forty-three states.[17] Although these figures represent tremendous increases in recent years, if Marland's estimates are accurate, between 39 and 63 percent of the gifted and talented student population is still not getting special help in schools. As a result of this neglect, many gifted and talented students drop out of school at rates far exceeding the rates of dropout for their nongifted peers. Many of those who stay in school become bored, apathetic, and unchallenged. The result is that many of our brightest and most talented minds are being turned off or underdeveloped. It has been only recently that school districts have begun to make serious efforts to identify gifted children and to develop special programs for them.

Types of Programs

Current educational programs for gifted and talented students are quite varied. Some programs establish special schools that are designed only for gifted or talented students and which have special admission requirements. In such schools, stimulating courses can be devised and taught without concern for students who might be unable to keep pace, and teachers as well as students can be recruited specifically. Schools for the performing

---

[16]*Education of the Gifted and Talented,* Sidney Marland, ed. Report to the Congress of the United States by the U.S. Commissioner of Education (Washington, D.C.: U.S. Government Printing Office, 1972), p. 10.

[17]"Newsnotes," *Phi Delta Kappan* 62 (February 1981): 464.

arts, such as the one depicted on the television show *Fame*, are examples of such special schools.

Other programs adapt and enrich the regular school curriculum for gifted and talented children by grouping these students together for all or part of their instruction. This option is normally more flexible and practical than special schools. Classes can be established on a continuing or short-term basis, in any subject area, with the intention of either enriching or accelerating the student. A major advantage of such classes is that they reduce the variance among the students, both in ability and interest, thus making it easier to plan instruction. Since 1972 Johns Hopkins University in Baltimore, Maryland, has been operating with great success special classes for mathematically gifted children. In literature and the humanities, special classes have been used to permit deeper exploration of issues not normally covered in regular classes. The "Great Books" program has been used as a supplementary curriculum for gifted children at the secondary level, for example.

Still other programs are designed as out-of-school programs for gifted and talented youngsters who may have exhausted the resources of their particular school. Internship or work experiences with such professionals as physicians, engineers, and lawyers can provide valuable insights and learnings not available in regular secondary schools. Museums, theaters, ballet, art shows, nature excursions, and other cultural experiences can also serve to supplement the regular school offerings for gifted and talented students.

Identification of the Gifted and Talented

When special programs and services are provided for gifted and talented children, there exists the problem of how to identify children who might qualify. Experts have recommended the following tools, in descending order of preference:

1. individual intelligence test scores
2. earlier achievements, including academic record
3. teacher nomination based on observations
4. standardized achievement test scores
5. scores on creativity tests
6. scores on group intelligence tests[18]

A cautionary note: there is a danger of letting the *tools* used to locate the children become synonymous with the *definition* of gifted and talented. To avoid this potential danger, teachers and administrators must take the position that they study and interpret what data the tools provide rather than take the data at face value and use them for hard and fast cutoff points.

[18]Maynard C. Reynolds and Jack W. Birch, *Teaching Exceptional Children in All America's Schools* (Reston, Va.: The Council for Exceptional Children, 1977), p. 220.

Whether or not a child is to be recommended for a special program is a decision that should be made by the responsible teacher and other professional educators, based on their objective and subjective appraisals of the student, the nature of the gifted program or activity, and the atmosphere in which the student lives and goes to school. Parents should be included in discussions. The point is that the complexity of the variables involved requires that individual decisions be made by professionals using their best judgments, rather than according to arbitrary, predetermined cutoff points on tests.

The Role of the Regular Classroom Teacher

If your school or school district does have special programs and activities for gifted and talented students, you may be expected to work with resource teachers to help prepare individualized educational plans for these students. It is more likely that you will discover certain students in your class to be gifted or talented and, lacking any special programs, you will be responsible

for teaching these students as part of your regular class. What do you need to know?

1. Recognize that gifted and talented pupils generally learn the standard curricular skills and content quickly and easily. They need teaching that does not tie them to a limited range. They need teaching that is not preoccupied with filling them with facts and information, but allows them to use the regular class as a forum for research, inquiry, and projects that are meaningful to them.

2. Realize that these students are persistently curious. They need teachers who encourage them to maintain confidence in their own ideas, even when those ideas differ from the norm.

3. Teach these pupils to be efficient and effective at independent study, developing the skills required in self-directed learning and in analyzing and solving problems independently.

4. Help students to apply complex cognitive processes such as creative thinking, critiques, and pro and con analyses.

HUMBLING CASES FOR CAREER COUNSELORS

Creative and imaginative people are often not recognized by their contemporaries. In fact often they are not recognized in school by their teachers either. History is full of illustrations to give guidance counselors pause. Consider some of these:

Einstein was four years old before he could speak and seven before he could read. Isaac Newton did poorly in grade school, and Beethoven's music teacher once said of him, "As a composer he is hopeless." When Thomas Edison was a boy, his teachers told him he was too stupid to learn anything. F. W. Woolworth got a job in a dry goods store when he was 21, but his employers would not let him wait on a customer because he "didn't have enough sense." A newspaper editor fired Walt Disney because he had "no good ideas." Caruso's music teacher told him, "You can't sing. You have no voice at all." The director of the Imperial Opera in Vienna told Madam Schumann-Heink that she would never be a singer and advised her to buy a sewing machine. Leo Tolstoy flunked out of college; Wernher Von Braun flunked ninth-grade algebra. Admiral Richard E. Byrd had been retired from the Navy as "unfit for service" until he flew over both Poles. Louis Pasteur was rated as "mediocre" in chemistry when he attended the Royal College. Abraham Lincoln entered the Black Hawk War as a captain and came out as a private. Louisa May Alcott was told by an editor that she could never write anything that had popular appeal. Fred Waring was once rejected for high school chorus. Winston Churchill failed the sixth form (grade) in school.

Probably these people were identified as low achievers in school or as misfits on their job because of problems of relevance.

Milton E. Larson, *Phi Delta Kappan* 54 (February 1973): 374. Reprinted by permission.

5. Expand your ideas concerning what instructional materials are available. Consider businesses, religious groups, national parks, universities, factories, museums, libraries, and resource people as potential instructional materials, in addition to the textbooks and reference books available in the school.

The characteristics of gifted and talented children, particularly when they appear in regular classes, challenge the breadth and depth of a teacher's skills and professionalism. It is no easy task to be able to direct the work of these children in widely divergent areas, to support and guide them in further inquiry, and to keep them accepted as members of a class group. It is challenging, but oh so rewarding!

A FINAL WORD: THE FUTURE OF AMERICAN EDUCATION

It is almost impossible to summarize a book that treats as many different topics as this one does, so no such attempt will be made. Instead, it might be useful to try to look ahead to speculate about what directions American education may take in the next ten or so years. It is important for us to realize that change in education is usually slow to come about, so ten years from now schools will probably more closely resemble our current educational scene than they will appear different. Recognize also that future gazing is at best a risky enterprise. Despite this caveat, we offer the following:

- Education will continue to suffer from fiscal problems that will curtail much experimentation and development.

- There will continue to be a search for the most appropriate curriculum and agreement on what is meant by "the basics."

- Elective courses will continue to decline, and there will be continued emphasis on strong academic curricula.

- The most dramatic change will be in the use of microcomputers as they become a part of school life and as students and teachers alike develop computer literacy.

- There will be less emphasis on training people for specific jobs in industry, and more emphasis on training people who are flexible and who can plan, adapt, and know how to learn.

- Educational systems will continue to seek ways to provide equal educational opportunities through school finance reforms, alternative schools, multicultural and bilingual education programs, mainstreaming, and programs for the gifted and talented.

In spite of the fact that the United States has created the greatest system of education the world has seen, many challenges remain. We hope that you will become one of the dedicated educators who seek to meet those challenges.

All education springs from some image of the future. If the image of the future held by a society is grossly inaccurate, its educational system will betray its youth.

— ALVIN TOFFLER —

Discussion Questions

1. Are you familiar with any alternative schools? Would you like to teach in one? If so, what kind?

2. What positive benefits can you see resulting from having volunteers participating in the schools?

3. Have you ever operated a microcomputer? Do you believe that computer literacy for teachers will be a necessity in the future? Why or why not?

4. How might the goals of multicultural education be implemented in the classroom? Do you agree with the basic assumption of bilingual education—that is, that children who do not speak English should receive instruction in their native language until they can speak English? Why or why not?

5. What problems and opportunities do you think mainstreaming will present to regular classroom teachers?

6. Are you familiar with any programs for gifted children? How do they differ from the curriculum for regular students?

For Further Reading

Gold, Milton J., Carl A. Grant, and Harry N. Rivlin. *In Praise of Diversity: A Resource Book for Multicultural Education.* Washington, D.C.: Teacher Corps and Association of Teacher Educators, 1977.
  Explores basic concepts of multicultural education and discusses the various ethnic groups that American society comprises.

Kirk, Samuel, and James J. Gallagher. *Educating Exceptional Children*, 4th ed. Boston: Houghton Mifflin, 1983.
  Includes a contemporary, brief overview of salient issues in special education, including mainstreaming and programs for the gifted and talented.

Passow, A. Harry, ed. *The Gifted and the Talented: Their Education and Development.* Seventy-eighth Yearbook of the National Society for the Study of Education. Chicago: University of Chicago Press, 1979.
  An excellent volume on the issues, programs, and problems related to educating gifted and talented youngsters.

Phi Delta Kappan 62 (April 1981).
  An issue containing several articles on alternative schools.

Phi Delta Kappan 63 (January 1982).
  An issue containing nine articles on computers in education.

Index

sources of information on, 38, 45–46, 56–57
steps in seeking, 41–47
summer, 40
see also Career(s); Salaries
England, *see* Britain
Engle v. *Vitale*, 413
Enrollment, school
black, in post-Reconstruction South, 126, 127
declining, 32, 36, 364
fluctuations in, 31, 32
private school, 36, 37, 117, 153
Environment(s)
conflicting, 161–162
heredity and, 160, 231
interactive, 161
and learning, 160–161
school as, 160–162
Epictetus, 67
Epistemology, 68–69
Escapism, forms of, 383–388
Essentialism, 79–82
as teaching philosophy, 81–82
Ethics, 70
Evaluation, student, 293. *See also* Testing
Evening Hour of a Hermit, The (Pestalozzi), 10
Evolution, theory of, 69
Existentialism, 82–85
as teaching philosophy, 84–85
"Existential moment," 82
Expectations
of beginning teachers, 284, 287
in moral education, 420–421
Experience
and career choice, 7–9
personal, and goals of school, 143–146
vicarious, 8, 9
Extracurricular activities, 179–180, 199

Facilitator, role of, 312–313
Factory, school as a, 147
Failures, labeling children as, 162
"Fame" (television show), 8, 444
Family, changing structure of, 378–380
working mothers, 343, 398

Federal aid to schools, 253–254, 256, 414–415
Female academies, 111, 117
Films, 8
Financing, school, 153, 255–258
and accountability, 411–412
reform, 257–258
Finkelstein, Barbara Joan, 100
Flanders, Ned, 169–171
Flanders's Interaction Analysis, 169–171, 194
Flexibility, 326–327
Florida, textbook adoption in, 225–226
Ford, Gerald, 438
Ford Foundation, 392
Foreign language curriculum
audiolingual approach, 212, 213
Soviet vs. U.S., 222
Foundation for Education Assistance, 254
Foundations, career opportunities with, 52
Fragmentation, 335
Franklin, Benjamin, 101, 110–111, 125
"Freaks," 181–182, 183
Freedmen's Bureau, 125
Freedom, limits on student, 164–165
"Frills," in curriculum, 214.
See also Back-to-basics movement
Fuchs, Estelle, 265–266
Functional illiteracy, 222, 408
Funding, for schools, 153. *See also* Financing, school

Gallagher, James, 172–173
Galloway, Charles, 175–176
Gallup poll, 407
Gardner, John, 142, 156
Gelles, R. J., 382
Getzels, J. W., 306
Gifted and talented children
classroom teacher and, 445–447
identifying, 444–445
programs for, 443–447
special classes for, 444
Ginott, Haim, 176, 329
Glass, Gene V., 179
Glasser, William, 161–162, 329
"Golden Rule, the," 242

Goodbye, Mr. Chips (Hilton), 8
"Good citizens," as goal of education, 24, 26–27, 77
Goodlad, John, 168–169, 219, 344
Governance of schools, 237–241
business and, 246, 250–252
and control, 237, 241–254
federal government and, 253–254, 256
informal pressure groups and, 243–248
legal responsibility for, 237
at local level, 237, 239–241, 242–243
and parent-teacher groups, 249–250
principal and, 248
by professional educators, 241–243
at state level, 101, 237–239
superintendent and, 240–241, 242, 243–248, 251, 269
Government, U.S.
aid to private schools, 414–415
aid to public schools, 253–254, 256
and bilingual education, 435, 436
education careers in, 36, 51–52, 53–54
and education for handicapped, 438
roll of, in education, 201, 235, 253–254
see also Supreme Court, U.S.
Graham, Grace, 251
Grand Rapids, Michigan, John Ball Zoo School, 187–188
Gray, J. Glenn, 351
"Greasers," 181, 183
"Great Books" approach, 72–73, 444
Great Cities School Improvement Programs, 392
Gross, Neal, 244, 246
Group process, in classroom, 330
Group study, in continuous learning, 353
Growing Up on Television (Moody), 386
Guidance, in career choice, 9

Hall, Edward, 174
Handicapped children
mainstreaming of, 437, 438–442
nineteenth-century treatment of, 437–438

Luther, Martin, 346
Lyon, Mary, 111

McAshan, H. H., 89
McGuffey Readers, 102
McLaughlin, M., 433
McNeil, John D., 206
Magnet school programs, 184–185, 397–399
Mainstreaming, of handicapped children, 437, 438–442
Malcolm X, 211
Man: A Course of Study (Bruner), 202–203
Mann, Horace, 102, 360
life and work of, 122–123
Marijuana, 384–385
Marland, Sidney, 442–443
Marsh, D., 433
Marvin, M., 404–405
Massachusetts, early education in, 96, 106, 121. *See also* Boston, Mass.
Massachusetts Board of Education, 123
Mastery learning, 228–229
"Math anxiety," in teachers, 18–19, 433
Mathematics curriculum, 114, 207, 223
"new math," 207
Soviet vs. U.S., 221
use of computers in, 210
Mather, Cotton, 125
Mayer, Frederick, 95
MAZE (computer program), 210
Media, 8, 385–386
as teacher, 349
"Melting pot" theory, schools and, 150, 433–434
Metaphysics, 67–68
Method, value of, 75
Microcomputers, 207, 428–433
in simulations, 431
teacher's response to, 431–432, 433
as word processors, 212, 431
see also Computers
Middle colonies
history of education in, 96, 99–100, 121
Latin grammar schools in, 109

private venture schools in, 96, 100, 109, 110
teachers in, 119
Middle schools, 115–116
Amherst (N.H.) Middle School, 186–187
Mill, John Stuart, 178
Miller, George, 203
Milton (Mass.) Academy, 210
Minnesota Teacher Attitude Inventory, 282n
Minorities
bilingual education programs and, 434–436
educational neglect of, 124
educational opportunity and, 103, 124, 389–397, 437
history of education for, 103, 110, 124–132
test performance of, 129, 389–390, 435
Minority children
educational opportunity for, 389–397, 437
self-fulfilling prophecy and, 391
Missionary schools, 129
Modeling, in moral education, 419–420
Momentum, in classroom management, 335
Montessori, Maria, life and work of, 398–399
Montessori schools, 399, 426
Moody, Kate, 386
Moral education, 409, 415–422
in common schools, 104
"four Es" of, 419–422
history of, 416–417
teacher's role in, 419–422
More Effective Schools Program, 392
Motivation, for teaching, 6–7, 10–28
case studies in, 15–28
dialogue on, 14
Moving schools, 97, 107
Multicultural education, 132, 433–435
Murphy's Law, Instructor's guide to, 295–298
Music curriculum, 213–214

Nash, Ogden, 378
National Assessment of Educational Progress, 389, 435

National Association for the Advancement of Colored People, 128
National Association of Manufacturers, 251–252
National Board of Popular Education, 121
National Commission on Excellence in Education (1983 report), 222–223, 409
National Defense Education Act, 213
National Education Association, 38, 347, 356–361
and AFT, 364–365
Code of Ethics, 358–359
Committees (1890s), 105, 113–114
and control of education, 241, 242–243
Educational Policies Commission, 142, 143
goals of, 356
political power of, 357–360
position on aid to private schools, 414
study on motives for teaching, 27
Task Force on Bilingual/Multicultural Education, 437
Teacher Opinion Poll, 406
National Institute of Education, 333, 403, 406
Beginning Teacher Evaluation Study (BTES), 166, 333
National Institute on Drug Abuse, 384
National School Volunteer Program, 427
National Science Foundation, 205, 209
study of teaching methods, 168, 206
Nation at Risk: The Imperative for Educational Reform, 222–223, 409
Native Americans, education of, 124, 128–129
New England, colonial education in, 96–98, 109
New England Primer, 97, 98, 102
New math, 207
"New poor," 379
Newton, Isaac, 446
New York Board of Regents, 243
New York City, compensatory education in, 392
New York Times, 417
Normal schools, 121, 123, 124, 126

PHOTO CREDITS

An Invitation to Respond

In the previous editions of *Those Who Can, Teach,* we included a form with which students evaluated the book and provided us with feedback. Many of the changes made in this edition were based on these student evaluations. Please help us respond to the interests and needs of future readers by completing the questionnaire below and returning it to College Marketing, Houghton Mifflin Company, One Beacon Street, Boston, MA 02108.

Kevin and Jim

Please tell us your overall impression of the text.

	Excellent	Good	Adequate	Poor	Very poor
1. Was it written in a clear and understandable style?	_____	_____	_____	_____	_____
2. Were difficult concepts explained?	_____	_____	_____	_____	_____
3. How would you rate the cartoons and illustrations?	_____	_____	_____	_____	_____
4. How does this text compare with texts you are using in other education courses?	_____	_____	_____	_____	_____
5. Did the book's informality help your reading?	_____	_____	_____	_____	_____

Can you cite examples that illustrate any of your above ratings?

_____

_____

Were there any chapters or features that you particularly liked or disliked? If so, why?

_____

_____

Were there any topics that were not covered that you believe *should* have been covered?

_____

_____

Do you think this book has influenced your career choice? Which way? And how?

_____

_____

Which chapters did you read because they were required by your instructor?

_____

Which chapters did you read on your own?

_____

We would appreciate any other comments or reactions you are willing to share with us:

_____

_____

_____